THIS FLAME WITHIN

THIS

also to Thuy Linh Tu for helping me situate my work within Asian American studies, and for understanding the weight of carrying my father's history. Finally, I am grateful to Ella Shohat, who offered invaluable feedback on an early iteration of this project. Thank you, Ella, for being at the forefront of developing diasporic feminism and paving the way for scholars like me. Your work has illuminated lines of inquiry that I have been following ever since.

I have been lucky enough to benefit from the intellectual labor and support of outstanding NYU faculty members Crystal Parikh, Andrew Ross, Manu Goswami, Kristin Ross, and Aisha Khan. Thank you for creating an intellectual atmosphere in which I was able to thrive. The camaraderie and shared political outlook of my peers also made graduate school far more pleasant than I imagined it could be. Thank you to my cohort Thulani Davis, Justin Leroy, Claudia Sofía Garriga López, and Stuart Shrader, and to Liz Mesok, Zenia Kish, Emma Kreyche, Marisol LeBrón, Eva Hageman, Leticia Alvarado, A. J. Bauer, Sam Ng, and Amita Manghnani for much solidarity and inspiration.

When I first set out to do research for this book, I wouldn't have gotten very far without the support of my cousin Melanie Goldstein, who generously hosted me twice at her home in Maryland, and my cousin Rachel Platt, who lent me her car so I could drive around the Virginia suburbs conducting interviews. Thanks to both of you for coming through!

Many people helped to connect me with interview subjects, shared archival documents, or otherwise recognized the significance of this project and supported me along the way: Narges Bajoughli, Fahimeh Gooran, Negar Mottahedeh, Hamid Dabashi, Nina Farnia, Anne McClintock, Grace Kyungwon Hong, Macarena Gómez-Barris, Atefeh Akbari, Bahaar Ahsan, and Michael Letwin—thank you! My appreciation goes also to Hirad Dinavari, at the Library of Congress, and to the librarians at Howard University's Moorland-Spingarn Research Center, at UC Berkeley's Bancroft Library, and at Stanford University's Hoover Institute. In addition, I am grateful to the non-Iranian activists who remembered the ISA and shared their stories with me: Victoria Wong, Camelia Odeah, Margaret Leahy, Mike Haire, Kate Lombardi, Ann Schneider, and Stephanie Weiner.

The process of writing this book has been long and arduous, but it has also created many pleasurable opportunities to build new relationships. I was the beneficiary of a University of California President's Postdoctoral Fellowship in Asian American Studies at UC Davis, where I worked closely with the brilliant Sunaina Maira. Thank you, Sunaina, for championing my work as part of Asian American Studies, for reading earlier versions of this book and providing detailed suggestions for a path forward when I felt rather lost, and for your warmth, friendship, and kindness. Your political commitments and radical scholarship have shown me what is possible in this profession.

Perhaps the most exciting title I will ever hold in my life was thanks to Naghmeh Sohrabi and Gregory Childs, who awarded me an Andrew Mellon Postdoctoral Fellowship in Comparative Revolutions at Brandeis University. What a year we had of transnational and interdisciplinary conversations! I am deeply grateful to Naghmeh for her own work to transform the historiography of the Iranian Revolution and for the many hours she spent reading, commenting on, and talking with me about my work. Thank you for welcoming me, challenging me, and believing in me. My appreciation also goes to Vivian Solana Moreno for her dedication to feminist anticolonial scholarship and her valuable feedback on my project. And to Kym, Vivek, and Maya: thank you for providing such a lovely home away from home! Your generosity and hospitality were unparalleled.

My ability to function as a scholar has been contingent upon the peace of mind that comes from knowing that my child is in good hands. Thank you, Marzieh Rahimian, for taking care of my baby so I could write. Your support for me and my family in those early days of parenting made it all possible. Thank you Saba Yazdanian, Claudia Gaviria, and Molly McIntyre for countless hours of childcare. Thank you to my mother, Lesley, for all those weekday evenings you were there while I was at Brandeis. We couldn't have made it through that year without you! My deep gratitude goes also to Amy Mathews, who took charge of remote learning for an entire school year while I finished the book.

I have had the opportunity to present portions of this book at conferences and at universities due to many generous invitations over the years. Thank you to Evelyn Alsultany, Sarah Gualtieri, Keith Feldman, Gayatri Gopinath, Persis Karim, Marianne Hirsch, Andreas Huyssen, Payman Jafari, and many others for creating spaces for me to share my research. In particular, I want to extend my sincere gratitude to Ali Mirsepassi and Arang Keshavarzian for including me in several NYU Iranian Studies Initiative events and projects over the years. I have greatly appreciated the chance to be in conversation with both of you and with the community of scholars you have assembled.

My editor at Duke University Press, Courtney Berger, was kind enough to snap up this project in its early stages and to wait patiently, meeting with me year after year, until I figured out how to tell this story. Thank you for listening to me work through numerous problems in the manuscript and for your unwavering confidence that I would finish this book! Thank you to Duke editorial assistant Sandra Korn, and project editor Susan Albury, for guiding me through the final steps to make this "book" an actual book. My sincere gratitude goes to Elizabeth Terzakis for meticulous proofreading that sharpened my thinking and my prose.

I would never have thought I could write a book at all but for the magnificent Louise DeSalvo, whose approach to the craft of writing opened up new worlds for me. In her classroom at Hunter College, I found my writing sisters, Kym Ragusa and Jade Sanchez-Ventura, who have been with me on this journey ever since. Thank you for lifting me up again and again.

This book went through many drafts and I was assisted along the way by the invaluable feedback of several people I want to acknowledge. Afshin Matin-asgari, who wore many hats as historian, mentor, interview subject and friend, encouraged me to pick up the threads of the story that only he had told thus far. He offered a model of intergenerational mentoring and collaboration that is all too rare. Thanks to the support of Barnard College, I was able to benefit from the wisdom of Afsaneh Najmabadi and Elizabeth Bernstein, who gently pushed me toward greater clarity. It was a special honor to work with Afsaneh, whose scholarship and life history have been deeply meaningful to this project. I am grateful also to Behrooz Ghamari-Tabrizi and Alex Lubin for careful and critical readings of the manuscript at key stages in this process.

There is another unique category of comrade-scholar-friends whose ears I have talked off at various points while grappling with one or another problem in the writing of this book. Thank you Sahar Sadjadi, Golnar Nikpour, Yumi Lee, Mitra Rastegar, Golnar Adili, Anne McClintock, Elizabeth Terzakis, Madiha Tahir, Rupal Oza, Ujju Aggarwal, and Ashley Dawson for caring about me and about this project.

Craig Willse went deep into the weeds of my sentences with me and we came out the other side with a book! Thank you for helping me to overcome many difficulties and write the book I wanted to write. Nadine Naber was my dream-come-true reader and a powerhouse writing coach, thanks to whom I made major breakthroughs with the manuscript.

I finished the book while teaching in the Women's, Gender, and Sexuality Studies department at Barnard College, where I have received phenomenal support from my extraordinary colleagues: Janet Jakobsen, Beck Jordan-Young, Elizabeth Bernstein, Neferti Tadiar, and Marisa Solomon. It has been an honor and a pleasure to join your ranks and I can't imagine a better home for me in academia than with all of you.

My gratitude goes to Setareh Shohadaei for her extensive research assistance, and also to Solby Lim and Alex Volgyesi for additional research support.

I have been lucky enough to count on the support of a wonderful community of friends in New York City. When pandemic parenting threatened to derail my writing goals, Rachel Knopf-Shey and Mandy Ikert each offered up their apartments as writing spaces without hesitation. When our kids were remote-learning at my place, Aine Doddy and Jonathan Rooke took me into theirs, and we all worked at home together. I thank Amita Nagaraja, Gregg Walkes, Linta Varghese, Roop Roy, Danny Katch, Lucy Herschel, Meredith Kolodner, Yasmine Farhang, Bitta Mostofi, Jaya Vasandani, and Jeremy Benjamin for being part of the network of friends that sustained me.

Sierra Stoneman-Bell has been with me through thick and thin long before this book began, and I will always be grateful for her unwavering confidence in me. My heartful gratitude goes also to a courageous and kind group of people who helped me find my way: Anne, Mike, AL, Cecilia, Rose, Deborah, Sheree, Tina, Marissa, Dan, Brenda, Rebecca, Azi, Vida, Nadine, Monisha, Devora, Marion, Suja, Teresa, and Mary. Thank you for listening.

I want to give a special acknowledgment to Nadia and Younes Benab, like an aunt and uncle to me as a child, who were there when I needed them and who loved my family even when things were hard. Younes's contributions to this book were foundational.

My extended family in Iran have kept me grounded these many years. We nurse the pain of separation and rejoice when we are together. Farkhondeh, Nasrin, Keikhosro, Parisa, and Vista—you are always with me in my heart. Thank you for taking me into your family after a lifetime as strangers. What once felt impossible, now seems miraculous.

Ann, Nigel, Ginny, and Sofia: thank you for welcoming me into your family and for your unwavering, loving support.

To my parents, who instilled in me the power of critique: I wouldn't know about this history or have the chutzpah to write about it without the two of you. Mom, thank you for teaching me how to write and helping me in countless ways to get to this point in my life. Baba, thank you for my revolutionary upbringing. Because of you, I have always known that one way to express Iranian identity in the United States is to work against racism and empire.

Finally, endless gratitude to my sweetest ones, Ashley and Sholeh, who remind me every day that life can be joyful and the struggle is worth it.

This book is for all the children of revolutionaries.

Introduction
Before We Were "Terrorists"

On February 15, 1977, six members of the Iranian Students Association (ISA), along with a small group of Americans from the Revolutionary Student Brigade, chained themselves to the inside of the crown of the Statue of Liberty and unfurled two giant banners (see figure I.1).[1] The larger one read "DOWN WITH THE SHAH." To the right, a smaller banner demanded "FREE THE 18," a reference to a group of political prisoners who had just been arrested in Iran. The ISA was a coalition involving several thousand Iranian student-visa holders living in the United States who were determined to end Washington's political, economic, and military aid to the Shah's regime. They channeled this determination into a political force through conspicuous acts of protest, such as the occupation of the statue that epitomized America's democratic promise to the world. By draping an iconic monument to American exceptionalism with a condemnation of a dictatorship that was also a major US ally, these young men and women turned their outrage into a visual spectacle of American hypocrisy. They hoped this spectacle would resonate widely as a call to action.

An accompanying press release issued by Vietnam Veterans Against the War made the expectation of solidarity clear. "The American people," it stated, "have no interest in dominati[ng] other countries as the American rulers do, [*sic*] instead their very interest is in joining with other people to fight against our own rulers who perpetuate the same misery in this country as well as abroad."[2] This sentiment was echoed in an article that appeared shortly afterward in the ISA's English-language magazine, *Resistance*, explaining that

Resistance

A publication of I.S.A.U.S., Member of Confederation of Iranian Students (National Union)

VOLUME FOUR FEBRUARY, 1977 SUPPLEMENT TWO

Iranian and American Students Seize Statue of Liberty in Support of 18 Iranian Patriots

The dictatorial regime of the Shah of Iran is finding it more and more difficult to carry out his barbaric repression of Iranian people in the face of mounting international condemnation of his fascist rule. And he is worried. Very worried.

RECENT KILLINGS, ARRESTS GIVE RISE TO FRESH WAVES OF OUTRAGE

Announcements by government- controlled press in Iran disclosed in the last few weeks several new political murders and arrests at the hands of the Shah's secret police.

To begin with, two patriots who had been in prison for an unknown period of time were summarily executed. Mr. M.H. Abrari, and Ms. Z. Gholhaki, whose arrests had never been announced previous to their deaths, and had been kept in an unnamed prison, were the victims. Ms. Gholhaki is the second woman known to be executed on political grounds after the Shah's takeover through the 1953 CIA coup. Many more women, of course, have died in the struggle against the regime both inside and out of prison, though only two have been victims of political executions known to date.

In another announcement by the regime of the Shah it was revealed that Mr. B. Aram, one of the leaders of the revolutionary *Organization of Mojahedeen of the People of Iran* was gunned down along with two other members of the same organization (Mr. M. Shafieha and Mr. H. Bagheri) in a confrontation with Shah's SAVAK and police. Seven others have been arrested in the same incident.

The cold-blooded killings had resulted from what has come to be known as house raids in Iran. An example, typical of these vicious measures,

Figure I.1 *Resistance*, February 1977. ISA file, Social Protest Collection, Bancroft Library, UC Berkeley.

the occupation was intended to "dramatize the hatred and disgust of the Shah and US policies toward Iran felt both by Iranian and American people."[3] The article's broad and confident assertion that "Iranian and American people" shared viscerally negative reactions—"hatred" and "disgust"—toward their own respective governments, rather than hostile feelings toward one another, reveals the presumption of a shared affective disposition and internationalist sensibility that would, after the revolution in Iran just two years later, become almost unimaginable.

By the time of the Statue of Liberty occupation in 1977, Iranian student activists had already spent sixteen years working to convince the Americans around them that they were on the same side in a global contest over the future of humanity. On one side was the US government, its brutal war in Vietnam, its coterie of allied dictatorships across the Third World, and its entrenched racist power structure at home; on the other side were popular liberation movements in Africa, Asia, Latin America, and the United States. The ISA invited Americans to add Iran to the map of concern and affiliation that had motivated so many to act against US imperial power in Southeast Asia. If enough Americans expressed outrage at US complicity with the authoritarian regime in Iran, ISA members hoped, Washington might withdraw its support and weaken the Shah to the point that the Iranian people could overthrow him.

Hence the need for dramatic acts of protest that could attract attention to the cause. Chained to the inside of Lady Liberty's crown for over five hours, Iranian students and their American friends waited for a crew of reporters to arrive. Instead, all ferry services to the island were suspended. The Coast Guard went so far as to intercept a private boat full of journalists to prevent them from conducting interviews.[4] According to *Resistance*, Coast Guard Captain J. L. Fleishell declared a "security zone" around the perimeter, in his words, "because of the presence of known terrorists on Liberty Island."[5] The unnamed ISA author conveys surprise at this choice of words: "Why would he say that? How did he know? What made these people 'terrorists'?"[6] As the article points out, the students carried no weapons and made no threats. The article's indignant questions, however justified, transport today's reader to a very different geopolitical era, before the words *Iranian* and *terrorist* had become virtually synonymous in the American media and popular imagination. At the time, Iranians were not generally regarded as threatening or violent. From the mid-1950s until the mid-1970s, Iran was a hopeful site of American largesse toward developing nations, and Iranian students in the US were welcomed as harbingers of Iran's ascent to the rank of a modern, capitalist nation—that is, if they were noticed at all. Scholars and media commentators routinely assume that the term *terrorist* first stuck to Iranians in the US after the taking of American hostages in Iran in late 1979. In fact, it was used against leftist Iranian students in 1977 who expressed public outrage about US complicity with the Shah's dictatorship. This earlier iteration reveals the enduring political motivations behind the selective use of this term as a slur against individuals and groups who oppose hegemonic state power. Before Iranians in the US were labeled "terrorists" they were revolutionaries.

The ISA's occupation of the Statue of Liberty raises several questions at the heart of this book. First, how was it that militant anti-imperialist activists emerged from the ranks of privileged foreign students whose raison d'être was to assist in the Westernization of Iran? Second, how did these students come to align themselves with a wide range of other liberation movements, and what did this solidarity look like in practice? Third, how did the history of the ISA become marginalized to the point that it is a virtually unknown part of the story of the Third World Left in the US, and how would that story change if the ISA were part of it? Finally, how might the ISA's legacy become meaningful to the contemporary Iranian diaspora in the US? I address these questions through an investigation of the lived experiences of Iranian student leftists in the United States from the early 1960s through the 1978–79 Iranian revolution. This investigation draws on archives and interviews to write Iranian foreign students into the historiography of Third World internationalism in the US and to gain a deeper understanding of what it meant to organize one's life around the project of revolution. It also examines the tensions and disappointments of that era, particularly the apparent tendency of anticolonial revolutions to betray the women who fought for them. The ISA thus becomes a case study of the gender and sexual politics of the anti-imperialist Left and reveals a far richer and more complex story than one of simple male domination. This wrangling with the past is also a provocation to rethink contemporary Iranian diasporic subjectivity, feminism, and transnational solidarity. My major contention is that the neglected history of Iranian revolutionaries in the United States can help to reorient diasporic identity away from nationalism, assimilation, and exceptionalism, and toward affiliation with multiple, ongoing freedom struggles—in the US, in Iran, and around the world.

In the pages that follow, not only do the activities of a nearly forgotten movement come into focus, but the affects and emotions that made it possible resurface from the hidden archives of memory and the fading mimeographed pages of activist ephemera. *This Flame Within* invokes both the powerful ferment of an Iranian revolutionary movement that occurred within the borders of the United States *and* the animating, embodied force of affect in forging political subjects and movements. It is the exploration of what I call "revolutionary affects" and how they transform subjectivity that compels this study and imbues it with significance beyond the Iranian context. If we want to better understand how collectivities form around the goal of social and political revolution, then the registers of affect and emotion carry valuable information. This study of the ISA thus addresses the much larger question of how and under what conditions affective attachments to revolution come to be shared in common, making it possible for people with very different experiences and histories to imagine their struggles and futures as interdependent. Below I describe my research process and the conceptual terminology I assembled in order make sense of what I found.

Becoming Revolutionaries

Before they were revolutionaries, Iranians in the US were students, including my father, who arrived in Washington, DC, in 1960 to attend Howard University. He participated in ISA meetings, rallies, and marches, as well as actions large and small against anti-Black racism, colonization, and war. It was from him that I first learned about the existence of an Iranian student movement in the United States. My father seemed to embody the spirit of those years of connection across difference, rejecting narrow forms of Persian nationalist identity in favor of the broadest possible identification with all those who suffered because of global capitalist expansion. As a graduate student, I wanted to learn more about the ISA, its role in undermining US support for the Shah, and its role in the post-World War II era of decolonization. Crucially, given the polarizing gender and sexual politics of the Iranian Revolution in which these students participated, I wondered what a study of this movement might have to teach us about the broader tendency of postcolonial states to reconfigure and reinforce, rather than dismantle, patriarchal forms of citizenship. How, I wanted to know, did former ISA members feel about this traumatic history, which drove many of them into permanent exile?

My research led me to ISA archival materials at Stanford University, University of California–Berkeley, and the Library of Congress. Among the many pamphlets, fliers, and periodicals available in Persian and in English, the ISA's English language journal, *Resistance*, which was published regularly throughout the 1970s, proved invaluable as a record of how the ISA attempted to galvanize the Americans around them. I was also fortunate enough to gain access to the personal collections of several former ISA members, including Younes Parsa Benab, Leyli Shayegan, Nancy Hormachea, and Parviz Shokat. I looked in less obvious places, too, such as the San Francisco State Strike archives and the archives of campus newspapers, and was rewarded for my efforts. In particular, coverage of the ISA in UC Berkeley's *Daily Californian* and Howard University's *The Hilltop* provided rich material for addressing the impact of ISA activism on American student politics more broadly. In addition to these print sources, I also analyze a short documentary film about the women's uprising in Tehran in March 1979, in which some returning ISA members participated. The original Persian audio is difficult to hear, but reveals affects and experiences marginalized by the French voiceover and English subtitles. My close reading of this film centers the voices of the Iranian women featured in it, voices that have been all but buried by the dominant narratives of victory and defeat that attend the Iranian Revolution.

Above all, as I set out to learn about the ISA, I wanted to hear directly from participants and gather their memories into a new kind of archive. Over the course of several years, I interviewed thirty former ISA members: twenty men and ten women. These interviews were usually conducted in person and lasted an average of three hours, sometimes with additional follow-up sessions. I also interviewed six non-Iranian activists who had worked with the ISA. It quickly became clear that I could interview dozens of Americans who fit this description, as the ISA was fondly remembered by many leftists of that generation, but this would have become a different project. Listening to former ISA members talk about their activist years, I was repeatedly struck by the strength of feeling that lingered decades later. I was interviewing people who had been profoundly affected by growing up under a US-backed dictatorship. Their encounters with state repression and with different traditions and moments of resistance in Iran left them searching for a way to act against injustice. The ISA became the way, a vehicle for transforming students into revolutionaries.[7] But how did this happen and what did it feel like in practice? And how might those feelings inform present and future diasporic orientations?

In order to address these questions, I read the affects and emotions embedded in the memories of former ISA members, as well as in print and video materials, as an "affective archive." I borrow this concept from queer feminist scholars, in particular Gayatri Gopinath and Ann Cvetkovich. Gopinath understands affect as the force of desire that transgresses the boundaries of nation, race, gender, and sexuality, making legible marginalized histories of the interconnections between different forms of oppression and differently targeted populations.[8] She locates the formation of marginalized subjectivities in the body's affective capacity to remember that which official histories must forget, and in small, everyday acts that are too often excluded from notions of the political.[9] I take my understanding of the subversive potential of affect as a site for reading alternative diasporic histories from her work. Cvetkovich's attention to the "emotional histories that lead people to activism" has also been formative in my approach to charting an affective history of the Iranian student Left in the US.[10] The registers of affect and emotion reveal complex and often contradictory responses to the experience of revolutionary activity—from joy to grief to ambivalence to disbelief—that belie tidy narratives of success or failure. Far from offering a static picture of how things really were, feelings attached to certain memories of collective struggle in the 1960s and 1970s change along with geopolitical conditions and sensibilities, becoming available for new interpretations. An "affective archive" of the ISA can help to make sense of the risks that were taken, the sacrifices that were made, and the feelings that suffuse diasporic political consciousness today.[11]

This Flame Within reads this archive for what I call "revolutionary affects," those visceral intensities generated by experiences of repression and resistance that remain latent within the body. For former ISA members, revolutionary affects are the embodied remains of the intertwined experiences of imperialism, dictatorship, and diaspora. Revolutionary affects form the basis of the transnational theory of revolutionary subjectivity offered in this book. Before I elaborate, I must first explain what I mean by *affect,* a term rarely used outside specialized scholarly circles. Affect refers to the way the body, which includes the "mind" or brain, registers the impact of coming into contact with people, places, objects, and ideas. Affects are outward and relational, rather than internal or fixed, and they are manifest physically—as a sensation (or lack thereof), a gesture, a facial expression, a stance, an orientation in space. They are always present; indeed, as Jonathan Flatley points out, we are always in an affective state (or mood) of some sort, although we may not know exactly how we got there.[12] The sociologist Deborah Gould explains that an affective state is "often experienced, as Raymond Williams wrote, 'at the very edge of semantic availability,' felt as 'an unease, a stress, a displacement, a latency.'"[13] I would add to this list affective states experienced as pressure, excitement, anger, fear, and melancholia, by which I mean an unwillingness to let go of someone or something that is lost, like a loved one, a sense of belonging, or a moment of freedom. Rather than understand "negative" affects and feelings—such as anger and melancholia—as counterproductive or unhealthy, I draw on cultural studies scholarship that explores the subversive knowledge, subjectivities, and collectives that can emerge from an open and ongoing engagement with loss.[14] Our affective states, what Williams famously called "structures of feeling," can register the "tension between dominant accounts of what is and what might be, on the one hand, and lived experience that contradicts those accounts."[15] They may be the first sign that all is not well, that something needs to change.

Affect and *emotion* are not identical terms. Some scholars draw a sharp distinction between the two, arguing that affect is inchoate and loaded with potential, whereas emotion represents the cohering of affect into a definite form of expression.[16] Affect may be open-ended, but it is, nonetheless, always social. As Gould writes, "affect is a body's processing of social conditions."[17] Sara Ahmed has illustrated how this processing provides the raw material for political emotions: we might experience something that puts us in an affective state of unease—an incident of harassment, for example—but only realize later, when we come to recognize the experience as part of a system of discrimination, that we are angry about what happened.[18] We also might want to better understand how that system works in order to make sense of how we have been affected. Coming into contact with others who share our affective state can channel our affects in particular directions, toward particular political ideologies and organizations. Social movements, Gould argues, provide an "emotional pedagogy ... a guide for what and how to feel and what to do in light of those feelings," and can, moreover, "authorize selected feelings and actions while downplaying and even invalidating others."[19] This is the case no matter where a social movement falls on the political spectrum. Seen in this way, the ISA became compelling because it offered an explanation for the affective states of Iranian students who had trouble accepting a US worldview that hinged on support for dictatorship and because it provided a plan for action. Affect thus became a conduit toward new political horizons, new ideas about what kinds of feelings and actions were permissible and desirable.[20] In the chapters that follow, I have sometimes found it necessary to draw a distinction between *affect* and *emotion*—for example, when discussing childhood memories of ISA members or changing feelings ascribed to the same memory. At other times I use the two terms together because they are both equally relevant to my analysis of revolutionary subjectivity.

The concept of revolutionary affects refers to the sensorial material out of which a revolutionary consciousness can later be fashioned *and* to those affects that attach to and fuel the project of making a revolution. Michael Hardt argues that affects "illuminate ... both our power to affect the world around us and our power to be affected by it, and the relationship between these two powers."[21] The term *revolutionary affects* describes precisely this relationship, encompassing the power of being impacted by the world such that one is out of sync with the dominant order *and* the power to sustain revolutionary activity designed to change that same order. The revolutionary affects of former ISA members provide an archive of the United States' disavowed empire in the Middle East and the efforts by a group of foreign students to bring that empire down.

Revolutionary affects describe a theory of revolutionary subjectivity that is not predictive but rather historical and analytical. Affective potency lingers and can animate the body later on in ways that are impossible to foresee.[22] In the absence of revolutionary ideas and organization, revolutionary affects flow elsewhere or dissipate. In other words, revolutionary affects do not cause a person to adopt a revolutionary ideology or join a revolutionary organization; and yet it may be impossible to fully understand why certain ideologies and organizations become compelling enough to reorient the lives of thousands of people at the same time without paying attention to the affects they mobilize and circulate.[23] After all, not everyone who reads Marx becomes a Marxist. Or as Flatley points out, "insights about one's political oppression are unlikely to motivate resistance unless they can be made interesting and affectively rewarding."[24] Just as socialist and communist ideas offered Iranian students a method of "reading" their formative memories and the affects that remained, the concept of revolutionary affects offers an approach to reading history, a method of interpreting the data I accumulated through in-depth interviews with former ISA members and through archival research. By telling their stories, and opening themselves up to the affects and feelings that attend them, ISA veterans produced, in the words of Cvetkovich, "political history as affective history, a history that captures activism's felt and even traumatic dimensions."[25] These are the dimensions that do not appear in conventional histories of modern Iran or of US-Iran relations, but that left each of these young people longing for justice. Here I give just a few examples.

Sitting quietly in a room in Tehran, a ten-year-old Jewish girl named Jaleh Behroozi tried to make sense of why her brother, an artist, had been tortured by SAVAK (Sāzemān-e Ettelā'āt va Amniyat-e Keshvar), the US-trained secret police force. As she worked this horror over in her mind, she sat next to a different brother who was translating *The Diary of Anne Frank* into Persian. She read each page as he handed it to her. It is this moment that Jaleh recalls when she talks about how she lost her faith in God and became interested in the idea of self-emancipation. The atrocities of the European Holocaust, the violence of dictatorship, her brother's body in pain—these experiences affected her in ways she hardly understood at the time. Years later in diaspora, the affects and emotions that remained would fuel her decision to commit her life to a revolutionary movement that promised to put an end, once and for all, to regimes that torture.[26]

Among the thirty former ISA members interviewed for this book, many could still describe specific encounters with state repression in Iran in the aftermath of the 1953 CIA-backed coup, events that occurred many years before they came to study in the US. They recounted memories of martial law and the sting of tear gas, of relatives disappeared, of friends, teachers, and neighbors imprisoned and tortured. Farid, a former ISA member now based in New York City, recalled a recurring scene from his childhood in Tehran: "We would see the tanks, we would see the soldiers in the streets. These were all in front of my eyes, and then the question, why are they doing that? Why are they there?" These formative experiences, and the troubling questions they raised affected how individuals reacted when they came across subversive ideas, texts, and organizations—whether in Iran or in diaspora. The recollections of some former ISA members evoked even earlier moments of Iranian opposition to autocracy, charting a subterranean leftist genealogy that reaches back through generations of repression and resistance. During the first half of the twentieth century, Iran was a nexus point for the transnational circulation of radical ideologies and movements, including the formation of Asia's first communist party among Iranian migrant workers in the oil fields of Baku in 1920. Both the persistence of visceral memories of state violence *and* affective attachments to earlier moments in the modern Iranian freedom struggle illustrate how the making of revolutionary subjects unfolds over time through a complex entanglement of the intimate, the historical, and the geopolitical.

The desire for national liberation among Iranian students challenged the hierarchies of class, as thousands of middle- and upper-class Iranian students in the US became concerned with the liberation of the vast majority of poor Iranians back home. Members of the ISA were affectively attached to a broad yet powerful notion of "the Iranian people," which included those left out of the version of progress the US and the Shah were promoting. These attachments to the impoverished and exploited masses proved far more compelling than Western degrees or the promise of individual career advancement. As I discuss in chapter 5, this class rebellion included a rejection of bourgeois forms of femininity associated with a Westernizing dictatorship and made possible new gender roles for women within the student movement. Revolutionary affects, including the desire for equality and belonging in an alienating and unjust world, facilitated the transformation of thousands of Iranian students into revolutionaries.

Affects of Solidarity

In the course of my research, I found that former ISA members had not only engaged in actions geared toward overthrowing the Shah, but also participated in a wide range of other movements. This is how Jalil Mostashari, a former ISA member at Michigan State in the mid-1960s, described his activities: "The Black struggle was a part of the total international struggle for me. It was not only them. Sometimes the UAW [United Auto Workers] needed people on their picket line in Detroit. When Arab students had an action, we would participate in it. When we had an action, they would participate in it. Eritreans would come with us. Afghan students would come with us. Some people from Bengal—they were leftists—they would come with us."[27]

When I asked him what motivated this level of commitment to so many different causes, he looked me in the eyes, held my gaze, and spoke with the gravity of someone expressing a sacred truth: "If you want people to sympathize with you, you have to sympathize with them at the time of their need. You cannot just say things; you've got to believe it, really, in your heart. You have to have this flame within you that can warm others. You cannot say it with your tongue; it doesn't move anybody." This book takes its title from Jalil's words and from the description of the relationship between affective energy and political action embedded within it. To "believe" something "really, in your heart" describes an affective state that blurs the mind/body divide structuring Western enlightenment notions of subjectivity. To have "this flame within" is to embody a politics of solidarity as animating energy that burns, warms, and moves people toward others with whom they sense something shared.

I developed the concept "affects of solidarity" to describe embodied attachments to the liberation of others. Affects of solidarity are generated when revolutionary affects, or desires for revolution, circulate and converge across different populations and movements. It is important here to distinguish between affects of solidarity and emotions like pity or guilt that might accompany altruism or charity. Solidarity enables people who do not occupy the same position in a global or national hierarchy of power to imagine themselves as sharing something in common—a common enemy perhaps, or a common stance against injustice, or a common vision of the future. David Featherstone defines solidarity "as a relation forged through political struggle which seeks to challenge forms of oppression."[28] Solidarity, he explains, is transformative and relational, proceeding across the uneven terrain of race, gender, nation, and empire, bringing new political possibilities into being.[29] Solidarity does not automatically eradicate or transcend those divisions and can sometimes reproduce them, but it can also reroute our affiliations and attachments away from dominant hierarchies and toward new forms of connection.

By paying attention to affects of solidarity we can better understand how the power of solidarity "from below" emerges. If affect refers to our ability to be affected or changed by the world, and also our ability to effect change, then the question becomes: how and under what conditions is affect mobilized toward acts of solidarity? There may be a material basis for different groups of people coming to identify with one another and act collectively, such as a common interest in fighting a company that pollutes the environment and busts unions (for example, the "Teamsters and Turtles" coalition of union members and environmentalists that opposed NAFTA). But this kind of co-incidence of immediate, material interests is not always present or necessary for solidarity to occur. There was no immediate, material interest at stake when Iranian students marched with their American counterparts against the US war in Vietnam as they were not in danger of being drafted. I argue that the affective states mobilized and generated through acts of solidarity have the power to redefine the very notion of "interests," to change how we perceive our needs, desires, and commonalities. Affects of solidarity encompass a range of sensations and orientations toward the Other that are compelling precisely because they facilitate a new feeling of mutuality, connection, and collective power. This is how affective attachments to the well-being of others become rewarding and transformative, even among people who may previously have understood themselves to hold disparate or conflicting concerns.

The element of mobility that characterizes affect is perhaps most crucial to my formulation. Affects of solidarity accumulate and circulate, building in intensity and picking up new meanings as they move. Affects of solidarity draw people together from widely differing contexts and facilitate joint political action across the boundaries of race, class, gender, sexuality, religion, language, and nationality. They describe the affective state or mood that made Third World internationalism possible. Iranian student activists in the US were deeply affected by the conditions they encountered in diaspora, by the rebellions underway on and off college campuses. Depending on where they landed, ISA members had the opportunity to participate in mass movements against racism and war. Their activities constitute a missing piece of Afro-Asian studies historiography, bringing West Asian solidarity with African American and African liberation into focus. Like their American activist peers, Iranian students were influenced and inspired by the prolif-eration of Third World anticolonial movements and searched among them for models to adapt and follow. In turn, ISA members contributed to the shared feelings of militancy and solidarity among a larger leftist milieu by exposing the hidden brutalities of the alliance between the US and the Shah, and, along with Arab and Arab American students, by placing West Asia and North Africa on the map of activist affiliation and concern. In this way, they deepened and expanded an internationalist political culture that thrived by making connections between domestic and imperial forms of subjugation and by linking vastly different sites of resistance. These connections were sometimes material—as when the Shah was funneling weapons to suppress anticolonial struggles in Southern Africa—and always affective.

Among the most active Iranian students, Third World Marxism became the primary interpretive lens for their experiences in Iran and in the US. Even though the ISA was imagined as a coalition representing the interests of all Iranian foreign students, by the late 1960s many leading ISA activists were also affiliated with a handful of underground leftist parties. These par-ties followed various interpretations of Marxism-Leninism and Maoism. Some supported guerilla struggle while others looked to rural peasant movements or to the urban working class as the agent of change. By 1975, the competing influences of these parties, and disagreements among them, would cause the ISA to split. Despite this fragmentation, the Iranian anti-Shah student opposition would continue to grow and to deepen its connections with other revolutionary movements.[30] The fact that the ISA came to be dominated by Third World Marxism created a shared ideological framework with the rest of the US Third World Left, facilitating what Cynthia Young has called the "multiple translations and substitutions" necessary to "close the gaps between First and Third World subjects."[31] My argument is that analogies between the conditions faced by inhabitants of racialized urban space in the US and those of the colonial countryside, between Black and Brown Americans and the peasantries of Asia, Africa, and Latin America, were lived and felt as affects of solidarity, and that this force allowed dispar-ities and inconsistencies to recede in the construction of a deeply rewarding revolutionary imaginary.

However, even as affects of solidarity crossed national, racial, and other sites of difference, they did not necessarily transcend them. In the 1960s and 1970s, affects of solidarity did not attach equally to all liberation move-ments. Notably, feminist and gay liberation movements were not common areas of affiliation and solidarity for the Third World Marxist Left, including for the ISA. Rather than idealizing solidarity, this study explores these gaps and contradictions in order to better understand how affects of solidarity attach to some struggles and not others. I thus contribute to queer and feminist interventions into Afro-Asian studies by exploring how affective dissonance within movements became a launching point for challenges to hetero-patriarchal ideas and forms of organizing.[32]

Crucially, as my research shows, affects of solidarity do not necessarily stem from the same experiences of oppression; Iranian foreign students like Jalil were not targeted by racism the way that African Americans were, for example, and yet they could still identify with and support "the Black struggle." That "flame within" could emanate from vastly different encounters with injustice and still attract people to the same meetings and demonstrations. When it came to the divisions between men and women, however, solidarity was often conditional upon adherence to masculinist definitions of proper revolutionary activity. These were the conditions that gave rise to Third World and women-of-color feminism.[33] Below I apply my affective theory of revolutionary subjectivity to analyze the structures of feeling that facilitated, and impinged upon, solidarity between women and men in the ISA.

Affect, Gender, and Feminist Critique

The terms of belonging for women and men in the ISA reflected a set of feelings about the particular relationship between class, gender, and sexuality produced in the context of Western intervention in Iran. Class, gender, and sexuality, while not the only markers of difference among ISA members, emerged in my research as the most persistent challenges to building a united movement. New forms of revolutionary subjectivity both transgressed and reinforced the boundaries of traditional gender roles and class divisions. In the 1960s, as the first generation of Iranian feminist scholars of modern Iran have shown, the Shah co-opted the discourse, and even some of the demands, of Iranian feminists and imposed a top-down agenda that rested on thoroughly gendered notions of modernization.[34] The link between femininity and modernization crystalized in the figure of the Westernized bourgeois woman, adorned with a miniskirt and makeup. For opposition movements, religious and secular, this figure fused femininity, upper-class status, and imperial intervention into the quintessential symbol of the corruption and degradation of Iranian society under the Shah.[35] Anti-Shah forces from across the political spectrum railed against this figure and offered ways for women to regain their self-respect via adherence to particular revolutionary ideologies and gendered forms of participation in revolutionary activity. For the Marxist Left, women could never really be free until the larger socioeconomic system was transformed. Yet, within Marxist organizations, as Iranian feminist scholars have discussed, women's experiences were highly contradictory. On the one hand, becoming part of a clandestine movement for human liberation was exciting and empowering, especially when compared with life as a bourgeois housewife valued only for her sex appeal and reproductive capacity.[36] On the other hand, the Left remained male-dominated in leadership and outlook, invested in a hierarchical approach to liberation that subordinated the "woman question" to the anti-imperialist struggle.[37]

Hostile feelings toward the Westernized femininity promoted under the Shah's reign traveled with Iranian students to the US and fueled attachments to anti-capitalist, anti-consumerist ideals. Adherence to these ideals was also the manner in which mostly upper-class student activists tried to show that they had truly sided with the "toiling masses"—a population, the ISA routinely pointed out, which included millions of women. These women performed backbreaking labor in fields and dusty workshops and did not wear miniskirts or makeup. The exploited masses of women thus served as a noble foil to the "West-toxified" woman complicit with the Shah's regime. Feelings about class and gender were inextricably linked to feelings about the intertwining of imperialism and dictatorship, and were embedded within the revolutionary affects mobilized by the ISA in diaspora. Class and gender differences within the organization were mediated through affective attachments to new forms of revolutionary subjectivity, which were supposed to make those differences less visible and, therefore, less threatening to the unity of the movement. Through an ideology of "gender sameness," men and women repeated the notion that they were "the same," meaning already equal. Their "sameness" was supposedly achieved by mutual dedication to and participation in the cause, and through a tacit, if routinely broken, agreement that "serious" revolutionaries had no time or interest in the distractions of sexual desire and intimacy. Yet in practice, the ideology of gender sameness manifested as what Parvin Paidar has called "masculinization": for the good of the revolution, women would cut their hair short and wear clothing that hid the shape of their bodies.[38] At no point were men supposed to change the way they looked or acted to become more like women. Many women felt uncomfortable about such double standards, including those surrounding the sexual practices of men versus women, but willingly participated anyway. My research illuminates the affective investments women had in these gendered forms of revolutionary subject-making, which were not unique to the Iranian context.

Memories of gender sameness, masculinization, and efforts to side with the oppressed classes are loaded with contradictory sensations, affective dissonances that index deeply gendered states of being. Affects, to borrow Flatley's words, "come into being only *through* categories of class and gender" because these social formations "are woven into our emotional lives in the most fundamental way."[39] We must speak, then, of the intersectional character of revolutionary affects—affective experiences of state repression and resistance in Iran—which reside in bodies continuously impacted by patriarchy, compulsory heterosexuality, and class divisions.[40] While the men and women I interviewed recalled the joy that came from feeling part of a revolutionary family, estrangement, surprise, dismay, and regret toward the past often emerged as well, and sometimes in the course of a single memory. These "negative" feelings are certainly products of hindsight, inextricable from the events and experiences of the past forty years, and yet these feelings also reference affective states of ambivalence, tension, and discomfort that existed at the time. Sometimes these feelings drove efforts toward institutional and cultural change within the ISA and the Iranian Left. More frequently, they remained in an inchoate and unnamed affective register until conditions changed and they became available as sources of feminist critique and mobilization. As I argue in chapter 6, this is what happened in Tehran in March 1979, when a revolutionary women's uprising seemed to appear out of nowhere, catching all established parties off guard.

Given the demonization of Iranian society and culture as particularly oppressive to women, and the weaponization of this discourse by Western imperial countries, I have found it necessary and productive to adopt a relational approach that makes visible similarities between the gender and sexual politics of the Iranian internationalist Left and other diasporic and anticolonial revolutionary movements. In the United States, Iranian students were active alongside many non-Iranian movements that were also grappling with gender, sexual, and class divisions within their ranks. Iranian leftists were far from alone in reproducing existing hierarchies, demanding gendered forms of sacrifice in the name of unity and gendered forms of unity in the face of state repression. For the Third Worldist Left of the 1960s and 1970s, revolutionary affects attached to ideas, leaders, and organizations that represented the most compelling responses to oppressive conditions at the time. Across all racial, ethnic, and national groups, those responses were often bound up with the oppressions they sought to overcome, even as they offered animating visions of another possible world. Placing the gender and sexual politics of the ISA within this broader context undermines the reductionist, ahistorical blaming of Muslim culture as the source of gender and sexual oppression in Iran and on the Iranian Left. My research shows that the revolutionary affects of avowedly secular ISA members were embedded within social formations (gender, sexuality, and class) that were reconfigured at the intersection of imperialism, dictatorship, and diaspora. My argument is that this analysis of the relationship between affect and political processes must impact how we study the Iranian diaspora before and after 1979.

An Intersectional Approach to Iranian Diaspora Studies

The changing dynamics of US imperialism and dictatorship in Iran have been, since the US replaced Britain as the dominant imperial power in the middle of the twentieth century, the driving force behind the migration of Iranians abroad—whether as foreign students or as exiles, immigrants, and asylees—and the central problematic around which Iranian diasporic identity, culture, and politics have been organized in the US. Imperialism and dictatorship both stand in the way of freedom and justice for ordinary Iranian people, who might yet wish for a future that is neither a US neo-colony nor an Islamic republic. This is true whether US empire and dictatorship are in alignment, as they generally were during the reign of Mohammad Reza Shah, which is the focus of the current study, or whether these power structures are locked in a bitter and highly unequal conflict, as are the US and Iran today.

With so much emphasis generally, and understandably, placed on the rupture of the 1979 Iranian Revolution, many of the continuities between the pre- and postrevolutionary periods have been overlooked in ways that may distort our understanding of diasporic consciousness and political possibility. *This Flame Within* offers an approach that views major geopolitical shifts in US-Iran relations not so much as a before and after, but as different iterations of a crisis brought on by the incompatibility between "US interests" and popular democracy. I understand "US interests" as the mandate to intervene militarily, economically, and/or politically anywhere in the world to maintain the profitability and competitive edge of US capitalism and to suppress any entity considered threatening or even slightly unfavorable to this agenda. It is this agenda that has been so sympathetic to dictatorships around the world, including that of Mohammad Reza Shah, who was empowered to crush all opposition. And it is in this context that anticolonial opposition forces come to treat internal dissent as a vulnerability, as a weakness to be stamped out in the face of the continuous threat of state repression and foreign domination. Whether US interests were in alignment with the goals of the Iranian state or not, it was the interactions between state repression and imperial aggression that created the conditions for Iranian migration to the United States from the 1950s through to our current moment.

This integrated and dynamic way of framing a longer historical arc of displacement builds on over three decades of scholarship constituting the still-emerging interdisciplinary field of Iranian diaspora studies. In their introduction to a special journal issue on the topic, Babak Elahi and Persis M. Karim traced the shift from the use of terms like *exile, refugee,* and *immigrant* to the term *diaspora* within literary and sociological scholarship on Iranian populations abroad. They argue that the use of diaspora allows for investigations of Iranian experiences outside Iran that are organized not only in relation to Iran, but also in "mutually transformative" relationship to various host countries *and* to communities of Iranians within them.[41] Elahi and Karim carve out space for the study of the Iranian diaspora not primarily as a subset of Iranian studies, but as a field that "situates Iran and Iranian culture in the continuum of more global diasporic consciousness."[42] My emphasis on an intersectional approach to Iranian diaspora studies is a provocation to develop this nascent field further precisely by engaging analyses drawn from the global context of multiple diasporic experiences.[43] These include systemic critiques of capitalism, empire, racial formation, and the politics of gender and sexuality produced by scholars of Black and Third World feminisms, Asian American studies, Arab American studies, and queer-of-color diasporic critique. One of the most important insights I draw from these bodies of work is the need to expose and resist the hierarchical binary between West and East that creates conditions in which the diasporic racialized subject must either assimilate to the higher civilizational order or be rendered abject/threatening. To reject this logic in relation to the Iranian diaspora means to tackle directly the geopolitical polarization between the US and Iran that exerts massive pressure on our diasporic culture, politics, and subjectivity.

An intersectional approach to the Iranian diaspora would reject the notion, so common among the generation of Iranians who came to the US in the immediate aftermath of the 1979 revolution, that Iran has been "lost" to a uniquely oppressive Islamist state and that the US constitutes its polar opposite—a space of exceptional freedom.[44] Aside from the obvious Orientalism inscribed in this view, it removes the Islamic Republic from the political battles which brought it into being and also exempts it from the larger context of postcolonial dictatorships across Asia, Africa, and Latin America.[45] The corresponding construction of the US as "free" disregards the structural brutality of settler colonialism, white supremacy, poverty, mass incarceration, and the rampant gender and sexual violence embedded in every sector of US society. Furthermore, this dominant "polar opposites" paradigm cannot account for the complicated role of US empire in the rise of undemocratic postcolonial governments, whether formed with US support or in reaction to US imperial power.

At the same time, an intersectional Iranian diaspora studies framework departs from a still potent strain of anti-imperialism, which insists the job of Iranians in the US is only to denounce US aggression and not to discuss the domestic repression that shapes Iranian society. This position makes transnational solidarity with Iranians living in Iran impossible, for it refuses to respond to popular opposition to and alienation from the Iranian government and offers no support to grassroots activists persecuted for contesting policies that are anathema to even the most broadly defined progressive agenda.[46] Furthermore, it aligns the Left in the US with the Iranian government, conceding the political terrain of concern for repression in Iran either to liberal human rights advocates—who often take for granted the benevolence of US influence abroad—or to pro-war media outlets and politicians.[47] The leftist diasporic mandate to only criticize "our own government," meaning the US government, is driven by the legitimate fear that saying anything negative about Iranian society can and will be used as a justification for sanctions, war, and US-sponsored "regime change."

This amounts to a transnational version of an argument that has long circulated among oppressed and targeted groups: that we must not air our "dirty laundry" in front of those who would seize on any excuse to do us harm. Women-of-color feminists have had to engage with this argument as a condition of possibility for their very existence.[48] From the 1977 statement of the Combahee River Collective, to anthologies like *This Bridge Called My Back* and *Colonize This!*, to the work of Arab and Arab American feminists like Rabab Abdulhadi, Evelyn Alsultany, and Nadine Naber, women-of-color feminists in the US have responded to the "dirty laundry" debate by arguing that our movements against racism, economic exploitation, and imperialism will become stronger and more effective if we also oppose gender and sexual oppression.[49] Even more than this, women-of-color and Third World feminists have demonstrated that racism, capitalism, and empire mobilize and depend on particular constructions of gender and sexual difference in order to justify and carry out their operations of power.[50] My aim in this book is to continue this work by addressing multiple, "interlocking" or "intersecting" forms of oppression that impact Iranians and by refusing to rank or silence systemic injustices.[51] The agenda of those who would do us harm is an operating constraint and a workplace hazard, demanding that we make it as difficult as possible for our ideas and activities to be co-opted.

An intersectional Iranian diaspora studies framework addresses this set of challenges by drawing on several branches of feminist thought and practice. These include the theoretical and conceptual tools of women-of-color feminism developed in a US context, in particular Black feminism, which can be productively adapted to the transnational relationship between the Iranian diaspora and Iran. By illuminating the multiple sources of oppression and inequality that structure US *and* Iranian societies, we can refuse to side with either government and open up new spaces of mutual connection and solidarity. An intersectional approach to the Iranian diaspora also builds on the frameworks of postcolonial feminist scholars and applies them to the diaspora, looking at how gendered discourses of Orientalism and modernity impact people displaced to the heart of empire. Feminist scholarship on West Asia and North Africa has demonstrated the centrality of gender and sexuality for delineating the categories of West and East and for positioning the masculinized West as dominant over the feminized East. Leila Ahmed, Leila Abu-Lughod, and Deniz Kandiyoti, among others, have argued that gender and sexuality in Muslim-majority nations—and in particular, gendered forms of dress like hijab—become politically loaded markers of difference mobilized for distinct, often competing ends by anticolonial governments and by Western imperial powers.[52] In postrevolutionary Iran, the unequal legal status of women, state-imposed hijab, and specific Islamized ideals about women's roles in the family and in society are crucial to the state's notions of citizenship and sovereignty and to its anti-imperialist ideology.[53]

Postcolonial and transnational feminist scholars have also critiqued the shifting discourses of US imperialism and its co-optation of women's rights.[54] As the world witnessed to disastrous effect in Afghanistan, the US has marketed war and occupation as necessary preconditions for the liberation of Muslim women.[55] Transnational feminists have done the difficult work of analyzing gender and sexual oppression across the violent divide of Global South and Global North, generating incisive critiques of the gender and sexual oppression on which imperialism, neocolonialism, and corporate globalization rest.[56] The challenge for an intersectional approach to the Iranian diaspora is how to counter the deadly combination of Orientalism,

Islamophobia, and imperialism, all of which rely on gendered systems of meaning for their legitimacy, while also engaging with the real problems women and gender and sexual minorities in Iran face. In fact, Iranians living in Iran also confront this challenge, and there is much to learn from the variety of strategies of resistance that different groups have used to advocate for internal change from below.[57]

This is also not a new problem, since authoritarian rule and imperialist intervention have characterized Iranian society for more than a century. There is a rich tradition of Iranian feminist scholarship by Afsaneh Najmabadi, Eliz Sanasarian, Parvin Paidar, Haideh Moghissi, Homa Hoodfar, Minoo Moallem, Nima Naghibi, and others who have parsed the gender and sexual politics of the Pahlavi dynasty (1925–79), of the various opposition tendencies that called for its overthrow, and of the Islamic Republic that took its place.[58] State-building ideologies, as well as opposition movements, all have a politics of gender and sexuality—that is, ideas about the "natural" and/ or "proper" roles and attributes ascribed to the constructed categories of "woman" and "man," which are enforced and regulated in particular ways. This scholarship reveals many similarities between supposedly antithetical regimes and ideologies, and works to shift debates over gender and sexual oppression away from the familiar dichotomies of West versus East, secularism versus Islam. Indeed, both the monarchists and the leftists in Iran shared a similar teleological narrative of Third World development; the major difference was over who should benefit from the resulting abundance.[59] Women's rights were always subordinated to these narratives of developmentalist progress, either circumscribed by a modernizing dictatorship or subsumed under the "primary" project of national liberation.

An intersectional framework expands upon this legacy of Iranian feminist scholarship on twentieth-century Iran by responding to three sites of concern at the same time: American imperial pretentions to saving Muslim women; the repressive policies and attitudes regulating gender and sexuality in Iran; and the repressive policies and attitudes regulating gender and sexuality in the US.[60] This approach can lay the foundations for an unapologetic, anti-imperialist approach to understanding and supporting struggles around gender and sexual equality in Iran on the basis of an engagement with related struggles in the US (and elsewhere). The ISA's multifaceted and multi-sited critique of imperialism and dictatorship, and its consistent practice of making connections between oppressive conditions in the US and in Iran, is, therefore, a necessary starting point for an intersectional feminist approach to the Iranian diaspora in the US.

Re-Periodizing the Diaspora

Members of the ISA were part of the first mass migration of Iranians to the United States, which was composed of student-visa holders scattered across Europe, North America, and parts of West and South Asia. I refer to this population as a diaspora, even though the temporary nature of their student visas ensured that most of them returned home when their studies had finished.[61] Many could not go home, however, because their political activity had made them targets of the Iranian government. Nadine Naber's theorization of "diasporas of empire" highlights the fact that this population of foreign students was produced by the economic and political priorities of US imperialism in Iran and draws our attention to the ways that "empire inscribes itself on the diasporic subject within the domestic (national) borders of empire."[62] Throughout this book, I explore the inscription of US empire on diasporic subjectivity in the form of the turn to revolutionary politics. The inability for some foreign students to return home safely was a side effect of their political activity in response to Western-backed authoritarian modernization. It was this formation that produced a foreign student diaspora in the first place.

From the late 1950s, following the CIA-backed coup in Iran, through 1980, tens of thousands of Iranians came to the US to study—more than from any other nation.[63] At the time of the revolution in Iran, there were approximately 50,000 Iranian students enrolled in American colleges and universities.[64] I call the diasporic students of this era "imperial model minorities" (see chapter 2) because they were supposed to model the benefits of US-sponsored development in the Third World as an alternative to national liberation movements. Iranian imperial model minorities were encouraged to adopt a US worldview, and their presence in the US was considered evidence of the success of US Cold War hegemony. Rather than only viewing the nationally bounded space of Iran as the site of revolutionary opposition to the alliance between the US and the Shah, this study of the ISA shows that the process of "losing" Iran as a watchdog for US interests also unfolded in diaspora, in the US itself.

The revolutionary affects of ISA members left them alienated from the mainstream of Iranian and US societies and fueled a vibrant diasporic counterculture that has been almost completely left out of studies of the Iranian diaspora.[65] Until very recently, scholarship on the Iranian diaspora in the US was chiefly concerned with the immigrant population that fled the 1979 revolution and its aftermath.[66] Traumatized by revolution and war and often persecuted as "counterrevolutionaries" by the new Iranian government, this latter group developed an exilic culture oriented around deep animosity toward the Islamic Republic and nostalgia for the era of the pro-Western Shah. The majority of these immigrants leveraged their upper-class backgrounds and advanced degrees to achieve notably high rates of economic success.[67] They tended to embrace what I call a "Persian imperial identity" constituted around an attachment to a so-called Aryan racial heritage associated with the pre-Islamic Persian Empire and a disassociation from Arabs and other people of color in the US.[68]

While it has largely been through literary writing that a more complex picture of Iranian American/diaspora identity has emerged, academic scholarship is only just beginning to attend to a wider variety of affiliations.[69] Neda Maghbouleh's groundbreaking sociological study, *The Limits of Whiteness: Iranian Americans and the Everyday Politics of Race*, revealed how racism and Islamophobia whipped up during the 1979–80 hostage crisis and in the aftermath of the 9/11 attacks have disrupted the process of assimilation for younger generations and produced alienation from the Persian imperial identity of Iranian immigrant parents and grandparents.[70] In this context, new racial identities and solidarities with Arabs, South Asians, African Americans, and other people of color, sometimes organized around a pan-Muslim affiliation, have become available to Iranians in the US.[71] These findings are all the more interesting if we understand them as a contemporary iteration of "affects of solidarity," a diasporic orientation that resonates with the pre-1979 period and the story of the ISA.

The capacious internationalism practiced by the ISA exemplified an anti-imperialist worldview that linked the US and Iran as sites of resistance to unjust state power. Such a view offers a radical alternative to enduring notions of a clash of cultures or civilizations, of Islam versus the West, that have cast an indelible shadow over how the Iranian Revolution, Iranian diasporic subjectivity, and US-Iran relations have been understood ever since. While these Orientalist logics stretch back to the beginnings of European incursion into Asia, they have been reinvigorated by the US-Iran standoff, now in its fifth decade. Both Washington and Tehran continually reinforce the idea of a fundamental cultural difference between the two nations, with each government competing to claim moral superiority over the other. In what has become a familiar script, the US accuses Iran of promoting and sponsoring terrorism, revising the Truman Doctrine's mandate to fight "communism" anywhere in the world in order to legitimize a permanent, global "war on terror." The Iranian government counters by declaring itself the main obstacle to US imperialism in the Middle East, the champion of the oppressed. It then folds this rhetoric into official justifications for domestic repression in the name of national security and for its own regional imperial interventions. This polarizing context exerts a structuring constraint over global politics today, limiting the political horizon to a choice between accepting US hegemony or aligning with some form of Islamic governance.

Two examples illustrate the stakes of finding a way out of this impasse. First: In 2009, when a pro-democracy movement erupted in the streets of Iranian cities, the Iranian government quickly labeled it a Western imperialist conspiracy and unleashed a violent crackdown on dissent. This is a script the Iranian government has followed each time its citizens rise up to demand structural change. Second: During the popular uprising in Egypt in 2011, the specter of Iran hovered overhead, an ever-present deterrent against the complete dismantling of the military dictatorship. Iran, many people argued, was proof that the sudden overthrow of a pro-Western authoritarian regime could result in something even worse: an Islamic republic. This logic shares much in common with Margaret Thatcher's famous declaration at the end of the Cold War: "there is no alternative." This phrase, which became known by the acronym TINA, has been used to assert that any attempt to create an alternative to Western capitalism inevitably leads to totalitarianism. Today, by running an authoritarian state in the name of "revolution," the Iranian government helps to discredit the idea of "revolution" altogether. After the broken promises and bloody betrayals of so many postcolonial states, it *can* seem as if there is no alternative to joining the US world order, waging the war on terror, embracing neoliberal economic policies, and intensifying the militarization of everyday life. Ironically, even while it maintains independence from US domination, the Iranian government pursues its own version of austerity, privatization, and the hyper-policing of public space. This can indeed make it seem like there is no alternative outside the hegemonic logics of authoritarian capitalism, whether in secular or religious garb.

Working against the cynicism of TINA doctrines old and new, this book revisits the period leading up to the shift in US-Iran relations from special friends to arch enemies in order to recuperate the sense of political possibility and dynamism that enlivened an era of revolutionary internationalism. It draws on this history to reframe the "US-Iran conflict" as a long, unequal, and deeply fraught relationship that originates with US efforts to control Iranian resources and the larger Persian Gulf region. In the chapters that follow, I analyze the impact of this relationship on the Iranians who joined the ISA and explore the web of affective, material, and ideological connections that facilitated solidarity between the ISA and other liberation movements.

By paying attention to how the material, the affective, and the ideological interact in the making of revolutionary subjects, movements, and practices, we can better understand how rebellions can erupt from within spaces of privilege, turning the celebrated figure of the Iranian imperial model minority into an anti-imperialist revolutionary, or, according to the US Coast Guard, a "known terrorist."

A Methodology of Possibility

This Flame Within is concerned with both recuperating a diasporic movement of Iranian revolutionaries in the United States and with critiquing that movement at the same time. But how can this be done? Surely one must decide to be *for* something or *against* it, to either redeem or to condemn. The overwhelming majority of former ISA members I interviewed took a different approach, and I listened while they grappled with who they had been and what they had done. The memories I gathered were filled with feelings of regret, shame, and grief as well as joy, elation, and hope. I developed what I call a "methodology of possibility" to analyze both the "positive" and "negative" feelings associated with the Iranian leftist past for their productive, future-oriented potential. A methodology of possibility allows a non-teleological approach to reading an archive, one that is attentive to memories, affects, and emotions marginalized or erased by dominant accounts of the failures of revolutionary leftist movements.[72] It shares an affinity with the queer futurity José Muñoz describes as a mode of critiquing the "devastating logic of the here and now," recuperating hope as something always on the horizon.[73] A methodology of possibility takes the collective feeling of hope or possibility itself—however fleeting or naive—as a legitimate object of study, as a way of rethinking the legacy of anti-imperialist revolutions.

The legacy of the Iranian Left—before, during, and after the 1979 revolution—is a site of tremendous affective and emotional discord among the Iranian diaspora, and any discussion of the ISA is likely to trigger an avalanche of strong feelings among readers directly impacted by the events of the period. The Left was heavily persecuted—by the Shah and by the Islamic Republic—and was unable to survive the revolutionary period with its organizations, members, and ideas intact. With a few notable exceptions, ISA members echoed the major Iranian leftist parties in offering uncritical support to Ayatollah Khomeini in his capacity as the leader of the revolution.[74] As a whole, the organized Iranian Left did not marshal its forces, limited though they were, to advocate for a more democratic postrevolutionary society or to defend equal citizenship for women and religious and ethnic minorities.[75] Many volumes have been written about the reasons for these failures, attributing them to dogmatism, disconnection from Iranian society, the stifling conditions of state repression, a fundamental misapprehension of Khomeinism, and a suicidal naivete.[76]

The postrevolutionary generation of Iranian feminist scholars cited earlier emerged from this experience of betrayal and disappointment to produce ground-breaking work on the politics of gender and sexuality at the intersection of imperialism and dictatorship. While the organized Left of the ISA's generation has been discredited and crushed, Iranian feminists, labor activists, students, and others persist in organizing and agitating for the society in which they want to live. The economic warfare of the US sanctions policy in Iran, and the constant threats of American military intervention, undermine the prospects of these activists and grind the population into despair. At this bleak moment, it is all the more important to recuperate a history of thousands of young Iranians who imagined, and even glimpsed, a future for Iran that was neither a monarchical client state nor a theocratic dictatorship. A methodology of possibility allows us to generate new meanings from the ISA's fraught and flawed legacy, to claim the mistakes as much as the successes as part of a diasporic inheritance for future generations to parse and transform.

As illustrated above, the affective archive I have assembled from interviews with former ISA members makes possible a comparative, transnational, and intersectional feminist critique of Third Worldist Marxism, which, I argue, can strengthen our future movements against multiple, interlocking oppressions in the US and in Iran. At the same time, the memories gathered in this book reveal a set of feelings that force us to contend with the Third World leftist experiment as it was lived and experienced from day to day, rather than as a prelude to some inevitable failure or betrayal. Stories of collective self-sacrifice, dedication, and discipline index ways of being in the world that are only possible when the logics of capitalist individualism lose their hold and a passion for justice shapes new forms of subjectivity. Shahnaz, who joined the ISA in Northern California, did not lament the time she spent in prison in Iran after the revolution. Instead, she declared, "That experience is one of the greatest of my life!" and described with palpable joy the community of women she had the chance to know behind bars. She, like so many women and men of her generation, had devoted her life to the cause of freedom and was willing to suffer the consequences. This is just one example of an affective attachment to revolutionary ways of being in the world that has endured alongside devastating loss.

Many such examples emerged in the course of my research, compelling me to make sense of melancholic attachments to revolutionary activity that have been marginalized by the dominant narrative of leftist failure and complicity. I borrow the term *resistant nostalgia* from Marianne Hirsch and Leo Spitzer to describe affective attachments that disrupt the dominant forms of diasporic nostalgia for pre-revolutionary Iran, for the "good life" lived under the Shah.[77] Resistant nostalgia allows us to engage with a sustained longing for a freedom that never arrived, an ongoing attachment to a wild and uncompromising desire for a different, better world. In this way, memories of revolutionary subjectivity, sociality, and solidarity can become part of the terrain of diasporic consciousness and identity, with implications for how we view the past and the future. Indeed, the resistant nostalgia of some ISA members makes it necessary to tell the story of the Iranian revolution itself differently. Memories of participation in the women's uprising in Tehran in March 1979, in which tens of thousands of women took to the streets and mounted the first open challenge to the consolidation of a new Islamist government, contain another set of possibilities for what might have been.[78] They gesture toward an intersectional anti-imperialist politics that began to emerge from within the revolutionary process itself. By using a methodology of possibility to center these fleeting days of protest (see chapter 6), new sources of knowledge about the postcolonial relationship between gender, sexuality, and national sovereignty that resonate far beyond the Iranian context become available; and new losses, which continue to shape diasporic subjectivity and politics today, become visible.

Resistant nostalgia is out of sync with neat stories of leftist failure. It pushes us to question the political stakes of how the past is remembered and how the permissible scope of subsequent political action is determined. Resistant nostalgia, as a key aspect of a methodology of possibility, keeps alive the memories, affects, and emotions generated in moments when collective aspirations for human liberation are still abstracted from any actually existing state form. These moments remind us that the outcomes of revolutions are unpredictable rather than inevitable. Resistant nostalgia expresses affects that refuse to be vanquished even in a period of defeat. The words of Egyptian activist Alaa Abdel-Fattah offer a heartbreaking contemporary example. Writing from his prison cell in Cairo in 2016, five years after his arrest for participating in the uprising that ousted US-backed President Hosni Mubarak, Abdel-Fattah ended his despairing account of a lost revolution with these incisive words: "But one thing I do remember, one thing I know: the sense of possibility was real. It may have been naive to believe our dream could come true, but it was not foolish to believe that another world was possible. It really was. Or at least that's how I remember it."[79] *This Flame Within* takes that "sense of possibility" seriously as something "real": a revolutionary affect attached to a memory—however fleeting—that just might harbor our best hopes for the future.

Organization of the Book

The chapters of this book follow the transnational journey of Iranian foreign students and the movement they built. Chapter 1, "Revolutionary Affects and the Archive of Memory," reads formative experiences of dictatorship and US empire in Iran as an archive of revolutionary affects *and* a partial genealogy of the modern Iranian freedom struggle. This chapter argues that Iranian student radicalization must be understood as a transnational process that began in Iran—a place that was itself a site of regional and international circulation of revolutionary movements, ideas, banned literatures, and democratic aspirations, as well as technologies of imperial and state repression. I examine the relationship between affect, memory, and diasporic politics, and argue that melancholic attachments to pre-1979 moments of popular resistance continue to circulate revolutionary affects across the generations.

Chapters 2 and 3 focus on the formation, development, and impact of the ISA on public opinion, discourse, and institutional practices in the US. In chapter 2, "Revolt in the Metropole," I examine the unexpected consequences of the migration of foreign students—and their revolutionary affects—to the US at the height of the Cold War. The chapter names this population "imperial model minorities," a revision of the immigrant "model minority" category that shifts the site of proscribed normativity from the domestic sphere of citizenship to the transnational sphere of empire. I investigate migrant radicalization as a response to the cooperation between imperialism and dictatorship, rather than only as a reaction against racial discrimination and assimilation in the US, and trace the history of the ISA's emergence as an opposition organization. Chapter 3, "Making the Most of an American Education," draws on interviews, ISA publications, and mainstream and student newspapers to analyze ISA actions designed to expose the complicity of US universities, law enforcement, and government with state repression in Iran. I argue that the ISA played an important role in undermining American popular support for US influence in West Asia by bringing the spectacle of torture and suffering in Iran into the public sphere in the US. This chapter also draws on mainstream media coverage to analyze the backlash against the ISA among ordinary Americans, pundits, and politicians. The ISA's militant, leftist opposition to the relationship between the US and the Shah triggered a racist, xenophobic reaction years before the taking of American hostages in Iran.

I then turn to look at the extensive cross-pollination that occurred between the Iranian foreign-student opposition, the US Left, and diasporic anticolonial movements. Chapter 4, "The Feeling and Practice of Solidarity," draws on interviews with former ISA members and other former activists of the era, campus newspapers, ISA literature, and activist ephemera to excavate ISA participation in the anti-Vietnam War, Black liberation, and Palestine liberation movements. I look at how revolutionary affects among disparate groups of people converged into powerful affects of solidarity that made mutual support and affiliation into a way of being in relation to others that shaped everyday life. This chapter contributes to feminist and queer interventions into Afro-Asian studies, a field that has not focused on the gender and sexual hierarchies within revolutionary organizations. Resisting the notion that revolutionary militancy is always already masculinist, I argue that acts of solidarity were affectively rewarding for women as much as for men. This chapter departs from a celebratory mode of studying the high points of Third World internationalism *and* from the narrative of leftist failure that weighs so heavily on the Iranian experience. Instead, it argues that the cross-pollinations between the ISA and non-Iranian leftist movements evidence forms of affinity across difference that provided the context for the later emergence of feminist and queer revolutionary politics.

Chapter 5, "Political Cultures of Revolutionary Belonging," looks at the internal political culture of the ISA and the Iranian leftist groups operating within it. I theorize the "revolutionary time" that reoriented ISA members away from the linear march of authoritarian developmentalism and analyze how the urgent imperative to bring about a revolution infused the management of gender and sexual difference in the ISA.[80] This chapter situates the everyday gender and sexual practices of the ISA, such as "gender sameness" and "masculinization," within the broader leftist milieu in which these students lived and organized. By using a comparative, diasporic framework, my analysis undermines facile religious or cultural explanations for persistent sexism within the Iranian left and allows for a serious engagement with the affective investments of women themselves in contradictory forms of gendered revolutionary subjectivity.

Chapter 6, "Intersectional Anti-Imperialism: Alternative Genealogies of Revolution and Diaspora," looks at what happened when ISA members returned to Iran to participate in the unfolding process of revolution. The chapter focuses on the mass uprising of women in Tehran in March 1979, which posed the first major challenge to the curtailing of democracy by the revolutionary government. I argue for the centrality of the women's uprising, which has been minimized in the historiography of 1979, to understanding the trajectory of the Iranian revolution overall. Through close readings of interviews, movement literature, and video documentary footage, I argue that these events constitute a neglected part of a genealogy of Third World revolutionary feminism that has implications for diasporic and anti-imperialist politics today.

The concluding chapter, "Revolutionary Affects and the Remaking of Diaspora," follows the fragmentation and disorientation of the Iranian student Left under conditions of postrevolutionary repression—conditions that led the majority of my interviewees to return to the US. I utilize a methodology of possibility to explore the political potential of revolutionary affects that live on in diaspora, where they have been marginalized by the prevalence of hostile feelings toward the revolution and the Left. I argue that the affective attachments of former ISA members to the possibility of an Iran that was neither a US client state nor an Islamic republic illustrate resistant nostalgia, a form of exilic nostalgia that disrupts the normative Iranian diasporic nostalgia for the "good life" under the Shah. This chapter reprises the major concepts and arguments within the book as a whole and ends with provocations for reimagining the way Iranians in the US might relate to the traumatic history that has produced our diaspora. I consider the implications of resistant nostalgia—as a means of maintaining an open relationship to the political hopes of the previous era—for contemporary diasporic affective and political orientations.

A Note on the Interview Process

Among the Iranians I interviewed, some individuals requested the use of pseudonyms or the omission of their last names, and I have honored these requests. While they came from families with varying degrees of religiosity, all of the men and women I interviewed were from the Shi'i Muslim majority except two Jewish women and one Sunni man. The majority were from upper-middle class or upper-class backgrounds. Most, but not all, were members of ISA chapters in Northern California, Washington-Baltimore, New York City, or Texas-Oklahoma. All but three were also members of transnational underground leftist parties. Currently, twenty-nine of the people I interviewed live in the US and one lives in Iran.[81] Although the details of their lives differ in important ways, as a cohort they are survivors of the persecution that followed the establishment of the Islamic Republic of Iran. This book would not have been possible without their willingness to share their memories of revolutionary activity and their reflections on this tumultuous period of their lives. I am profoundly grateful for their generosity and trust. It is important to acknowledge, of course, that memory is slippery, ephemeral, and contested, and to be aware that it is always filtered through present concerns and adapted to particular audiences.[82] As Maurice Halbwachs, who developed the concept of collective memory over seventy years ago, wrote, "the mind reconstructs its memories under the pressure of society," and in the case of former ISA members, both US and Iranian societies have been hostile to the leftist politics that once defined their lives.[83] I treat the memories of those who shared their stories for this book as a living archive of how subjects negotiate that which cannot be forgotten, the hopes that have not died, the wounds that do not heal.

It is also important to note that the relationship between interviewer and interviewee shapes what memories are shared and how. Halbwachs noted precisely this facet of the workings of memory when he wrote, "most of the time, when I remember, it is others who spur me on."[84] Inevitably, my own interests and concerns shaped the direction of the interviews and, thus, the process of selecting and crafting the stories that were told. My approach to those I interviewed was evidence of the transmission of revolutionary affects across borders and generations. I disclosed to the former ISA members I interviewed that my father had been involved on the periphery of the movement during his student days at Howard University (although only three people remembered him). For many of them, I became "like a daughter," a sentiment I heard again and again. At the same time, several of my interviewees also remarked that I was quite unlike their actual children, many of whom, they felt, were not particularly interested in the history we were discussing. Invariably, I was asked to account for this difference, which set me apart in their eyes from my generational peers. I was open about my own history of political involvement; like the men and women I interviewed, I too joined a revolutionary organization in college and devoted many years of my life to the large and small causes it championed. The major difference, aside from the specificity of the Marxist traditions to which we had each adhered, was that my membership had not coincided with a global revolutionary conjuncture; the personal and political stakes were much lower for me than they were for this older generation of Iranian activists. However, my intimate familiarity with leftist political cultures, often with the same texts and historical debates in which my interviewees had immersed themselves when they were young, allowed for an ease of conversation and omitted any need to explain or defend the choice to make revolutionary politics the center of one's life. The fact that I left my organization after twelve years but did not renounce this part of my past meant that I also shared their ambivalent and melancholic relationship to the Left. I carried my own resistant nostalgia—for my lived experiences of collective struggle and for a previous revolutionary era that ended before I was old enough to participate. This shared affective state or affinity provided a sense of safety, leading some of the people I interviewed to talk about particularly painful memories for the first time and even to express a sense of solace that comes from (finally) feeling understood.

One brief exchange illustrates this dynamic. Jaleh Pirnazar, a Jewish woman who was a member of the Northern California branch of the ISA, described her parents' opposition to her revolutionary activity. Knowing that I also have a Jewish mother, she was curious about how my mother had reacted to my all-consuming approach to activism. I told her that my mother was very disappointed that I went to college and spent so much of my time protesting instead of studying. Jaleh said that this was exactly how her parents had felt, that she was wasting her opportunities in the US. I added that I did not think I had wasted my time and began to list some of the campaigns in which I was proud to have participated, such as preventing campus police from carrying guns, organizing Palestine solidarity actions, and supporting a local teacher's strike.

"But these are all good causes!" Jaleh said, interrupting me. She nodded to show her approval, not unlike a proud mother might.

"We did a lot of good things," I continued, "but sometimes I look back and think—"

"You would have done it differently," she said.

"I would have done it differently. At the time, it was just about—"

"Becoming accepted in a cause that is so good." We sat quietly for a moment. Jaleh had finished my sentences, and now she smiled, as if to affirm that we each knew just how the other felt. The feeling we shared was the starting point for the study that unfolds in the chapters that follow.

1

Revolutionary Affects and the Archive of Memory

I met Jalil Mostashari by accident in fall 2011, in the midst of the Occupy Wall Street encampment in downtown Manhattan. It was indeed a chance encounter, for Jalil lives in Tehran and was only in the US briefly to visit his son, an activist involved in the occupation of Zuccotti Park. I found Jalil, who appeared at ease and rather delighted, sitting on the steps of the park among a group of Iranian foreign students offering this advice: "Social movements, they are like rainwater. They are imbibed by the earth, and the spring comes out somewhere you don't expect. It has been raining here; you have the spring there. These are all connected to each other. Do not think of a social movement as a one-time finishing act." This metaphor aptly describes the subterranean legacy of Iranian democratic and leftist movements in the twentieth century, which emerged in the course of the interviews I conducted for this study. During severe droughts of intense state repression that destroyed these movements organizationally, they survived in the underground of memory, a trickle just strong enough to nourish future generations.

Memories of former members of the Iranian Students Association (ISA) thus form part of a much larger archive of the circulation of revolutionary affects in twentieth-century Iranian society. In an effort to understand the conditions of possibility for the creation of an Iranian revolutionary movement in diaspora, this chapter examines the process of politicization for Iranian foreign students as a transnational phenomenon that began in Iran. Iran was not a hermetically sealed place with a purely national culture, but rather a site of influence for multiple empires as well as for revolutionary ideas and movements from within and beyond its borders. When I asked former ISA members I interviewed, "How did you become political?" the responses came in the form of childhood memories of state-sponsored violence and collective resistance that were still charged with fear, grief, joy, and defiance. References to previous generations of activists influenced by the Russian Revolution of 1917 also popped up, like Jalil's springs, in unlikely places, revealing the intergenerational transmission of revolutionary affects even in the absence of organizational continuities. These references evoke the ISA's prehistory, a collective history of struggle and defeat and a melancholic refusal to accept that defeat as the end of history.

In the accounts that follow, I note how these affective legacies were incorporated in different ways into the subjectivities of two generations of revolutionaries who span the two decades of the ISA's activity. The first generation includes those foreign students born in the 1930s and 1940s, who were old enough to remember the 1953 CIA-led coup in Iran and who came to the US in the 1960s. The second generation, born after the coup, arrived in the US in the 1970s. I interviewed eighteen people born before 1953 and twelve born after. The seven narrative excerpts included here are weighted toward the first generation because of the longer historical arc this older cohort could recall. The archive of memories I assembled is not intended to represent the experiences of thousands of members of the Confederation of Iranian Students (National Union) (CISNU) across several countries or even across all ISA chapters in the US; rather, these memories are individual explorations of a larger phenomenon: the complex and unpredictable interaction between dramatic historical events and the intimate experiences of everyday life that shape people into political subjects. My interviewees remind us that history is mapped onto bodies, which register the sensations and moods of a certain time and place and then keep going, bringing affects and emotions from one context to another, offering up new interpretations of the past from the always shifting vantage point of the present.

The movement of memory—its selectivity, changeability, erasures, and disjunctures—may be all the more apparent for the exile or the refugee who cannot return to the places that are being remembered, who can only conjure up the past that was home from the ongoing displacement of diaspora. Migration, as a mass phenomenon produced by the ravages of capitalism and empire, war, revolution, and dictatorship, has posed a challenge to the normative association between memory and place that has been foundational to the construction of national memory as a shared, collective past grounded in a specific geography.[1] Diasporic memory, however, is characterized by distance, scattering, and fragmentation, and scholars have had to account for the ways it "cannot be contained within the traditional, nation-state format of memory studies."[2]

This study of the marginalized experience of the Iranian Left in diaspora draws on recent theories of memory and migration, which have emphasized the potential for diasporic memory to commemorate precisely that which has been excised in the process of constructing a collective national memory.[3] Viewed in this light, migrant memories are no less authentic or valid because of the distance that separates people from the places they remember. If there is a fixed point in time and space that matters for how we interpret memory, it is the present rather than the past. As Julia Creet argues, "memory is where we have arrived rather than where we have left."[4] Paul Ricoeur reframed the link between memory and place as relational, arguing that memory becomes an archive of what happens when the body moves from place to place, encountering new moods, audiences, and social environments.[5] This relationality makes it possible for some memories to interrupt nationalistic narratives of unified identities, including those new forms of nationalism that cohere in diaspora. The memories of former ISA members, I argue, reveal the affective dissonances and political fragmentations that characterize both diaspora and home.

If "movement is what produces memory," then when former ISA members share their memories of politicization during the time of childhood in Iran, they are also sharing evidence of the impact of the journeys they have taken and the diasporic locations where they have arrived and settled.[6] Regardless of their official legal status, former ISA members tended to speak in ways that are exemplary of refugee memories. As Nergis Canefe writes in her study of Pakistani and Iranian Muslims in Canada, they tend to convey "a home country and society . . . as a place where there remains an unfinished struggle for justice and change."[7] For people largely removed from direct political participation on the ground in Iran, "collective memories framed by the exilic condition provide the context within which this struggle continues from the diaspora."[8] Childhood memories of home are thus layered with meanings accumulated at every stage of the journey, which are reinterpreted in the context of the polarized politics of diaspora.

I have borrowed Marianne Hirsch and Leo Spitzer's term *resistant nostalgia* to characterize the affective and interpretive work that Iranian diasporic memories of revolutionary possibilities can do in relation to dominant narratives of nation and diaspora.[9] Resistant nostalgia as a revolutionary affect is deeply melancholic, constituting a persistent attachment to the democratic Iran that might have been *and* to the experiences that informed a commitment to revolutionary politics. Becoming political in the 1960s and 1970s meant engaging with an inheritance of loss: during the first half of the twentieth-century in Iran, each generation tried and failed to liberate the country from the interdependent forces of (indirect) colonialism (*este'mar*) and dictatorship (*estebdad*). These losses continued to exert a powerful, politicizing pull, especially on those who could remember the feelings of victory before the defeats, making it possible for revolutionary affects to flow from one generation to the next. The 1953 coup d'état remains an especially powerful site of resistant nostalgia—as a moment of the loss of Iranian political and economic independence, but also as the event precipitating the destruction of mass democratic and communist movements.

Upon arriving in the US, Iranian foreign students often discovered that Americans had no knowledge of Iranian society or of the US government's role in forcibly reshaping it. In this context, a melancholic attachment to loss became a source of informal education for American classmates and friends, doubt spreading like cracks in the edifice of US exceptionalism. Especially in the early years of the ISA's activity, it was common for Iranian activists to find their American peers entirely ignorant of the coup and of the democratic movement that had been sacrificed to Washington's preference for a pliable shah. Of his classmates at Michigan State University, Jalil said, "They didn't even know where Iran is!" Hamid Kowsari, who came from Tehran to Berkeley, California, and joined the ISA in 1963, remembers his shock at the "astonishing ignorance" of his American classmates: "Every day I would tell people [about the coup]. They didn't know. They were wondering if I was telling the truth." Like Freud's melancholics, Jalil, Hamid, and many others would not stop talking about how they had been affected by an empire the US continually disavowed.[10] A refusal to let go of these losses, to accept and bury them, was common among those who joined the ISA. Collectively and individually, on their demonstrations and in their publications, they insisted on remembering what was lost, what—and who—had been taken away.[11]

Whereas Freud deemed melancholia abnormal, the melancholic preoccupations of ISA members appear here as an example of what David Eng and David Kazanjian call "a realistic response" to the ongoing injustices of imperialism and dictatorship.[12] For ISA members, the past was not over and dead but alive in "the body's capacities to act, engage, and connect"— to affect and be affected.[13] The interview excerpts that follow engage with affect and memory as a living, embodied archive mediating between past and present, home and diaspora, individuals and collectives. They were of course produced in response to what Ricoeur called "the injunction to remember" generated by the interview process itself, where the order to remember necessarily turns memory into an ethico-political project.[14] "It is justice which extracts from traumatizing remembrances their exemplary value," he writes, "and it is this project of justice that gives the form of the future and of imperativeness to the duty of memory."[15] I understand the "duty of memory" in the context of my interviews with former ISA members as a means of participating in an unfinished struggle for freedom in Iran, as a manifestation of fragmented and contentious diasporic politics, and as a mode of intergenerational transmission. The seven wide-ranging accounts that follow thus describe the transnational process through which some children grew up and became revolutionaries far from home. These excerpts of memory continue the circulation of revolutionary affects—including the melancholic attachments of resistant nostalgia—as part of a diasporic inheritance.

The Education of a Stonecutter

Jalil Mostashari (b. 1940, Kermanshah; ISA chapter: East Lansing, Michigan; party affiliation: none)

Jalil was born into a Shiʻi merchant family in the provincial capital of a Kurdish-speaking area of Iran near the border with Iraq. The radio in his home picked up Iraqi stations, filling the rooms with Arabic music from across the region. Jalil attended a religious school founded by merchants from the bazaar, including his father, and became a devout Muslim. Jalil is old enough to have witnessed the rise and fall of the two major political movements that would shape Iranian opposition politics for generations to come. The first was the Iranian communist party, known as the Tudeh Party, which, on the eve of the 1953 coup, had over 25,000 members and hundreds of thousands of sympathizers in and around its many front organizations.[16] Tudeh was formed in 1941 during the Anglo-Soviet invasion of Iran when the British removed Reza Shah and replaced him with his son, the twenty-two-year-old Mohammad Reza Shah. The young Shah issued a general amnesty for all political prisoners, including the communists, who promptly launched Tudeh upon their release. The other opposition formation was the National Front, a coalition of religious and secular groups founded by Mohammad Mosaddeq in 1949, which led the oil nationalization movement and gained control over the government through elections in 1951.

Jalil could still recall the atmosphere of that time: "We all, Iran, became political. Eighty percent of our teachers were *Tudeh-i*. Members, supporters, sympathizers and that sort of thing. Of course, bazaaris were mostly Mosaddeqi, like my father. Schools gradually became leftist. People had become very excited [about] being able to fight the greatest power of our time, the British. So everybody was involved. Even my nanny. And we were not in Tehran. We were in fifth province, a Kurdish town. But Tudeh had the whole city, all the high schools. You couldn't be anything else except for Mosaddeqi. I was Mosaddeqi." As he recalled the widespread affiliation of ordinary Iranians—his nanny, his teachers, students, bazaar merchants like his father—with democratic and communist ideas, Jalil beamed with pride. His affective attachment to memories of a high point of mass political mobilization in urban, provincial, Kurdish Iran brimmed with resistant nostalgia for a time when ordinary people felt empowered to challenge both empire and dictatorship. This was the history he wanted me to know, as we sat in a college classroom in New York City, before he returned home to Tehran. The interview thus provided a chance for Jalil to pass on the impact of encounters with repression and resistance that shaped his own revolutionary trajectory. The ways in which he remembered the mass movements of the early 1950s intervened in how the past is understood today. Not only did he insist that we remember the democratic possibilities derailed by the coup, but the affects embedded in his memories also reintroduce those possibilities into the present. Jalil's revolutionary affects bring the anti-imperialist democratic aspirations of millions of Iranians flooding into our contemporary moment, when the future is too often imagined as a choice between an Islamic republic and US domination.

In July 1952, when the Shah attempted to block the full constitutional powers of the office of the prime minister, Mosaddeq resigned in protest. For three days, cities across the country rose up in open rebellion. Tudeh mobilized its significant forces to join the uprisings. Jalil remembers those three days well, for they offered a brief, but transformative, lesson in the power of collective resistance: "We were all there when Kermanshah people fought the police. I was then twelve years old. We would bring a wheelbarrow and collect stone pieces and bring them to the street so that the people could throw them at the military police. Our town was a garrison town. A border town, always a garrison town. Many people were killed that day. I stupidly took refuge under a tank that was stationary. Where else to go? And I lost one of my shoes. When I came out it got stuck there. I came home with one shoe." Affected by the militancy of those around him, Jalil was willing to risk his life to fight for democracy. He was lucky to lose only a shoe. The experience of becoming a participant in this uprising, and of the deaths of people with whom he identified, was profound and formative. The immediate lesson was one of victory: these popular rebellions succeeded. The Shah reappointed Mossadeq to the role of prime minster.

However, just over one year later, in August 1953, the British and the Americans would engineer a coup and restore the Shah to his throne with more power than ever before. In the midst of the chaos of the coup, Jalil remembers how the spirit of collective resistance flourished once more on the brink of defeat. In August 1953, the Shah had called his troops to the capital to help quell unrest, leaving Kermanshah without any military presence. Jalil recalled: "On Wednesday, Thursday, Friday [August 19–21, 1953], the town was in the hands of the people. No police were there, nobody. People were ruling the town. This is the only town in the whole country which was not run over by the army." This time, however, Tudeh did not mobilize to defend Mosaddeq, a decision that would prove fatal.[17] Yet, for Jalil, the historic defeat of the coup contained within it the memory of popular self-rule in his city, the kernel of a truth he has held on to ever since and that has oriented him toward a multitude of revolutionary movements.

As a thirteen-year-old, Jalil began a quest to understand what had happened to him, to his city, to the country as a whole. After visiting clerical leaders from several different religions, he finally found what he was looking for:

> They told me there is this *sang tarash*, a stonecutter. They told me this guy teaches philosophy. I told myself, I have seen *sang tarash*; they can't even read. At any rate, he wouldn't accept me. I had to bring in many, many people as intermediaries to vouch for me that I'm not police, that I am okay, I'm son of such-and-such person in the bazaar and all this. Finally, he accepted to see me in the evening at his house, which was in an unbelievably dilapidated place. He had a room with his wife and one child and he was around thirty-some years old. He started teaching philosophy, materialism, in simple words. Very nicely without a book! There was no book! He would put his sugar cube in his mouth and drink his tea and tell me why he believes there is no creator and cannot be any creator. He would bring me examples from Persian poetry. He would bring me examples from Koran. He was well versed, unbelievable. Apparently he was trained at the age of fifteen or sixteen by an old communist of Lahuti Khan's.

Jalil had stumbled across the roots of a revolutionary genealogy buried in his hometown. "This goes back to 1910," he explained, to the first wave of Iranian communism decades before the formation of Tudeh. Jalil went on to summarize the history of Bolshevik infiltration of the Tsarist Cossack brigades, which occupied parts of northern Iran, including the Azerbaijani city of Baku, during the second decade of the twentieth century. These Bolshevik cells fraternized with Iranian troops, including Major Abulqasim Lahuti, who became a Marxist while serving in the Iranian gendarmerie. Jalil wanted me to understand the education of this stonecutter by Lahuti's comrades in Kermanshah as more than just a localized quirk of history. This was the underwater spring he was referring to the day I met him at the Occupy Wall Street encampment. He wanted me to understand the deep roots of communist ideas in Iranian society and to share his attachment to a narrative of a long Iranian freedom struggle that must continue.

My own research into Lahuti Khan retraced the contours of an Iranian transnational opposition. By 1917, when the Russian Revolution brought the soviets to power, the preceding years of organizing and education had created a radical Iranian current that spread out from Baku—the center of a booming oil industry that drew thousands of displaced Iranian workers—via Bolshevik cells in the Russian army and Cossack brigades all the way to Kermanshah. It was there, as a member of the gendarmerie stationed in his hometown, that Lahuti Khan attended clandestine meetings of revolutionary soldiers and helped to organize a joint committee of Russians and Iranians to oppose British military incursions into western Iran.[18] In 1920, Lahuti traveled to Baku to participate in the Comintern's historic First Congress of the Peoples of the East.[19] The Iranian situation received particular attention because the congress coincided with the declaration of the Soviet Socialist Republic of Gilan, an Iranian province on the Caspian Sea. Without permission from the Comintern, the Jangalis, a broad "anti-imperialist front" uniting Bolshevik sympathizers with populist nationalists and anti-Russian Iranian clerics, had seized power after the Red Army evicted occupying British troops. The Jangalis then entered into negotiations with the Bolsheviks that led to the founding of the Iranian Communist Party, the first communist party in Asia, which sent representatives to the gathering in Baku.

The congress famously affirmed the central importance of "Eastern" liberation movements to the global revolutionary socialist project, exemplifying the anti-imperialist internationalism of the Russian Revolution's early years. Recent scholarly efforts to chart cross-pollinations and solidarity between African and Asian liberation movements have highlighted the important interventions made in Baku by Jamaican revolutionary Claude McKay and Indian Marxist M. N. Roy, among others, during crucial debates over the relationship between national liberation (decolonization) and socialism.[20] The fact that the congress occurred at the same time and in the birthplace of Iranian communism expands the scope of these celebrated Afro-Asian connections and shows how the roots of the Iranian Left are intertwined with the inception of anticolonial Marxism, which pushed beyond the European context.

It was in 1922, just after the Iranian Communist Party was officially banned, that Lahuti Khan's chance came to lead a socialist uprising in Tabriz, the urban center of Iranian Azerbaijan. The soviets withheld support and the rebellion was swiftly put down by Reza Shah's army. This defeat marked the end of this first phase of socialist activity in Iran and was decisive for the successful consolidation of a centralized, authoritarian state. Over the next twenty years, the combination of repression and Stalinist purges nearly liquidated an entire generation of Iranian communists.[21] The rainwater sank deep into the earth.

And yet, Jalil's first-hand experiences of popular resistance and self-determination compelled him to seek out his unlikely teacher, a stonecutter who was also a living link to an earlier era when the gendarmerie had been infiltrated by Iranian socialists inspired by the Russian Revolution. A spring bubbled up where it was least expected. Lahuti's failed attempts to make a revolution in Tabriz had succeeded nevertheless in preserving and spreading Marxist thought across more than three generations. Even the poetry he wrote while living in exile in Tajikistan would inspire revolutionaries of the future. Rahim Bajoughli, part of the second generation of ISA activists and another interview subject for this book, described reading Lahuti's banned verses as a pivotal part of his politicization as a teenager in the 1960s.

These enduring affective attachments to an Iranianized Marxism disrupt the binaries between East and West, indigenous and foreign, so often used to discredit the Left as inauthentic. The marginalized history recounted above recasts Iran as a transnational site for the development and exchange of socialist ideas contemporaneous with the period of the Russian Revolution. Jalil's memories also illustrate the relationship between affect and revolutionary subjectivity. Without the embodied, lived experience of state repression and resistance, Jalil would not have gone searching for a political framework that fit his mood, and fugitive Marxist ideas would not have found so many eager adherents among his generation of Iranian students. Affect, rather than political continuity in organization or ideas, made it possible for the legacy of an exiled and failed revolutionary like Lahuti to travel with Jalil to Michigan State University, where he organized the ISA chapter from 1963 to 1968. The next section further illustrates this dynamic by focusing on affective encounters with events surrounding the 1953 coup in Iran as a catalyst for revolutionary consciousness.

Blood, Books, and Binoculars: Scenes from the
Coup in Tehran

When the first generation of ISA members were children, the 1953 coup that deposed Prime Minister Mohammad Mossadeq was something that happened not so much to the nation as to their families, their friends, their neighbors. Intimate, partial encounters with the coup and its aftermath made sharp tears in the fabric of society, through which they glimpsed the raw violence of imperial power. Affective and emotional responses to what they witnessed, and sometimes directly experienced, as children and adolescents became charged with political meaning into adulthood. Among the people I interviewed, visceral impressions of the coup and its aftermath often returned as narrative points of departure for a journey of political awakening that would lead them to the ISA in the United States and then to the revolutionary underground back in Iran. While the three stories discussed below all took place in Tehran, they delineate different paths toward radicalization. The first two reflect the pervasive influence of the Iranian Left before the coup and come from individuals who had Tudeh members or sympathizers within their families. The third story, which completes this section, comes from someone with family members tied to the Shah's regime. Becoming a part of the student opposition abroad could, therefore, represent a continuation or a break with the political orientation of one's family. In either case, joining the ISA (and the underground leftist groups) became a way of making meaning out of these traumatic memories and finding an outlet for the affects and emotions that remained. All three of these accounts come from former ISA members who were active in the Bay Area, a reflection of the networks I was able to tap into for my research as well as of the large size and national influence of the ISA's Northern California chapter.

Hamid Kowsari (b. 1944, Hamadan; grew up in Tehran; ISA chapter: Northern California; party affiliation: UIC)

"By the time I was seven years old I was already political," Hamid said, recalling his participation in the oil nationalization movement before the coup. "I would organize my little friends and we would go around the streets with chalk and we would write 'Long Live Mosaddeq' on the walls." Hamid's upper-middle-class family was steeped in politics: his father, a carpet exporter, was pro-Mosaddeq, while several members of his mother's family were members of Tudeh. He grew up reading poetry and the daily newspapers aloud with his father and siblings, following radio news broadcasts, and listening to his father's accompanying commentary.

Hamid was nine years old in 1953. In mid-August, like many Tehranis of his class background, he was on vacation with his family in a village outside the city. "There was a beautiful field around the *meydun* (square) full of wild-flowers. Groups from Tehran would gather there, group by group, singing, playing music," he recalled. On August 19, "We were listening to the news, and then all of a sudden the program was interrupted." Hamid's father sent him to the *meydun* to find out what was going on. By the time I got there, the radio had already announced the coup," Hamid said. That evening, people gathered among the wildflowers as usual but there was "no music, no singing, nothing. Everybody was there. Some people were openly crying, including my older sisters who were at that time fourteen and fifteen years old. There were some thugs who had gathered at the corner of the square and were shouting 'Long live Shah' and 'Death to Mosaddeq.'"

Later that same night, Hamid was awakened by the sound of voices. All the lights were on in the house. His mother's cousin Hashem had arrived unexpectedly:

> [Hashem] was an active member of the Tudeh Party and they [he and his family] had rented another house maybe half an hour from us. Those thugs, knowing he was active, had attacked his home and he had managed to escape. The next morning he left and went to Kermanshah into hiding. He was later on arrested and he was in jail, I don't know how many years. I remember my mother used to go to jail to visit him. I even remember one time she came back and she had brought some clothes that were bloody. He was tortured. Back in Tehran, arrests had already started. We would hear someone's husband or son had been taken. It was a really sad time. I remember how bad it was. Even when I went to school in the fall, school was not the same.

The lively, hopeful energy that had permeated Hamid's social world during Mosaddeq's tenure as prime minister was gone. His teachers were scared, depressed; his neighbors reeling from the arrests of loved ones. His cousin's blood-stained shirt, material evidence of the state-sponsored torture of someone he knew well, arrived in his house. Looking back on these memories, Hamid said: "I'm pretty sure it had a lot of effect on me. Six years later, I was in the streets fighting with the cops. I'm pretty sure it had a lot to do with that. I remember the first demonstration that I went to was in 1959. I was about fifteen years old. That started a series of demonstrations from 1959 to 1963. I participated in all of them. That was actually when I became really political." The demonstrations Hamid participated in were evidence of the thaw in the post-coup atmosphere made possible by pressure from President Kennedy in the context of the Cold War. As an increasingly indispensable US ally, the Shah was not to commit flagrant human rights violations that might be damaging to America's reputation as the defender of the "free" world.[22] Presented with even the slightest opening, anti-Shah sentiment began to manifest in demonstrations and open-air meetings to demand free elections.[23] Thousands of university students, and even high school students like Hamid, participated:

> All of [the demonstrations] were attacked. They would beat us with clubs and the wooden part of their rifles. We would hit and run, just with fists and sometimes stones. They did shoot a few times and they killed—one time they killed two students, one time they killed a teacher—but usually they were not shooting. One time they hit me, and they cut my head. There was blood all over my shirt when I came home, and my younger sister opened the door and started crying. I didn't get arrested, but some of my friends were arrested. It was not as bad as when they started the real suppression in '63.

The blood-stained shirt, this time Hamid's, returns in this memory as a rite of passage for a teenager who had chosen to fight the shock troops of dictatorship. The desire to understand why one is being hit on the head, why so much blood is being spilled, and what to do about it fueled a process of political transformation for a generation of young activists.

The blows of police batons had a profound effect on Hamid, pushing him to seek out revolutionary frameworks to make sense of what was happening. He began reading books from abroad that had been translated into Persian, a transnational intellectual journey he could take even before leaving home:

> When I was little, we used to read a lot of novels, and my hero was Robin Hood. So then during this period of 1960 to '62, I had heard about Castro and all that. Jean Paul Sartre went to Cuba just after the revolution and wrote a book [published in 1961]. I read it in Persian—it would mean *The War of Sugar in Cuba* in English—and, in that book, Castro in the beginning was very revolutionary. He had started distribution of land among the peasants, starting with his own family's land. Sartre explains all these things in that book. I said, "That's a modern Robin Hood!" So

it was a small step for me to take from Robin Hood to Castro. I became a Castroist and Guevarist. Soon I became convinced that armed struggle is the only way. I started talking with my classmates, who were also radicalized, about this. But we thought we should go to all the [unarmed] demonstrations anyway."

Already an activist, already acquainted with revolutionary ideas and literature from other places, Hamid arrived in Berkeley, California in 1963, and immediately began organizing people around him. He was eighteen years old. At first he enrolled at McKinley High School to learn English, then spent two years at Vallejo Junior College before transferring to San Francisco State College in 1965. Hamid would go on to participate in the student strike that took place there in 1968–69 (see chapter 4). However, even before he joined any movements or organizations, Hamid set out to educate the Americans around him. "Every night in the dormitory we would sit down, two of us from Iran. We would gather students and discuss politics." His first demonstration in the US was a picket outside the Sheraton Hotel in downtown San Francisco to demand equal employment opportunities and pay for Black workers. "I was the only foreigner there. That's how I got involved in the American movement. It was the beginning. Later on, when the antiwar movement started, of course, I became very active in that. I viewed the Vietnam War just as I viewed the coup against the Iranian people: it was imperialist aggression." The ability of affect to facilitate connections across differences—of time and place as well as culture and language—is a recurring element in the formation of revolutionary internationalist orientations, as I illustrate further in the examples that follow.

Jaleh Behroozi (b. 1947, Tehran; ISA chapter: Northern California; party affiliation: UIC)

In contrast to the narratives by men discussed thus far, Jaleh's earliest memories of political awakening took place in the interiors of her upper-middle-class family's home rather than in the street or the *meydun*. She first learned about the brutalities of political violence indirectly; her older brothers were the early protagonists of her story.

My father was a businessman. Of course, my mom never worked. We were a very traditional family, a Jewish family. There were seven of us. Not super religious. Actually, our family was culturally active—music, painting—they were all artists. I am the odd one. One of the issues that made me politically aware was that my brother was arrested and tortured very hard when he was sixteen and I was ten. That brought something. I was in sixth grade. It would have been 1956–57 that they arrested him, after the coup d'état. My brother had friends in Tudeh Party. He was going to their meetings; he was the youngest, and he was an artist and through his artwork he got to know a lot of progressive people who were much older than him.

Jaleh's childhood home, anchored in bourgeois gender roles, was suddenly jolted by the violence the state enacted against her brother's body. Under the Shah's dictatorship, even wealth and status did not necessarily make a person safe. This fact offers a window into how and why so many middle- and upper-middle-class Iranian students turned against the regime. It was rarely an abstract, theoretical objection that moved them, but more often the lived experience of the arbitrariness of state power. Here we see how a US Cold War policy of anti-communism, personified by the CIA-trained Iranian secret police, took material form in the torture of children. In her effort to explain her brother's marginal relationship to the banned Tudeh Party—"he was the youngest, and he was an artist"—Jaleh's old grief and indignation resurfaced. She wanted me to know that her brother was not a threat, not even really a party member—in other words, entirely inno- cent. The unfairness and the horror of what was done "brought something," introduced affects and emotions, that stayed with her, later facilitating her departure from the imperial model minority script *and* the gender roles that structured the bourgeois family.

Jaleh's awareness of state violence expanded outward, beyond her family, beyond Iran, even while she was still a child:

> After [my brother was tortured], I started to learn about the Holocaust. At that point my eldest brother, who was in England, came back to Iran, and he translated *The Diary of Anne Frank*. While he was trans- lating it, I started reading it; every page as he would translate, he would give it to me to read. That story made me really anti-God. I thought if there is any god, then why this kind of thing happens, this kind of dis- crimination happens? I remember very clearly that that was so strong and powerful for me, the image, and the impact that the Holocaust had on me. And I became anti-religion, and anti-God.

A Jewish girl in Iran learned about the intimate details of the life of a Jewish girl in the Netherlands through the transnational movement of her oldest brother, who had been a foreign student in England, and of a text, which underwent multiple translations. Sitting quietly next to her brother, Jaleh read page after page, struggling to absorb the full impact of the words, to comprehend the scale of injustice, of loss. This account of childhood politicization resists a separation between the domestic and the political, a key characteristic of feminist historiography, and illustrates how small, sometimes silent moments can contain within them traumatic shocks that shatter one worldview and make room for another.

Jaleh's memories then skip ahead to her time as a student at Tehran University in the mid-1960s: "In the last year of my participation in university, two or three political people started to talk to me. I suppose they felt there was some humanistic emotions in me and that's why they started to talk to me. And during the four years of college in Iran, I started learning about liberal philosophy and Jean-Paul Sartre—at that point [these ideas] were really common in Iran. Those things helped also for me to become involved." The fact that there were "political people" looking for new recruits on campus, and the popularity of authors like Sartre, reveal that even after the demonstrations between 1961 and 1963 were suppressed, in what may have appeared as a period of consolidation and strength for the Shah, the revolutionary affects of many college students were cohering into plans for a new opposition movement.

Jaleh became an activist at UC Berkeley soon after her arrival there in 1968. "The issue of political prisoners [in Iran] was the strong motive for me" in joining the ISA. The affects that remained from the time of her brother's torture were mobilized into concrete work against the Shah's policy of torturing dissidents. And her feelings about injustice on a larger scale, which first emerged as she read *The Diary of Anne Frank*, also led her to act against the oppression of others. When the United States began bombing Cambodia in 1969, Jaleh was among the ISA members at UC Berkeley who formed a coalition with former members of Students for a Democratic Society (SDS) and Palestinian and Ethiopian students. "We were in Iran House [the local ISA headquarters] when we heard about [the bombing]. We all went into the streets and we had street fights for three or four days," she recalls. "We would take part of the street, then the police would take it back. We would take the [UC Berkeley] Student Union, and then they would take it back. All Iranian students were really active; it was thousands of us." This "us" may have referred to the protesters in general, rather than just to the Iranians among them, for no single ISA branch could claim thousands of members. The ambiguity of the grammar, the potential for slippage between or conflation of "Iranians" and a larger "us," illustrates the ways that the movement of revolutionary affects made possible new forms of political affiliation not confined to national origin. "We believed we were allies with whomever was anti-imperialist," Jaleh explained for my sake, for such thinking was simply common sense at the time. The power of revolutionary affects to foster these new sites of attachment and solidarity reconfigured class allegiances, turning elite young people into sharp critics of the upper echelons of Iranian society. In the example that follows, alienation and estrangement from family resulted from childhood memories of the complicity of the Iranian bourgeoisie with imperialism and dictatorship.

Parviz Shokat (b. 1944, Tehran; ISA chapter: Northern
California; party affiliation: UIC)

Parviz's story underscores the transnational character of the journey from imperial model minority to revolutionary, taking him from Tehran to Oakland, California, back to Tehran, then to France, and finally back to Oakland, where he became active in the Iranian and broader US student movements. His journey also highlights the ways that proximity to power and privilege can provide a close-up view of injustice and propel a young person far away from home, both geographically and politically. Parviz happens to be a descendant of ministers of the Qajar dynasty—which ruled Iran from 1785 to 1925—though his casual, humble demeanor carries no hint of this elite pedigree. His family was largely made up of politically conservative army men. "I think my father was the exception," Parviz said. "He was pro-Mosaddeq, although he died when I was about ten so I didn't know him that long." His family's affluence and political ties meant that, as a boy, Parviz knew "some of Mosaddeq's people" and, at the same time, his uncle was an adviser to the Shah. Unlike the other ISA members I interviewed, his memories of the coup take place *before* and after it occurred: "The night before the coup, I happen to have gone with my aunt and her husband to a party near Shemiran [a wealthy enclave in northern Tehran] at [army officer and future SAVAK chief, Nasser] Moghadam's house. I later found out that Zahedi [the general who would lead the coup and replace Mosaddeq as prime minster] was there that night. I saw these Chevys that belonged to the American consulate and some prominent people that were there that night. So I knew that Americans were very much involved in those things." As a nine-year-old guest at this party, Parviz certainly could not have understood the significance of who was there, nor did he know what was about to happen. However, as events unfolded, this memory would become firsthand evidence of the US role in the plot to overthrow Mosaddeq.

Parviz was also privy to a scene from the overthrow itself: "From the roof of our house, I could see Mosaddeq's house. I remember I was standing there with binoculars looking into the house when thugs attacked the house and people were just tearing things up and taking them away. I still remember what I saw. A lot of them passed by our house carrying chairs and carpets, things like that." Alone on his rooftop, Parviz observed the immediate aftermath of what a former US embassy official who photographed the scene called the "bloodiest spot in town" on the day of the coup.[24] Outside Mosaddeq's house, guards battled "the attackers" (hired thugs) for five hours, and the bodies of the fallen were displayed in the streets.[25] Parviz witnessed more than just the ransacking of the deposed prime minister's house; the destruction of rooms and the looting of possessions in broad daylight symbolized the desecration of Iranian democracy, and the vandalism foretold a new era of state terror. Peering through his binoculars, Parviz was affected by the violence he saw. This memory became part of a series of encounters that would alienate him from the world of power and privilege into which he was born.

Parviz understood from a young age that there were two sides in a conflict going on around him; the strange thing was that they were both present in his family. After the coup, his father would go every day to attend Mosaddeq's trial while some of his cousins had been directly involved in carrying out the overthrow. The same aunt who took him to the party on the eve of the coup also had leftist friends who came to her when they needed help:

> After the coup, only a few days after, there were two Armenian activists that were very close friends of my aunt and they were apparently at least some of the translators of Marxist-Leninist books into Farsi and they were in danger. They brought suitcases of books to our house and burned them. We couldn't even destroy the covers to the books because they were very well made. We had to separate them. So this dichotomy of being with the people who were part of the coup and also with these people my aunt was trying to help was very interesting.

To help his aunt protect her friends, Parviz assisted in the destruction of books he would seek out and read just a few years later when he became a Marxist-Leninist in the United States. In the secretive frenzy of tearing off covers and burning pages, he also encountered the fear and desperation of these two activists whose lives were in danger.

In 1958, when he was only fifteen years old, Parviz planned to leave Iran to attend Oakland Technical High School in Oakland, California, continuing a tradition among the upper classes of Iranian society of sending their teenage children abroad for high school. Before he left, he was taken to the Shah to say goodbye. The Shah said to "study industrial engineering and come back to Iran soon. But I came here and became very much against him," Parviz said, chuckling quietly. Parviz thus bears the distinction of having directly defied the Shah's personal advice when he chose to abandon his imperial model minority role and join the opposition.

While he was living in a boarding house and going to high school in Oakland, Parviz looked for ways to engage in politics. "I started a Democratic club at Coalinga Junior College. I was in the radical Democratic Party at the time." He might well have dedicated his energies to a mainstream political career, either in the US or in Iran, and fulfilled the promise of a successful imperial model minority. But then, after six years away, he went home to Tehran for the summer.

It was 1964, a time of increased repression after the crackdown on the demonstrations in 1963. "I became very disenchanted with the situation," Parviz said: "I remember I thought that Iran was almost like a colony except the colonialists could speak the language of the people. It was very, very divided. Near our house, there was a large area in the northern part of Tehran where squatters were living. They were living in almost caves made with cardboard. In fact, when I was there, they had access to the main throughway where there was water and the neighbors got together and built a wall so they wouldn't have access. So those things got me very angry." The extreme inequality of combined and uneven development, which Western-backed modernization imposed on the Third World, was mapped onto the streets of Parviz's neighborhood.[26] Iran's condition of being "like a colony except the colonialists could speak the language of the people" exemplified the indirect and disavowed forms of empire that characterized US Cold War imperialism throughout much of the Third World. When Parviz's wealthy neighbors built a wall to keep clean, running water from the poor, they became like colonizers siphoning off natural resources for themselves. Parviz tried to raise these issues with his powerful relatives and their friends but quickly hit another kind of wall: a lack of political will to make change.

Parviz stayed in Iran through the fall of 1964, long enough to witness another burst of popular resistance in the form of the Tehran taxi workers' strike. There is one memory in particular that appears to have reoriented him away from mainstream politics and toward the Left:

I think the thing that really affected me was they raised the price of petroleum from five rials to one toman—doubled it. That caused the taxi drivers to go on strike for a few days. Then it happened that our car was in a garage and one afternoon about 2 o'clock, with the driver that we had, we went to the garage to pick up the car. While I was in that garage, people in civilian clothes, but they were clearly army people, came and took the taxis out. There was one guy that was taking care of the garage, and it was closed. It was in the afternoon; nobody was there. This young kid who was the caretaker there had the keys. They got him and beat him up and put him in a closet and locked the door, and took the taxis out, and I saw that. So that really pissed me off. Then, in the afternoon, they were saying on the radio the strike is over, the taxis are back. But at the same time, they did increase the price of oil anyway. That made me really mad. I became very much against the Shah and the whole system.

Still shaken up by this experience, Parviz left Iran by train and made his way across Europe. "I was like the later hippies with a beard traveling around with very little money," he recalled. He arrived in France in time to join some of the first demonstrations against the Vietnam War. He began reading Marxist literature and learning about contemporary revolutionary movements. "I just wanted to do something that hopefully would make a difference in the world in the future," he said of that period of travel and intellectual exploration. In 1965, he returned to live in Berkeley, enrolled at Hayward College, and joined SDS. In 1967, while participating in Stop the Draft Week with SDS, he met the ISA. "Before that, I had the idea that Iranians were not interested in politics. I was very disappointed with everybody, and I just didn't associate with them. But then I met some Iranians on the demonstrations, and I was really excited that these people are political too."

Finally, Parviz found other Iranians who shared his affective relationship to Iranian society under the Shah—the alienation, the anger, and the eagerness to bring about change. He threw himself into the anti-Shah movement while also remaining active in the broader Bay Area political scene. Along with Hamid, Jaleh, and her future husband, Ahmad Taghvai, he became a founding member of the Union of Iranian Communists, one of the underground groups that would come to dominate the ISA. In the Northern California ISA branch, he would meet other young Iranians who had also repudiated family connections with the Shah and his government and forever jettisoned the life of power and privilege that had been waiting for them.

The Shock of the Leaflets

Zohreh Khayam (b. 1948, Tehran; ISA chapter:
Washington, DC; party affiliation: unnamed faction
sympathetic to Fadaiyan)

Zohreh experienced the contradictions of the relationship between dictator-ship and Cold War imperialism as she tried to assert her values and beliefs in the classroom, first in Iran and then as a high school exchange student in Wisconsin in 1965–66. As a seventeen-year-old in the US, she was able to assess the "Western values" that were idealized and promoted in Iran under the Shah up close, quickly bumping up against the limits of liberal democracy. When she returned to the US five years later as a master's student and joined the ISA, she carried with her memories of imperial encounters in both countries that undergirded her activism.

Zohreh was born into a middle-class Muslim family. Her mother was a teacher and her father worked for the National Bank of Iran. Although she was only four and a half at the time of the coup, she remembers the feelings and affects that suddenly swirled around her, disrupting her family's beach holiday in Babol-Sar on the Caspian Sea in August 1953: "I remember a lot; my long-term memory is very good. I remember that adults were really feeling very anxious about what was happening. I kept hearing the word *coup d'état*. At that age, I obviously didn't know Dr. Mosaddeq and his way of thinking. We were exposed to the official publicity about the Shah and his court, the Shah and the Queen and all of that. But all I knew was that the anxiety on the part of the adults about where the country was going was striking to me." The reactions of the adults closest to her were her first premonitions of the repression to come. Although her family were not members of a political organization, "we had anti-Shah feelings," Zohreh explained, feelings that led her to question authority in many forms.

In her early adolescence, she began to publicly assert herself against religious ideas:

> My family was a modern thinking family. I never owned a headscarf, or the *chador*. One of the things I was always taught by my mother—both my sister and I were taught one theme: women have to be economically independent. And this is back in the early fifties. That was her thing. Obviously, the way that Islam looks at women is very different, even though some people have progressive interpretations of that. So I would question a lot. By the time I graduated high school, I was determined

not to believe. Now the question was whether I was an atheist or an agnostic person.

As was common among urban middle-class, educated families in Iran at the time, Zohreh equated "modern thinking" with secular thinking. As a teenager, she felt empowered to directly challenge the religion teacher at her school: "I would start by saying to the teacher, "I have a question for you." And the teacher would say, "What's your question?" And I would say, "I don't believe in God. Do you?" And that would open a whole conversation because he was a believer, he was teaching it. But yet he himself was exposed to a lot of modern values and modern aspects of life. That was the context that I grew up in."

Though critical of the Shah's dictatorship, Zohreh and her family were uncomfortable with the religious character of the June 1963 anti-Shah demonstrations, which erupted after Khomeini gave a speech denouncing the Shah as a dictator and his White Revolution reform package as anti-Islamic (see chapter 2). Khomeini was arrested and eventually exiled, while the regime violently suppressed the protests.[27] This "June 5th" uprising, which historian Ervand Abrahamian has called a "dress rehearsal for the Islamic Revolution of 78–79," represented the first open resistance to the Shah since the 1953 coup and also established anti-regime clerics as a center of opposition activities.[28] While the government's brutal response was designed to instill fear in the population at large, Zohreh's feelings about the actual demonstrations were ambivalent. One of Khomeini's major criticisms of the Shah's reform package was the provision granting women the right to vote. Zohreh remembers:

That was the first manifestation of traditionalism against modernism. And that was something that really was very influential on me, that whole event. One of the things that I remember was that when we had social studies class, we had a book, and they were talking about who couldn't vote in the elections. And it was very interesting. Women couldn't vote, minors couldn't vote, and people with mental illness. So my thinking was: well, I understand that I am a child and I shouldn't vote, but as a woman, why shouldn't I be able to vote? You have to remember that in the context of culture in my family, that women have to be economically independent, that contradiction had always been there, and as a child I couldn't articulate this, obviously. But the events of that year, that uprising, were very consistent with what I had feelings against in my learning and my educational process. I felt very bad about it. The sentiment at the time in my family was also against the Shah. But we were opposed to what Khomeini was talking about, what they called the uprising. To me it was a very backward and ill-intentioned move on the part of religious fundamentalists in Iran, though some people thought it was an anti-dictatorial process.

Zohreh narrates her experience of the 1963 uprising as one of alienation from both sides. The manifestation of anti-Shah sentiments as a call for the exclusion of women from full citizenship rights left no room for her "modern," upstart vision of how she might carve out a place in society. The Shah's dictatorship, likewise, was a barrier to the freedom of thought and expression in which Zohreh sought to engage equally with men. In her account of her political life, the bad feelings that marked this moment foreshadow more bad feelings to come. In 1979, as Khomeini's faction maneuvered to consolidate power, Zohreh helped to launch a leftist women's organization to resist both imperialism and the gender discrimination promoted by the new government (see chapter 6). As a teenager, however, there was little she could do except to look for like-minded people with whom to share her negative emotions about the dictatorship, about religion, and about the different limitations each placed on women. When the Shah's reform package was pushed through, Zohreh was dismayed. "Even the right of women to vote was not celebrated by someone like me because I was thinking that rights are not given but we have to take our rights," she explained. Indeed, the ISA would consistently argue that "voting rights" in a system that banned dissent meant little in the lives of most women (and men).

Zohreh was among those college students who found their way to opposition circles after 1963, when the Shah ramped up repression and censorship. "By the time I had graduated high school and went to the University of Tehran in sociology, I was part of the resistance movement; at least I saw myself as being part of that," Zohreh said. "We knew by instinct that so many things were going wrong, you know, so many things were imposed by the government. The interesting part was that we didn't have any theoretical knowledge of what a democratic society is like, but we had exposure at the time to Western culture." Here, "Western culture" did not only refer to the pro-US newspapers, magazines, and movies or access to American consumer goods that saturated the Iranian urban middle class. It also included literatures of resistance to oppression and exploitation in the West. "At that time, I had some progressive exposure because I read," Zohreh explained. "I wanted to land on the side of people who were oppressed and all of that.

I read a lot of Dostoyevsky. I think the sense of associating myself against exploitation and oppression really came from him. I also read some Tolstoy and Victor Hugo's *Les Miserables*." These books had an enormous impact on Zohreh's life, teaching her "that people are complex, and you can be giving, you can be loving, and you can be ethical in so many different ways. These are the values that I learned aside from the values that I was taught by my parents."

Zohreh's values were challenged and refined through the direct experience of life in the West several years before she joined the ISA:

> I came here as a seventeen-year-old for the first time, as an exchange student. I stayed in the United States for a year and I went back. That was actually after eleventh grade in Iran. School year 1965–66. I was placed with a very conservative, Republican family. At the time, the Vietnam War was going on. I was in Jamesville, Wisconsin, which is half an hour south of Madison. I was in Jamesville High School, which at the time had 600 students. In my journalism class, there was a lot of interaction between pro-Republicans and pro-Democrats, which I wasn't really used to in terms of different party affiliations debating each other. So it was very fascinating to me. I asked our teacher, I understand that people affiliate themselves with Republicans and Democrats, but can you please explain to me how they are different in the nature of what they want? What's their desire that makes them different? Believe it or not, not the teacher and not the students, who really were trying to debate hard, argue hard, could answer that question. And they all shook their heads and it was an interesting moment.

Coming from a dictatorship rooted in the direct censorship of political parties, Zohreh expected more from what was supposed to be the greatest democracy on earth. In the US she encountered the dominance of a world-view that narrowed the spectrum of political thought without the need for overt state intervention. She recalled another example: when she wrote a paper against the death penalty that year, "there was a whole lot of reaction because at the time you couldn't even talk about that." Her views on the right of the state to execute its citizens proved far more "liberal" than those of her American classmates, whose affective attachments to their government and its two major parties still anchored their political lives.

Zohreh was generally treated well by her host family, but they clashed over her position on the US war in Vietnam. In her debate class, she and her partner had been charged with arguing the case against the war. "When I came home and I told my family that we won the debate, the reaction was so cold and so discouraging. I never forgot that," she said. This reaction led her to a deeper understanding of the differences in how she and the Americans around her felt about the way power, resources, and state violence were unevenly distributed:

> One of the things that I remember is that when I was arguing within my family and my friends, they really were oblivious or ignorant about what was going on politically. I remember a conversation with the father of the family. In fact, it started with the question of Vietnam, and I was asking how in the world United States is staging a war so far away from their country when they are not threatened. You have wars when you're defending yourself—that makes sense. But the Vietnamese hadn't done anything to Americans. Very bluntly, the father of the family, who was a very conservative Republican, told me, that's because Vietnam is influenced by the Russians, and we are spreading our influence territory. So when I had a discussion about oil in Iran, his response was, Iran is a backward country, what are you going to do with your oil? It was a sense of entitlement to natural resources, and there was a sense of entitlement about creating that area of influence for Americans. To me that was very bold and arrogant.

From debate class to the family dinner table, Zohreh was affected by the imperial attitudes around her, and she was not afraid to argue her perspective. It was a comment from the daughter of the family that would one day leave her speechless:

> The worst treatment that I got in that home was from the young woman who was my age. We were in the car going back home, and she knew my sensitivity toward the Vietnam War, and she said something, to this day it hurts me. [The father was preparing to take a new job with the Eversharp pen company.] One of the things the daughter said was, "You know, dad, you can advertise Eversharp pens as a pen that works with the ink of Vietnamese blood." And that truly made me sick. I mean, physically, I was sick. So from then on, I decided to back off because I was living with that family.

What might be casual banter to some can affect another person's body like the sudden onset of illness, like a physical hurt. In this moment of affective dissonance between herself and this American girl, Zohreh glimpsed a moral and political worldview in which the Vietnamese could not be imagined as fellow human beings. She recoiled in disgust.

Upon her return to Iran, where she studied sociology at Tehran University, Zohreh became involved in student activism in support of the Tehran bus workers' strike in 1967. "We got on the street and protested. One of the things that really impacted me seriously was a student put himself on fire and died. It was huge. Many of our friends were arrested during that time." Self-immolation, like arrest and torture, materialized resistance in the body, generating loss, grief, and also a demand for justice among those who survive, those who remember.

In 1971, Zohreh returned to the US to begin a master's degree in economics at the University of Maryland and joined the ISA. She recalled her first ISA action, a demonstration against the Shah's 2,500-year celebration of the Persian Empire:

> We had people pick me up from College Park, Maryland, and we came to DC, and I volunteered to distribute leaflets, and that's when the shock came. We were distributing leaflets, and people were not taking them, and I was thinking, "We are distributing leaflets! How come people are not interested?" In Iran, people were starved for pieces of information, especially if it was underground. During my university years [in Tehran], a lot of people really had leaflets in hand writing. We didn't have access to copy machines and things like that. We would rewrite. If I got a leaflet, I would rewrite it in multiple copies to distribute. So for me, coming from that background, I was shocked that somebody would refuse a political leaflet!

Zohreh's painstaking, intimate relationship to handwritten leaflets and their risky, clandestine distribution in Iran contrasted with the lack of interest among the Americans walking past her in Washington, generating another moment of affective dissonance, a "shock" that she remembered still. It is the shock that comes from realizing you have been shaped by a set of political realities unknown to the people around you. In that moment, Zohreh saw that the challenges she faced as an activist in Iran, where the threat of prison and torture hung over her with every leaflet she rewrote, were very different from the obstacles she and her ISA comrades confronted in the US. Over the next nine years, Zohreh would work hard to educate Americans about what their government was doing in Iran, trying with each leaflet, each speech, each demonstration, to create within them an affective and emotional response that would move closer to her own.

New Heroes for a New Generation

Farid Ashkan (b. 1953, Arak, grew up in Tehran; ISA
chapters: Austin and Lubbock, Texas, and Chicago;
party affiliation: Fadaiyan majority)

Farid had a somber and deliberate way of talking about his past, as if each sentence carried a heavy burden. Listening to him I was reminded that revolutionary affects have been largely discredited among many Iranians as a wrongheaded passion that led young leftists to support Khomeini, and, because of Khomeini's subsequent persecution of the Left, to contribute to their own destruction. Farid's youthful support for the armed Marxist guerilla movement in Iran was not a light or easy topic for him to discuss, fraught as it was with former attachments to ideas and organizations that have been judged harshly by history. Yet, it was precisely the ability of revolutionary affects to live on, long after painful breaks with a specific ideology, strategy, and organization, that struck me as most significant. Resistant nostalgia for a time when the armed struggle was a source of inspiration and hope was, for Farid, entirely compatible with his own critical analysis of what went wrong. This form of melancholic attachment made it possible for discredited ways of being in the world to become legible again in diaspora, unbounded by party lines or membership, persisting as an embodied continuity of affect that could not be repudiated.

When I asked Farid how he became political, he replied, "It started with daily life." Farid was from a middle-class Muslim family, the son of a policeman who was religious and a supporter of the Shah. His first memory of larger political events going on in the immediate world around him occurred on June 5, 1963, during the anti-Shah protests. Unlike Zohreh, Farid was not in a position to critically evaluate what was happening at the time. Partly because he was not exposed to anti-Shah sentiment at home and partly because he was five years younger, he was not aware of the political issues at stake. His memories are sensory impressions of life under dictatorship. He realized something was wrong when his daily routine was disrupted. His father's assistant came to pick him up from elementary school because the school buses were not running. Along the half-hour walk home, Farid saw barricades and demonstrations and heard the sounds of gunshots nearby:

> This is always in my mind. I remember the turmoil in the streets. I remember the smell of the tear gas. I still do. I remember right after that my father had retired and took us on our first travel abroad. We went to

Germany by bus. This was like a week after *panzdah-e khordad* [June 5 on the Iranian calendar] and still the big cities like Tehran, Tabriz, Sanjan were under curfew [following the protests]. I remember when we would pass through the big cities, we would see the tanks. We would see the soldiers in the streets. So these were all in front of my eyes, and then the question: Why are they doing that? Why are they there? I think I was either in fifth grade or fourth grade, about ten years old. And it's literally in front of my eyes even up to this point. I remember all those things. They were in back of my mind somewhere. When you see things like that, you can never forget as a young kid. So obviously that had something to do with [how I became an activist]. No doubt about it.

The sights, smells, and sounds of the regime's repressive apparatus registered in his body, "in front of my eyes," "in back of my mind." Impossible to forget, these memories became part of Farid. It would take him several more years to find answers to the questions that arose in him as a child bearing witness.

He was too young to join protests supporting the bus workers' strike of 1967; however, in 1970, when Farid was in junior high school, new demonstrations broke out against increased bus fares and offered a chance to directly participate in opposition activity:

Immediately, because everything in society was ready for that, it exploded. Starting from Tehran University, it went on to the rest of the universities in Tehran. Then some other places like the bazaar were affected. So next day, we came to school, and we said we have to close the school to go join the students from Tehran University. As soon as we went out of the school, the principal called the police and said the students have revolted. So when we came out, the police were there, riot police, for the first time at our school, with full riot gear. So, nicely we came out of the school, and we just walked about ten to fifteen feet and started saying "*Marg bar Shah*" [Down with the Shah]. It wasn't the bus thing. That was just an excuse. It was the opposition to the Shah, that's what it was. We would use any excuse.

Despite their youth and the nonviolent nature of their protest, the police attacked the students. "I didn't get beaten up," Farid says, "but a good friend of mine, Hamid, got beaten up by the baton a couple of times. We didn't get arrested, but we were not able to join the Tehran University students because, by the time we got there, [the campus] was completely surrounded [by security forces]."

The scope of Farid's informal political education expanded dramatically when he attended a high school founded by an older generation of communist sympathizers and was suddenly surrounded by classmates who were immediate relations of former Tudeh Party members. Through them, the living memory of the Iranian communist movement's ideas, traditions, and mistakes was transmitted and debated by a new generation of radicalizing young people. Farid and his friends formed secret reading circles to share copies of Russian novels purchased from the Soviet embassy, as well as Iranian literature by the iconoclast novelist Sadegh Hedayat and socialist folklorist Samad Behrangi.

On February 8, 1971, when Farid was in his junior year of high school, something extraordinary happened. Thirteen armed men launched an assault on a remote gendarmerie post in the town of Siahkal in Gilan province on the Caspian Sea. The guerrillas killed three policemen and freed two of their jailed comrades. With this brazen attack, the Organization of Iranian People's Fadā'i Guerrillas (the Marxist Fadaiyan) declared war on the Shah's regime. Gilan, site of the fleeting socialist republic of 1920, once again became the flashpoint for an effort to undermine the central government. The state responded by executing thirteen people, including two who were already in prison at the time. The turn to armed struggle occurred as a result of the police state conditions that prevailed in Iran in the 1960s, which prohibited the formation of mass opposition parties like Tudeh or the National Front. The guerrilla movement, composed of Marxist as well as Islamist and Islamic socialist organizations, drew members primarily from the educated middle class.[29] "Thus they took up arms," historian Ervand Abrahamian writes, "not because of economic deprivation, but because of social discontent, moral indignation, and political frustration."[30] Its members were predominantly in their teens and twenties, and they wanted change to come quickly. They were a major force in the development of a "new Left" inside Iran.

Farid and his friends "were very much affected by the guerrilla movement" and joined an underground student circle linked to the Marxist Fadaiyan. After Siahkal, "we started making leaflets and distributing them in high school." The word *fadaiyan* translates roughly as "self-sacrificers," or those willing to give their lives for people's freedom. The figure of the fadayi—resolute, courageous, and willing to make the ultimate sacrifice in service to the people—mobilized the revolutionary affects of a generation of students. "Being a fadayi guerrilla was a big thing. It wasn't a small thing. It was huge," Farid recalled. I asked if they were his heroes. "Of course!" he said without hesitation. And yet, his feelings about this movement were a complicated tangle of loyalty, admiration, and grief: "They were the smartest and most intelligent people. And then they got killed. It's enormous what was lost from that movement because of the wrong tactics and analysis that they had at the time. But no regrets. It was a time that needed those kind of actions [sic]. It wasn't just for Iran; it was all over the world. I mean we had a Ché Guevara in the world as a person who still is associated with honor and someone who is always on the side of the people. So I was very much involved with this." When Farid talked about the guerrillas, it was with the difficulty of unresolved emotions that have stayed with him through the ensuing decades of exile in the United States. He remembered not only his first brush with the movement in high school, but also his later involvement during the Iranian Revolution itself, when he was a student organizer for the Marxist Fadaiyan majority faction in Tehran. He spoke with effort, the strain visible on his face as he attempted to recuperate the bravery, the passion, and the integrity of his fallen heroes, while also offering a sober assessment of the grave errors they made.

The guerrilla movement proved that the Shah's regime was vulnerable. It inspired and radicalized many young people like Farid, but it was not an effective catalyst for mass action and would play almost no role in the events that led to the overthrow of the Shah. In the years between Siahkal and the beginning of the revolutionary upheaval in fall 1977, 341 guerrillas were killed, including thirty-nine women.[31] Perhaps by comparing these fallen fighters with the legendary Ché, Farid intended to bestow upon them a degree of legitimacy he felt had eluded them. Perhaps he meant to suggest that, like Ché, they had expressed affects and emotions that were righteous, genuine, and necessary, even now, with the benefit of hindsight.

Farid's account then shifted to a more matter-of-fact tone. The Marxist guerrillas of his generation were responding to all that had come before them, he explained: "The radical Left and the communist movement and noncommunist Left, in the sense of tactics not necessarily ideology, was in answer to the inaction of Tudeh. They had the power, actually, and they didn't use it properly, so they lost a huge opportunity. Our mission was, whatever we want to do, we want to do it against Tudeh's policy and behavior, because they did a disservice to the Left."[32]

Farid recalled how the weight of history hung over his generation, compelling them to define themselves against the political strategies that led to defeat in 1953. Despite this, Farid did not deny the crucial role that Tudeh played in the development of the Iranian revolutionary movement: "The Left in Iran has one history. It starts from 120 years ago, from the enclave in the north of Iran during the Constitutional Revolution and it just continues [through] the Group of 53 [who became communists in prison in the late 1930s] and comes to the establishment of the Tudeh Party and comes to the Fadaiyan and the rest of the people who were related directly or indirectly. Some refuted the past, some didn't, some were half and half. That is the Left." Farid thus summarized the genealogy explored throughout all of the memories presented in this chapter. This blunt assertion of the Iranian Left's shared history emphasized continuity despite waves of repression and a tradition of bitter factionalism. If there is but one legacy to inherit, then the way each generation, or each organization, reinterprets and acts upon it cannot be separated from this history as a whole.

This inheritance inevitably consists of personal and political losses that are often intertwined and inseparable, and that imbue revolutionary affects with their melancholy character. For Farid, his support for the Fadaiyan as a teenager would result in the loss of Iran as his home and the loss of family ties. "My family became very aware of my anxiety, and they were very worried, especially my father. When I was seventeen, I was in constant confrontation and clashes with my father. We never got along because of this, never did. The older I would get, the more radical I would become, and the more conservative he would become." Tensions came to a head during the Shah's outlandish commemoration of two-and-a-half millennia of the Iranian monarchy in October 1971, an event that came to symbolize the decadence and corruption of the regime (see chapter 2). This was also Farid's last year of high school, and the Shah's celebration brought Farid's relationship with his father to the breaking point. All retirees from all of the Shah's armed forces were required to decorate their homes with flags and lights. When Farid's father told him to go hang the lights on their house, "I said, it's either going to be the lights on this house or its going to be me living in this house. So you have to choose between these two. If you put the lights, I'm going to leave. He put the lights up, and I left for the first time. I was seventeen." His parents spent twenty-four hours searching police stations and hospitals. They found him at his aunt's house the next day. "I went back home with the condition that he has to remove those ornaments, and he did," Farid said.

Still, Farid resisted going abroad. "I didn't want to leave, actually. I didn't take an entrance exam. I gave them two options: I want to become a pilot, or I want to go to United States. The reason I wanted to become a pilot was I thought that was the most effective way I can help. I knew of the Tudeh Party's military wing [in the 1940s], how effective they were and how much influence they had. I knew people who were like that." Ultimately, he did not pursue his ambition to build a clandestine Marxist cell in the Shah's air force, an updated version of the Bolshevik cells in the Cossack brigades. Instead, he took an English exam and left Iran for Texas in 1973. "From early on, from touching the ground here, I got involved in political activity," he said. Farid's story of quotidian encounters with state repression and the coming into consciousness of the possibility of resistance reprises elements present in each of the preceding interview excerpts. Taken together, these memories offer insights into the politicization of children as a broad social phenomenon. Indeed, as the final narrative excerpt below illustrates, the pressures and paranoia of dictatorship could force children to become political actors even before they were fully aware of what was happening.

Down with Math!

Behzad Golemohammadi (b. 1956 or 1957, Hamadan;
ISA chapters: Oklahoma and Northern California;
party affiliation: UIC and, later, Fadaiyan majority)

Behzad's father began working as a tailor at age six, and his mother learned the same trade at age eleven. His family's working-class background set him apart from the majority of the first ISA generation; it was not until the second generation of students who came to the US in the mid-1970s that significant numbers of Iranians from less affluent backgrounds could finally afford to send their children abroad. Through his family, Behzad was exposed to communist ideas from a young age. In fact, it was a communist who first brought his parents together:

> I had an uncle who was very active in the Tudeh Party, and when they were young they were working for him as a tailor. That's where my mom and dad met, in my uncle's shop. He was active in Hamadan. He was arrested and almost executed. Luckily, due to all kinds of circumstances, he was able to be saved. This was around the time of the coup. I heard about it. I had like six uncles on my dad's side and three on my mom's side, and we'd get together almost every week. Hush-hush talk, don't say loud so the kids will hear. Always political talk. My dad was never religious. My mom still prays, but she's not that strict. In Hamadan, we attended the Jewish school from kindergarten until we left. My mom was very open-minded.

In this brief description of his family life, Behzad offers a window into a secular, leftist working-class milieu. Histories of communist organizing and state repression came alive at weekly family gatherings, as adults traded memories, opinions, and arguments, and Behzad listened. He became "very sympathetic to Tudeh. At the time, Tudeh was the Left of Iran. So that became the base of a lot of us in the next generation who became active."

Scenes from Behzad's teenage years in Tehran invoked the fabric of daily life under the Shah's regime. Moving from home to high school and back again, he would pass in front of Tehran University, the epicenter of periodic student unrest. "I always saw these big platoons full of soldiers parked outside. Occasionally, I would see them chasing the students. Many times I saw them arrest students. One time I remember, we were playing soccer on this field, and this girl came running there, and they came after her and arrested her there. They pulled a gun in front of me. So you get exposed to these things and you know the atmosphere of dictatorship." The "atmosphere of dictatorship" condensed in the militarization of public space. Behzad came to expect the sight of soldiers outside the university, sometimes running after unarmed students. But the arbitrariness that characterizes authoritarian regimes also caught him off guard, appearing out of place in the spaces of childhood play: a gun in a soccer field; one particular girl disappeared before his eyes. In the course of their ordinary, everyday activities, children became witnesses to the crimes of the state against the people, preventing a separation between childhood and politics.

Almost any activity, it seemed, could take on political dimensions in this context, and what might otherwise be considered normal adolescent grievances could garner hyperbolic reactions from the authorities. When I asked Behzad if he had been politically active in Iran before he went to the United States, he recalled an incident in which dissident intentions had been mistakenly ascribed to him and his classmates:

> Thursday afternoons and Fridays was our weekend. Thursdays, usually [during] the last two hours, we had sports or something relaxing. We were looking forward to that. For whatever reason, they set up our mathematics class right on Thursday afternoon. Our class was big, eighty kids. So some of the kids decided to go on strike. Our high school, Takht-e Jamshid, was actually inside Park-e Farah (now Park-e Laleh). We decided to all go to the park instead of class. The vice-principal, the doorman, they came and chased us, and we all went running. So Saturday morning when we went back to class, they brought a SAVAK member to interrogate us to

find out who told us not to go to class. They kind of push you in a way. They thought that some organized leftist group or something … they were very, very paranoid. So there was no organized political activity, but things like that kind of pushed you to think what the heck is going on? I just don't want to have math on Thursday afternoon!

Behzad did not expect to be interrogated by a member of the secret police in his very own school, and the affective remains of this surprising betrayal have stayed with him ever since. During his time in the ISA, when he was targeted by SAVAK and by the FBI, he absolutely refused to be intimidated (see chapter 3). It is possible that his family connection to Tudeh may have provided sufficient impetus for his political activity as a foreign student in the US. But his own encounters, as witness and as suspect, with the repressive forces of the regime undoubtedly affected his orientation to the world around him. They "pushed" him toward becoming exactly what the state feared: a dedicated member of the student opposition. When Behzad joined the ISA in Oklahoma in 1976, he did not hold "any personal grudge against the Shah." His involvement came from "wanting to have freedom. Because we grew up in a hush-hush society. As a young student, it seemed like the right thing to do, and the more we got involved and more friendships, solidarity with people we associated with. … It was exciting because here we could freely discuss political issues, which we couldn't do in Iran. It was like a flourishing of ideas, opinions, of a side that was kept in the dark." From the "hush-hush" conversations in his childhood home to noisy demonstrations in the streets of the imperial heartland, Behzad finally found an outlet for his feelings about a childhood indelibly marked by dictatorship.

Conclusion

The child psychiatrist Robert Coles, who spent decades working with children in conflict zones around the world, once wrote, "Those of us who want to understand how children grow up to embody the political and ideological variations of this planet … would do well to recognize that … a political inclination has a 'developmental history.'" This was not the same as a "developmental imperative," he warned, for "in the lives of individuals and nations alike there is simply no way of knowing at what moment an apparently unremarkable, even unknowable set of feelings or attitudes will suddenly appear, to everyone's surprise, as utterly critical and persuasive in the life of a person or community of people."[33] The revolutionary affects of thousands of Iranian foreign students caught the Iranian and US governments off guard, animating a revolt in the heart of empire through the organizational vehicle of the ISA. If not for the repeated outbursts of dissent in Iran and the formation of CISNU as part of a global movement against imperialism, these affects might have remained "unremarkable, even unknowable." Through the narrative accounts former ISA members gave of their own politicization, I have traced a "developmental history" of the diasporic Iranian student movement as an affective history, a history that lives on in memories of formative encounters with state repression and collective resistance.

The result is both an intimate archive of the lived experience of US-backed dictatorship *and* a genealogy of secular democratic and leftist organizing that has been marginalized by official histories in both the US and Iran. A close reading of just a handful of former ISA members' childhood memories meant revisiting the spread of Bolshevism across parts of Iran and the localized uprisings of the early 1920s, as well as the mass communist-led organizations and oil nationalization movement of the late 1940s and early 1950s. While not every person interviewed encountered the legacy of these events as a child or adolescent living in Iran, it is worth noticing how, and the extent to which, the affects, emotions, and lessons from the past *were* transmitted to the generations of foreign student activists of the 1960s and 1970s. Despite the "hush-hush" conditions that prevailed in the Shah's police state, individuals had distinct memories of when it felt like change was possible, whether it was the stonecutter teaching Marxism in his one-room hovel or the old communists in Behzad's family whispering about what Iran was like before the coup. For those who could remember, the short-lived nature of the victories wrought by democratic and leftist movements seems to have enhanced the hopeful, optimistic feelings attached to them. During the long, dark years of reaction that followed, grief over what, and who, had been lost, mixed with anger and indignation over the daily injustices of an autocratic state backed by imperial power. These expressions of resistant nostalgia maintain an open relationship to a past that has been marginalized within the largely pro-Shah post-1979 diaspora.

Seen in this light, CISNU represents a diasporic continuation of the longer struggle narrated in the interviews, and the interviews themselves register and transmit revolutionary affects that have been circulating in Iranian society for over a century. Indeed, one ISA poster asserts this legacy explicitly, reproducing iconic portraits of key leaders from the Constitutional Revolution accompanied by the slogan "We continue the struggle."

Figure 1.1 "We continue the struggle." ISA poster depicting leaders of Iranian Constitutional Revolution. Courtesy of Shayegan Family Estate.

Compelling explanations for the losses Iran had suffered were provided by revolutionary politics and organization in diaspora. But the appeal of such politics and organization, which demanded high levels of discipline and self-sacrifice, remains abstract without an understanding of how individuals felt about the world and their place within it. Access to literatures of dissent, like the writings of Ché Guevara or Samad Behrangi or Dostoyevsky, was certainly an important element in the radicalization of some young Iranians. But the desire to seek out and read certain books over others, the willingness to risk the consequences of possessing banned books, and what those books came to mean had a great deal to do with the ways that these readers had already been affected by the oppressive conditions of their society.

This chapter has argued for the central role of revolutionary affects in a transnational story of the making of children into revolutionary subjects. The memories analyzed above narrate a quest for justice that moved from Iran to the US, back to Iran during the revolution, and then back to the US, where all but Jalil currently reside. These narratives must be understood in the context of contested diasporic responses to the US-Iran conflict. As Nergis Canefe writes in her discussion of the political stakes of refugee memory, "for these individuals, who paid a heavy personal price to remain alive and who are acutely aware of the conditions in political regimes that are prone to produce many more refugees like themselves," the act of remembering home "symbolize[s] a public devotion to justice and change in the diaspora."[34] That devotion may no longer be attached to the same ideologies and organizations as it once was, yet its power remains as a revolutionary affect circulating in diaspora with unknown, and perhaps unlikely, impacts on future generations. It is this methodology of possibility that anchors this study, as a critical engagement with history that can inform new diasporic orientations today. During the period of the alliance between the US and the Shah, the visceral, embodied remains of encounters with repression and resistance in Iran found expression in CISNU abroad and unleashed a new subversive force in the heart of empire.

2

Revolt in the Metropole

The SAVAK agent was done listening and now began to dictate a letter that Sina, an undergraduate at Tehran University, would have to write and sign if he wanted permission to study in the United States.[1] It was 1975, and the Iranian state, including its secret police force, SAVAK, was having trouble with its students. Tehran University was a hub of unrest, and Iranian students outside the country were also causing problems, exploiting every opportunity to embarrass the Shah. How to determine, then, which students would prove loyal once they left home and which ones might try to tarnish the Shah's reputation abroad as an enlightened monarch shepherding his people toward modernity?

Sina posed an obvious risk. He had already been arrested during a campus protest against the Shah in Tehran. The protest was no lunchtime picket; it had lasted three days and ended in a police riot. Sina had been identified as one of the leaders. Sitting in his prison cell, he was grateful that his friends had not recruited him to join one of several underground Marxist organizations that were gaining influence among the more active students. He readily admitted that he did not have the requisite secretive personality, for he quickly became emotional. At least if they torture me, he thought, I will have nothing to reveal. As it happened, things never got to that point. The president of the university himself telephoned SAVAK. "This must be a mistake," he insisted, and he heaped praise on this dissident student who was, nonetheless, at the top of his class.

Sina was released from jail, but the authorities placed a travel ban on his passport. When he was accepted to a university in the US South, he presented himself at the local SAVAK office to ask for the ban to be removed. The SAVAK agent was open to Sina's request but with some conditions, which he dictated so rapidly that Sina worried that he would not have time to consider the content of what he was about to sign. Luckily for him, there was a fair amount of repetition. Sina wrote that he promised not to join the Iranian Students Association in the United States, only to follow that with another promise not to join the Confederation of Iranian Students. Since the first organization was an affiliate of the second, the SAVAK agent must have been trying to eliminate any possible loopholes. Fine, fine, Sina thought, let's get on with it. The agent continued his dictation: "If someone from the Confederation approaches me, I will report—." Sina stopped writing. "I promise that I will not join the Confederation, but that's it," he said. He searched for a way to avoid escalating the situation. "I want to serve my country," he said. "Each of us should do this in the best way he can. Each should do his own job. My job is to serve Iran as a scholar. Your job is to be a spy. Each is legitimate. But you should not become a scholar, and I should not become a spy." The agent accepted this argument. Within a week after arriving in the US, Sina approached the first Iranian he saw and asked, "Is there a Confederation chapter here?"

In this anecdote, Sina described the dominant Persian national-imperial script that featured an essential, starring role for Western-educated Iranians. The mandate to "serve my country" by becoming a scholar was the injunction to embody the very notions of progress that rested on the suppression of democracy, on the equally essential role of the SAVAK agent who was also serving his country. Sina, and the tens of thousands of Iranian students who came to the US after the CIA-backed coup in 1953, were the privileged subjects of the alliance between the US and the Shah. Iranians with Western degrees were handsomely rewarded with top positions in the military, economic planning and development, and the expanding national university system.[2] This chapter looks at how a powerful opposition movement erupted from a significant minority of a population that was central to US-Iran relations, the Shah's ambitions, and US Cold War policy. I argue that revolutionary affects found collective expression as alienation from the political mainstream of both Iranian and US society, and as the desire for fundamental change. The melancholic refusal to forget the role of the US in the development of the police state in Iran found new outlets in the context of burgeoning student movements on US college campuses and around the world.

This transnational account of the formation of the Iranian Students Association (ISA) and the dedicated activism of its members sheds new light on the US-Iran foreign policy arrangements enshrined in the term *special relationship*, an indirect mode of imperialism that relied on notions of mutual interest and diplomacy rather than military invasion or occupation.[3] The term *special relationship* was meant to elicit happy, hopeful feelings. By understanding the special relationship as something lived and felt in Iran and in the US, I argue that this term in fact indexed competing affects and worldviews. A significant minority of Iranian students who arrived in the US refused to align themselves with the normative affects governing the alliance between the US and the Shah and became a thorn in the side of empire. Far away from home, experiences of repression and resistance in Iran manifested through the ISA as an affective attachment to the Iranian freedom struggle that fueled twenty years of sustained organizing in diaspora.

This chapter draws on queer and feminist scholarship concerning the relationship between affect and activism in order to theorize revolutionary affects as embodied practices that bring new political subjects and possibilities into being. I take the ISA as a case study in the centrality of affect to revolutionary subjectivity and argue that what Brigitte Bargetz calls the "political ambivalence of affect" is central to the power and potential of social movements to change consciousness and material conditions.[4] Revolutionary affects may not always *feel* good, but they nonetheless become rewarding when they are shared. Outrage, fear, self-sacrifice, grief, urgency, the joy of speaking truth to power and of belonging to a group of like-minded people—such affects and emotions have the potential to reorient subjectivity away from the reproduction of capitalism and empire and toward other possible futures. They also have the power to circumscribe revolutionary subjectivity. Revolutionary affects that hold people and movements together attach to certain issues and causes over and against others, center the voices and feelings of some people while silencing others, and may well disqualify concerns that are deemed "secondary," "individualistic," or in the case of the Marxist students at the heart of this study, "bourgeois." As Bargetz warns, "social and political structures circulate through affect," which, therefore, also transmits "those powers and forces that inhibit political agency."[5] In other words, affects permeate and attach to the hierarchies that organize our societies and that tend to undermine the much-sought-after unity of grassroots movements. As I discuss in chapters 5 and 6, affective attachments to the Iranian freedom struggle and to belonging within Iranian student organizations tended to obscure and reinscribe gender, sexual, and class hierarchies precisely through affective appeals to revolutionary discipline and unity.

Rather than romanticizing revolutionary affects, I apply a methodology of possibility to recuperate a legacy of dissident subjectivity and subversive action among diasporic Iranians that was powerful yet flawed. This chapter focuses on the ISA's formation and development into a revolutionary force that would change the ways Americans thought and felt about the special relationship between the US and Iran. In what follows, I will first show how the revolutionary affects of Iranian students transformed a complicit population—what I call "imperial model minorities"—into the source of a new opposition movement. Then I will offer an overview of the movement, charting the shift from a reformist to a revolutionary orientation. I begin by explaining the particular role of the imperial model minority during the Cold War and the affective dissonances that emerged from tensions embedded in this category. Given that the post-1979 Iranian diaspora has been overwhelmingly made up of educated members of the middle and upper-middle classes, it is of particular significance to theorize revolutionary subjectivity that emanated not from the marginalized, or the dispossessed, but from those who were celebrated as evidence of the successful incorporation of minority subjects into a pro-US world order.[6]

Imperial Opportunities

Despite the bloody coup that paved the way for the US to become the major foreign power in Iran, the resulting alliance was shrouded in the language and affects of friendship and included, from the beginning, the opportunity for Iranians to study abroad. The aptly named American Friends of the Middle East (AFME) was one of the first entities to assist in recruiting foreign students. Funded by the CIA's International Organizations Division, the AFME opened an office in Tehran on the eve of the coup and, by 1955, was placing hundreds of Iranian students in US universities.[7] Soon students could and did apply directly to schools in the US, and by the late 1950s, over 1,000 Iranians were studying in the country.[8] In the immediate aftermath of the coup, and with a budget supplied by the CIA, the AFME founded the Iranian Students Association (ISA) in order to make sure that Iranian students in the US maintained their loyalty to the Shah.[9] At the same time as the CIA was busy assisting the Shah in crushing dissent, reorganizing the military, and establishing the new secret police force that would become SAVAK, it also set in motion the mass recruitment and monitoring of Iranian foreign students. In order to understand how the ISA transformed from these complicit beginnings into an opposition movement deeply influenced by the revolutionary Left, it is first necessary to ask why the American and Iranian governments actively supported the recruitment of Iranians to US institutions of higher education. How did these students fit into the vision for Iran's future promoted by both Washington and Tehran?

The American education of tens of thousands of Iranian students was a critical component of the forms of imperial power the US relied on throughout the Cold War. The Iranian template—a CIA-backed coup, the installation of a pliable dictator, the establishment of a CIA-trained police, military, and/or paramilitary force—was adapted and applied in many other countries, from Guatemala to Congo to Vietnam to Chile. In the aftermath, US-sponsored development promised a fresh start on the road to Western-style prosperity, effectively rationalizing the political violence used against anticolonial movements and governments. There was no hope of delivering on this promise, however, without the cultivated talent, skills, and allegiance of an indigenous class of professionals with Western degrees.

Iranian boosters of industrial and commercial development were keenly aware of this need. For example, J. H. Behdjou, the executive vice president of the Iran-American Chamber of Industry and Commerce, wrote in the *Los Angeles Times* that the billions of dollars in "joint American-Iranian business ventures" depended on "perhaps the most important of many cultural ties between the two countries, the vast number of Iranian students now studying in American institutions."[10] As historian Paul Kramer notes, after World War II, US government agencies, educators, and public intellectuals deemed foreign students "critical actors in the global politics of the Cold War and decolonization" and "prospective agents of US influence in the world to which they would eventually return."[11] Indeed, Kramer argues that "the key to US domination ... was the affective capture of these aspirants and their training" in what Walter Lippman, who popularized the term *Cold War*, called "the universal principles of freedom."[12]

Foreign students from across Asia, Africa, Latin America, and the Caribbean gathered in the imperial metropoles of US college campuses, where they were called upon to model the universal human benefits of an American education—as individuals and for the nations from which they came. They can be understood, then, as "imperial model minorities," a transnational corollary of the domestic "model minority" citizen.[13] Both of these categories came into being during the Cold War, and both were coined as part of attempts at assimilating non-white peoples into narratives of American exceptionalism, though across different geographic scales. As many scholars have shown, US media celebrations of the relative economic success of some Asian Americans labeled "model minorities" were mobilized to rebut the searing critiques of structural inequality and racism made by the civil rights and Black Power movements.[14] If the domestic model minority ideal was wielded in order to obscure the systemic oppression that remained after civil rights legislation, then the "imperial model minority" was mobilized to mask the harsh effects of economically polarizing modernization and state-sanctioned repression in allied Third World nations. Foreign students personified the supposedly friendly, mutually beneficial arrangements that accompanied US intervention abroad.[15] They may have needed a Western education to remake their societies, but ordinary Americans also needed them in order to become emotionally and politically invested in the new US role as leader of the "free world."

In the 1950s, white Americans had to be taught to attach happy, hopeful feelings to the increasing presence of young scholars from US-allied nations. Learning to feel good about foreign students, especially those from non-white and/or non-Christian countries, was part of learning to feel good about the new US role as global hegemon. Concerned Americans formed groups like the Southwest Area Council of International Students in order "to help foreign students know Americans, and vice versa, with the knowledge that lasting peace can be achieved only if the peoples of the world understand and cooperate with one another."[16] In Los Angeles in February 1954, this organization hosted a reception for 500 community leaders at the home of the University of Southern California chancellor. Three student representatives from each of forty different countries, attired in "native costume," had been selected to help host the event. The evening's entertainment included musical and dance performances by students from Afghanistan, India, France, Nigeria, England, and Iran, a lineup that reflected the breadth of US postwar influence. Similar events were held around the United States in the mid-1950s under the auspices of the nonprofit Institute of International Education, which operated student exchange programs with seventy-four other nations as early as 1953.[17] Sometimes these receptions were bastions of the political elite; however, events for the broader public were also common, offering what one *New York Times* headline called "A 'Live' Lesson in Foreign Relations" to thousands of residents of college towns.[18] At these local gatherings, Americans became "the beneficiaries of their own civic efforts" and challenged their "misconceptions about foreign countries."[19]

As invited and honored guests, foreign students became recipients of a burgeoning fascination with parts of the world most Americans had never thought about before.[20] The affective experience of welcoming foreign students, and appreciating and learning about their cultures, helped to erode American isolationism, ignorance, and "old-fashioned" (that is, overt) racial prejudice. The affects of friendship that infused these encounters worked to position Americans as gracious and hospitable hosts, rather than citizens of an empire. Iran's relative invisibility in the American political and cultural lexicon before the 1950s lent added significance to interactions with Iranian foreign students. By socializing with them, Americans had the opportunity to embody Cold War doctrines of global integration and personally express friendship toward representatives of a new and important US ally.[21] In the 1950s, encounters with Iranian foreign students on campuses and through civic organizations tended to be emblematic of how most Americans understood US postwar expansion in Iran and elsewhere as a series of "exchanges that benefitted all parties."[22]

In this context, Iran and Iranian foreign students were not uniformly racialized according to older European Orientalist scripts that positioned "West" and "East" as polar opposites. Instead, they were incorporated into the contradictory project Christina Klein has called "Cold War Orientalism," which often promoted "the ideal of East-West friendship."[23] Rather than entirely displacing notions of Western superiority and Eastern inferiority, however, Cold War Orientalism relied on "a logic of affiliation as well as difference."[24] In the late 1950s, Cold War Orientalism encompassed the doting media coverage of the Shah and his glamorous, young bride, Soraya, as well as the "handsome" Iranian Ambassador Ardeshir Zahedi, his wife Princess Shahnaz, and the lavish, star-studded parties at the Iranian embassy in Washington.[25] A taste for Persian carpets, Persian caviar, and Iranian fashion designers catering to Washington and Hollywood elites revealed an apparent affinity between a rising imperial power and the trappings of Persian royalty promoted by the Shah and his emissaries.[26] The American elite could indulge in the fairytale of the Persian empire and revel in their own feelings of imperial grandeur at the same time, while the American public could feel generous and proud for helping to uplift the Iranian nation.

The potentially troubling fact of the world's indispensable democracy celebrating and aiding a repressive monarch was, at least temporarily, resolved in the figure of the Iranian "imperial model minority," whose American education would enable them to gradually bring modernity—and perhaps one day, liberal democracy—to Iran. The assimilation of Iranian foreign students into the US vision for "progress" in the Middle East, therefore, exemplified Cold War Orientalism's embrace of the Eastern Other as sympathetic and knowable. In addition, Iranian foreign students arrived during the apex of what Mary Dudziak has called "Cold War racial liberalism," a new racial doctrine of tolerance intended to improve the US image abroad by addressing criticism over the treatment of racial minorities at home.[27] As figures of hope for an American-sponsored era of peace and prosperity, Iranian imperial model minorities became part of the postwar experiment in accepting racial difference, mobilizing "positive" affects among their hosts in support of the integration of non-European, non-Christian populations into a global capitalist system dominated by the US.

Yet, the category of the imperial model minority, like that of the model minority citizen, was often overwhelmed by the very contradictions it was meant to erase. The process of recruiting and educating imperial model minorities, in Kramer's words, "sometimes spilled off the rails, when screenings failed to prune student radicals and dissenters"—as was the case with Sina and many other Iranian students—"when students' lateral solidarities overtook hoped for vertical loyalties, [and] when encounters with the US state and civil society proved alienating rather than binding."[28] The history of the ISA offers a fascinating instance of this "spilling off the rails." Because of the gender politics of modernization in Iran, which mandated western urban styles of dress, the imperial model minority revolt was a rebellion against prescribed class and gender roles, especially for women in the ISA, who found an escape from the norms of westernized bourgeois femininity in new forms of revolutionary subjectivity (see chapter 5). Members of the ISA stood on the path of progress that would have led them to lucrative jobs and marriages back home, and chose instead to sit down and block traffic. These activists challenge the common association of the model minority figure with an uncritical investment in the entrepreneurial logics of upward mobility and US exceptionalism, offering a window into how members of a privileged minority group decided to do everything in their power to overthrow the social, economic, and political order they were charged with spreading. I now turn to the crucial role of affect and emotion in this process of political reorientation, examining how new forms of diasporic subjectivity emerged from the lived experience of the contradiction between access to opportunity and the subverted Iranian sovereignty that allowed for that access.

Crashing the Party

The revolutionary affects of Iranian imperial model minorities were out of sync with the dominant mood attending the relationship between the US and the Shah described above. Much like the "alien affects" Sara Ahmed attributes to migrants who arrived in England from former British colonies after World War II, the foreign students who formed an opposition movement in the US found that they did not feel the way they were supposed to feel in response to the promise that assimilation in the metropole would sustain and spread happiness in Iran.[29] The justifying logic of the US Cold War project in Iran was indeed that it would make everyone happier, opening up a brighter future for all Iranians. As the Iranian prime minister, Asadollah Alam, told *Time* magazine in 1963, "in twenty years Iran's current spate of reforms will produce a Western standard of living."[30] This was, in a nutshell, the promise of the good life held out to the Third World as an alternative to communism.

The assimilation of imperial model minorities was thus bound by what Ahmed calls "the happiness duty"—that is, the "positive duty to speak of what is good" about the US-Iran special relationship, which is also "a negative duty not to speak of what is not good, not to speak from or out of unhappiness."[31] As Ahmed points out, "histories of empire ... are erased under the sign of happiness."[32] Violating the "happiness duty" was the first manifestation of revolutionary affects among the ranks of the elite student diaspora. Melancholic attachments to democracy and sovereignty undermined by the coup, as well as anger and alienation from the US-backed dictatorship, disrupted the affective capture of a significant minority of foreign students. By expressing their unhappiness with the current configurations of power, they "embod[ied] the persistence of histories that cannot be wished away by happiness" or by the imperial affects of friendship and hospitality described above.[33]

Iranian imperial model minorities became sources of unhappiness for officials from the Iranian and American governments, despite the efforts of the AFME and the Iranian embassy in Washington to keep them in line via the pro-Shah ISA. By 1960, the AFME withdrew its funding for the ISA in dismay over student criticism of the US role in the 1953 coup.[34] The Iranian ambassador to Washington, Ardeshir Zahedi, who was also the Shah's son-in-law, then moved to reassert the ISA's pro-regime character by stepping in to finance and attend its eighth annual congress in Ypsilanti, Michigan.[35] There, in the last days of August 1960, with 170 students assembled, representing colleges in twenty-five different states, Zahedi lost control.[36] While the ambassador fumed in front of them, opposition students gave pro-Mossadeq speeches and won the key leadership positions in the organization.[37] The new leaders rewrote the ISA's constitution and took over writing and publishing *Daneshjoo* ("university student"), the ISA's monthly Persian-language journal.[38] What had previously been a pro-establishment mouthpiece now became an organ of the nascent diasporic student movement. The new ISA constitution declared political independence from both Tehran and Washington, and called for Iran to join African and Asian nations in a policy of nonalignment toward both Cold War superpowers.[39] Revolutionary affects thus manifested as declarations of solidarity with broader Third World aspirations for independence and self-sufficiency. This solidarity emanated from Iranian desires for sovereignty as well as from the historical experience of the Soviet and British occupations of Iran during World War II. It also expressed an affective attachment to the liberation movements of others (see chapter 4).

Just a few months later, in March 1961, the Iranian embassy's annual Nowruz party became the scene of a public break between the ISA and the regime from which there was no going back.[40] The elaborate and formal Iranian New Year festival was the most high-profile annual celebration of imperial model minority status and the stability of the Shah's regime, at which Iranian foreign students and officials mingled with American dignitaries under Zahedi's watchful eye. After the upset in Ypsilanti, however, the new ISA leadership felt emboldened to disrupt business as usual. Mohammed Eghtedari, an ISA member at Howard University who was active from 1961 through 1979, was in attendance that night and recalled events that would become part of the story of the ISA's militant origins. Saddegh Qotbzadeh, a key student leader in the transformation of the ISA into an opposition force, led the impromptu protest.[41] According to Mohammed:

> All of a sudden, when the master of ceremonies was talking on the microphone, [Qotbzadeh] just went up there and grabbed the microphone and started sloganing pro-Mossadeq and saying things against Zahedi, saying things against the Shah. And then some people, his supporters, they turned the switch, and all the lights went off and all the plates went up! The whole party was disrupted! Police came in, arrested a lot of people, including some embassy people because they didn't know who was who. Thereafter, we, the Iranian students, did the [annual] New Year [celebration], and from then on we said that we have taken one castle away from the Iranian regime.

This was the beginning of the ISA's dominance over diasporic celebrations of the most important Iranian holiday, which would become the ISA's major fundraising event every year. As Parviz Shokat, a member of the ISA in Northern California and a student at Hayward College, said, "After a couple of years, the embassy or anyone close to the government could not put up a Nowruz party. It was only ISA everywhere in the US."

This incident is instructive for thinking through the relationship between affect, subjectivity, and politics at the core of this book. By crashing the party, and apparently even going so far as to slap Zahedi in the face, Qotbzadeh and his friends unleashed revolutionary affects into a place where they didn't belong. In order to understand just how disruptive this was, it is important to note that the Iranian government felt threatened enough to retaliate by refusing to renew the passports of those involved.[42] Rather than intimidating others into silence, however, this punishment ignited the first of many ISA defense campaigns to come. The same outrage that "ruined" the Nowruz party mobilized other Iranian foreign students. Based on this confrontation, the ISA recruited a whole new cohort who now had the confidence to bring their unhappiness into the public sphere in the form of collective protest.

Affect, as this chapter illustrates, is part of the workings of hegemony *and* is crucial to disrupting it. Jacques Rancière has called attention to the way that power operates through the "distribution of the sensible"—that is, by partitioning the world according to which bodies, voices, actions, and senses are permissible and which are not.[43] Bargetz reformulates this concept as a "distribution of emotions" in order to highlight the ways that the normative ordering of the world depends on distinguishing "between whose feelings constitute the existing distribution of the sensible and whose feelings are excluded."[44] In the existing distribution of emotions, Iranian imperial model minorities were supposed to embody the celebratory mood of the alliance between the US and the Shah, to aid in the circulation of happy feelings. But, as Bargetz argues, the circulation of affect is also the basis for acts of disruption, or what Rancière calls "emancipation"—a rupture of the existing order through an assertion of equality from those who have been excluded.[45] The revolt of Iranian imperial model minorities offers an additional insight, for it was precisely based on their *inclusion* in the existing order that the affects and emotions they introduced were so disruptive. The students who ruined the party were supposed to be there, just as they were supposed to be on the campuses that they turned into sites of protest. By introducing affects and emotions that were impermissible, Iranian foreign students "embrac[ed] the power of disturbance that is based on the premise of equality."[46] This exemplifies what Bargetz calls an "affective politics of emancipation," which brings new political subjects into being.[47] By acting on affects and emotions that disturbed the dominant order as if they were already a legitimate part of the public sphere, Iranian students positioned themselves against that order. Their alien affects accumulated revolutionary meaning as they circulated. In fact, this process was unfolding across the Iranian student diaspora in Europe as the circulation of revolutionary affects facilitated the making of new opposition formations.

• In 1960, the year of the Ypsilanti congress that marked the ISA's breaking point with the Iranian regime, Iranian student activists in England, Germany, and France came together to form the Confederation of Iranian Students.[48] In 1962, this entity met with the ISA at a joint congress in Paris, where they launched the Confederation of Iranian Students (National Union), known as CISNU, which claimed to represent 13,000 Iranian students in Europe and 6,000 in the United States.[49] In addition to its concentration of members in Europe, Canada, and the US, CISNU also had members in Turkey by 1966 and in India and Japan by the mid-1970s.[50] Once formed, CISNU immediately established ties with the Organization of Tehran University Students (OTUS) and positioned itself as an extension of the domestic Iranian student movement that just happened to be outside Iran's borders.[51] A message of solidarity was then sent by OTUS on behalf of "students of the blood-drenched Tehran University and militant students from other cities."[52] This was a reference to the violence meted out against Iranian students who had participated in several protests beginning with a 15,000 strong commemoration of "Student Day" in 1961, which had turned into a protest against the Shah's hand-picked prime minister, Ali Amini.[53] "Student Day" honored three students killed by the Shah's troops during a protest in 1953 against the visit to Iran of then Vice President Richard Nixon, and became an important recurring date around which to organize.[54] After this show of student opposition in 1961, the regime responded to student protests with paramilitary invasions of the campus—for example in 1962, when hundreds of students were injured and the university's top administrators resigned in protest.[55] The bravery of these students, and the tremendous state violence used against them, inspired some of the first actions among Iranian students abroad, including an ISA demonstration at the United Nations and occupation of the Iranian embassy in Washington.[56] As these events illustrate, CISNU functioned as more than just a corporate body representing dissident foreign students. As one ISA pamphlet published in 1971, after a decade of organizing, explained: "Because of the severe political repression in Iran and the highly censored press, the Confederation of Iranian Students has been the only organ through which the Iranian people have been heard by the people of the world. The activities of the Confederation are a part of the struggle of the Iranian people for freedom and independence—in actuality it is the struggle extended abroad."[57] The ISA, and CISNU more broadly, understood itself to be a necessary and integral part of this struggle, amplifying the voices of those who were being suppressed, and embodying a living connection between "the Iranian people" and the rest of the world. This connection was sustained through revolutionary affects, embodied and visceral desires on the part of thousands of imperial model minorities to work for "freedom and independence" back in Iran. With this compelling mission, the ISA turned the imperial model minority mandate to "serve my country as a scholar," as Sina put it, inside out. As one ISA pamphlet explained: "When the Shah allows Iranian youth to leave the country, he aims to have them return to Iran as educated intellectuals who will serve his dictatorship with their newly acquired skills. However, the ISA enables its members to become more fully aware of the regime's true nature and prepares them to return to Iran to support the people's movement."[58] While the ISA developed a multifaceted critique of the Shah's policies domestically and of his role as a watchdog for US interests in the region (and beyond), the movement's ability to recruit members and sustain high levels of activity was, in Bargetz's words, "based on affective dissent and inspired, or even driven, by a longing for transformation, that is, for a different distribution of the sensible."[59] In other words, unhappy feelings about the present fused with hope for a future in which Iran might be free of both imperialism and dictatorship. Below I offer an overview of the movement before turning to significant moments in the ISA's history and its "affective politics of emancipation," which were both transnational and diasporic.

Overview of the ISA

According to Afshin Matin-asgari, who is both a historian of CISNU and a former participant in the group, the Iranian student movement "was the most active and persistent force of opposition to the Shah's regime during the two decades prior to the 1978–79 Revolution."[60] Initially constituted as a broad umbrella group without a stated political orientation, akin to a student union claiming to represent the interests of *all* Iranian students,

CISNU quickly became defined by its anti-Shah activities and grew into the largest Iranian dissident movement abroad. In fact, it was the only legal Iranian opposition formation from 1963, when government troops suppressed anti-Shah demonstrations in Iran, until 1971, when the Shah decided that enough was enough and banned the group outright. A prison sentence of three to ten years was the punishment for membership.[61] As the level of risk increased, and the more visible members could no longer return home safely, the movement only grew in size and militancy. Deeply impacted by opposition activities within Iran, especially the start of guerrilla struggle in 1971, Iranian foreign-student activism sustained its militancy and urgency through 1979.

The US was thus a critical site for the Iranian anti-Shah student movement because of the amount of aid money—over $2 trillion between 1953 and 1979—given through government and bilateral agreements, and because it hosted by far the largest number of Iranian foreign students.[62] Approximately 80,000 Iranians attended college or university in the US at some point between 1960 and 1977, comprising the largest national group of foreign students in the US and about half of the total number of Iranians studying abroad.[63] As a result, the ISA became the largest of CISNU's national affiliates. In 1978, the Iranian government estimated the size of the student opposition abroad as between 5,000 and 6,000, approximately 10 percent of the total number of students studying outside Iran.[64] Precise membership numbers are not available for local ISA chapters; however, attendance at annual ISA congresses is one way to gauge the movement's growth over the course of almost two decades of organizing. Delegates attending the ISA's tenth annual congress at the University of California's Berkeley campus in 1963 represented 800 members from twenty-four chapters (additional chapters were unable to send delegates).[65] At the thirteenth congress in 1966, held in Los Angeles, fifty-one delegates representing approximately 2,550 members attended from chapters in New York, Washington, DC, Northern California, Southern California, New England, Chicago, Minnesota, Connecticut, and elsewhere.[66] In 1973, sixty delegates representing 3,000 members from thirteen chapters plus an additional 500 students attended the ISA's twenty-first congress held in Chicago.[67] By December 1977, when Iran was already racked by the strikes and demonstrations that would lead to the Shah's downfall, an ISA congress was held at a fairground in Oklahoma City. *Resistance*, the ISA's English-language periodical, reported that over 2,500 Iranians from across the country attended the seven-day proceedings.[68] Behzad Golemohammadi, a student at Oklahoma State and an ISA organizer in the Texas-

Oklahoma region at the time, recalled that the frigid weather and ensuing illness of many participants failed to dampen their enthusiasm. "We talked and talked, day and night!" he said.

These numbers do not accurately reflect the ISA's political and ideological impact on the Iranian diaspora, which was disproportionate to its size. One reason for this was the organization's pervasive and highly visible presence. Chapters sprung up in every part of the US, wherever there was even a small concentration of Iranian students. Members of chapters organized in the 1960s, such as in Northern California and Washington, DC, tended to come from middle-class and upper-middle-class families in Tehran, or other major cities, who could afford to finance a Western education. For them, imperial model minority status was an extension of the class privileges that they already enjoyed in Iran. For Iranians from less affluent backgrounds, it was a path to upward mobility that promised to transform their family circumstances and futures significantly. By the mid-1970s, the oil boom made it possible for the children of white-collar oil workers from the south and west of Iran to attend college in the US.[69] The influx of these students from the lower middle class enabled the Texas-Oklahoma ISA chapter to grow into a significant base of anti-Shah activism that was also imbued with a different class and cultural character than other regions. The children of oil workers were not only angry about US support for the Shah's dictatorship, but also about the economic insecurity of their families and the shocking concentrations of wealth they saw in the US. These ISA members arguably had much more to lose then their upper-middle-class comrades in rejecting incorporation into the imperial model minority script, and they injected a degree of militancy into the Texas-Oklahoma region that would reverberate throughout the movement as a whole.

Both CISNU and the ISA were numerically and politically dominated by men, although small numbers of women played active and important roles in organizing and leading meetings, acting as official spokespeople to the media, and serving on committees and in elected positions of leadership. For example, in 1966, Zohreh Kaviani, a student in West Germany, was the first woman elected to CISNU's international secretariat by the annual congress, which was "[the organization]'s highest source of authority."[70] Prior to her election, in 1965, CISNU supported a meeting of the first Congress of Iranian Women in Cologne, West Germany, and declared its intent to establish a separate international organization of women that would focus on women's rights in Iran and promote women's participation in CISNU itself.[71] This was at a time when American women in radical student groups such as Students for a Democratic Society (SDS) and the Student Nonviolent Coordinating Committee faced ridicule and abuse for raising issues of women's equality and sexism within the movement.[72] The independent women's organization floated by CISNU never emerged; however, some of the women who were active in CISNU would later attempt to launch similar formations in Iran during and after the revolution. Chapters 5 and 6 describe these efforts as well as the broader gender and sexual politics of the ISA as they manifested in organizational policies and practices and in the daily lived experiences of active members. However, it is important to note here that the overall gender disparity in membership partially reflected the fact that the foreign student population as a whole was overwhelmingly male, especially in the 1960s. This began to change by the 1970s, when more women traveled abroad to study. During this second decade of the movement, Jaleh Pirnazar, an Iranian Jewish woman studying at UC Berkeley, was elected to serve as secretary of publications for the whole of the ISA in the US. Eventually, most chapters had a minority of women members, although the extent to which they challenged male leadership and advocated for themselves as women varied widely from chapter to chapter. In 1976, after several years in which the international leadership of CISNU had been all men, Vida Samiian, an Iranian student who had been active in the ISA at the University of California–Los Angeles, moved to Germany and was elected to the five-member secretariat of one CISNU faction. She was charged with the task of overseeing all of the organization's publications and media relations.

At a time when many student groups received funding from either the US or the USSR, CISNU's financial independence remains a point of pride for many former members.[73] Ali Hojat, who was active in the Northern California branch, emphasized that "after thirty to forty years, they haven't found a single document that shows [CISNU] received any money from any government." Like CISNU, according to Parviz, the "ISA was totally self-sufficient in terms of money. That's very surprising to a lot of people now. I don't blame them for not really believing because it was very effective without [taking government funds] and that was very unusual." Indeed a CIA report on the antiwar movement of the 1960s confirms the financial independence of CISNU, stating "Most of the funds apparently come from membership dues."[74] The combination of dues, donations from sympathizers, and fundraisers, such as annual Nowruz parties attended by thousands of people across the US, sustained the budget necessary to produce publications, fund travel to congresses, defend members facing deportation for their political activities, and rent ISA headquarters.

These headquarters were known either as *Khane-e Iran* ("Iran house") or *Khane-e Daneshjoo* ("university student house"). Members scattered in smaller towns and colleges came together for large, regular meetings in these regional organizing centers. For example, ISA members at Oklahoma State University in Stillwater and at the University of Oklahoma in Norman would travel to the *Khane-e Iran* in Oklahoma City every weekend. According to Behzad, who was active in the late 1970s, there would be "like a couple hundred people sitting there, a big crowded store front and everybody smoking. The more heated the discussion became, the more they smoked." Especially in cities such as Berkeley and Washington, DC, which were organizing centers for the broader US student and progressive movements, *Khane-e Iran* became a hub of activity for Iranian and non-Iranian supporters. In Northern California, Jaleh Behroozi, a Jewish UC Berkeley student, and Ahmad Taghvai, a Sunni student at Richmond College, remembered Tuesday night meetings at the Berkeley *Khane-e Iran* would attract hundreds of people, drawing from among the chapter's 300 members plus hundreds more sympathizers. In Washington, DC, the *Khane-e Iran* attracted similar numbers. In New York City, while the New School for Social Research was the campus hub of ISA activity, there was also a *Khane-e Iran* on Fourteenth Street and Sixth Avenue. Wherever the ISA established a headquarters, it became a space for public forums and joint events with other groups, and for members to do the daily work of running the organization—including holding committee meetings and study groups and working on ISA publications. It was at the *Khane-e Iran*, as much as at informal gatherings in student apartments and cafes, that members educated themselves, developed leadership, and strategized about what campaigns to undertake and how to maximize their visibility.

By the mid-1970s, a majority of ISA members would become affiliated, to varying degrees, with a leftist party that either already had members working illegally inside Iran or that was planning to launch such work as foreign student members returned home. While other smaller parties also existed, those that dominated the ISA through their supporters included: the Marxist Fadaiyan (Sāzmān-e čerikhā-ye Fadā'i-e ḵalq-e Irān); the Revolutionary Organization (Sāzmān-e enqelāb-e hezb-e tūde-ye Īrān), a group that split from Tudeh and became Maoist; a faction of the National Front (Jebhā-ye Mellī-e Īrān), remnants of Mosaddeq's old nationalist-liberal party that had been radicalized and adopted Third World Marxism; and the Union of Iranian Communists (Etehādi-e kommūnisthā), a Maoist group that, unlike all of the others with roots in Iran, was a distinctly diasporic formation founded by Iranians in Northern California.[75] Some ISA chapters in Texas in the early 1970s also included members of the Mojahedin, an Islamic guerrilla group that split when a section of its membership became Islamic Marxists.[76]

Like many other student movements, such as SDS in the US (which split in 1969), or the National Union of Students of France (which split in 1971), CISNU grappled with internal tensions over its political orientation and purpose that raised fundamental questions about the relationship between social movements and political parties. By the mid-1970s, bitter factional disputes among the various leftist parties operating within CISNU erupted over a series of issues—most importantly, over whether CISNU should maintain itself as a broad student union or whether it should itself become an explicitly revolutionary formation. Even though all of the parties making up the Iranian new Left were variously Marxist-Leninist in their political outlook, CISNU congresses were consumed by rivalries and disagreements among them. The context for the rise of this sectarianism matters: as resistance in Iran reemerged in the 1970s, and under the weight of tragic mistakes made by the previous generation of Iranian leftists, Iranian student activists in the US felt a vital urgency to organize around the correct political line, to get it right this time. Nothing less than human liberation was at stake, and each party was quick to label opinions that differed from its own line "counterrevolutionary." In such a climate, strong personalities and wounded egos also played a role in the breakdown of political relationships among members. Over time, it became harder to sustain unity or make room for dissent within CISNU as a whole, and the organization finally split in 1975.

Rather than the split precipitating the movement's decline—as was the case when SDS split, for example—Matin-asgari has shown that, in fact, the opposite occurred: the diasporic anti-Shah student movement grew numerically, expanded its influence among Iranians and non-Iranians, and increased its tactical militancy.[77] Former ISA members interviewed for this study lamented the bitter tenor of the split, but noted that the overall effect was to unleash even more activity. In the US, rival ISA factions, each claiming to be the true representative of Iranian foreign students, competed for members among the growing numbers of new arrivals, sometimes going so far as to meet students at the airport and bring them directly to a political meeting.[78] In a sign of just how much the anti-Shah movement was in dialogue with American progressives and leftists, one side in the split went to the trouble of writing and publishing a fourteen-page pamphlet in English called "On the Question of Splits in the Iranian Students Association," which tried to persuade readers of its democratic principles and positions by recounting a series of internal debates.[79]

Ironically, given the acrimony that the different Iranian leftist groups (now organized into different ISAs) felt toward one another, everyone declared their adherence to the principles of solidarity and unity on which CISNU was founded. When a member of the Iranian royal family visited the US, or when it was necessary to defend political prisoners in Iran, each ISA undertook all-out mobilizations, sometimes bringing thousands into the streets. Perhaps because of this, many of the former ISA activists I interviewed continued to refer to the movement as "the ISA" or "the Confederation," even when discussing the period after the split. In the living archive of memory, an affective attachment to the movement as a whole has created a tendency to put the organization back together, to reassemble its coherence in order to reminisce about the high points of struggle and praise the ISA's democratic ideals.

A powerful refrain of resistant nostalgia for unity and democracy within the Iranian student movement emerged as an enduring attachment to a somewhat idealized version of the ISA. During the interviews I conducted, the ISA came to represent an important counterpoint to the hierarchical tendencies of Iranian leftist parties and to the broader authoritarianism of Iranian society. Mohammed Eghtedari recalled the democratic spirit the ISA aimed to embody and project during its early years. When "we opened up *Khane-e Iran* in 1963 or [19]64 in Adam's Morgan area [of Washington, DC]," he said, "a student who was an engineer, Karbazchi, he put the motto there: *Tajamo asas khane-e Iran ast*. 'Gathering is the only principle of Iran house.' That was the only slogan, no other slogans. That was a good place for us." Jaleh Pirnazar emphasized aspects of the organization that she saw as unique and noteworthy within the Iranian context: "I think there should be one decent dissertation written about this mass movement that was democratic when all around us was autocratic, dictatorial, and so on. It was egalitarian. It was pro-women. It was pro-national and religious minorities. If you were a Kurd or a Turk, so much the better! We loved you! Because you had been oppressed all your life." This attitude permeated a diasporic movement that privileged political orientation over and above the national, ethnic, religious, class, and gender identities that often divided Iranians back home. While these differences did manifest in diaspora in more or less subtle ways, they were also subordinated to the larger project of organizing to sever the alliance between the US and the Shah. According to Zohreh Khayam, who attended graduate school at the University of Maryland and Howard University, "The ISA was a wonderful haven for the young people who came to the United States. We had people from a variety of class and cultural backgrounds. It was a wonderful alternative way of living and thinking and we were really effective in mobilizing the young people." For thousands of Iranian students, the ISA became a home away from home, a chosen political family that persisted—despite sectarianism, dogmatism, and the endurance of gender and class hierarchies—in interrupting imperial business-as-usual.

The Arc of Radicalization

Members of the ISA were relentlessly active in the public view, whether through demonstrations, hunger strikes, or other forms of protest. These activists' location outside the geographic space of Iran served to accentuate their feelings of responsibility and accountability to the movement back home. Knowing the risks their counterparts in Iran faced every time they gathered in the streets, ISA members felt obligated to take full advantage of the more favorable conditions for opposition activities that existed in the US. While the following chapter reviews major ISA campaigns and actions, here I chart the process through which the ISA came to adopt a revolutionary outlook and set of demands.

Younes Parsa Benab recalled that early ISA demands were far from radical. Younes came to the US in 1960 from a middle-class family in Tabriz, a city known for its secular cosmopolitanism, and joined the ISA chapter in Washington, DC while studying at Howard University. He was active until the ISA dissolved in the aftermath of 1979 and has published a two-volume genealogy of the Iranian Left in Persian.[80] Younes remembered the tepid tenor of the ISA demonstrations he helped to organize in the early 1960s:

> When I go back to our documents, and I look at it, our demand was very, very limited. Unbelievably! In fact, when I tell my friends now, they laugh. Our demand was that the ambassador of Iran in the US, Ardeshir Zahedi, should send a telegram to the Shah demanding that Dr. Mosaddeq, who is in exile in a village very close to Tehran, should have a right to come to Tehran whenever he's sick to visit his doctor. Ardeshir Zahedi, in front of my eyes, told our delegation of students that this is disrespect. You are asking me to send this telegram to my wife's father.[81] That was his answer. So what did we do? We got dispersed [i.e., sent away].

This anecdote captures the ISA's initial efforts to support the deposed leader of Iran's most successful democratic movement and to generally work within a legal framework that did not challenge the legitimacy of the regime as a whole. It also makes apparent that revolutionary affects have no correct or predetermined political expression, but pick up new meanings as they move between bodies and objects.[82] An affective attachment to a letter that is summarily dismissed can turn into a dismissal of the authority rejecting the letter. And this intensification of emotions and sensations also changes the subjectivity of the protester in the process.

Four major factors would contribute to the shift from reform to revolution as an orientation for the ISA. The first was the animosity of the Iranian government toward its protesting students, regardless of the modesty of their demands. Newsreel footage from an ISA protest in San Francisco in 1961 illustrates this dynamic. At a time when the Shah had suspended parliament indefinitely, an ISA spokesperson told a reporter, "We are asking for constitutional rights and freedom.... All we are asking is to stop threatening against the students. ... And stop canceling out our money and canceling out our passports. We are not overthrowing any government."[83] These references to SAVAK and Iranian embassy harassment of students living in the US highlight the transnational dimensions of Iranian state repression and show the regime's determination to silence even mild forms of opposition. Nonetheless, in January 1962, a three-hour ISA sit-in at the Iranian embassy "demanded the resignation of the Prime Minister [Ali Amini] and freedom for Mosaddeq," but did not denounce the Shah.[84] In January 1963, forty-five ISA members again occupied the Iranian embassy and launched a hunger strike when the new ambassador refused to initial a copy of their protest letter to the Shah opposing "the substitution of a referendum for the re-opening of parliament."[85] Leading ISA member Ali Fatemi shouted "Down with the Shah!" as police dragged him, along with thirteen other protestors, outside and hauled them off to jail.[86] This would soon become the main slogan of the movement, once all hope for democratic reform was gone.

The second development that pushed ISA members toward revolutionary conclusions occurred on the US side of the special relationship. As Matthew Shannon has documented, leading ISA members worked hard to persuade the Kennedy administration to push for democratization in Iran. For a brief period, it seemed like they were getting somewhere. In January 1962, Attorney General Robert Kennedy met with an ISA delegation, which convinced him to cancel his upcoming visit to Iran.[87] The Shah, alarmed by this news and by other ISA protests, immediately recalled Ambassador Zahedi to Tehran.[88]

When the Shah came to the US that spring, ISA pickets were waiting for him at airports in Washington and New York, but a planned demonstration in front of the White House was canceled "as a courtesy to President Kennedy."[89] While ISA leaders had the ear of the attorney general, the National Security Council ultimately blocked any moves that would undermine US support for the Shah or make US aid contingent upon democratic reforms.[90] In 1963, President Kennedy "sent congratulations to the Shah of Iran" for his so-called White Revolution, a package of reforms that further concentrated power in the hands of the dictatorship.[91] While the ISA would continue to work with several progressive members of Congress in the years to come, never again would its members get this close to the inner circle of a sitting US president.

Disappointed with President Kennedy's response, the ISA relentlessly attacked the idea that the White Revolution was evidence of peaceful progress in Iran. For example, Dariush Shadman, president of the ISA chapter at the University of Illinois, published an article in English in *Daneshjoo* in 1964 that sought to expose "Iran's False Image." The author maintained that between 1955 and 1962, Iran's debt rose from $10 million to $500 million, and a majority of villages still had no electricity, no hospitals, doctors, or schools. He quoted a 1963 article in the *New Statesman* that explained how severely the Iranian economy had been distorted by inflation and reliance on "US surpluses." "Only oil and American aid keeps it going at all," the excerpt concluded. "Is this "economic progress?" Shadman asked his American readers.[92]

President Kennedy persisted in promoting a very different narrative, celebrating the Shah as a great modernizer engaged in "the struggle to better the lot of [his] people."[93] This view was compatible with the anticommunism that guided Kennedy to push for more foreign aid. As he stated in a message to Congress in April 1963, "our military and economic assistance to nations on the frontiers of the Communist world—such as Iran, Pakistan, India, Vietnam and free China—has enabled threatened peoples to stay free and independent, when they otherwise would have either been overrun by aggressive Communist power or fallen victim of utter chaos, poverty and despair."[94] In return for financial and political support, the Shah extended diplomatic immunity to *all* Americans living and working in Iran, a standard protocol of US overseas interventions since at least the late nineteenth century. This immunity applied to civilians working in industry as well as the 12,000 "advisers" tasked with training the 250,000 members of the Iranian army—an early template for partnerships between the US military and local forces in the region that would proliferate decades later during the "war on terror" in Afghanistan, Iraq, and Pakistan.[95]

The third factor propelling the ISA toward a revolutionary orientation was the return of popular, open opposition beyond the campuses in Iran, which had effectively been suppressed since the coup. Criticism of the White Revolution and of the law granting immunity to US nationals became catalysts for a domestic Iranian uprising. In June 1963, Ayatollah Khomeini was thrown in jail after he publicly denounced the Shah's policies as acts of colonial submission.[96] While he did not call for the Shah's overthrow until a few years later, his speech and subsequent arrest triggered opposition demonstrations among students, workers, peasants, and religious groups, which were brutally repressed by the Shah's troops.[97] Members of the ISA publicized the uprising along with condemnations of the Shah's repression.[98] They agreed with Khomeini's attacks on the immunity law and also with his attacks on the expansion of voting rights to women, though not necessarily for the same reasons.[99] While *Resistance* supported suffrage as "a major demand of Iranian women since the early 1900s," it argued that "suffrage in general has no significance" under a dictatorship that prohibits free elections.[100] Khomeini cast women's suffrage as un-Islamic and as part of the "Westernization" that had undermined Iranian sovereignty.[101] Subsequently, CISNU made contact with Khomeini in exile in Iraq in 1965 and consistently campaigned to free jailed Islamist protesters.[102] Even after the ISA took on a decidedly Marxist character, with an exodus of the most devout students to Muslim student organizations in the mid-1960s, the organization generally supported the "progressive clergy," including Khomeini, all the way through the initial period of the revolution itself. This strategy, considered necessary in order to maintain a "united front" against imperialism, was also an expression of the revolutionary affects circulating among the ISA. If Khomeini was able to mobilize masses of people, then he deserved the support of every serious revolutionary.[103]

After the 1963 uprising, ISA and CISNU publications meticulously documented and commemorated every eruption of popular protest in Iran. Every strike and demonstration, every arrest, trial, sentencing, and execution of activists that happened in Iran was a call to action for the student movement abroad. While striking bus workers braved bullets and arrest in Tehran in 1970, for example, ISA members launched a hunger strike and printed a leaflet proclaiming, "We shall continue the struggle; this is our duty."[104] In 1971, the struggle took on a new character when Marxist and religious guerrilla organizations launched their first armed attacks. In particular, the attack on a gendarmerie post carried out by the Marxist Fadaiyan in the northern Iranian town of Siahkal deeply impacted Iranian students, both in Iran and across the diaspora.[105] Affective attachments to the heroism and boldness of the Fadaiyan also indexed the impact of anticolonial guerrilla movements in Palestine and elsewhere. As I discuss in detail in chapter 4, this global context was the fourth factor contributing to the transformation of imperial model minorities into revolutionaries.

While the ISA's approach to the US government shifted in the course of the 1960s from hopeful engagement to alienation and anger, the group consistently encouraged ordinary Americans to identify with the Iranian people and their freedom struggle, rather than with Cold War doctrines of American exceptionalism or with the Shah's celebrity allure. They wanted Americans to know what was being done in their name, and publicly performed their critique of the special relationship in the hopes of spreading their mood of outrage more broadly. When the Shah made his customary trip to the White House in 1967, President Lyndon B. Johnson commended the monarch for "winning progress without violence and without any bloodshed, a lesson that others still have to learn."[106] Members of the ISA protested outside with signs declaring, "Shah was installed by CIA," "Iranians want bread not weapons," and "Free Political Prisoners."[107] Four ISA members were arrested protesting the Shah's visit to Congress and later held a press conference "to complain they were mistreated" by police.[108] Other ISA members maintained a vigil outside the Capitol, and the organization vowed to picket at every stop on the Shah's North American tour.[109] Revolutionary affects moved between the coup in 1953, the plight of imprisoned dissidents in Iran, and the police harassment of ISA members themselves, as compounding sources of anger, alienation, and militancy. By 1968, an explicit call for the Shah's overthrow was added to the CISNU platform and the organization defined itself for the first time as "anti-imperialist, democratic and popular."[110]

In 1971, the Shah's decadence soared to fantastic new heights. As previously mentioned, the monarch decided to commemorate 2,500 years of the Persian Empire with a lavish celebration staged among the ruins of the ancient ceremonial city of Persepolis and financed through the state treasury. The ISA responded with a flurry of protests and counterpropaganda, as if they hoped to crash the party from afar. In San Francisco, the lead banner on the ISA march through downtown read, "A Hungry Nation Does Not Need a 2500 Year Celebration." At the corresponding protest in DC, one ISA member carried a sign that read simply: "The majority of the families in Iran live in one room."[111] In a pamphlet produced for the occasion, titled "People's Living Conditions, the Reason for Struggle," the ISA reported that, while the Shah was feasting with 600 international dignitaries on food and wine imported from Maxim's in Paris, "75% of households have no electricity; 85% are not supplied with water."[112] Life expectancy in Iran, the pamphlet stated, was thirty-eight years and malnutrition was widespread. It continued, "Despite all this starvation, the Shah spent ... $1.3 million alone on bar glasses for his guests."[113] Another ISA leaflet from 1971 asked, "What are the people suffering from?" and answered, "the infant mortality rate is 50%, there is rampant contagious disease, low wages, extreme poverty, high percentage of illiteracy, which are common features of all countries exploited by imperialism."[114] For the ISA, the failures of the White Revolution were predetermined by the interests of dictatorship and empire that guided them.[115] Yet, no matter how bleak a portrait ISA pamphlets and periodicals painted of the poverty and repression in Iranian society and the formidable military power the Shah had amassed, the organization always advanced the optimistic perspective that these conditions "will certainly add to the revolutionary fervor of the people."[116] In fact, the ISA had been conducting itself with great fervor even before it adopted the explicit language of revolution, as the organization attempted to redefine US-Iran relations from the bottom up.

Conclusion

Unruly and ungrateful, Iranian imperial model minorities who joined the ISA did not spend their time in the US absorbing the great achievements of Western civilization. Rather, they applied themselves to disrupting the distribution of emotions undergirding the Western civilizational project and its particular Cold War doctrines of friendship and racial liberalism. The combined failure of imperial and royal efforts to capture and channel the affects of these young people reminds us that even the most powerful states and empires cannot control or predict the character and sources of dissent. While the ISA was initially established in order to monitor allegiance to the Shah among the student diaspora, the Shah's emissaries abroad, including Ambassador Zahedi, proved woefully unprepared for the rebellion that erupted. The creation of a diasporic wing of the anti-Shah movement from among the ranks of elite imperial model minorities was a direct result of the impact on these students of repression and resistance in Iran, and their subsequent inability to align themselves with the project of capitalist development, anticommunism, and authoritarianism that made the US-Iran alliance so important to both governments.

There was nothing inevitable about the radicalization of the ISA, as I have shown, and few students arrived in the US in the early 1960s already committed to revolutionary politics. However, as demands to work through the existing Iranian constitution and institutions provoked hostility and attack, as the US government doubled down on its support for the dictatorship, as Iranians back home risked their lives repeatedly to express their dissent, and as anticolonial movements around the world became sources of inspiration and solidarity, Iranian activists in diaspora responded with increased hostility toward the Shah and demands for his overthrow. The desire to stand with the Iranian people—even when that meant facing suspended passports, arrest, threats of deportation, and the inability to return home safely—propelled a shift in the diasporic movement toward revolutionary opposition to the Shah and to US imperialism more broadly. Imperial model minorities who became committed ISA activists ultimately found the Iranian freedom struggle more compelling than their studies and the prestige that awaited them back home. I now turn to look in more detail at their effort to undermine the US empire from within, at their successes, and at the backlash that followed.

3

Making the Most of an American Education

In June 1964, an audience of graduates, friends, and families gathered outdoors at the University of California–Los Angeles commencement ceremony to revel in the promise of a bright future. But not everyone was in the mood to celebrate. The Shah of Iran was also to be awarded a degree that day, the Doctor of Humane Letters, and, as the UCLA administration prepared to honor him, ISA members and their supporters prepared to protest. Weeks earlier, the local ISA chapter had launched a campaign to disinvite the Shah.[1] This campaign sometimes utilized the language of American exceptionalism, hoping to convince American students to act on their ideals as if they really did apply universally. In May, an ISA leaflet addressed to "All fair-minded people and student organizations at UCLA seriously interested in upholding the principles of academic freedom" argued that the Iranian people's struggle to be free of the US-backed dictatorship was "essentially identical with the battle fought by the courageous American people from the dawn of their independence to this day for extending the area of human freedom and happiness."[2]

Two weeks later, having won the support of the student governing body, the ISA went on the offensive. The organization issued a leaflet asserting the absolute incompatibility of democratic ideals, like academic freedom, with the Shah's regime. Titled "Why the Shah Should Not Be Invited to UCLA," this two-page leaflet provided detailed evidence of the violent repression of dissent in Iran and on Iranian campuses excerpted from mainstream US magazine and newspaper reports and other sources.³ This exemplified the ISA's systematic efforts to make the suffering of ordinary Iranians not only visible but also affectively compelling, the catalyst for a redistribution of emotions that would reorient Americans away from the Shah and toward solidarity with, in this case, Iranian students who were trying to access higher education in Iran.

When the UCLA administration refused to back down, the ISA took advantage of the mass audience provided by the commencement ceremony in order to turn the stadium into the scene of one of its most spectacular actions. Hamid Kowsari, an ISA member who was based in Northern California but was also involved in planning the protest, explained: "We talked with the progressive Americans who were getting a degree that as soon as the Shah started giving his speech, all those American graduates started walking out. Around that time, some antidrug organization had printed something about Ashraf [the Shah's sister] importing heroin into Iran. One of these [progressive] Americans had a flight license. We rented a small plane and he flew it over the stadium, with the banner 'Need a Fix, See the Shah.' Police helicopters flew to force him down, and he wouldn't land, so that even attracted more attention!" Amid the deafening sound of helicopters dueling above, local police and SAVAK agents violently removed students who unfurled anti-Shah banners inside the stadium, while other students left to join the protest of hundreds of Americans and Iranians gathered just outside.⁴

As this incident illustrates, when the revolutionary affects of Iranian foreign students intervened in the constitutive blindness of Americans toward US empire, the responses varied widely. Iranian students were able to mobilize significant support from some Americans, especially on campuses, while also facing stiff institutional resistance and enduring surveillance and direct repression from US and Iranian security forces. Eventually, the size of their movement, the militancy of their tactics, and the content of their message would trigger a major backlash. Years before the Iranian revolution and the taking of American hostages at the US embassy in Tehran, anti-Iranian sentiment would sweep through US society in direct retaliation against this group of imperial model minorities who had gone drastically off script.

This chapter documents ISA campaigns in three areas designed to educate the American public and sever the alliance between the US and the Shah: protests against close ties between US colleges and universities and the Shah's regime; self-defense campaigns of ISA members targeted for their activism; and campaigns against Iranian state repression, primarily to free political prisoners in Iran and expose SAVAK activities in the US. Not only do these organizing efforts represent the major spheres of ISA activity, but, taken together, they reveal the power the diasporic student wing of the Iranian opposition had to undermine a linchpin of US Cold War strategy in a region of strategic importance to global capitalism. Through the examples provided below, I illustrate the remarkably disruptive force of Iranian revolutionary affects as the source of what Lisa Lowe called an "immanent critique" of an empire that most Americans either did not acknowledge or believed was a vehicle for spreading their most treasured ideals.[5]

While this chapter highlights a variety of responses to ISA activism, the final sections focus on efforts to suppress, punish, and banish Iranian students for their political activity. This backlash expressed imperial affects of victimization and innocence, as politicians, journalists, and the public came to resent this group of imperial model minorities who, in their refusal to assimilate, soured the happy, welcoming feelings of their hosts (see chapter 2). Members of the ISA became the target of university administrations, the US government, and SAVAK, another beneficiary of an American education.[6] As a CIA report on the ISA from 1970 acknowledged, "Those who are in the forefront of anti-Shah activities are well known to Iranian authorities and most of them find it impossible to return to Iran."[7] In the process of visibly and noisily exposing US support for the Shah's regime, ISA members would also test the limits of Western liberal democracy within the US itself and lay bare the links between state repression in the US and in Iran.

Targeting the "Imperial University"

The strategy of shaming and embarrassing the Shah and the universities honoring him played an important role in popularizing a critique of what Sunaina Maira and Piya Chatterjee have called the "imperial university."[8] The ISA helped to undermine the ability of the US academy, "as a presumably liberal institution," to cultivate a liberal, educated base of support for US imperial intervention.[9] As Maira and Chatterjee explain, this support is usually organized around "legitimizing notions of Manifest Destiny and foundational mythologies of settler colonialism and exceptional democracy."[10] However, by the late 1960s, radical student activists were challenging the nationalism and racism of college curriculums and the central role of universities in reproducing unequal power relations. Through the antiwar movement, students also learned about the complicity of their universities in the defense industry and the violence meted out in Southeast Asia. A series of galvanizing campus strikes around the country in 1968–69 popularized an analysis of universities as legitimate targets for revolutionary change.[11]

The role the ISA played in educating Americans about the "imperial university" has been largely absent from this narrative. In the early to mid-1960s, when opposition to the war in Vietnam was still quite small, and the suffering of the Vietnamese people was remote, ISA actions exposed Americans to a group of foreign students who denounced atrocities committed in their country with full US support and the complicity of US institutions of higher education. The Chinese American activist Victoria Wong offers just one example of the lasting impact of the ISA's early actions: "The very first demonstration I ever witnessed was by the Iranian Students Association protesting at my older brother's graduation at UCLA [described above]. Their impassioned, unified chants against US imperialism opened my very young eyes to the world way beyond my reactionary agri-corporate hometown of Salinas, CA." Wong would go on to cofound the Asian American Political Alliance in 1968, a key organization in the emerging Asian American movement. Looking back on her student activist years, she wrote, "I believe the ISA was in many ways the vanguard student organization in the early 1960s that paved the way for the student and anti-imperialist movement, not just in this country but worldwide."[12]

Nowhere did the ISA have a greater opportunity to make their case against the Shah than on the campuses where they lived, worked, and studied, and they seized on this strategic location with all of the passion and outrage they could muster. US universities played a crucial part in sustaining happy, hopeful feelings about *pax Americana*, and the alliance between the US and the Shah in particular, through the ritual practice of awarding the Shah honorary degrees. By 1979, the Shah had accumulated degrees from the University of Michigan (1949), Columbia University (1955), the University of Pennsylvania (1962), New York University (1964), the University of California in both Los Angeles and Berkeley (1964), the American University (1964), Harvard University (1968), George Washington University (1974), the University of Southern California (1975), and Pepperdine University (1977). At each institution, the Shah donned the robes of a graduating doctoral student and gave lofty speeches revolving around the same theme: there was "no better way" than educational exchanges to "strengthen the bonds of friendship between my people and the people of this great country … and preserve the peace of the world."[13]

These performances commemorated a web of financial and institutional ties between US universities and the Iranian state, but relied for their legitimacy on what Sara Ahmed has called an "affective economy," or the circulation of affect "between objects and signs" through which they "increase in affective value."[14] The transfer of positive affects attached to the university, as an institution epitomizing the values of liberal humanism, to the Shah, worked to intensify associations between the Shah and those same values. As these affects moved between the university and the Shah, they generated happy feelings about the US as a global power. Under the sign of the universal good of higher education, and with the requisite pomp and circumstance, the alliance between imperialism and dictatorship became a noble and dignified example of a universal ideal of human progress.[15]

This repetitive awarding of honorary degrees highlights the importance of the non-Western world to dominant conceptions of the university as an unquestioned good. Critical university studies scholars Abigail Boggs and Nick Mitchell have argued that this conception rests on "fantasy-scenarios" that erase the historical binding of US universities to the material and ideological projects of settler colonialism and white supremacy, from the dispossession of Indigenous lands on which to build these institutions, to the profits from and presence of slave labor which allowed them to operate.[16] Even as racialized minorities in the US had to struggle for access to higher education, and to diversify all-white faculties and the white, Christian, male canon, the heartfelt welcome given to the Shah and to Iranian imperial model minorities reveals the imperial scope of what Roderick Ferguson has called "affirmative modes of power."[17] Ferguson identifies these as efforts by universities to incorporate, instrumentalize, discipline, and valorize racial, ethnic, gender, cultural, and other forms of difference.[18] While Ferguson is primarily concerned with how universities responded to domestic revolutionary student movements that challenged racial and gender exclusions, the affective economy that circulated shared values between the university and the Iranian monarch shows how the demands of empire worked to hone affirmative strategies for the absorption of difference. "Affirmative modes of power" that normalized the presence of Iranians in the hallowed halls of Western knowledge production also normalized US Cold War influence in the Third World as part of a pedagogical process of spreading enlightenment.[19] This occurred precisely during the so-called golden age of higher education "from the 1960s to the 1970s ... when the university was imagined as a form of redress in the absence of broader forms of wealth distribution."[20]

As the figure of the imperial model minority makes clear, the ideal of the university as the site of redress was leveraged on a global, rather than only a national, scale as the crucial site of hope for Third World development. The relationship between the Shah and US universities during this "golden age" warrants more than just a critique of Orientalist area studies programs funded by the US government.[21] Not only in the drive to produce expertise about the Orient, but also in the happy inclusion of the "foreign" Other within the physical spaces, ritual practices, and affective economies of US universities does the universal good of higher education become fully implicated in the project of empire.

When ISA members protested honorary degree ceremonies, they sabotaged the affective economy of the Cold War "special relationship." They brought injustices committed against Iranian students, workers, peasants and political prisoners into ceremonial spaces as a charge against the university's liberal humanist claims, enacting their affective attachments to "the people" instead of to the regime. The revolutionary affects that circulated among Iranian imperial model minorities ruptured the linear temporality of progress, according to which the 1953 coup and the repression that followed would disappear into a past left behind on the road to a better future, one that these very students were meant to embody and create.

The ISA also publicized and condemned the material ties between US institutions of higher learning and the Iranian monarch. These included large financial gifts from the Shah and US university-led programs to provide professional and technical support to diverse sectors of the Iranian economy and military. A few examples include the Shah's establishment of a $1-million-dollar endowed chair in petroleum engineering at the University of Southern California, a gift of $900,000 to Stanford University to start a satellite communications system in Iran, and the establishment at Harvard of the Iran Center for Management Studies to "produce personnel for key government posts and financial establishments" in Iran.[22] The University of California system vied for multimillion dollar contracts as well. As a 1975 article in UC Berkeley's student newspaper the *Daily Californian* put it, "The nationwide university rush for the oil producing countries' research and development money is on."[23] The *Chronicle of Higher Education* reported in 1977 that approximately fifty US universities had signed seventy-four agreements with the Iranian government to work for "departments or organizations, including those that deal with science and education, energy, radio and television, police and the military."[24] The ISA publication *Resistance* introduced notions of suffering and injustice into the public conversation, calling the hundreds of millions of dollars given by Iran to these institutions "the blood, sweat, and toil of the impoverished Iranian people."[25] In return, *Resistance* explained, "the fascist dictator, the Shah, and members of his corrupt and decadent family" received honorary doctoral degrees.[26] Every time the Shah arrived to pick up another award, the ISA was there to cast a pall over the proceedings, transforming campuses into battlegrounds over the Shah's image and over the allegiances of American students.

The ISA was usually unable to prevent or abrogate the many deals between the Shah and US institutions of higher education. However, there are a few documented cases of at least partial success. In 1976, the *Daily Californian* reported two stories of ISA victories. In February, a front-page story explains that Iranian recruiters from the Iranian Helicopter Company "failed to keep their appointment with Iranian engineering students" at UC Berkeley. According to ISA spokesperson "Mohommad Mobarez"—a pseudonym, meaning "Mohammad the militant"—"The recruiters are agents of the Shah who want Iranian students to return to Iran to work for the fascist military machine there."[27] Upon hearing of plans for an ISA protest, the recruiters "failed to arrive" and the protest was canceled. "We scared them away before they had a chance," "Mobarez" said.[28] In April, the *Daily Californian* covered Iranian students' objections to the $100 million in "educational services given to the Shah" by US universities and noted, "Student protests last fall at the Southern Massachusetts University over a plan to use the campus as a training ground for the Iranian Navy led officials there to cancel the program."[29] At Old Dominion University in Norfolk, Virginia, word got out about a program to train the Iranian navy there. There was no local ISA chapter, only one member, Haydar "Radical" Paykari, who called ISA activists in Washington, DC, and Maryland for help. Mohammed Eghtedari remembered receiving that call and organizing with two other ISA members from different factions to go down to Norfolk. This was after the ISA split in 1975 and, according to Mohammed, "although different groups were opposed to one another at different levels, we cooperated because of personal relationships." The three friends addressed an assembly of faculty and students. After hearing their appeals, the university "decided to cancel the whole program at Old Dominion," Mohammed said. That such outright success was rare shows just how committed US universities were to the alliance between the US and the Shah's regime.

Campus Crackdowns

The ISA's campus activism sometimes led university administrations to respond with punitive measures—from banning tabling privileges and withholding student club status to the suspension and expulsion of ISA members. Expulsion put students at risk for cancellation of their visas and subsequent deportation, although these potentially dire consequences rarely came to pass. Iranian activists, coming from a society where they could not speak or organize freely, fought any attempt to curtail those rights in the US. Local chapters mobilized to defend themselves and relied on help from their political allies. Ahmad Taghvai, active in the Northern California chapter, described a joint defense campaign with Students for a Democratic Society (SDS) on behalf of two ISA members suspended for their activism at a college in San Luis Obispo, a place he remembered as "so conservative that they only had two hippies in the whole city." Posters announcing a protest for the day of the student appeals court had been put up ahead of time by SDS. "If you watch the famous movie, *The Russians Are Coming!*, the SDS posters were something like that," Ahmad said, laughing. "People were scared, sitting in their houses on that day, looking out from their windows. They had never had a protest in this city. Different radio stations from San Francisco and LA were there to broadcast everything live. So probably this is one of the big things that happened in Obispo's history. After all, the university had to take back their vote [to suspend the students] and we won." The delight Ahmad took in recounting this memory illustrates how the collective disruption of American complacency could indeed be a pleasurable experience.

While ISA members might have enjoyed the feeling of shaking Americans out of their ignorance, they also had to defend themselves from the repercussions. The National Lawyers Guild was frequently called upon to represent ISA members fighting for their First Amendment rights against suspension and expulsion. The following examples also indicate the extent to which Iranian foreign students were active on non-elite campuses. As the sheer number of Iranian students ballooned throughout the 1970s, less competitive students looked for institutions with open enrollment policies, and less affluent students looked for cheap tuition. In 1978, the ISA won a lawsuit against Texas Southern University, a historically Black college in Houston with an active ISA chapter, forcing the president to rescind a ban on demonstrations issued in response to anti-Shah protests on campus.[30]

At Bee County College, in the tiny East Texas town of Beeville, ISA members caused what *Texas Monthly* magazine called an "international incident" when they occupied the campus gymnasium to protest complaints brought against them by the administration. The incident began as a meeting in the gymnasium with the college president, Grady Hogue, who presented the students with a list of complaints including "failure to pay rent, bad checks, unauthorized phone calls to Iran on college telephones, unlawful filling of private mailboxes with the Iranian Student Association newspaper *Resistance*, intimidation of non-Iranian students by Iranian students, and cheating on college examinations."[31] Hogue asked the students to resolve these issues among themselves and left the building. The ISA members did not leave. They objected to the accusations as well as to the fact that the administration had refused them permission to form a student club on a campus where Iranians made up 10 percent of the total student population of 2,000.[32] A crowd of American students waiting outside, who were unable to attend regular physical education classes due to the impromptu ISA sit-in, grew agitated. Hogue called in the police and had all 103 Iranian students arrested. The students filled the jail cells in four South Texas counties and continued their obstructionism by giving the police false names. The college expelled eighty-five of those arrested.

Practically overnight, the "Ad Hoc Committee to Defend the Beeville 103" was formed through the ISA and the Committee for Artistic and Intellectual Freedom in Iran, an entity founded by Iranian Trotskyists that was able to mobilize prominent Americans opposed to the Shah. Suddenly, Bee College was inundated with letters from former Attorney General Ramsey Clark, Kate Millet, Benjamin Spock, Philip Berrigan, Noam Chomsky, Allen Ginsberg, and Edward Albee, among others, defending the civil rights of Iranian students.[33] After initially losing the case, the National Lawyers Guild won on appeal; the charges were dropped, and all students were reinstated.

This case illustrates the national profile Iranian anti-Shah students had among American progressives and the resulting ability of the anti-Shah movement to leverage significant grassroots support. It also reveals the complicated attitudes of small-town Texans toward the presence in their midst of politically militant and culturally foreign students, who had apparently tried to negotiate the price of rent and tuition as if they were haggling in a bazaar. *Texas Monthly*'s reporting on the "Beeville 103" discusses a series of cultural misunderstandings between Iranians and Americans on and off campus, portraying the students' militancy as an almost comedic overreaction to the quaint ignorance of the townspeople when it came to Iran. Mocking ISA accusations that the Bee College president might be cooperating with the CIA, the reporter observed, "he didn't appear to be collaborating with anyone accept the mailman, who is frankly getting tired of hauling bags full of letters out to the college."[34] Despite this breezy, dismissive tone, the article attempted to contextualize the students' protest in a way that might educate its American readership:

> It is doubtful that many people in Beeville follow the politics of Iran or the policies of Shah Mohammad Riza Pahlevi [*sic*]. It is even more doubtful any of them were aware that the Shah, in January and February, had ordered military suppression of two violent revolts in the provincial Iranian cities of Tabriz and Qom. But the Bee County Iranians did know about these things. ... The ISA had been split into factions for years, but all its members agree on two principles: the Shah is a dictatorial killer supported by the United States government, and the people of the United States should know about it.[35]

The militancy of ISA members could thus be construed as legitimate, and even strategic, although it manifested revolutionary affects out of sync with everyday life in Beeville. While they may not have won over many local residents—at least not according to the *Texas Monthly* report—the ISA nationally was buoyed by this and other small victories, and by an outpouring of support from their allies on and off campuses. From Berkeley to Beeville, Iranian student activists felt absolutely justified in telling anyone who would listen how angry they were about what was happening far away, in the place they called home.

Iranian State Repression across Borders

The ISA's exposure and condemnation of the systematic torture of political prisoners in Iran was arguably their most powerful expression of revolutionary affects, which succeeded in galvanizing Americans on and off campuses. Torture, in a word, shattered the affects of friendship that attended the alliance between the US and the Shah; benevolence had been a smokescreen for barbarism. By the mid-1970s, the Shah had an "image problem" in the Western media.[36] In 1975, amidst a massive military buildup, the Shah made Iran an official one-party state, further alienating wide sections of Iranian society. Protests on Iranian campuses and actions by the Fadaiyan and Mojahedin were met with regime violence, hundreds of arrests, and defense campaigns by opposition groups abroad, including the ISA.[37] Also in 1975, Amnesty International published a widely cited report condemning the

Iranian government as one of the worst human rights abusers in the world.[38] The report gave the same figures that the ISA had been circulating, claiming there were between 25,000 and 100,000 political prisoners in Iran. Although Amnesty made clear that they were not able to confirm such figures, these were the numbers subsequently used in major exposés in *Time* magazine and the *New York Times*.[39]

The ISA wanted ordinary Americans to know and care about what was happening to Iranian dissidents on the other side of the world and to feel responsible for acting on their behalf. The publications and placards of the ISA consistently displayed the names and faces of prisoners who could still be saved, and memorialized those who had been executed.[40] *Resistance* reprinted prison memoirs translated into English with graphic descriptions of torture, sometimes accompanied by photographs.[41] Torture was invoked with characteristic aesthetic boldness in ISA flyers advertising upcoming protests. One leaflet for a demonstration against the Shah's 1973 visit to the Nixon White House featured a cartoon portrait of the Shah and Empress Farah dressed in royal regalia with a blindfolded political prisoner hanging from a noose in the background (figure 3.1). The image of a lynching was meant to shock people into action, and, in the context of the US in the 1970s, would have resonated widely as the epitome of horrific violence.

Campaigns to free particular political prisoners or lighten their prison sentences were the central way the organization provided material, rather than only symbolic, support to the opposition in Iran.[42] Using a variety of strategies—from demonstrations to sit-ins to hunger strikes—ISA actions shone a light on the darkest reaches of the Shah's dungeons. Pressure generated by CISNU in the US and Europe did, in fact, help to save the lives of Iranian dissidents on more than one occasion. In 1965, after large CISNU protests in defense of two intellectuals facing the death penalty, the Shah backed down and commuted their sentences to life imprisonment.[43] The lives of two jailed members of the Tudeh Party were also spared as a result of mass public pressure organized by the student movement abroad.[44] In 1968, eight Iranian students were saved from execution by an extensive CISNU-led campaign.[45]

In the 1970s, in response to Iranian student organizing efforts, Amnesty International, the National Lawyers Guild, and the Geneva-based International Commission of Jurists sent observers to Iran to witness trials and interview prisoners.[46] These delegations faced harassment from the Iranian government and were sometimes expelled from the country; they invariably returned with firsthand accounts of kangaroo courts and evidence of tortured

Figure 3.1 ISA File, Social Protest Collection. Bancroft Library, UC Berkeley.

prisoners.[47] These accounts were circulated by CISNU in its publications, and mainstream media outlets, including the *New York Times* and the *Washington Post*, reported on their findings.[48]

In June 1976, Iranian students in Geneva occupied the Iranian consulate, seized 2,800 classified documents, and leaked them to the press.[49] While CISNU chapters from England to India had long been gathering their own evidence of SAVAK activities, there was now irrefutable proof.[50] In the US, a special *Resistance* pamphlet was devoted to publicizing this newly verified information. Photographs of SAVAK agents, including Colonel Rafizadeh, the US station chief, appeared alongside revelations about SAVAK's tactics. The pamphlet revealed that *lubia*, "string bean" in Persian, was the code word for SAVAK in the US, and it reported covert plans to launch pro-Shah student organizations in an effort to undermine the ISA.[51] The pamphlet ends by condemning the US government's "half-hearted denial of 'having found no evidence' of SAVAK activities here" and urging Americans to put pressure on their own government to "disclose all information about SAVAK activities here in the US."[52]

Then, in October, the subject of torture in Iran suddenly entered the living rooms of millions of American viewers of the CBS Sunday night news magazine *60 Minutes*. Anchorman Mike Wallace interviewed the Shah in Tehran, repeatedly questioning the visibly uncomfortable monarch about his policies on torture.[53] The Shah casually admitted that in Iran, as in Great Britain and elsewhere, the state sometimes tortured its citizens.[54] He attempted to say that physical torture no longer occurred, but refused to say when it had ended. The Shah also admitted that SAVAK agents were operating in the US. Wallace then turned directly to claims that the ISA had been making for years: that they were targeted by the Iranian secret police in the US:

WALLACE And are they here for the purpose of checking up on Iranian students?

SHAH Checking up on anybody who becomes affiliated with circles, organizations hostile to my country …

WALLACE And they are here with the knowledge and consent of the United States Government?

SHAH I think it is.[55]

Wallace then abruptly shifts gear, asking the Shah if he is aware of a secret CIA study that "portrays the Shah as a brilliant but dangerous megalomaniac."[56]

Bijan, an ISA organizer in Texas, remembered this interview as a breakthrough moment for the ISA and for US-Iran relations. "They called him a dictator in the news. You could hear that on CBS. As a result of our activities, the press was not 100 percent in line with the State Department." Claims by the ISA about SAVAK torture in Iran and the surveillance and harassment of Iranian students in the US had become common knowledge and were causing a flurry of public outrage and calls for accountability. Mainstream dailies kept the pressure on, with Jack Anderson and Les Whitten writing a series of articles in the *Washington Post* under headlines such as "CIA Seen Abetting Foreign Agents" and "Iranian Secret Police Dirty Tricks."[57] The State Department launched an inquiry "to determine whether Iranian officials were conducting themselves in any way that conflicted with their diplomatic status," and the Senate Select Committee on Intelligence began investigating "the clandestine activities that have reportedly been conducted in the United States by the intelligence agencies of 'friendly' foreign governments."[58] Indeed, SAVAK was only one of many foreign spy agencies from "friendly" nations actively working against diasporic student movements; operatives from South Korea, the Philippines, Chile, and Taiwan also targeted opposition activists in the US.[59] As one "intelligence expert" told *US News and World Report*, "They have people here just as we do in their countries."[60] Another "knowledgeable intelligence source" said, "You name it, they do it. And they do it here."[61]

"We were very aware of SAVAK's existence among our ranks and outside of our association," said Jaleh Pirnazar. "And we were quite aware of their connections back home. They had called our parents. They had asked them to intervene, asked them to cut funds for us." In addition to pressuring parents to punish their wayward children, SAVAK engaged in a range of other, sometimes bizarre, strategies. In one sinister episode, SAVAK planned to set fire to the ISA headquarters in the Dupont Circle neighborhood of Washington, DC. The agency sent a letter from a fake "Iranian Anti-Communist Organization" to the building manager warning that there was going to be an "explosion" and attempted to lay the blame in advance on the ISA. The manager left a copy of this strange letter for his Iranian student tenants with the advice, "Kindly read it and be made aware that somebody's out to get you!"[62]

A more common tactic used to try to scare Iranian students and keep them in line was the use of informants. Only after the revolution in Iran would the US Senate finally release a report admitting that SAVAK had at least 3,000 informers spying on roughly 30,000 foreign students.[63] Fear of informants generated an atmosphere of paranoia that could sometimes fuel false accusations against political enemies within the movement. Shahnaz, active in Northern California, said, "some of them [our suspicions] were right and some of them were assumptions." She felt that the ISA was particularly vulnerable at large gatherings, such as the annual Nowruz fundraisers, where anyone could enter with a ticket. "When people were going back to Iran, [they discovered that] SAVAK had that information about who is who," she explained. Farid, active in Texas and Chicago, recalled the painful story of a good friend and roommate in the US who, when he returned to Iran, had been pressured into giving SAVAK the names of five ISA members, including Farid. Because of this, Farid said, "I knew I was banned to go back." At least this friend was honest enough to tell his former comrades what he had done. "After that we banned him and disowned him even to this day," Farid said, and looked as if the pain of that betrayal was still palpable.

Nicky Nodjoumi recalled another incident in New York City: he was one of eight ISA members who met secretly to plan an occupation of the Iranian United Nations Mission at Rockefeller Center early the following morning. When they arrived, "the whole block was policemen. They expected us." The Iranian diplomats had barricaded themselves in an office, but ISA members still tried to read out their list of demands, even as the police read them their rights. "Either we were bugged or somebody informed on us," Nicky said. "To this day, we don't know."

When Nicky returned to Iran in 1975, SAVAK interrogated him in a deserted house every day for three months, allowing him to go home each night: "In that interrogation, I saw all the pictures from the demonstrations [in New York]. They would point and ask me, 'Who is this? Who is this?' Someone had warned me that if you go to Iran, this might happen. So you know the names that they already know, that already came out a couple of years ago. Just say those names. So I would say those names. It was revealing how much they knew, how many pictures they had of our activity." This was not unique to New York City. Nancy Hormachea, an American who joined the ISA in Texas, said SAVAK's presence was well known in Houston. "Every Friday there would be [an ISA] demo outside the consulate in Houston and they would come down and take photos and take names." Behzad, who organized ISA chapters in Oklahoma, said, "Obviously we were being spied on because when I went back, they knew who I was." With "scores" of agents posing as Iranian diplomats and an unknown number of informants operating in the US, it is no surprise that a majority of the former ISA members interviewed for this study had SAVAK files.[64]

The SAVAK agents deployed in the US benefited from an atmosphere in which the domestic repression of leftist organizations was already a central task of American law enforcement agencies. As the ISA pointed out, one of

SAVAK's most common overseas tactics involved "collaborating with the police of the other countries to forcefully suppress the activities of [CISNU]."[65] In 1977, court papers revealed that the ISA had "been a target of an elaborate spy operation for seven years," and a year later civil liberties activists revealed that the ISA was one of 200 groups under surveillance by the Los Angeles Police Department.[66]

By 1977, the US government was so concerned about ISA activities that it sent the FBI directly to the homes of activists. Behzad recalled such a visit to an apartment he shared with several ISA members in Stillwater, Oklahoma, in fall 1977, just before the Shah's annual visit to Washington:

> They came and said, "We know you're active and Shah is our guest. We don't want anything to happen to him. If something happens, we're going to hold you accountable." I'm sure they did this elsewhere, if they came to Stillwater. There was nothing going on there! We expected it. Because we had the notion that this is a police state in the US, and in Iran, both. So when they came it was not a surprise to me. In fact, I was a little late, so when I got home, I saw the FBI guy sitting at our coffee table with a couple of my roommates. We took it as a joke. I remember we were making fun of him as he was talking, giving him very odd answers and chuckling, and then after he left we had a big laugh. How stupid they were … as if we were going to tell them what we were about to do. We were getting ready to go to Washington. [*laughs*]. We had a big laugh, but they were serious.

Behzad's lack of surprise stemmed from the direct experience he and other ISA members had of different forms of state surveillance and repression in Iran and the US, and from an understanding of the linkages between them. This vantage point is crucial to an intersectional approach to Iranian diaspora studies in that it challenges the binary opposition between Iran as exceptionally repressive and the US as exceptionally free. Behzad, like thousands of other Iranian foreign students, ran afoul of both the Iranian and US governments, and their experiences undermine the "clash of civilizations" narrative that came later.

Despite their apparently amused response in this instance, ISA members did learn to take certain precautions, particularly since the temporary nature of a diaspora of foreign students meant that they were always preparing for their eventual return home. After the Shah outlawed membership of CISNU in 1971, even sympathizing with the movement could subject family members back in Iran to "intimidation, threats, confiscation of property and business, and imprisonment and torture."[67] "Therefore," one ISA pamphlet

CIS Defends Patriots

SUPPORT IRANIAN STUDENTS ASS.N HUNGER STRIKE
TO SAVE THE 10

STOP TORTURING POLITICAL PRISONERS IN IRAN

SUPPORT THE JUST
STRUGGLE OF THE
CONFEDERATION
IRANIAN STUDENTS

By Larry Morris—The Washington Post

Masked Iranian students fast at the United Methodist Church, 4th and I Streets SW, to protest political conditions in their country.

The confederation of Iranian Students, in response to the Shah's recent campaign of terror in Iran, has waged an extensive defense campaign. We have learned through years of experience that unless immediate mass action is taken to defend the political prisoners in Iran, they will surely face death by execution. The main purpose of all of the actions taken by the CIS and its supporters, is to p supporters has been to pressure the regime into submitting to two demands. The damdns two demands. The demands are that the Iranian government:
1) Cancell all executions of patriots now on trial; and

of patrios now on trial; and
2) Allow a team of medical and legal observers into Iran to investigate the physical and legal conditions of political prisoners and also to investigate the prison conditions.

15 Days Hunger Strike

On Feb. 14, two hunger strikes were launched in Washington D. C. and Paris to protest the executions and to generally express solidarity with the Iranian patriots. 140 students joined in these hunger strikes which lasted for 14 and 15 days. At

6

Continued

Figure 3.2 Parviz Shokat collection, Box 3, "ISA Hunger Strikers with masks." Hoover Institution Archives, Stanford University.

states, "in all the demonstrations, hunger strikes and other activities organized by the ISA, all Iranian participants are advised to wear face masks to prevent recognition" (see figure 3.2).[68] In ISA meetings, due to the possible presence of informants as well as the potential for SAVAK to pressure individuals for information once they returned to Iran, "no one is addressed by his family name. It often happens that even the closest friends do not know each other's last names."[69]

The masks, in particular, attracted attention. Jaleh Pirnazar explained, "We didn't have fancy masks or anything. A brown bag would do, with a couple of holes." The masked protesters became something of a fixture, Jaleh recalled: "the ISA downtown, angry, fist raising, 'Down with US'—that was part of the San Francisco scene. Some years ago, I saw some books about political posters [and movements] in SF. [The] ISA was there—a long line of us looking almost scary." As early as 1967, these masks became a staple of ISA rallies and marches, lending the movement a high degree of visibility, and even theatricality.[70]

The chilling spectacle of the crudely made masks continually drew attention to police repression as a transnational project.[71] The masks demanded commentary, and campus and mainstream media reports often dwelt on their significance. For example, a 1976 *Daily Californian* report on a twelve-day ISA hunger strike at UC Berkeley protesting death sentences for ten dissidents in Iran notes, "The hunger strikers wear masks covering their faces to protect their identity. Another ISA member said the Shah of Iran has spies in the Bay Area, and the strikers are protecting themselves from the Shah's police when they return to Iran."[72] Under a photograph of masked ISA protestors carrying banners and placards condemning the execution and torture of dissidents in Iran, the *Los Angeles Times* included in its caption the following explanation: "A spokesman for the group said they wore the masks to avoid being imprisoned in the event they return to Iran."[73] The expectation of return worked to collapse the geographical spaces of the US and Iran and to undermine the notion that the US was the land of freedom. Members of the ISA dramatized the relationship between the US and Iran as one that rendered them unsafe in either location. Most importantly for the ISA's critique, the masks gave aesthetic form to the specter of torture and execution of Iranian political prisoners haunting the imperial metropole.

The feeling of accountability to political prisoners back home was so strong for Iranian student activists in diaspora that they sometimes created new moments of crisis, placing themselves at additional risk of state repression and deportation, all in the hopes of reaching even wider audiences with their message. The sense of urgency was like a physical need. This is how Jaleh Pirnazar described the decision of the Northern California ISA chapter to occupy the Iranian consulate in San Francisco on June 26, 1970: "We had been itching to do something, something grand, something that would even involve arrests. Something that would make it big, and it did make it big. We had all the channels in San Francisco. We had prime time news and so on. So we were itching and we were looking for an excuse." Forty-one Iranian students were arrested during the occupation. According to one CISNU pamphlet, the "case of the 41 was perhaps the single most successful endeavor by Iranian students in the US to bring the issue of political repression in Iran to the attention of the American public."[74] By bringing the repressive forces of the US state down upon their own bodies, these students hoped they could make Americans share the feeling that something unbearable was happening every day in their name.

The arrested ISA members were shocked to learn that they faced multiple felony charges. Parviz explained, "We were charged with horrendous things—kidnapping, burglary, everything! I guess kidnapping was the biggest." Seven Iranian women and thirty-four men were taken to the city jail in downtown San Francisco where, according to Parviz, "we raised such hell that I remember the chief of police late at night went and asked the judge to release us and have us come back for the trial. There were too many of us and we were chanting, yelling, and screaming." Eventually a grand jury indicted the students, and the Iranian government canceled their passports.

The ISA's defense campaign became an opportunity to mobilize Iranian and non-Iranian supporters against the "collaboration" of "the grand jury," "the DA of SF and the Iranian Counsel General."[75] Protests were organized to illustrate this collaboration—for example, by marching through downtown San Francisco from the US immigration office to the Iranian consulate. One such demonstration included speakers from the Progressive Labor Party, Arab Student Association, and Students for a Democratic Society.[76] Other protests were held in Chicago, Boston, Washington, DC, and New York City. At UC Berkeley, the ISA organized a revolutionary film series to raise money for legal fees, featuring Eisenstein's *October: Ten Days That Shook the World* and *Strike*.[77] Every ISA article, flyer, leaflet, and statement to the media made sure to link the struggle of "the 41" against detention and deportation with demands to free political prisoners in Iran. "We finally plea bargained [down to a misdemeanor charge] and all went to prison for a month and half," Parviz said. The Iranian consulate returned all forty-one passports and no one was deported.

The ISA's strategy was to publicize attacks on its members as a sign of the movement's growing power, as evidence that they were undermining the official narrative about Iran's march toward prosperity. In 1973, Babak Zahraei, an ISA member active in the anti-Vietnam War movement, spoke out on television about the plight of political prisoners in Iran. He was charged with "subversion and conspiracy" and told by the Immigration and Naturalization Service (INS) that "there was a plane waiting for him and that he was going to be handed over to the Iranian government."[78] After a successful public campaign, all the charges were dropped, and Zahraei went on a victory tour, stopping at more than eighty college campuses to link the harassment of foreign students to the inherent injustice of the Shah's regime.[79]

By the late 1970s, the US government was particularly vulnerable to the accusations that the ISA was making. Still reeling from its defeat in Vietnam, domestic public outrage over atrocities carried out by the US military, and the lies and corruption of Watergate, US government officials knew just how delicate and necessary it was to lead a national recovery of faith in the benevolence of US global power. It was in this context that President Carter declared "human rights is the soul of our foreign policy."[80] By this time, however, the ISA's analysis had reached mass circulation. Prominent intellectuals like Bertrand Russell and Jean-Paul Sartre had written articles about torture and economic inequality in Iran, and major US daily newspapers consistently reported on the growing concerns of human rights lawyers and senators over what exactly the US government was supporting in the name of progress.[81] Student newspapers like the *Daily Californian* ran multiple articles about SAVAK harassment of Iranian students in the US. The fact that a major student daily was essentially helping to disseminate the political perspective of a small group of Iranian revolutionaries is testament to the ISA's success at generating negative feelings about the alliance between the US and the Shah among some sections of American society. But this mainstream support was soon overshadowed.

Unruly and Ungrateful

As early as 1975, some mainstream US media coverage began to portray the ISA as menacing, communist, and violence-prone, and individual right-wing politicians, most notably Representative Larry McDonald, a conservative Democrat from Georgia, denounced the ISA and called for the deportation of ISA members. "There is no legitimate excuse for allowing these revolutionaries to remain in this country," he told the House of Representatives, and demanded that the State Department expel "this category of person."[82] However, the major turning point in public opinion came in November 1977, when the Shah and the Empress appeared with President Carter at the White House for what would turn out to be the last royal visit.

Even before they arrived, the *Washington Post* repeatedly alerted its readers that as many as 18,000 Iranians were about to descend on the nation's capital, eliciting the concerns of law enforcement, the Secret Service, and the Parks Department about the risk of a major confrontation.[83] The upcoming demonstrations of November 15–16 would be different from previous anti-Shah rallies, the paper warned, because they would "mark the first time that any sizable pro-Shah groups also will be present."[84] The stakes, scale, and potential for violence were made legible to readers with reference to the last great domestic battle over US foreign policy, from which the nation was still reeling: "The shah's visit comes amid some of the most intense preparations for street demonstrations here since the days of the Vietnam antiwar movement."[85] By invoking recent memories of mass demonstrations against the US government, the paper also stirred up strong feelings of betrayal, anger, and fear that had already fueled a nationalist retrenchment against the liberal Left in defense of US imperial power.

Following the events, the *Washington Post* ran a front-page story portraying the protests as utter mayhem that resulted in injuries to ninety-six demonstrators and twenty-eight police officers: "Thousands of Iranians ... turned the streets around the White House into a battleground of scattered but bitter and bloody violence. ... Stick-wielding youths viciously attacked each other. Tear gas floated across the Ellipse and White House grounds. Trash fires burned on Pennsylvania Avenue. ... From before dawn until long after dark, the thousands of pro- and anti-shah demonstrators ... marched in serpentine lines ... protestors bellowed a cacophony of political slogans in English and their native language, Farsi."[86] An adjacent photograph, spanning the width of three newspaper columns, appeared to show hundreds of masked anti-Shah students charging forward with raised poles and sticks in their hands.

Buried in the newspaper's coverage was the claim by a spokesman from one ISA faction that SAVAK agents had instigated the violence by infiltrating the anti-Shah protest, shouting insults, and throwing sticks at protesters. "Our friends moved forward in self-defense," the spokesman said. "The police on horseback intervened, but they attacked only the students."[87] Such a claim carried little weight, however, against reports that anti-Shah students commandeered wooden planks with protruding nails from a nearby construction site to use as weapons, that a sixty-six-year-old man was hospitalized with a fractured skull, and that injured pro- and anti-Shah demonstrators had to be separated to prevent them from assaulting each other at a local hospital.[88] Sniper teams were hastily deployed on the White House roof and the Secret Service shut down part of Pennsylvania Avenue.[89]

The anti-Shah movement declared victory, not realizing, or not caring, that Iranian revolutionary affects were woefully out of sync with the feelings of the American public at large. As one Iranian woman told the *Washington Post*, "We succeeded in smashing the Shah's demonstration."[90] Indeed, the ISA's coverage of the protest was nothing short of triumphant. "Mr. 'Human Rights' Meets King Torture," read the front-page headline of *Resistance*. The lead story described the ultimate battle between the ISA and its combined enemies: "The scene was fitting. Tear gas, riot police, SAVAK agents, paid supporters, FBI, Secret Service, Immigration and Nationalization Service, [and] US Park Police had all been brought together."[91] Arrayed against these formidable foes were approximately 8,000 ISA members and their supporters, the largest mobilization in the history of the Iranian student movement in the US.[92]

Resistance celebrated the ISA victory against pro-Shah forces by publishing the now-iconic photograph of the Shah and Carter getting tear gassed in the Rose Garden on its front page (figure 3.3). The police had fired the tear gas to disperse the students; however, the gas blew toward the official proceedings. In the photograph, the Shah's face is buried in a handkerchief as he tries to wipe away his "crocodile tears."[93] For the anti-Shah student movement, this image instantly captured the Shah's weakness, Carter's complicity, and the momentum of an opposition that could no longer be dismissed or suppressed. "The world knows of the Iranian students and their movement now," one anti-Shah student told the *Washington Post*.[94] "Across the US, people know of the struggle. They see it. They see it on television last night in Europe too, and most important, in Iran they see us and know we fight on."[95] Reports came in of people in Tehran "rejoicing" when they saw images of the protests.[96] For millions of Iranians, in Iran and abroad, the chemical tears shed by Carter and the Shah evoked the genuine tears of political prisoners and of the families of those executed by the regime. Iranian student revolutionaries saw they could reach into the heart of power, and they saw that it was vulnerable.

But the mood of the American public was shifting in a different direction. The November 1977 demonstrations unleashed an unprecedented and widespread torrent of xenophobic nationalism toward Iranian foreign students, challenging Cold War Orientalist discourses of friendship and assimilation. One letter to the editor from a Lawrence Forsyth is worth quoting at length, for it exemplifies the affects of an offended imperial host that were soon to become widespread and undergird calls for a government crackdown:

> Of the many "out of" signs—"US out of Persian Gulf," "Savak out of US," "CIA out of Iran"—on display around the White House during the

Resistance

A publication of I.S.A.U.S., member of Confederation of Iranian Students (National Union)

Volume Five   December 1977   Number One

The scene was so fitting. Tear gas, riot police, SAVAK agents, paid supporters, FBI Secret Service, Immigration and Naturalization Service, U.S. Park Police had all been brought together. The Occasion: The Shah of Iran's 2-day visit to Washington, D.C. on Nov. 15 and 16. After all, what else but the Shah rates such welcome by President Carter? This month's issue of Resistance is wholly devoted to news and analysis of Shah's U.S. visit, its goals, its results, and the movement against it. Due to its importance, each significant aspect surrounding the trip has been analyzed in a separate article.

Mr. "Human Rights" Meets King Torture

Washington, D.C., for all practical purposes is the Shah's second home. On November 15 and 16, Washington became an armed camp much like Iran itself in order to allow the Shah to visit. Ever since his ascension to power in the 1953 CIA coup, the Shah has met every U.S. president—Roosevelt, Truman,Eisenhower, Kennedy, Johnson, Nixon, and Ford. Each visit symbolized a further intensification of the U.S. Government domination over the life of the Iranian people.

Yet besides the disgusting ceremonial aspects of such visits, eventually serve to cover-up even more disgusting talks that take place between

them behind closed doors, there are extremely important political, economic and military decisions that are made behind the backs of the people. These decisions greatly influence the daily lives of both American and Iranian peoples, but neither the Shah nor any U.S. president, being what they are, will come out and tell the truth about these deals and decisions. They try to turn things upside-down, confuse the issues, and prettify these ugly agreements so as to carry out their holy mission to extract even more profits from people's back-breaking work, while attempting to portray all this as

being in "everyone's interest."

For example, the Shah-Kennedy meeting resulted in the so-called "White Revolution," a comprehensive economic and military program resulting from the "Kennedy Doctrine" that has ruined Iran's agriculture, industry and commerce. Johnson followed in Kennedy's footsteps with more of the same.

Nixon's Doctrine brought massive militarization of Iran when the Shah was turned into the regional gendarme of the U.S. in the Persian Gulf region. The Shah's meeting with Ford resulted in the Rastakhiz Party. The Shah

abolished the so-called "opposition" parties which had, in fact, been set up by him previously, and announced the formation of a "one party" system of political organization under which the adult population of Iran was given three "choices": to join, to leave the country, or to go to jail. The party, of course, would be organized on the basis of three "principles": recognition of the Monarchy, recognition of the so-called "constitution," and acceptance of the Shah-Kennedy "White Revolution," all of which amounted to nothing short of

(Continued on page 2)

Figure 3.3 Iranian Leftist Students Association of America Collection, Library of Congress. Donated by Parviz Shokat.

Shah's visit, one was sorely needed but conspicuously absent: "Iranian Students Out of US."

How long must we tolerate this band of ruffians who hurl invective upon the American people and their government, threaten to destroy the White House, despoil our sidewalks and buildings with their slogans, turn our parks into jungles and assault American citizens while hiding behind masks? Surely such actions run counter to the provisions under which their student visas were granted and, if that's the case, they should be deported. They and Savak deserve each other.[97]

By lumping "the American people and their government" together as victims of anti-Shah students, the author imposes a nationalist framework the ISA had long argued against. His assertion that Iranians threatened to destroy a sacred American institution and "turn our parks into jungles" reveals the racial and civilizational hierarchy embedded in his argument, which bolstered the conclusion that Iranian students should be sent back to face possible torture and execution in Iran. Other letters similarly dehumanized Iranians in order to justify the suspension of their constitutional and human rights, calling the protesters "illegal aliens" and demanding mass deportations.[98] That there was no mention of Islam or Khomeini, or a single reference to Iranian culture, in any of these citizens' tirades shows the extent to which Iranian students were vilified as part of the secular Left. The state of the wider right-wing resurgence in US society was already such that this association alone was enough to render them terrorists, uncivilized, and unwelcome.

The sheer size of the Iranian student population in the US, something many Americans had apparently been unaware of until they saw the large numbers at the demonstrations in November, became a major cause for alarm. A *New York Times* article highlighting the number of Iranian students in the US opened with a recap of the students' "noisy, occasionally violent demonstrations outside the White House" and maintained that these students, who were mostly "members of factions of the Iranian Students Association," were "among nearly 50,000 Iranian students in this country." The article cites an INS spokesman giving the following statistics: "there were 17,200 Iranians here on valid student visas, far more than any other country ... [and an] estimated ... 27,000 or so 'to the best of our knowledge have overstayed' when their visas expired or were rescinded."[99] These large numbers, the lack of INS certainty about them, and the agency's complacency toward those without valid paperwork all became evidence marshaled against Iranian students in the weeks and months to come.

The *Los Angeles Times* went much farther in its open attack on the ISA, running an opinion piece by a syndicated columnist based in Washington titled "Do the Iranian 'Students' Ever Study?"[100] Again, the affects of an aggrieved imperial host who has been overly generous to his undeserving colonial guests come to the fore:

I recall no parallel to the current situation in which untold thousands of Iranian students (estimates run from 23,000 to 60,000, and even our own government professes not to know) have virtually taken over some schools and moved into organized, hostile street protests in our country.

That noncitizens would be allowed the same privileges anywhere else—in Moscow, Paris or, of course, Tehran—is absurd. ... Yet here in Washington we are exceedingly courteous to thousands of obnoxious outsiders who flaunt red banners with symbols intentionally reminiscent of the hammer and sickle, except that one of the implements depicted is instead an AK-47 automatic rifle. ... [W]hile these may be students, they are by no means kids. They surely are not nice, unless clubbing people with sticks fits the category. And most important, to be frankly xenophobic, they are not even ours.[101]

The columnist attacked the legitimacy and integrity of the imperial model minority that had been entrusted with the noble mission of studying and learning from the most advanced, democratic society in the world. Instead, these students had betrayed their host country, which had acted with far more generosity and fairness than any other country would have. Rather than assimilating the benefits of a Western education, Iranian students had "taken over," turning institutions of higher learning into a base from which to unleash Marxist-inspired hostility on America's streets. The tone of panic over how many Iranians were present in the US ("our own government professes not to know") invoked the latent hysteria of a "red scare" and bolstered calls for a government crackdown. Iranian imperial model minorities were thus summarily disqualified from their privileged and protected status, paving the way for a "frankly xenophobic" response.

Anticommunism, nationalism, and xenophobia combined to create a new logic of exclusion against Iranian students. By 1978, a national climate of overt hostility toward Iranian anti-Shah activists enabled the police to resort to measures that had rarely been used against Iranians before. At an ISA protest in Chicago in May, 182 ISA members were detained by police. The *New York Times* reported, "In what officials acknowledged was a relatively unusual action, all of those who were detained but not formally charged were turned over to the Immigration and Naturalization Service for investigation of their alien status."[102] In August, a demonstration of up to 6,000 Iranian students outside the office of the *Los Angeles Times* demanded that the newspaper correct what activists perceived to be biased coverage against the revolutionary movement in Iran. The police attacked, resulting in thirty serious injuries and 171 arrests.[103] Media reports characterized the protest as "a bloody melee," in which students shouted, blocked traffic, and "ignited two sidewalk fires in front of *The Times*."[104] The paper published a single letter sympathetic to the protesters, in which the author pointed out a disturbing "paradox": police had recently protected a march of Nazis in Chicago, but Iranians "risking their lives to inform us of the brutal ruler of their land" were pushed, kicked, and dragged while lying tied up on the pavement.[105] The other six letters brimmed with xenophobic vitriol toward these "guests," and each one included an emotional call for the deportation of all Iranian students.[106]

1979: Revolution and Reaction

On January 2, 1979, with the Shah increasingly powerless against the sustained momentum of mass demonstrations and strikes in Iran, 2,000 ISA protesters marched on a mansion in Beverly Hills where the Shah's sister, Ashraf, and his mother had taken refuge. Afshin, who had been active in the Los Angeles ISA, was already back in Tehran where anti-Shah demonstrators faced lethal violence in the streets. He phoned his cousin, an ISA member in Los Angeles: "I remember I had told my cousin, 'People are dying here. The situation is pretty bad. Do something you guys.' He said, 'Tomorrow watch the news, and you will see something.' The something was attacking Ashraf's house. That had a good effect in Iran. It was like, these bastards, anywhere they go, we're going to get them, even in the heart of Beverly Hills." Vida Samiian, who had served on the international CISNU secretariat in the mid-1970s and was then a graduate student at UCLA, was one of the organizers of the Beverly Hills march and also the ISA's media spokesperson, a role she held on and off throughout the 1970s: "Before we started marching, a reporter asked me, 'Is this going to be a peaceful action?' I said, 'Yes, of course. These are just students who want to express themselves.' But then, when we got to the gates outside the house, it was like a mob that went out of control. There was nothing I could do. People were just so angry at what the regime had done. They even smashed that reporter's car that was like a Porsche or something." Hundreds of Iranians, many of whom were not ISA members and whom Vida had never seen before, smashed the gates and set fire to patches of lawn, some attempting to avenge the deaths of loved ones killed in Iran by the Shah's troops.[107] The local police, in the presence of agents from the State Department and SAVAK, unleashed the most violent response the Iranian student movement ever received in the US, using tear gas, high-pressure fire hoses, and police vehicles. Shahnaz, a former ISA member in Northern California, recalled what happened: "The police cars attacked us. I was there. I remember we were coming up the hill when the cars came at us." The *New York Times* reported: "A woman demonstrator was reportedly dragged 20 feet by a patrol car of the Los Angeles County Sheriff's Department after it struck her. One witness said the car was moving through a column of demonstrators at about 35 miles per hour."[108] The police ran over dozens of students and arrested seven, sending forty-five to the hospital with broken limbs and fractured skulls.[109]

Iranian students had threatened one of the wealthiest, most exclusive communities in the US. In a front-page story, the *Washington Post* quoted a neighbor who witnessed what became known as the "Battle of Beverly Hills": "I looked out the window and saw people climbing all over the house, and there was smoke and flames all around. I don't know why the authorities don't come in here and round them up and ship them back to where they came from."[110] This sentiment, which had been expressed numerous times in the mainstream media since the November 1977 demonstrations in front of the White House, was about to become official government policy.

On January 4, Senator Lloyd Bentsen of Texas expressed his outrage in a letter to Attorney General Griffin Bell: "They are guests in our country and when they mock our hospitality with a blind and violent disregard for the law, I want them sent home."[111] The next day, the *Washington Post* reported: "Reacting grimly to Tuesday's anti-Shah riot in Beverly Hills, the Carter administration ... pledged to deport all Iranians guilty of violence in this country as fast as the law allows."[112] Attorney General Bell announced, "We are not going to put up with this kind of conduct by visitors to this country. All participants in such violence will be deported."[113]

Editorials and letters to the editor also reflected a new transnational twist in the hostility expressed toward anti-Shah activists: feelings about expressions of anti-Americanism in Iran began to attach to Iranian students in the US. The mainstream media (and the Carter administration), which had for so long refused to recognize the Shah's unpopularity among the Iranian people, were caught off guard by the onset of revolution.[114] As it became clear that the US was about to lose its major ally in the Persian Gulf to an Islamic revolutionary movement that explicitly and virulently rejected the US role in Iran, a feeling of bitter resentment gained currency among the American public.[115] Iranians' mass rejection of US-backed Westernization was equated with a rejection of modernity, and the violence that had occurred in Beverly

Hills was used to cast doubt on the future of an independent Iran. Again, numerous editorials and letters to the editor appeared in major national dailies condemning the failure of the protesters to have learned civilized behavior as part of their Western education, calling all Iranian students "terrorists," and demanding their deportation.[116]

President Carter ordered Attorney General Bell not just to deport the students arrested at the Beverly Hills action, but to investigate the immigration status of every single student-visa holder.[117] It quickly became apparent that the INS did not have a reliable count of the number of Iranian students in the US at the time, legally or otherwise. It could only estimate that out of a possible 50,600 Iranian students in the US, as many as 42,000 might not be enrolled in any college or university.[118] Outrage followed from officials and from the public, both over the large numbers and over the fact that the INS revealed itself to be in such a state of disarray. Attorney General Bell initiated a "crackdown" after viewing "televised reports of Iranian students battling police and setting a car afire" in Beverly Hills, and after "Secretary of State Cyrus R. Vance and Zbigniew Brzezinski, the national security adviser, [who] were angry, too ... suggested that it was time that Mr. Bell check into the immigration service."[119] He was "very upset at the 'antiquated' record-keeping system of the agency," which had only just come to his attention, and promised a full report on the status of foreign students in the US within one month.[120] Thirty-eight Iranian students were immediately arrested and deportation proceedings begun against them.[121]

The INS overhaul initiated in response to the "Battle of Beverly Hills" resulted in the automation of the agency, finally bringing it, in Bell's words, into "the modern world."[122] Promising that computers would help catch "illegal aliens," Bell told Americans that, while "it had been assumed that Mexicans slipping over the southern border accounted for most of the illegal aliens," he had "come to believe that perhaps as many illegal aliens are in the United States from a wholly different source: visitors and foreign students who enter legally with visas but who deliberately overstay and then disappear into the vastness of the country."[123] By tapping into racialized fears of "Mexicans slipping over the southern border," and then transferring those emotions onto foreign students, Bell reframed and expanded the source of the foreign threat to the nation. Assimilating foreign students into US society was no longer a desirable goal but a dangerous threat that had to be managed. In fact, their legal entry and potential for assimilation, their ability to "disappear into the vastness of the country," made these foreigners a potentially more difficult and intractable problem than those who could be stopped at a border without papers. Meanwhile, hysteria about the large numbers of foreign students only grew, with headlines like "Aliens Invading America's Campuses" appearing in the *Washington Post* as the first in a series of articles depicting the foreign student population as a sign that "things are getting out of hand."[124]

The INS "hastily hammered out a directive" stating that all foreign students had to be interviewed by an INS official or a university official "designated to act on behalf of the agency" in order to renew their visa status.[125] Whereas visa renewals previously had been processed by mail, now applicants would have to prove in person that they were enrolled as full-time students, that they had the necessary funding to support their stay, that they had not been working without permission, and "that [they had] not engaged in any activity deemed inconsistent with [their] continued presence in the United States as a student."[126] This directive was criticized for being so broad as to unleash a political witch hunt against foreign students.[127] Many faculty and staff advisers of foreign students working at colleges and universities insisted that they were not immigration officers and refused to help the INS carry out the thousands of interviews that would be necessary. The administrations of UCLA and the University of Southern California went so far as to ban INS agents from campus entirely.[128] Nonetheless, the INS interviews began with a focus on finding Iranians who had fallen out of status. In California, which had the largest concentration of Iranians, the State Assembly passed a resolution "prompted by recent Iranian student demonstrations in Los Angeles" that "foreigners who break the law during demonstrations and riots should be deported."[129]

Iranian students continued to mount protests throughout 1979 to show support for the revolution, to preemptively oppose US military intervention to restore the Shah, and to prevent the Shah from being granted exile in the US. The ISA no longer dominated these protests, however. Animosity between religious and secular students grew as the new government in Iran began persecuting the Left along with ethnic and religious minorities, and the police forcibly broke up clashes between opposing Iranian student groups in the US.[130]

Against the demands of the Iranian government and anti-Shah students in the US, Carter allowed the Shah to come to New York for cancer treatment in October. On November 4, 1979, a group of students in Tehran stormed the US embassy and the "hostage crisis" began. The "first overtly punitive action" in retaliation came from Greenville Technical College in Greenville, South Carolina, which "suspended its 104 Iranian students ... and told them they could not return until all the American hostages in Iran are released unharmed."[131]

Immediately, the INS came under intense pressure to quicken the pace of tracking down and trying to deport as many Iranians as possible. The agency instituted "an unprecedented special registration" program officially and exclusively targeting *all* Iranian foreign students, giving them thirty days to report to the INS "for a review of their status."[132] Newspaper reports heralded the possible "expulsion of several thousand Iranians."[133] Carter declared "he was canceling all visas issued to Iranians for entry into the United States" and Iranians en route to the US with valid visas were turned away at the airport in London.[134] Meanwhile, between twenty and thirty thousand Americans signed the Iranian Eviction Petition.[135]

Iranian students faced death threats, arson attacks, harassment, and assaults, which repeatedly made headlines. An Iranian student at Riverside City College in California was found shot in the head with his feet and hands bound.[136] When 900 members of the Muslim Students Association marched in Washington, DC, in November 1979, demanding that the Shah be extradited to Iran to stand trial, "they were jeered at, spit upon and shouted down as Americans finally found an outlet for expressing their anger at the takeover of the United States Embassy in Tehran," the *New York Times* reported.[137] The White House begged for calm, lest violence against Iranians in the US be used as an excuse to harm the American hostages in Iran.

Despite Carter's pleas, Americans organized anti-Iran rallies featuring slogans such as "Have a Happy Thanksgiving—Hold an Iranian Hostage," "Send in the Marines," "Expel All Iranian Students," "Death to Khomeini," "Camel Jockeys Go Home," "Arabs Go Home," and "Take the Oil and Shove It."[138] A gas-station owner in Long Island, New York, posted the following sign: "War—if Mr. Carter won't start it, we will. We do not serve Iranians or Pakistanis—bodily injury will be inflicted."[139] According to the *New York Times*, he kept "two pump-action shotguns at hand inside the station" to make good on his threat.[140] These examples reveal that Arabs, Iranians, and Pakistanis had become interchangeable targets of the racism and xenophobia that gripped the nation at the end of 1979, long before the twenty-first century global "war on terror" would rely on similarly muddled paranoia and desires for revenge against Muslims as part of its ideological architecture. When members of the Muslim Students Association attempted another march in Beverly Hills, "a mob of screaming, spitting Americans slugged, kicked and hurled pipe fittings ... routing their anti-shah protest and cheering as sheriff's deputies arrested 136 of the Iranians."[141] Anti-Iranian slogans that day included "Nuke Iran" and "This Thanksgiving Roast an Iranian."[142]

Congressional representatives in Orange County, California, were overwhelmed "by the volume and vehemence of calls" demanding that the US send in the Marines to free the hostages.[143] The president of the Transport Workers Union said in a telegram that "union members will stop servicing Iranian aircraft until the hostages are freed," and the International Longshoreman's Association said that "it was halting the loading on ships of cargo destined for Iran."[144] At New Mexico State University, a new group called Students against Terrorism rallied on campus to demand that the US government "revoke the visas of all Iranian students in the United States."[145] Flag dealers across the country reported a "run on Iranian flags in the United States" as they struggled to produce enough to meet the demand "coming from college campuses," where the flags were burned at anti-Iran protests.[146] Meanwhile, the Ku Klux Klan announced plans for an anti-Iranian rally in San Antonio, Texas.[147]

Despite the ferocity of the state and public backlash against Iranians, mass deportations never materialized. Out of the 54,486 Iranian students who reported to the INS, only 6,444 were found to be in violation of their visas and deportation proceedings were begun against over 4,000 of them.[148] Approximately 14,768 Iranians, including 2,204 students, returned voluntarily, and thousands more pursued various means of legalizing their status in the US, including as political asylees.[149] By April 1980, only nineteen Iranians had been forcibly deported.[150] After a protracted legal battle, the US Court of Appeals ruled Carter's special registrations program for Iranians legal under the Immigration and Nationality Act, but effectively ended forced deportations.[151]

Nonetheless, Iran, Islam, and terrorism were now virtually synonymous in the American popular imagination, replacing communism as the number one enemy of the nation. Attempts by some Iranian students to appeal to ordinary Americans and challenge resurgent US nationalism through signs such as "Yes to the US people, no to the US government" were met by hostile American students, who shoved the Iranians while waving American flags.[152] What began as attacks on the ISA for its loud, disruptive, and politically leftist demonstrations blossomed, after the revolution and taking of hostages, into what Mohsen Mobasher has called "Iranophobia," a pervasive set of anti-Iranian feelings loaded with Islamophobia and white nationalism that utterly transformed the lived experience of being Iranian in America.[153] It was into this affective landscape that Iranians fleeing the revolution would enter, and under these conditions that the post-1979 diaspora would establish itself as a permanent subset of the immigrant, exile, and refugee populations in the US.

Conclusion

This chapter has highlighted dramatic and militant actions taken by ISA members in order to sabotage the US-Iran special relationship and turn American public opinion against it. Revolutionary affects fueled a relentless pace of activity, as Iranian student activists expressed their rage at poverty and state repression in Iran, took pleasure in disrupting the "affective economies" of *pax Americana*, and acted on their enduring attachments to freedom for the Iranian people. Members of the ISA took full advantage of their location within powerful institutions complicit in upholding the Shah's dictatorship. By protesting the many symbolic and material ties between the Iranian regime and US "imperial universities," they transformed the opportunity to receive a Western education into the opportunity to educate Americans about the brutalities of US support for the Shah. This project included, above all else, exposing the torture and execution of dissidents in Iran and the efforts of SAVAK to undermine student opposition abroad. The ISA's critique of the transnational relationship between state repression in Iran and in the US and their exposure of collaboration among SAVAK and US immigration and law enforcement agencies, would, by the mid-1970s, make headlines in campus and national daily newspapers, and the Shah would come under increasing scrutiny for his human rights record. Through such coverage, and through raucous protests at every single public appearance the Shah made on his annual US tours, the revolutionary affects of Iranian student activists shook up US society, resonating with some and alienating others, eventually wreaking enough havoc to instigate a major backlash.

Chapter 2 discussed the happy, hopeful feelings Americans had learned to have about their non-Western Cold War allies and the imperial model minorities from those nations. Here I have shown how friendly feelings toward the Other, which were encouraged by doctrines of Cold War Orientalism and racial liberalism, turned sour. The more aggressively the ISA intervened in the constitutive blindness of Americans toward US empire, the more they triggered resentment, racism, and xenophobia—expressions of an aggrieved imperial host whose guests took advantage of the hospitality offered to them and ruined the relationship. Vehement calls for the deportation of Iranian student activists after the mass demonstrations outside the White House in November 1977 laid the groundwork for calls to surveil and deport all Iranian students, eventually spurring the INS to automate in order to better execute this task.

The ISA persisted in its militancy unabated until most of its members returned home to join the revolution, making way for the very different diaspora that emerged in the post-1979 period. A temporary diaspora of imperial model minorities, thousands of whom shared a deep affective attachment to revolutionary politics, was replaced by a diaspora defined by its abhorrence of the revolution they experienced in Iran. Rather than conclude the story of this earlier diaspora with the ultimate failure of the ISA to win the American people over to their side, this chapter reminds us that one of the most enduring legacies of Iranian anti-Shah student activism is the insistence on viewing "the American people" as sharing a common interest in peace and justice with "the Iranian people," rather than as de facto beneficiaries of an imperial arrangement. During the late 1960s and early 1970s, ISA activism did in fact resonate with the revolutionary affects that were already circulating in US society, as movements against racism and war gained momentum. It is to this broader milieu and the intensification and mobilization of "affects of solidarity" that I now turn.

4

The Feeling and Practice of Solidarity

It only took three swift kicks for the glass to shatter. One minute, a crowd of frustrated students stood outside the locked doors of the main administration building at San Francisco State College, pounding on the glass to the rhythm of their chant, "Hell no, no suspensions!" The next minute, ISA member and SF State undergraduate Khosro Kalantari smashed a hole in the bottom of the door with his foot and stepped carefully through the jagged opening. Hundreds of students filed in behind him, their cheers and chants echoing as they marched through the hallways.[1] This spontaneous building occupation, occurring on December 6, 1967, marked a steep escalation in the conflict between students and administrators that would erupt in a mass student strike less than one year later. As it happened, once Khosro broke through the glass, there was no turning back.

Iranian and American protesters had gathered that day to oppose the arrest and suspension of six members of the Black Student Union (BSU) and to denounce racism on campus. The six were involved in an altercation with the college newspaper staff over its disparaging coverage of Muhammad Ali and the Nation of Islam, as well as its editorial attacks on new affirmative action policies governing college admissions.[2] Student support for the six BSU members intensified when news spread that the administration had decided to reverse the unrelated suspensions of several white students. Outrage over this unequal treatment drew a politically heterogeneous group to the December rally, at which differences emerged between those who emphasized the lack of due process in the suspension proceedings and those who saw these suspensions as symptomatic of structural problems plaguing the institution as a whole. The Iranians were in the latter bloc. According to Hamid Kowsari, a member of the ISA's Northern California chapter and an SF State undergraduate at the time, they were hoping for a direct confrontation with the college authorities. Hamid summarized how he saw the ISA's role as the movement unfolded: "Our influence was to radicalize it, to be honest with you, to keep the strike going, not to compromise." I read this statement not as an effort by an Iranian to take credit for the strike, but rather as an illustration of the revolutionary affects that circulated between ISA members and some of the other activists around them, making possible a shared orientation toward confrontation and away from concessions.

The converging radicalisms of different groups of students was exactly what the college administration feared. Local news footage of the December 6 rally shows a staff member locking the building's doors from the inside and posting a "Closed" sign before the student protestors arrived—preemptive measures against the very occupation that Khosro would instigate. President John Summerskill was so shaken by the militant turn of the day's events that he decided to shut the entire campus down, telling a press conference that the students' behavior was "verging on civil insurrection."[3] Just prior to Khosro's brazen act, another ISA member also made a bold move to occupy the administration building, one that was not caught on camera. Parviz Shokat, an undergraduate at Hayward College, scaled the side of the building and climbed in through an open second-story window, hoping to find a way to let the protestors in. He did not expect campus police to be waiting just inside. They quickly grabbed him and escorted him downstairs. From the other side of the glass, Khosro saw the police holding his friend Parviz. "That's when [he] kicked in the door," Parviz said, "and they all came in, and the cops let me go."

Khosro's actions on this day foreshadowed the role he would play during the course of the strike. In what has become an iconic photograph of a mass mobilization on campus, Khosro stands in the front lines alongside Asian American, African American, Chicano, and other student leaders (figure 4.1). When the SF State strike committee issued a satirical leaflet in defense of leading activists, they included Khosro's name on a short list of those "WANTED FOR CRIMES AGAINST the STATE," warning the public about "these rebels . . . known to be extremely dangerous to society" (figure 4.2).[4] Among the list of crimes are "continual opposition to such key government

programs as suppression and exploitation of colored peoples, the war of extermination against the YELLOW PERIL, further expansion of our economic LEBENSRAUM in South American, Asia and Latin America." This flyer was just one example of how the strike was framed as an act of solidarity linking the fight against racism in the US to the fight against the racist logics of US imperialism. The inclusion of Khosro's name was just one indication of the extent to which ISA members, and their critique of US support for the Shah, were part of the Third World student Left of the era.

The white American activist Margaret Leahy, who was an SF State undergraduate affiliated with Students for a Democratic Society (SDS), remembered Khosro well: "People trusted him. He had no fear standing up for what he believed in. We were afraid for him because we knew if they arrested him, they would put a deportation hold on him and send him back."[5] The previous year, the ISA had successfully defended Khosro from a coordinated effort by SAVAK and the INS to deport him for violating the terms of his student visa by failing to maintain enrollment.[6] Those efforts, along with ongoing campaigns to free political prisoners in Iran,

Figure 4.1 Mass strike rally at San Francisco State (undated). Khosro Kalantari appears in the second row, third from the right. Social Protest Collection. Bancroft Library, UC Berkeley.

had successfully educated American activists such as Leahy about the harsh conditions facing Iranian dissidents under the Shah's regime. She remembered hanging out at *Khane-e Iran,* the ISA's organizing base in Berkeley, eating tangerines with Khosro and other Iranian activists and listening to them talk about what was happening in Iran. Through such informal gatherings, she came to understand the risks Iranian activists in the US faced due to cooperation between local law enforcement, immigration officials, and SAVAK. This knowledge proved indispensable when the police launched a series of campus invasions at SF State to suppress the student uprising. Along with thousands of other student strikers, Hamid, Parviz, and Khosro dodged police batons and ran for their lives as police on horseback charged into the demonstrations. "You would see blood everywhere around the campus," Hamid remembered. On January 23, 1969, the police arrested hundreds of students, including Khosro. Hamid, who was not himself arrested that day,

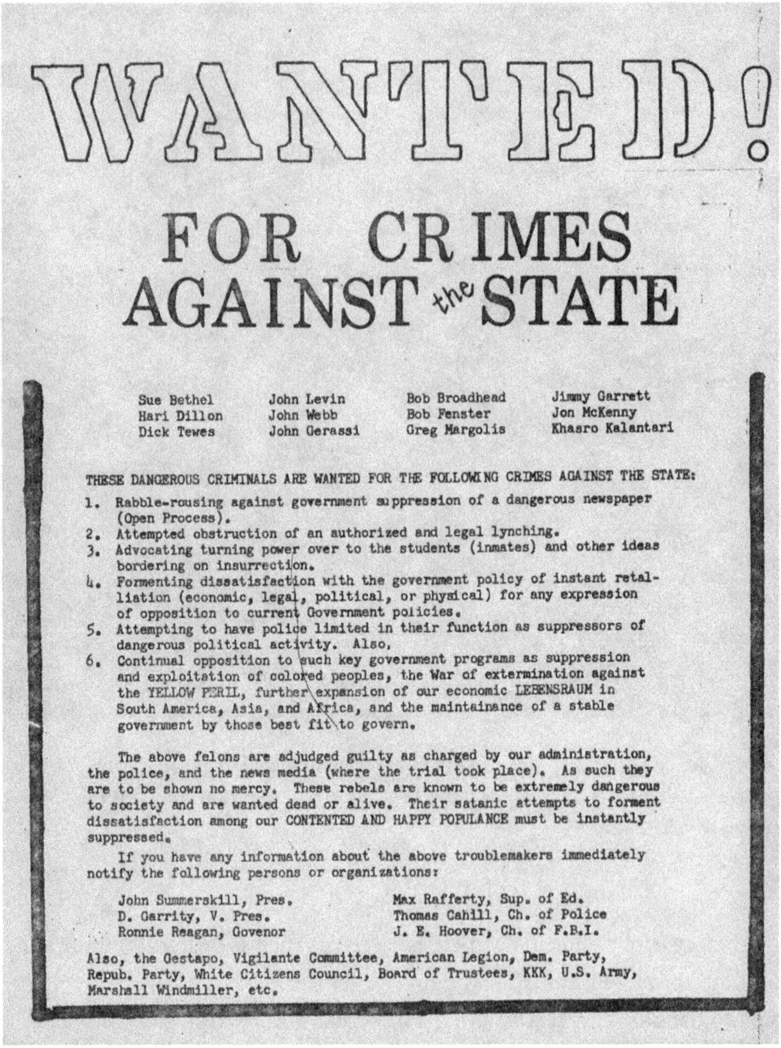

WANTED!

FOR CRIMES
AGAINST the STATE

Sue Bethel	John Levin	Bob Broadhead	Jimmy Garrett
Hari Dillon	John Webb	Bob Fenster	Jon McKenny
Dick Tewes	John Gerassi	Greg Margolis	Khasro Kalantari

THESE DANGEROUS CRIMINALS ARE WANTED FOR THE FOLLOWING CRIMES AGAINST THE STATE:

1. Rabble-rousing against government suppression of a dangerous newspaper (Open Process).
2. Attempted obstruction of an authorized and legal lynching.
3. Advocating turning power over to the students (inmates) and other ideas bordering on insurrection.
4. Fomenting dissatisfaction with the government policy of instant retaliation (economic, legal, political, or physical) for any expression of opposition to current Government policies.
5. Attempting to have police limited in their function as suppressors of dangerous political activity. Also,
6. Continual opposition to such key government programs as suppression and exploitation of colored peoples, the War of extermination against the YELLOW PERIL, further expansion of our economic LEBENSRAUM in South America, Asia, and Africa, and the maintainance of a stable government by those best fit to govern.

The above felons are adjudged guilty as charged by our administration, the police, and the news media (where the trial took place). As such they are to be shown no mercy. These rebels are known to be extremely dangerous to society and are wanted dead or alive. Their satanic attempts to forment dissatisfaction among our CONTENTED AND HAPPY POPULANCE must be instantly suppressed.

If you have any information about the above troublemakers immediately notify the following persons or organizations:

John Summerskill, Pres.	Max Rafferty, Sup. of Ed.
D. Garrity, V. Pres.	Thomas Cahill, Ch. of Police
Ronnie Reagan, Govenor	J. E. Hoover, Ch. of F.B.I.

Also, the Gestapo, Vigilante Committee, American Legion, Dem. Party, Repub. Party, White Citizens Council, Board of Trustees, KKK, U.S. Army, Marshall Windmiller, etc.

Figure 4.2 SF State Strike flyer. Social Protest Collection. Bancroft Library, UC Berkeley.

said that these students were placed in jail cells with the heat turned off and were sprayed with water hoses.

According to Margaret, Khosro was subjected to even worse abuse. As the person in charge of bailing out students arrested during the course of the strike—negotiating bond fees and raising money from supporters nationwide—she vividly recalled the mass arrests and extraordinary circumstances surrounding Khosro's imprisonment and release:

I was down at the bail office for three days working to get people out. Joe Gooden worked in room 201, which was the place that filed all the papers. We had become friends because I was always going in trying to get bail reductions. He called me and said, "Margaret, they've let the SAVAK into the jail. They've got Khosro. They've got pins up his gums and in his fingernails. Get him out now!" He had really high bail. Khosro had felonies on him, of course. He had hit a cop. My parents had left me a house when they died. They died when I was really young. I said, "I can cosign with my house." I never saw Khosro again because, when he was released, the Iranians drove him to Canada straight away. [The authorities] never foreclosed on my house. [The bail bondsman] said, "We got enough money from you guys." I never heard from Khosro again. Someone said they saw him in Paris one day. He was really worried about my house and offered to come back so I wouldn't lose it.[7]

Margaret's decision to place her own financial and housing security in jeopardy may have saved Khosro's life by preventing his deportation and further persecution in Iran. This willingness to sacrifice for another was one crucial manifestation of the revolutionary affects that moved between and among men and women from different racial, ethnic, and national backgrounds, and that made acts of solidarity both possible and deeply compelling.

This chapter investigates how the affects of solidarity described above shaped the everyday practices that made Third World internationalism into something lived and felt, a way of being in the world in relation to others. By focusing on the under-analyzed role of Iranian student activists in the movements that marked the heyday of Third World leftist organizing in the US, I highlight Iranian diasporic connections with other racialized populations as a vital part of the history of Iranians in the United States. These affinities challenge the "Persian imperial identity" that has held sway over the mainstream of the Iranian diaspora since 1979, and that relies on racial and class hierarchies to dissociate Iranians from poor and working-class people of color, especially Black people, Arabs, and other Muslim immigrants (see introduction). Aware of this current tendency, Ahmad Taghvai, who was active in the ISA's Northern California chapter, explained how much things have changed. "The image of the Iranians at that time was that they were all on the side of the civil rights movement," he said. "Not like now, when the image of Iranians is very conservative here."

Jalil Mostashari, a founding member of the ISA at Michigan State University in East Lansing, also offered his own experience of student activism as a counter to today's diasporic mainstream. "First I participated with the NAACP, then with CORE, and then the DuBois Club," he recounted. When I asked him what drew him to those organizations, he replied emphatically, "The Black struggle was part of the total international struggle for me!" He then went on to say, "You would be surprised to know that I was deputy chairman of the Muslim Students Association at Michigan State. The chairman was Pakistani." I asked him why he joined this group and he explained that he felt "an identity connection, a future, our future was to be the same. What does that have to do with religion? They knew that I'm not a Muslim. I was also a member of the Arab Students Association, an honorary member." Although Jalil came from a religious Muslim family, he became a communist as a teenager in Iran, part of a generation of young leftists who gave the ISA its decidedly secular character, as discussed in chapter 1. And yet, his ideological investments did not prevent him from identifying with and participating alongside Muslim students engaged in anticolonial organizing. Jalil's affective attachment to self-determination for Iranians also attached to self-determination for African Americans, Arabs, and Pakistanis. The circulation of affect made possible a set of relations based on ways of feeling about oppression. While experiences of oppression were always tied to specific conditions, histories, and identities, the affects that remained transcended the particular and found expression as Third World internationalism.

Affects of Solidarity, Coalitions across Difference

Affects of solidarity—by which I mean affective attachments to the liberation of others—are necessary for the emergence and sustainment of mass movements seeking systemic change. Drawing on interviews, student and mainstream media coverage, movement periodicals, and other activist ephemera, this chapter tracks the connections between the ISA and three major sites around which Third World internationalism coalesced: Black liberation, Palestinian liberation, and Vietnamese liberation. The Black liberation movement and the movement against the war in Southeast Asia became the most influential vehicles in the US for popularizing an analysis of the links between racial oppression at home and imperial domination abroad. The Palestinian movement was closest to home for Iranians, decisive for the fate of the region as a whole. The ISA played a role in connecting all three of these areas of struggle by bringing to the attention of American activists the Shah's crucial role as a watchdog for US interests in the Middle East and Africa.

Although the memories of ISA members who were active in Florida, Texas, Michigan, and Philadelphia enter into this discussion, large and long-standing ISA chapters in two locations—Northern California and Washington, DC—provided the most significant opportunities for Iranians to participate in the three movements and to experience them as interconnected. Northern California, the birthplace of the Black Panther Party for Self-Defense, was an epicenter of Black Power and anti-imperialist organizing against the Vietnam War. There were Palestinian and other Arab students actively organizing in support of Arab self-determination on campuses there as well. Washington, DC, a majority Black city with a politically active Palestinian minority, was significant as the site for national convergences of the mass movements against racism and war.

I approach this history of shared feelings and futures using a methodology of possibility to explore how the revolutionary affects of disparate groups overlapped and combined to generate powerful affects of solidarity. This era—marked by the Bandung conference of "nonaligned" nations in Indonesia in 1955, and punctuated by the Tri-Continental conference in Havana in 1966 and the formation of the Organization of Solidarity of the People of Africa, Asia, and Latin America—popularized Third World Marxism as an amalgam of antiracism, anti-imperialism, and anti-capitalism that urged a united front against US imperialism. This genealogy of Third World Marxism branches out from China, Cuba, Algeria, Congo, Vietnam, Palestine, and many other locations in what is now more commonly referred to as the Global South. By the late 1960s, Third World Marxism, sometimes referred to as Marxism-Leninism or Maoism, became the dominant political idiom for the student Left in Europe and North America, including the active cadre in CISNU.[8] Opposition to the Soviet Union worked to unite Iranian leftists with the US Third World Left, as many different organizations concluded that both superpowers were hostile to the socialism of colonized and formerly colonized peoples. Most of all, Third World Marxism articulated a shared hostility to the US government, which at the time backed authoritarian regimes in Iran, in the Arab world, and in Vietnam, while enforcing police state conditions in Black and Brown communities in the US.

This context enabled the popularization of the old Communist Party theory that racialized Americans constituted internally colonized peoples, sharing much in common with people in the Third World. As Cynthia Young has argued, the ability of Americans "to imagine and claim common cause with a radical Third World subject involved multiple translations and substitutions; it required the production of an imagined terrain able to close the multiple gaps between First and Third World subjects."[9] While the political ideology that provided these activists with a shared vocabulary has been examined previously, this chapter breaks new ground by looking at the role of affect in the production of that "imagined terrain" and offers a much-needed counterweight to the disillusionment, division, and co-optation that characterizes our current neoliberal era.

This analysis builds on the fact that, as Gayatri Gopinath points out, "generations of feminist and more recently queer scholars have long critiqued such pan-Third Worldist projects for their exclusions and hierarchies, both in their cultural nationalist and state nationalist forms."[10] Feminist and queer scholars have also extended these critiques to consider *internationalist* forms of Third World solidarity, revealing, in the words of Vanita Reddy and Anantha Sudhakar, an "almost-exclusive focus on men as political and historical actors in the construction of cross-racial solidarities."[11] *Bandung*, in a word, functions like a synonym for this era among scholars because the conference in 1955 articulated the project of solidarity as "a brotherhood of nations." However, as Abdel Takriti points out, the notion of "sister revolutions" was also popularized as a way of describing solidarity and interconnection.[12] Thus the gendered language of biological kinship was embedded in anticolonial movements and in the gender and sexual politics of the postcolonial states that made up the Non-Aligned Movement, which promoted particular gender roles for men and women as part of their nation-building programs.[13] Celebratory accounts of Afro-Asian solidarities have tended to romanticize or ignore the ways that male domination and compulsory heterosexuality structured these alliances and limited the meaning of freedom.[14]

Gender and sexual oppression within antiracist and anticolonial movements would propel the development of new forms of revolutionary feminism, including from within the Iranian leftist experience (see chapter 6). What is often lost in the circulation of this critique, however, is the fact that Third World feminism and women-of-color feminism would not have been possible without the mass participation of women in revolutionary movements. Rather than representing a rejection of revolutionary politics, Third World and women-of-color feminisms sought to develop, deepen, and expand revolutionary praxis to center the liberation of racialized and colonized women. As the Combahee River Collective Statement famously argued, "If Black women were free, it would mean that everyone else would have to be free since our freedom would necessitate the destruction of all the systems of oppression."[15] Such feminist interventions emerged as much from negative experiences of sexism, homophobia, and racism within movements as they did from ongoing attachments to the project of making a revolution. Third World and women-of-color feminisms thus rejected separatism as a political strategy and devoted tremendous energy to theorizing and building coalitions across difference. My exploration of affects of solidarity contributes to this genealogy of revolutionary feminist theorizing about how people who do not experience oppression in exactly the same ways might yet recognize the need for a common struggle against systematic injustices that are "interlocking."[16]

Informed by feminist and queer critique, this chapter rejects both celebratory narratives and narratives of failure as inadequate ways of engaging with the legacies of 1960s and 1970s Third Worldism. Instead, I investigate how affective attachments to the liberation of others generated new capacities for relating across difference. My argument here is that Third World solidarity was just as compelling for women as it was for men. Despite the pervasive male domination within the revolutionary movements and politics of the era, there was nothing inherently masculinist about militancy, outrage, defiance, and hope—even if male revolutionaries imagined there was. The affective rewards of mass resistance were not for men alone. Iranian women, like African American, Palestinian, Vietnamese, and white American women activists, were just as invested in the affects of solidarity that made large-scale social transformation feel possible. By tracking the circulation of affects of solidarity between Iranian and other liberation movements in the 1960s and 1970s, this chapter offers insights into the relationship between affect, subjectivity, and politics that may yet be crucial for the project of forging feminist and queer internationalisms today.

As Grace Hong and Roderick Ferguson have argued, "women of color feminism and queer of color critique profoundly question nationalist and identitarian modes of political organization and craft alternative understandings of subjectivity, collectivity and power."[17] This critique also highlights the uneven incorporation of some minority groups into the mainstream "norms of respectability" at the expense of others, such as the inclusion of imperial model minorities in higher education and the exclusion of many poor, racialized US citizens.[18] Using a methodology of possibility, I revisit the era that gave rise to minority nationalisms and homogenized notions of identity as a basis for revolutionary activity and argue that other ways of imagining affiliation and collective struggle were also present, even if they were not discernible as theoretical and political models at the time.

A closer look at the events at SF State forces us to question the dominant understanding of the strike as a coalition of distinct, internally homogeneous racial and ethnic groups. One of the strike's most celebrated innovations was the Third World Liberation Front (TWLF), which consisted of the BSU, the Latino Students Organization, the Filipino-American Students Organization, and the Mexican student group, El Renacimiento. This coalition understood the genocide of Native peoples, the enslavement of Africans, the direct and indirect colonization of Latin America and the Philippines, and the exploitation of Asian immigrant labor as linked by a common cause—the need to satisfy capitalism's insatiable lust for land, labor, and resources—and by the overlapping racist logics used to justify and perpetuate the horrors that ensued. These interwoven legacies continued to marginalize historically oppressed populations, in this case by denying them access to higher education and input into the content of the education on offer. Both the TWLF and the BSU issued strike demands that aimed to transform the college into a place where faculty and students of color could produce radical knowledge—new tools for dismantling the master's house.[19]

The ISA did not join TWLF. Unlike other non-white students at SF State, Iranians did not see themselves as a minority population struggling for the right to education. As imperial model minorities, access to education was the basis for their presence in the US. As noncitizens, they did not seek rights within broader US society based on their racial, ethnic, or national background, and they were always planning to return home. Strike demands focused on greater inclusion of racial minorities and minority perspectives within the college, issues that did not concern Iranian foreign students. "No, we didn't have those demands," Hamid said. "They were mostly for African American, Chicano, and Asian students." Iranians were not directly affected by the regimes of racism and dispossession that spurred other non-white students to action, but by forms of Cold War imperial intervention that were either covert or wrapped in the seemingly benign packaging of economic development and civilizational progress. A narrow perspective that views the SF State strike only as a domestic struggle over minority rights to equal citizenship renders ISA activism at the college invisible and obscures the influence of transnational and diasporic anticolonial movements on radical Americans of every background.[20] It also misses an opportunity to unpack and theorize the non-identitarian basis for Iranian solidarity with the strike.

By taking seriously shared affective states as a basis for joint organizing, new ways of understanding solidarity and difference emerge that do not rely on having the "same" experience of oppression. Rather than sharing common experiences of racism and exploitation in the US, Iranians and racialized Americans shared an affective response to unjust power. An affective approach to the revolutionary solidarities of the 1960s and 1970s emphasizes the open-ended capacity of bodies to respond to encounters with repression and resistance and the capacity for revolutionary responses to emerge from subjectivities marked by incommensurate histories and structures of oppression.

Affects are relational, circulating in unexpected ways, generating moods that shift how people see themselves, as well as those around them, and shaping a "common sense" about what is politically possible.[21] As Jonathan Flatley argues, "it is on the level of mood that historical forces most directly intervene in our affective lives and through mood that these forces may become apparent to us."[22] For revolutionary activists in the 1960s and 1970s, connections between domestic and imperial forms of domination generated a feeling and practice of solidarity, even without a deep historical understanding of the differences among those mobilizing together. Members of the ISA were drawn to the militancy of the TWLF because it resonated with their own oppositional feelings. By the late 1960s, the ISA had dispensed with hopes for "reforming" the Shah's regime (see chapter 2), and their revolutionary orientation pushed them away from mainstream civil rights organizations. The antiracism to which ISA members were attracted was not simply concerned with addressing the legacies of historic wrongs through greater minority representation and inclusion, but about fundamentally challenging the way power and knowledge circulated as a stepping-stone to systemic change. The revolutionary affects and convictions of Black and Brown student radicals resonated with the Iranians at SF State and elsewhere, inspiring them to take risks to help the movement succeed. It is to these sensed and felt dimensions of Third World solidarities that I now turn in order to further explore possibilities for mobilizing across multiple sites of difference.

Melancholia and Militancy

Militancy describes an affective response to the losses wrought by systemic oppression. As Douglass Crimp famously argued in the context of the AIDS crisis and debates over the appropriate activist response, "For many of us mourning *becomes* militancy."[23] Crimp argued for a form of militancy that permitted grief, that allowed activists to openly engage with multiple sites of loss under conditions in which new losses were being created all the time and activists often had to contemplate their own imminent deaths. Rather than pathologize melancholia as a malfunctioning of the subject's ego, David Eng and David Kazanjian have argued that the losses generated by "historic traumas and legacies of, among others, revolution, war, genocide, slavery, decolonization, exile, migration, reunification, globalization and AIDS" might be "full of volatile potentiality and future militancies," where militancy becomes both a force generating alternative futures and a reckoning with "what remains."[24]

Building on these formulations, I understand militancy as a revolutionary affect, a response to loss that is also an orientation toward ongoing injustices that continually produce new losses. As an affective orientation to loss, militancy encompasses a range of emotions, including grief, anger, joy, and hope, which contribute to a rewarding, collective mode of confronting the causes of loss in the context of social movements. Militancy registers and expresses the bodily intensities of that confrontation, circulating, resonating, and moving people toward and away from each other. Affects of solidarity might also be described as overlapping militancies, enabling very different people to identify with each other's losses and take action together. Affects of solidarity are thus a collective expression of melancholia, an affective response to "the loss of a loved person, or to the loss of some abstraction which has taken the place of one, such as fatherland, liberty, an ideal, and so on."[25] Members of the ISA refused to get over the depressed and fearful mood of the postcoup police state, creating an affective resonance with the freedom struggles of others who insisted on remembering the losses of genocide, slavery, colonization, and migration.

When describing their relationships with other movements, former ISA members spoke passionately, and sometimes wistfully, about their feelings of connection with other people's freedom struggles. Mohammed Eghtedari, an ISA member in Washington, DC, described what he considered a high point of his years as a student activist in the US. "You'll be amazed," he began:

> At All Souls Church in Washington, DC, Iranian Students Association is preparing for a demonstration [against the Shah's visit to the White House] and here are the chiefs of Indian Nations, maybe about twenty of them, sitting there with all the clothing special to them. They accepted us because we supported their activity. Anywhere that there was an injustice, we were in sync with it. They had come to Washington for their own issues and then when they noticed that Iranian students had a demonstration planned, and they knew that we are at All Souls Church, they all came there.[26]

As he spoke, Mohammed's facial expressions and gestures conveyed delight and surprise as if reliving that first encounter with the chiefs. The apparent pleasure he took in the act of remembering brought forth a form of Iranian diasporic subjectivity that has been marginalized since 1979. Feelings of connection and solidarity between a diasporic national liberation movement and an indigenous decolonization movement became possible because Iranian activists refused identification with the settler colonial state that had promised to transform them into imperial model minorities and to embrace them as the latest recruits to the civilizing project launched by Europeans centuries earlier. Instead, ISA members affiliated themselves with the ancestors of people who had been resisting that project since its inception. Mohammed narrates this memory without bothering to explain the political analysis that brought these groups together. Rather, he focuses on the unexpected joy he felt at the sight of the elaborately adorned chiefs assembled to support the ISA. What he remembers and wants to convey is that these very different people felt they had something in common and that this feeling meant that they would do things for each other even without being asked.

As Mohammed said, "Anywhere that there was an injustice, we were in sync with it." To be "in sync" with injustice as it manifests across time and space, one must be open to it, affected by it. This coincidence of reactions and responses occurred when the revolutionary affects of Iranian imperial model minorities attached not only to the anti-Shah movement but to other liberation movements as well. This process was not automatic but depended on the ability of Iranians to come into contact with other activists who felt similarly about the injustices that affected them, allowing them to experience a synchronicity. These affective, emotional, and political encounters had the potential to expand what Flatley calls an "affective map"—that is, a cartography of connections between people who share a melancholic relationship to loss.[27] Flatley argues that dwelling in loss, and attempting to understand the historical forces that have created the loss, can become "the very mechanism through which one may be interested in the world."[28] "Affective mapping," therefore, refers to "the historicity of one's affective experience" and is a means by which the intimate, personal effects of oppression can become recognizable as collective, political problems.[29]

The following example illustrates the work of affective mapping in forging solidarities. Zohreh Khayam, who joined the ISA in 1971 as a graduate student at Howard University in Washington, DC, related how a shared reaction to loss became the basis of joint organizing. "In 1973, when the coup against Allende in Chile happened, it was a no brainer," she said. Zohreh was from a middle-class family in Tehran and was unusual in that she had been a high-school exchange student in the US from 1965–66, as described in chapter 1. Despite the conservatism of her American host family, Zohreh had turned against the US war in Vietnam. Later, as an undergraduate in sociology at Tehran University, she became part of the student opposition. When she returned to the US for graduate school, she began at the University of Maryland and then transferred to Howard. Shortly after her arrival, she became an active ISA member and ace leaflet writer, eventually serving on the ISA's International Relations Committee. This was the committee responsible for outreach and solidarity with other organizations and movements. She described her participation in meetings and marches protesting Chilean dictator Augusto Pinochet's power grab: "It was a repetition of history for us. The same way the Americans had a coup against Dr. Mosaddeq, now this time they had it in Chile and it really was heartbreaking." A melancholic attachment to the pain and loss of the 1953 coup in Iran fueled shared affective and emotional responses to the pain and loss of others. For Zohreh and other ISA activists, "heartbreak" traveled along affective cartographies that were not based on ethnic, racial, or national identity, but on a militant response to the cruelties of economic restructuring and state repression in Chile as well as in Iran.

It is important to emphasize that militancy and melancholia describe states of heightened activity that can be intensely joyful. Indeed, as Freud noted, one component of melancholia is sometimes "mania," a situation "characterized by high spirits, by the signs of discharge of joyful emotion, and by increased readiness to all kinds of action" that can occur "when a man [*sic*] finds himself in a position to throw off at one blow some heavy burden, some false position he has long endured."[30] Fanon's writings on violence in the anticolonial struggle as necessary and transformative for the colonized, as a release of tension that is also a way of claiming one's full humanity, can also be understood as a melancholic response to the multiple losses produced by the colonial system.[31] For Iranian student activists, the ability to throw off the burden of living inside the Shah's police state, and to abandon the "false position" of an imperial model minority by joining the ISA, was exciting and produced an exuberance for organizing that was also present among other marginalized young people who joined activist movements. Indeed, what Émile Durkheim called "the euphoria of being in the streets" aptly describes the elation that can come from realizing one is not alone and from the hopeful feeling that one is participating in changing the world.[32]

Iranian foreign students, like Zohreh, who were unable to align themselves with the US-backed police state in Iran often found themselves in a parallel relationship to racialized and dispossessed Americans who could not tolerate the brutal status quo of US society. Under the conditions of social and political upheaval that prevailed on many college campuses, militancies converged like overlapping coordinates on an affective map of loss. Shared feelings of grief, indignation, and a persistent longing for freedom expanded these maps, charting new routes of connection and mutual concern. Each CIA-backed coup, each arrest of a political activist, each act of police violence brought new losses that were distinct yet also embedded in longer histories. Melancholic attachments to who and what was lost were imbued "with not only a multifaceted but also a certain palimpsest-like quality."[33] This meant that a melancholic attachment to one loss could reverberate with the militant remains of other losses occurring in different times and places to different groups of people.

One memory of the joint organizing between Iranian and Chicano/a activists that occurred in Texas in the 1970s helps to illustrate how affects of solidarity circulated and drew different communities together.[34] Kate, a white American leftist who organized with the ISA and dated an ISA member in Houston, commented on what she viewed as the typical process of assimilation for foreigners in the United States: "The first immigrant lesson was how to be a racist. That didn't happen in the Iranian community." She recalled an embattled demonstration against the police killing of a twenty-three-year-old Chicano man named José Campos Torres in Houston in 1977: "In true Iranian spirit, my boyfriend and I drove straight to the riot." This "true Iranian spirit" described the affects of solidarity through which Iranian student activists developed a reputation for supporting other people's struggles. Outrage about SAVAK torture and persecutions in Iran spilled over into outrage over police assaults on vulnerable populations in the US. The ISA's refusal to accept state violence in Iran flowed into support for others who wanted to stop state violence in the US. This dynamic helps explain how it was that some Iranians, who knew almost nothing about the history of racism in the US, felt a flash of recognition when they encountered Black people resisting racism.

Afro-Iranian Connections

Ahmad Taghvai joined the ISA shortly after arriving in Berkeley in 1968 and enrolling in Richmond College. It was "because of the problem of dictatorship in Iran that [Iranians] would become attracted to the civil rights movement," he explained, reflecting on an affinity he said was widespread among ISA members in Northern California. For Ahmad, however, there was also an additional, personal motivation for his feelings of solidarity: "What always really attracted me to the civil rights movement in America was this experience I had as a child. They kicked me out of school for being Sunni. They harassed us. I had to be careful all the time not to get run over or beat up. So when you leave home and you see such a movement of minorities for civil rights, you quickly become drawn to it." He could not help but feel affected by the injustice against Black people he witnessed, as it resonated with his own memories of mistreatment by a Shiʻi majority who perceived him as inferior. Ahmad carried with him the visceral, firsthand knowledge of what it felt like to be the target of violence that is both institutionalized and dispersed into the vigilante actions of the dominant group; hence his use of *they* to refer to both school authorities and his Shiʻi neighbors. The affective charge of these memories drew him toward the Black freedom movement.

Similarly, Sina experienced a powerful feeling of connection to African Americans. It was 1974, and he had just come from Tehran to a small city in the Deep South. "The first thing I noticed when I came to the United States was that Black people respond to police exactly the way Iranians do. We don't trust them. We consider them the enemy. We don't go to them. We solve our own problems and try to keep them out." When Sina agreed to drive a U-Haul for another recent Iranian arrival even though he did not have a license or know how to drive, he accidentally hit a parked car in a Black neighborhood. "I thought these guys are going to come out and jump on me. But these Black guys came out and they said, 'Go, go! Go before the police comes!' And I said, 'Oh, these are my people!'" This characterization of Iranian attitudes stemmed from Sina's experience living in the poor and working-class areas of southern Tehran. He proudly recounted his teenage years in Meydan-e Shush, a neighborhood scarred by poverty and neglect, where he "quickly picked up the language and demeanor of a *lotti*." The figure of the lotti, akin to the ruffian or gangster, can, in its more politicized iterations, also be considered an Iranian corollary to "the brothers on the block," evoking countercultural and subversive connotations of self-organization, irreverence toward official authority, and sexual appeal. Listening closely to his description of young African American men, the echoes of the lotti of south Tehran are also discernible: "In their swagger, I see a political figure of emancipation. In their swagger, I see an attitude about capitalism. I see an attitude about the whole arrangement and structure of the world, and I like that. It's not always pleasant when it's addressed at you, but, in and of itself, it's a beautiful thing." While Sina may have been indulging in a sweeping generalization, he nonetheless expressed feelings of recognition, admiration, and respect. The body language and "attitude" he described were familiar, a different version of the affects he had embodied as a young man, first in the streets of a heavily surveilled neighborhood in Tehran and later as a student activist in the ISA.

These reflections highlight the forms of revolutionary masculinity that were dominant at the time and that facilitated identifications between men across other sites of difference. The "swagger" Sina described and also knew intimately, manifested a bodily response to injustice unavailable to most women at the time, whether African American or Iranian. The aggressiveness, the hints of violence in that embodied "attitude about capitalism" resonate with Fanon's writings about the social transformation that "exists in a raw, repressed, and reckless state in the lives and consciousness of colonized men and women."[35] Gender certainly impacted the embodied form that this "attitude" could take, and the gendered performance of militancy became a source of recognition and affiliation for some Iranian men, including Sina.

Just as the "brotherhood of nations" described the way people from different Third World countries were supposed to feel about their interdependence, so the language of brotherhood also expressed affects of solidarity among men from different racial, ethnic, and national backgrounds. In Northern California, Hamid joined the BSU as an undergraduate at SF State in 1967. He recalled an incident in which Stokely Carmichael held a meeting on campus exclusively for Black students. "I went over there and the guy at the door didn't know me. Then some others came along, and they said, 'Hey, that's Brother Iranian. Let him in,'" Hamid recounted, laughing. "That's what they called me." Then he paused to reflect on how it felt to be welcomed into such a space of fraternal affection: "I wish I could live ten years like that and die and never find out what is reality," he said. The affects of solidarity that allowed him to feel a sense of belonging among a group of Black revolutionaries still resonated deeply with Hamid, expressing his melancholic attachment to the revolutionary energies and vision gathered in that room, which would dissipate a few years later. His honorary membership in the BSU came as the result of the credibility and trust he accrued through regular participation in antiracist protests. The first protest he ever attended in the US was at the San Francisco Sheraton Palace Hotel, where activists were staging sit-ins to demand good jobs for Black people.[36] During the 1968 SF State strike, Hamid would fight side by side with other BSU members in bloody clashes with police who routinely invaded the campus. These actions mobilized his own revolutionary affects, a militancy in the face of injustice and a desire to participate in mass social movements. Out of these shared affects, a feeling and practice of solidarity was forged.

The activists of the ISA became known for their ability to mobilize on short notice and their willingness to fight the police and go to jail. The first time Parviz was arrested was at a rally to free Black Panther cofounder Huey Newton in Oakland, California. "It was after the demonstration," he explained, "a policeman was hitting a very young girl on the street. We used to have these round wooden shields. I took one of those shields and hit the policeman on the back, and he fell on the street, and the woman got away and I got away." Rather than leave the area, however, Parviz joined a neighborhood patrol in Oakland that was monitoring police radios. He heard the cops say they were looking for him minutes before Oakland's "blue minis," the nickname for the Special Forces, turned up. "We went to Santa Rita [prison]," he said, "and there I refused to shave my beard, so they put me in solitary confinement. They poured water over me. It was twelve days."

Encounters with different forms of police violence, incarceration, and torture generated affects of solidarity connecting Iranian dissidents with the Black Panther Party for Self-Defense. The ISA's own experiences of surveillance and harassment by US law enforcement agencies, by the INS, and by SAVAK operatives in the US transformed a theoretical understanding of the limits of American freedom and democracy into something lived and felt. Members of the ISA were not persecuted by the United States in the way the Panthers and other Black activists were. They were not murdered in their beds by police or locked in prison for extended periods of time. However, the ISA was deeply concerned with the persecution of dissidents in Iran by SAVAK, some of whom were members of CISNU. One such case involved five CISNU members who had returned from studying in the United Kingdom in 1965, only to find themselves accused of plotting to assassinate the Shah.[37] They were thrown in military prison and threatened with execution. Thus there was a real and severe threat hanging over the heads of ISA members if they were deported or dared to return home. Iranian student activists always made sure to expose the links between torture in Iran and American foreign policy. Solidarity with the Panthers expressed the transnational circulation of revolutionary affects, attaching to political prisoners in Iran and to those in the US.

While a combination of political and material connections fueled Iranian activists' animosity toward US law enforcement, more immediately relevant were the shared feelings of responsibility toward jailed activists and indignation in the face of state repression. These feelings were reproduced and disseminated through constant campaigning to free political prisoners, making it possible for the Panthers and the ISA to regularly send members to each other's rallies and meetings in the Bay Area. As mentioned earlier, the ISA participated in the campaign to free Huey Newton, mobilizing for a mass protest on the first day of his trial.[38] In New York, ISA member and artist Nicky Nodjoumi recalled another means of showing support: "at the time when [leading Black feminist revolutionary] Angela Davis and [Black Panther cofounder] Bobby Seale were both in jail, I made a poster for them. You could see Bobby Seale's and Angela Davis's portraits. We spread it out, posted it everywhere. Gave it to all the political organizations" (figure 4.3).

Like other revolutionaries, Iranians looked to the Panthers as a source of hope and inspiration. An ISA message of solidarity in the January 1970 issue of the *Black Panther* describes the "momentum of the Black liberation movement" as one that "will not only mobilize the masses of Black people, but also all progressive people in US [*sic*]."[39] Midway through, the article abruptly shifts into an almost prophetic register: "Think of such a force; what power can withstand a force of millions of revolutionaries refusing compromise, and determined to destroy that which has denied their basic rights?"[40] This rousing, strident language contains more than just a message of solidarity; it expresses the hopes and desires of the Iranian student movement and of every other liberation movement underway at the time. While the article does not mention US support for the Shah or explain the link between foreign and domestic repression directly, the reader can *feel* the connection, for the author's own overwhelming desire for victory is bound up in the conviction that the Black movement must succeed.

Affects of friendship, as well as a confrontational approach to state power, helped to foster a working relationship between members of the ISA and the Black Panther Party. "I met Bobby Seale on the demonstrations," Parviz recalled. "We [in the ISA] were often the mediators; we were in between [not Black or white], and we had a lot of trust because we were very well organized and we were always showing up to the demonstrations." Bobby called me one day and said, "Parviz, we need your help." There were a bunch of Panthers surrounded, under police surveillance, and they needed some weapons and other supplies. He said, "'We can't go anywhere near them or we'll be arrested.' So I had this little Volkswagen, and I brought the stuff over to them." Here, affects of solidarity manifested not in rhetorical flourishes but in the delivery of material support, as Parviz placed himself at risk to transport weapons and supplies to a group of Panthers under siege. The

Figure 4.3 ISA poster. Original artwork by Niki Nodjoumi.

racial ambiguity of Iranian foreign students enabled Parviz to move freely through streets in which a Black person could not. Without any pretense to a shared racial experience, the militancy and discipline ISA members displayed in their political commitment to solidarity became the basis for trust and respect between the two organizations.

Parviz recounted another incident in which he was asked to play a supporting role. "Muhammad Ali was coming to speak at a rally in San Francisco. The Panthers wanted to stand behind him as he spoke, you know with their berets and the whole thing. Muhammad Ali didn't want this level of affiliation with them." According to Parviz, Seale turned to his friends in the ISA. "It was finally agreed that I would stand behind Ali during the speech and hold a poster for the Free Huey campaign," Parviz said. "And this is what I did."

The ISA also appealed to African American and other activists to support and identify with the Iranian freedom struggle. This is how an ISA leaflet from 1970 made the case:

> STOP ALL POLITICAL REPRESSION IN IRAN!!
> Political repression is not abstract. We have all been exposed to this, the most blatant form of repression. We need only name a few: The Los Siete, Chavez, the Panther 21, Bobby, Ericha, Angela; there are thousands more within this country. We all know this system is to blame, but few of us realize the manner in which this system manifests itself in the so-called underdeveloped countries—countries like Iran.[41]

This list of Black and Latino political prisoners, presumed to be of shared concern to Americans and Iranians, includes several women who are given prominence because of the persecution they faced as revolutionaries, not because of any particular concern with issues of gender justice or the impacts of racism on women of color. Instead, this list evinces the ways that solidarity moved along an affective map, charting connections with others who shared revolutionary responses to injustice. This could be a political strength and a political weakness at the same time, making mass movements possible while marginalizing important sites of difference that women of color feminists would identify as central to human liberation.

The leaflet goes on to describe the arrests of four Iranian students "awaiting execution for attempting to cross the border to join the Palestinian Revolution" (members of the "Palestine Group") and the arrest and "savage torture" of former ISA member Haj Rezavi in Iran.[42] The leaflet declares: "We need support in order to expose the fascist regime of the Shah and to save the 4 and the others in prison. . . . We invite all concerned people to join us."[43] In this way, the ISA positioned itself on the same side as the liberation movements of people of color in the US and attempted to mobilize the affects of solidarity circulating around them toward Iran and Palestine as sites of identification and collective action.

At least in Northern California, this strategy seems to have been effective. In 1971, when forty-one ISA members were arrested for occupying the Iranian consulate in San Francisco, UC Berkeley's BSU got involved in the defense campaign. The BSU sent a telegram to the Iranian embassy in Washington "deplor[ing] and condemn[ing] the oppressive tactics initiated against the students by the San Francisco Tac Squad, and sustained against them by the system with threats of prosecution, deportation, etc."[44] The San Francisco Tac Squad was the same force called in to beat up students at SF State during the strike just two years earlier, and it was notorious for routinely targeting Black Panthers and other activists. In this case, the ISA and the Black liberation movement faced repression from the *same* security forces. The BSU telegram ends with a message of solidarity, shouting in all caps: "WE SUPPORT THE IRANIAN STUDENTS AND DEMAND THE DROPPING OF ALL CHARGES AND THE CESSATION OF ALL IMPERIALIST ACTS AGAINST IRAN." While much has been written about the connections African American activists made between police repression "at home" and the US war in Vietnam, here we have an example of how a similar analysis informed Black students' solidarity with Iran. The BSU's telegram is just one indication of the extent to which the ISA's critique of the opaque forms of US intervention in the Middle East (coups d'état and the sponsoring of repressive dictatorships) entered the broader US leftist discourse. The telegram's language, tone, and style project a righteous indignation that nearly leaps off the page. It illustrates how affects of solidarity mapped transnational circuits of state repression and resistance across geographical sites, traversing the geopolitical and intimate scales of human experience.

The BSU telegram was not the only example of how the ISA succeeded in making the plight of political prisoners in Iran resonate with leading Black liberation activists in the US. In March 1972, Angela Davis sent a letter to the Iranian prime minister, Amir-Abbas Hoveyda, expressing dismay over a string of show trials and executions of dissidents in Iran.[45] "We have been closely following the political situation in Iran, and we have been in touch with the Confederation of Iranian Students," she wrote. The letter ends with the following explanation of her motivation in sending it: "We believe that the struggle to free political prisoners is international in scope, and we feel compelled to express our concern," she concluded, signing off on behalf of the National United Committee to Free Angela and All Political Prisoners.[46] Here, feeling compelled to act on behalf of another is not altruism or charity, but a shared affective response to injustice. It is the circulation of the desire for freedom across borders and categories of identity.

In Washington, DC, the ISA was able to connect to the Black anticolonial struggle in ways not possible in other locations. Howard University, a historically Black college, was a hub for imperial model minorities from across the decolonizing world. While the majority of foreign students at Howard came from Latin America and the Caribbean, the next largest group was from the Middle East, followed closely by students from Africa.[47] Younes Benab, a Howard undergraduate in economics and a founding member of the ISA chapter in Washington, DC, related the role that African and other foreign students played in his own development as an activist. "From the time I was involved with Iranian Student Association, I very naturally got in touch and in cooperation with other students from many different countries, specifically from Ghana, Congo, and Ethiopia," he said. The first time he attended a protest was in 1961, shortly after he arrived at Howard. "African students were demonstrating outside the Belgian embassy because they thought the Belgian authorities were responsible for the assassination of Patrice Lumumba in Congo. Later it was discovered that the CIA did it," Younes said. Students from many different Third World countries had a similar experience of having their democratically elected leaders overthrown, Younes explained: "In those countries, the leaders who came to power were like Mosaddeq types, they were fairly popular. Like Kwame Nkrumah in Ghana was very popular and he was overthrown in 1966. So all these students, they were active at Howard University before the coups in their countries. We were there after the coup in Iran, so we had tremendous sympathy for them." Younes also highlighted the close working relationship the ISA had with Ethiopian students. They "were like us," he said. "They were against their king, their Shah, and so we had a lot in common in that sense." State repression, including CIA-backed coups d'état, generated overlapping coordinates on the affective maps of students from very different places who refused to accept the loss of anticolonial leaders and the other possible futures they represented.

Like at SF State, ISA members at Howard also got involved in supporting African American student demands for institutional change, joining campus demonstrations and occupations that sought to transform the curriculum and increase the numbers of Black faculty. *Roshanai*, a Persian-language CISNU publication, featured a half-page photograph in 1968 showing Howard students scaling the edifice of the main administration building to hang a sign renaming their institution "Black University."[48] This image appeared in a photo spread displaying scenes of student protest around the world from that same year, evidence of CISNU's sense of itself as part of an internationalist young people's uprising and of the significance it placed on the US Black student "vanguard." Indeed, one-time Howard student Stokely Carmichael would become a national—and international—leader of this vanguard as a founding member of the Student Nonviolent Coordinating Committee (SNCC). Members of the ISA attended SNCC events and demonstrations on and off campus. Zohreh Khayam, a member of the ISA's International Relations Committee and a master's student in sociology at Howard at the time, was charged with reaching out to Carmichael to ask for an endorsement from SNCC. He invited her to share the stage with him in Howard's main auditorium, where she told the audience about the ISA's work and asked for their support.

The ISA's critique of the US-Iran "special relationship" also resonated with a broader student interest in charting connections between African and other liberation movements. Howard's campus weekly, *The Hilltop*, began covering ISA actions in 1971 and, throughout the 1970s, became a forum for connecting the Iranian opposition with African American and Third World freedom struggles. The names of many of the reporters who wrote about the ISA provide additional evidence that, by the mid-1970s, Howard was a politicized Black diasporic location.

On March 5, 1976, Marazere Ubani's *Hilltop* report on his interview with ISA member and Howard undergraduate Mohammed Eghtedari begins with a discussion of Iran's role in Africa: "Iranian students in the United States have vigorously protested measures taken by the Central Intelligence Agency-backed regime of the Shah of Iran who they say brutally suppresses the liberties of Iranian people and who overtly aids the apartheid regime in South Africa and Israel. The regime, they contend, is also supplying military hardwares [*sic*] and aircrafts to the military government in Ethiopia to combat the freedom fighters of Eritrea."[49] Mohammed also told Ubani that Iran was selling oil to South Africa in exchange for nuclear reactors, a central plank of the Shah's "African policy," which, he said, "means basically penetration by Iran into Africa." Mohammed argued that the Shah's "instigated role" was supposed to supplant what he called "Israel's dwindling influence in Africa" and that this exemplified Iran's position as "the second-best ally of the United States in the Middle East conflict."[50] In other words, US efforts to maintain hegemony in the Middle East were implicated in its efforts to do so in Africa. The stakes of the US outpost in Iran, therefore, were high not only for Iranians and their Arab neighbors, but for popular movements in Southern and Eastern Africa as well.

Two years later, *Hilltop* reporter Akpan Ekpo contributed to the "Eye on Africa" column under the headline "Shah of Iran: Enemy to Africa."[51] Ekpo discusses Iran's complicity with the racist regimes in both Rhodesia and South Africa, where Iran controlled two-thirds of the major oil refineries and ensured that supplies continued to flow. When a group of foreign ministers representing the Organization of African Unity tried to lobby the Shah to stop these oil exports, he refused to meet with them. "The Shah has made a blunder," Ekpo wrote:

> He should have sought the experiences of the Portuguese, the French, the British, etc. in Africa. The national wars of liberation in Angola, Mozambique and Guinea-Bissau uprooted fascism in Portugal. Shah's involvement in South Africa may assist in the destruction of fascism in Iran. We support vigorously the struggle of the Iranian people—workers, students, etc. against the dictatorial and fascist rule of the Shah.
>
> SHAH PAHLAVI IS AFRICA'S ENEMY.
>
> The struggle of the Iranian masses is our struggle, their victory is our victory.[52]

Righteous anger at the cruelties of these interrelated oppressive regimes pulses through each sentence, sometimes screaming in all caps, as the author "vigorously" asserts the feeling that Iranians and Africans would rise or fall together.

These and other articles reflect the breadth and depth of the passion and rage that undergirded Third World internationalism. Campus protests by the ISA were charged with this militancy and drew widespread support. A 1977 *Hilltop* editorial praises an ISA protest against President Carter's hypocritical human rights campaign, noting that Iran "has been exposed as a key link in covert shipments of US military supplies from Israel to Rhodesia, to the illegitimate minority government, to be used against Black freedom fighters. Therefore, the close relations of Iran and the US are important to Blacks in America."[53] After denouncing Howard University for awarding an honorary degree to the Iranian ambassador the previous year—an act bitterly opposed by the ISA—the editorial concludes: "The time has come for Black people in general and Howard students particularly, to exhibit the dedication and loyalty to freedom from oppression and repression that was demonstrated by the Iranian students and their supporters this week."[54]

When the Iranian Revolution finally succeeded in toppling the Shah, the *Hilltop*'s Sam Adeboye titled his column "Iranian People Should Be an Example for All" (figure 4.4).[55] The article celebrates the revolution's triumph and then notes, "As we all know, Iranians have been struggling for a long time to end the reign of terror by the oppressive regime of the Shah, which was created in Iran with the help of Western powers."[56] Adeboye's tribute to the Iranian revolution shows the extent to which some Black students had come to identify with the Iranian opposition and to understand it as, in the words of an ISA *Hilltop* column from 1977, part of "an era of the liberation movements of the peoples of the world."[57]

These examples of affinity with Black movements in the US and in Africa dramatically illustrate the overlapping coordinates on the "affective maps" of a generation of young revolutionaries.[58] The articles written by African diaspora students at Howard University transport us to a time when identifications among activists flowed not only from race, religion, nationality, or even the same experience of oppression, but from the visceral feeling that the losses already suffered would only continue to mount until the system of racial capitalism and imperialism was overthrown.

Palestine and Beyond: Arab Self-Determination

The question of Arab liberation was of paramount importance to the ISA in part because Iranian activists understood that the Shah's government posed a significant obstacle to its realization. Consequently, the ISA publicized the covert cooperation between Israel and Iran in its English-language pamphlets. One ISA report from 1973 includes this quote from the Danish new left magazine, *Politisk Revy*: "There also have been reports of an exchange of secret intelligence advisors between the two regimes. Israeli secret police, for example, have been instrumental in the training of Iranian SAVAK agents. The growing ties between the Iranian and Israeli regimes is seen as a first step toward possible joint military actions against independence movements in the Middle East especially in the Persian Gulf area [*sic*]."[59] By exposing the links between Iran and Israel, the ISA made the case that Iranians and Arabs faced the same constellation of repressive state powers. Revolutionary affects of Iranians and Arabs, including in the diaspora, converged in the desire for a region free of colonization and Western-backed dictatorships. For many Iranian leftists, the Israeli occupation of Palestine came to signify the ultimate injustice perpetuated by the alliance between the US and the Shah, the

Iranian People Should Be an Example for All

At last, the Iranian peoples' revolution has successfully up-rooted the last tap-root of oppression and imperialism in the Persian Gulf.

As we all know, Iranians have been struggling for a long time to end the reign of terror by the oppressive regime of the Shah, which was created in Iran with the help of Western Powers for the purpose of steady and continued economic exploitation.

The success of Iranian peoples' struggle to free themselves from the grips of the Shah and his backers is quite worthy of emulation by all who are still suffering today under the system which can best be described as "Slavery in a refined way." Iranians would not have succeeded if not for their unity and devotion to achieve their freedom at all cost.

They were murdered cold-bloodedly almost everyday by the Shah and also by his tap-root (Shahpour Baktiar) whom he left behind when he fled the country. Many were tortured and thrown into detention indefinitely without charges being preferred against them.

But in spite of all the atrocious tactics used against the determined Iranian people, they stood firm, and sacrificed their lives in thousands in order to achieve their political goal—FREEDOM.

They united as one indivisible group in spite of all odds against them. Their student organizations are extremely strong and devoted to the cause of freedom and democracy in their fathers' land. Their democracy was snatched away by the Shah with the great assistance of those Western governments, some of which happen to be human-rights advertisers.

If we should all look as far back as the era of institution of slavery and try to study the history of those involved in enslaving their fellow human beings, and also follow all the events of our present days, we will all be convinced that the entire western world has certainly projected itself as a great symbol of oppression and imperialism.

Anyone who has been watching the current episode of "ROOTS, the NEXT GENERATION," will be able to figure out the degree of our ancestors' agony.

They suffered because of the color of their skin, which was not of their own making. They suffered in the new land into which they were brought against their will, the land which later prospered through their sweat and labor. And, yet, they were not qualified to vote.

The same thing has been passed on to us because the present situation in South Africa and Rhodesia are both the carbon-copy of what happened in the "Next Generation of ROOTS." It is now a refined way of slavery, because direct slavery has long been outlawed, but indirect slavery is still existing today.

If you don't believe we are not in the world of indirect slavery, look at it this way:

(1) Direct slavery gave way to Colonialism

(2) Colonialism gave birth to Economic Exploitation

(3) Economic Exploitation gave birth to political oppression, and

(4) Political oppression, coupled with economic exploitation, both are equal to a "refined way of slavery."

The whole system seems to be in a cyclical form, a "vicious" circle, if you will.

This reminds me of one historian,

By Sam Adeboye

J.H. Parry, and his paperback book, titled "The establishment of the European Hegemony." He said that "The colonizing peoples of Western Europe looked out upon the world with eager and greedy confidence." If we look at the records of the Western world from the days of our great ancestors to present, we will see that the Western world still sees the world, through greedy eyes and attitudes of usurpation.

As we all congratulate the Iranian people for their achievement, we should also ask ourselves this big question: When will there be a strong and envious unity among the oppressed Black peoples all over the world?

We should all remember that one of our great leaders, Dr. Martin Luther King, sacrificed his life to restore dignity to the Black race. Dr. Kwame Nkrumah (Osagyefo) also did his best to project a positive image of the Black race. Brothers and sisters, when are we going to contribute our own quota to the restoration of dignity to the Black race?

Till then, between the oppressed, and the oppressors, the struggle continues.

Sam Adeboye is a senior in the School of Business, majoring in Accounting.

Figure 4.4 *The Hilltop*, March 2, 1979, 5. Courtesy of the Moorland-Spingarn Research Center. Howard University Archives.

starkest illustration of what it meant to say, as ISA periodicals often did, that the Shah was a "lapdog" of US imperialism. On and off college campuses, the ISA had ample opportunity to popularize this analysis by making solidarity with Palestine a central part of their movement.

The fall 1976 issue of *Iran Report*, the ISA's quarterly English-language journal, includes a lengthy appeal to defend the Palestinians and culminates in a list of medicines requested by the Palestinian Red Crescent Society with a bank account number and address where donations can be sent.[60] No fewer than five Palestinian groups sent official messages of solidarity to CISNU's seventeenth congress in Hamburg, Germany, in 1976, including one from the Palestinian Red Crescent Society's representatives in New York asserting, "The Palestinian revolution has an organic link with the Iranian armed struggle."[61]

In Washington, DC, Palestine House and *Khane-e Iran* were located just blocks away from each other in the neighborhood of Dupont Circle from 1968 until 1971, when the FBI shut the former down. Activists moved back and forth between both organizing centers, cosponsoring forums and planning joint demonstrations. At Howard University, an ISA-sponsored demonstration in solidarity with Palestine was the first Iranian activist initiative that made the pages of the *Hilltop*. The 1971 march through campus sought "the support of blacks in America for the Palestinian liberating [*sic*] movement in the Middle East."[62] During the protest, ISA members distributed a leaflet arguing the case for a "common cause and destiny," summarizing the plight of Iran under the thumb of Western imperialism, and concluding with a tribute to African American and Native American liberation movements "as an integral part of the world revolution."[63]

According to Mohammed Eghtedari, who participated in this march, the ISA's efforts to link revolutionary movements in the US to those in Palestine stemmed from the fact that Iranian anti-Shah students "unconditionally supported the Palestinian movement. Some students would take sides more with the PFLP [Popular Front for the Liberation of Palestine], or with George Habash [leader of a Marxist-nationalist faction of the PLO]. But in general, the Palestinian Liberation Organization was respected and we fully supported in every sense of the word, in terms of demonstrations. Whenever in a city there were no Palestinians, Iranians would go and demonstrate on behalf of Palestine." Sometimes, the desire to publicly identify with the Palestinian movement led ISA members to become targets of anti-Arab violence. As Mohammed recalled: "One time we went to New York to make a demonstration for Iranian issues but the majority of our students and organization in New York had brought slogans in support of the Palestinians. In fact, the Jewish Defense League from New York came and attacked the demonstration and several people got arrested. They thought we were Palestinian! Our slogans were so pro-Palestinian that they got confused." Sina remembered similar experiences on demonstrations in Philadelphia and New York: "I would usually carry the flag of the PLO. And because I went to *maktab* [religious school for Muslims] and I knew Arabic, I would be [chanting] '*Thora thora*,' 'Revolution, revolution until victory!' Many times because of that I was beaten up by Americans."

A leading Palestinian activist in Chicago, Camelia Odeah, remembered well the ISA's consistency and dedication. "They were more Palestinian than the Palestinians!" she said.[64] The ISA members' "fierce love for justice and equity put the Palestinian issue central to their work and their lives," she continued. "They were very genuine, they practiced what they preached." After the Israeli invasions and occupations of 1967 and 1973, activism around Palestine intensified among Arabs in diaspora, and many Iranians also felt compelled to act. According to Camelia, it was "the fact that people were uprooted and living in camps. ... [The ISA] saw the people suffering. They understood what it meant to have Israel in the region for the people in the region; they understood the close relationship between the Shah and Israel, [between] SAVAK and Mossad."

Camelia recalled traveling to Chicago as an undergraduate at Michigan State University after the 1973 Arab-Israeli War:

We came from all over the region for all night vigils, all night long, and demonstrations. I remember the hunger strikes Iranian students would have in solidarity with Palestinians and in solidarity with Iranian political prisoners. They would do this for days. Those types of activities were continual. If the oppression was the Shah or the Saudis or the Israeli occupation, they were all seen in one camp. In the past people used to say "US imperialism, Israel and the reactionary Arab countries." It was like one sentence. People would say this all together as the structures of domination that are oppressing our people. Now we don't even have that language. Back then, there was a deep respect and care for one another. I remember the Gulf students, they really cared about the Iranians and the Iranian students supported the Saudi students as much as they could. Everybody came together around Palestine.

This description of how affects of solidarity manifested as both feeling and practice offers an alternative to the Persian "Aryan" nationalism of the Shah, which asserted Iranian racial and cultural superiority over Arabs and which still circulates widely among Iranians today. Respect, self-sacrifice, empathy, and care mixed with anger and hope to forge a collective internationalist political culture that crossed national, linguistic, and ethnic borders. The assumption of commonality and connection became, in Camelia's words, a kind of "common sense" that was reaffirmed and reproduced through joint organizing: "You could say it was normal that we were close [Arabs and Iranians] because of our collective cultures from the region. Iranian/Arab divides were more of a joke about what to call the Gulf. Sometimes to be polite an Arab might call it the 'Persian Gulf' and vice versa. The Sunni and Shiite divide wasn't an issue. All these movements were a reflection of Mao Tse-tung or the Soviet Union, these were the ideas that were being discussed in the region. The core of it was liberation, emancipation from oppression, that's what brought people together." Cooperation between the US, the Shah, the Gulf client states, and Israel provided a structural basis for alliances among the diasporic opposition, while ideologies of Third World Marxism offered a common language for their movements. But without a deeply felt attachment to Arab self-determination as a goal in and of itself, it is difficult to explain Iranian participation in "all night vigils," hunger strikes, and demonstrations that subjected them to anti-Arab violence, or to understand their long-standing relationships with Arab foreign student and Arab American activists in cities across the US. Camelia's memories of the "continual" self-sacrifice, friendship, and commitment ISA members exhibited toward their Arab peers illustrate the power of overlapping revolutionary affects to create new forms of diasporic subjectivity and new political cultures of resistance and solidarity.

In this context, the ISA was able to work with many other organizations to make Palestine a visible, central part of the broader student revolt. A 1970 forum at San Jose State College featured speakers from Students for a Democratic Society (SDS), the Arab Students Association, and the ISA (figure 4.5).[65] In 1973, Israel shot down a Libyan commercial airplane over the Sinai and launched raids into Lebanon that killed Palestinian refugees and PLO leaders. The ISA joined with ten other groups, including the Organization of Arab Students, the Anti-Imperialist Coalition, Venceremos Organization, and the Ethiopian Students Association, to protest in front of San Francisco's Israeli consulate.[66] Later that year, on October 24, 1973, an ISA rally in UC Berkeley's Sproul Plaza was followed by an evening panel discussion and screening of a documentary about life in the refugee camps called, "Revolution Until Victory," which took

IMPERIALISM IN THE MIDDLE EAST &

APR 22 1970

On Saturday, April 25th, a seminar will be held at San Jose State College on: "Imperialism and the influence and penetration of Imperialism in the Middle East", "U.S. Imperialism's stake in Israel" and "The Evolution of the Palestine Question and the struggles of the Palestinian People."

The purpose of the seminar is to further our understanding of imperialism and the struggles of the Palestinian people against it.

Speakers from the Iranian Students Assoc., Arab Students Association and Students for a Democratic Society.

THE STRUGGLE OF THE PALESTINIAN PEOPLE

TIME :: SATURDAY APRIL 25, 1970   10:00 AM - 5:00 PM

PLACE :: SCIENCE 142, SAN JOSE STATE COLLEGE

ARAB STUDENTS ASSOCIATION (S. J. S. C.)
IRANIAN STUDENTS ASSOCIATION

Figure 4.5 ISA File, Social Protest Collection. Bancroft Library, UC Berkeley.

its name from the PLO slogan.[67] The flyer called for a "democratic, secular state where Jews, Moslems, and Christians can live together in justice and peace," an expression of hope in a "one-state solution" that was dominant on the Left at that time but that has been marginalized since the 1993 Oslo Accords. The final slogan at the bottom of the leaflet read, "Victory to the national liberation struggles of the Arab and Iranian peoples against imperialism and Zionism."

Former ISA member Jaleh Pirnazar, a Jewish woman who was an undergraduate at UC Berkeley, could still feel the sense of urgency and outrage that compelled her to take up the cause of Palestinian liberation, even though she alienated her pro-Israeli parents in the process: "1967 had just passed so it was very fresh. Land occupied, Palestinians being homeless and all—there was a very strong sentiment in all of the radical progressive movements. The Confederation [CISNU] embraced this and we worked in very close collaboration with Palestinians." She recalled the ISA's celebration of the Iranian New Year, the organization's annual flagship event, and how she worked to make Palestine central to the program. "I was musically talented in those days," Jaleh said: "I played the piano and I organized choruses. For our Nowruz [New Year] celebration we had huge parties; this was our major fundraising event [each year], and the chorus was one of the highlights. We practiced for months. We would have songs dedicated to the Palestinian movement. We learned Arabic to be able to sing these Palestinian songs." Shahnaz, a member of the same ISA chapter who studied at San Jose State College, also remembered these joint musical events: "I organized a choir with our people and with Palestinians, so we sang 'The Internationale' in three languages [Arabic, Persian, and English]. This was on campus at Berkeley. The nice thing was that, at the end of it, all of us sang at the same time. It was so beautiful." These choruses were embodied performances of affective attachments that made solidarity a politically necessary and deeply rewarding way of being in relation to others.

The identification of ISA members with the Palestinian cause can also be traced back to Iran, where a preexisting set of transnational connections already linked elements of both opposition movements. As ISA member and Howard University undergraduate Younes Benab explained:

> If you were aware politically in Iran, you belonged to two major groupings, two major blocks. One was communist, the Tudeh Party, and the other one was national liberation, like Mosaddeq and his followers. They were both solidly behind the Palestinian movement. Later, factions that broke away from Tudeh Party [after 1964], they all supported the Palestinian movement. So if you were in [CISNU], naturally you were either with the Tudeh Party or you were with *melligara* [i.e., the National Front, which supported Mosaddeq] or you were with the Revolutionary Organization that had split [from Tudeh]. All of them were supporting Palestine. If they had many, many disagreements on other things, on Palestine everybody competed to say, "I'm more pro-Palestinian than you are."

If ISA members inherited the pro-Palestinian legacies of the two major opposition tendencies in Iran before 1960, the PLO's turn to armed struggle exerted its influence on a new generation of Iranian activists disillusioned with both the Tudeh and the National Front. This soon led to tragic yet very concrete connections between the two liberation movements. In 1970, the ISA organized a march to protest the arrest of the "Palestine Group" in Iran. "We started from [the offices of the] *Baltimore Sun*, and it was all the way to Washington," Mohammed Eghtedari remembered.

The Palestine Group was composed primarily of university students in Tehran; their name expressed their political affiliations as well as their strategic aspirations—their desire to transport the PLO's organizing tactics to Iranian soil. In 1969, they planned to travel to Jordan or Lebanon to train with the PLO and then return to Iran to launch a guerrilla offensive. Before they managed to leave the country, however, they were discovered by SAVAK and arrested. Seventeen people were given lengthy prison terms. The ISA translated into English the final speech of that group's leader, Shokrollah Paknejad, delivered at his sentencing hearing in Tehran, and printed it in its entirety in a special pamphlet for mass distribution in the US. Paknejad unequivocally defended the group's intentions: "Yes, it is true that we were going to join the Palestinians to fight imperialism, which is responsible for the misfortune of the people of Asia, Africa, and Latin America. Palestine is a turning point in the anti-imperialist struggle in this region; and the secret of the final defeat of imperialism is to be found in these wars of liberation."[68] Here, the entire project of Third World liberation turns on the question of Palestine, a testament to the deep affective and emotional attachments a whole generation of Iranian leftists had to a struggle they understood to be both paradigmatic and exceptional. Paknejad also argues for the intertwined futures of Iranians and Palestinians, whose freedom could only be achieved through a regional revolutionary project connected to global transformations underway. Paknejad thus accused "the Iranian ruling elite" of "putting on trial the solidarity of our people and that of the world with the people of Palestine."[69] The affective capacity for solidarity was the real "crime" the accused had committed, which in and of itself constituted a threat to the ruling order. Paknejad was tortured in prison and given a life sentence, but his words circulated widely in the US and Europe as what Naghmeh Sohrabi deems a "clarion call," articulating the growing sense that the "national struggle against the Shah was inextricably linked to a global anti-imperial one."[70]

Decades later, affective attachments to Palestinian liberation still circulate in diaspora, embedded within the memories of former ISA members. As Zohreh Khayam explained:

> It is wrong, these people have been wronged. The irony was that we were all raised in those years, we were all against the Holocaust of the Jews and yet my thinking is when you're against something because it was oppressive and it was not fair, you learn from that experience, and you would become fair in your own behavior and treatment of others. In that case, the Israeli Jews were not, and their supporters were not. You see what I'm saying; it was the sense of fairness, and so there was a huge, huge sympathy for that movement over the years.

Zohreh contested the notion that the Nazi Holocaust necessitated a Jewish-only state; instead, her affective and emotional response to the genocide in Europe flowed directly into her opposition to the persecution of Palestinians.

Jaleh Behroozi, the Jewish woman described in chapter 1 who abandoned her religious faith after reading *The Diary of Anne Frank*, used similar moral language to describe her affinity with the Palestinian people. "The impact of [the] Holocaust for me was that religion was the reason that these things happened, these kind of divisions," she said. "I was just thinking of what is right and what is wrong, so defending the rights of Palestinians was significant because it was part of what is right and what is wrong for me." This assertion of "right and wrong" recurred in several discussions of Palestine with former ISA members. Sina put it this way: "What symbolizes everything that is wrong with the modern shape of the world for me more than anything else in the past thirty to forty years is the question of Palestine." He pointed to a pendant around his neck that symbolized his continued solidarity with Palestinians. "If you want to think about the figure of injustice in the modern world, it's that figure that you have to think about," he said. Vida Samiian, who played a leading role in the ISA chapter at UCLA, was also active in the local Palestine Solidarity Committee, along with Arab American and Arab foreign students "because it was the greatest injustice. I mean, the Shah was one thing, but Palestine—the dispossession, the occupation—it was unbelievable!"

While Palestine was the major site of Iranian-Arab affinity, it was not the only one. As early as 1962, the following political resolution was adopted as point four at the annual ISA congress in California: "Support the nationalist movement of the Arab People which with their successes in overthrow of corrupt regimes in Egypt and Iraq have shown the way and with heroic Algerian Revolution have added a new page to the glorious road of independence and progress [sic]."[71] This support would intensify over time along with Iran's increased involvement in regional politics. By the 1970s, Israel was not the only country to use US-made weapons against an Arab liberation movement.

When the Shah launched military interventions against popular uprisings in the Dhofar province of Oman and in southern Yemen, Iranian student activists in the US sought to publicize and condemn these actions as widely as possible. An ISA-authored opinion piece in the *Daily Californian* explains, "On Dec. 20, 1973, the Shah's troops, equipped and trained by the US Military Advisory Group, first invaded Dhofar, Oman." By that time, 90 percent of Dhofar had been liberated by the People's Front for the Liberation of Oman over the course of a nine-year conflict.[72] The article celebrates the achievements of the revolution, including "the establishment ... of a people's government," cooperative farming, reductions in illiteracy, and equal rights for women and men. It then goes on to explain that the Shah's intervention in Oman "has been intensified with a renewed and more vigorous attack on Dhofar as well as on the people's Democratic Republic of Yemen," an area of southern Yemen that declared independence in 1967.[73] In December 1973, and again in spring 1974, the ISA organized forums and demonstrations in San Francisco outside the Iranian consulate calling on the broader progressive American community to, as one flyer read, "Oppose the Shah of Iran's US-backed invasion of Oman" (figure 4.6).[74]

To compensate for the lack of mainstream US media coverage, the ISA's *Resistance* magazine ran lengthy reports in 1974 and 1975 detailing the economic, social, and political history of the country, the legacy of British colonialism, and the value of Oman to the US as a source of oil and as a strategic location from which to exert control over the Persian Gulf region. Written to agitate the conscience and incite people to act, these articles also summarized the decades-long resistance movement and explained how, at the behest of the US, the Shah had become "the gendarme of the region."[75] More than just acting on US orders, Abdel Takriti has argued that Iran's "unconditional support" of the Omani sultan reflected its own push to become a regional power.[76] One colorful passage from a 1975 article in *Resistance* describes the transformative effects of US weapons sales to Iran, which were fueling the Shah's imperial ambitions even beyond the Persian Gulf: "[The Shah] has become a monster turned into a Phantom, a Cobra, an octopus with steel tentacles spreading all over Iran and Oman, the Indian Ocean, and still

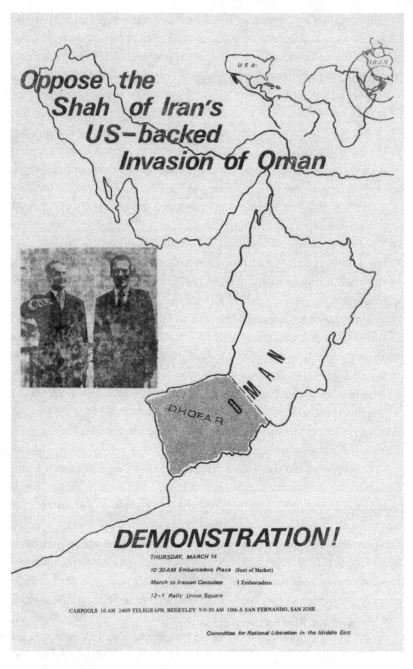

Fig 4.6 ISA Flyer, Social Protest Collection. Bancroft Library, UC Berkeley.

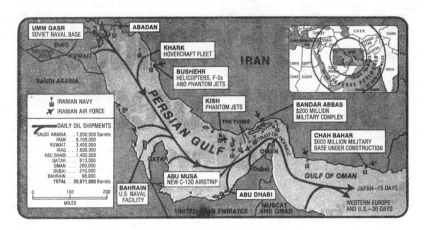

Figure 4.7 Parviz Shokat collection, Box 2, "Resistance Special Issue," 3, no. 1 (May 1975). Hoover Institution Archives, Stanford University.

expanding, meddling in Jordan and as far away as Ethiopia and Eritrea."[77] The ISA published a map showing Iran's role in the "unbridled arms build up raging in the area" (figure 4.7).

The results of a hyper-militarized Iranian regime proved devastating for the people of Dhofar, who were already suffering at the hands of the British-led "Omani" army.[78] As *Resistance* explained, "The Shah's invading troops have added misery, oppression, looting, raping, burning and destruction to the lot of a people who are already stricken with poverty, disease, and the chains of centuries old reaction."[79] Leftists inside Iran also felt a commitment to opposing their own government's regional imperial role. In the early 1970s, Fadaiyan guerrillas traveled from Iran to Dhofar to fight against the Shah's troops on the side of the Omani resistance. As Maziar Behrooz, historian of the Iranian Left, points out, "this meant that Iranians were fighting and dying on both sides."[80]

In December 1975, the ISA printed and distributed a one-page appeal from the Omani Red Crescent Society that described the harsh conditions of war and poverty afflicting the people of Dhofar, and asked for "speedy initiatives for urgent aid."[81] One year later, the fall 1976 issue of *Iran Report* published a letter from the Information Committee of the People's Front for the Liberation of Oman. "Dear Comrades," it begins and then goes on to confirm that the Omani Red Crescent Society had received the medicines sent by the ISA. The letter concludes, "we thank you, in the name of the Omani people for this kind support, and as always for your being in support to [*sic*] our just struggle against US Imperialism, British Imperialism, Shah's dictatorship and Arab reactionaries. Please receive our revolutionary greetings."[82] This list of adversaries illustrates the difference between charity and solidarity; the donation of medicines constituted mutual support for one crucial front in an interdependent revolutionary alliance against a coalition of reactionary state powers.

Given the historical and contemporary obstacles to solidarity between Arabs and Iranians, the legacy of this aspect of the ISA's work is particularly significant. The Islamic Republic of Iran has appropriated Palestinian suffering for more than four decades, mobilizing this issue to further its regional imperial ambitions and to shore up its image as the champion of the oppressed. The current Iranian government's commitment to Palestine is viewed in a cynical light by many Iranians, who are quick to point to the economic mismanagement, corruption, and human rights violations that produce suffering for ordinary Iranians on a daily basis. The unfortunate association of Palestine with the rhetoric and policies of a repressive government in Iran is compounded by longer histories of anti-Arab sentiment that are deeply embedded in the forms of Iranian nationalism promoted by the Shah. The extent to which the revolutionary affects of Iranian, Palestinian, and Dhofari activists overlapped in the 1960s and 1970s and mobilized regional solidarities was a significant blow to the dominant ideology of the Shah's reign. These affinities offer an alternative to the Persian imperial identity that has dominated the post-1979 diaspora.

In Iran, and in diaspora, Iranian leftists placed themselves in harm's way to protest the Israeli occupation of Palestine. They argued that the obstacles to freedom in Iran and in Palestine were directly linked through the US-Iran-Israel alliance and implicated the Shah's regime as a primary obstacle to Arab self-determination in ways that reverberated across the Left in the US. In their appeals to Americans, they made the comparison with Vietnam. The atrocities unfolding in Dhofar, according to *Resistance*, were "crimes which we are familiar with since the experience of US involvement in Viet-Nam [*sic*]. … It is the obligation of all freedom loving people to unite and expose these policies in order to prevent other 'Gulf of Tonkin' resolutions."[83] By writing and circulating such appeals in English, the ISA tried to mobilize the powerful affects of solidarity already circulating between Americans and the Vietnamese toward Arab revolutionary movements as sites of immediate concern and mobilization. Indeed, it was the widespread and militant abhorrence of US imperialism in Vietnam that made American support for Dhofari liberation seem possible at all.

Vietnam and the Defeat of US Imperialism

The ISA participated in antiwar demonstrations beginning in the early 1960s, shortly after it was reconstituted as an anti-Shah organization. In the mid-to-late 1960s, the ISA established organizational and personal ties with SDS. According to Ahmad Taghvai, ISA members in Northern California "had a very, very close relationship with SDS; SDS was an important point in this story. Some of our friends' girlfriends were from SDS, so it was a close connection." Friendships and romantic relationships overlapped with study groups, organizing meetings, and coalition-building to integrate the ISA into the left wing of the US antiwar movement. One joint ISA-SDS flyer printed in Berkeley in fall 1969 illustrates this. The leaflet first criticizes the liberal moratorium movement for labeling the war in Vietnam a "tragedy" rather than the result of a deliberate imperialist policy.[84] It then advertises three events: an SDS forum on imperialism and Vietnam, an SDS organizing meeting "to discuss Northern Calif. Regional SDS action with Iranian Student Assoc. against the Shah of Iran and US Imperialism," and a demonstration "against the Shah of Iran and US Imperialism in Vietnam"—all scheduled within a two-week period (figure 4.8).[85] The demonstration took shape as a rally at San Francisco's Federal Building followed by a march to the Iranian consulate to protest the Shah's visit. An ISA flyer for the action reads, "The Iranian people see the struggle of the Vietnamese and the Palestinian people as a just and victorious war against imperialism and pay their full support to these struggles."[86]

The ISA consistently attempted to link Vietnam, Palestine, and Iran, which was not always welcome in the antiwar movement. Younes recalled an incident from a demonstration in Washington, DC, in 1968:

> We, as Iranian student group, we went to join the antiwar movement at McPherson Square. I approached the leaders of the [demonstration]; one was white, the other one was African American. I asked them for permission, if it is possible for us to speak too? They said, "Sure. ISA is always welcome." So I said, "Well, I will consult with my friends, and we will pick someone to speak on behalf of ISA to make sure that you will know Iranian student movement is hundred percent behind antiwar movement." So after consultation, I returned, and I asked them is it all right for us at the same time to declare our solidarity with the Palestinian movement. They said, "No, no, that can create a lot of discomfort." So they were single-issue oriented.

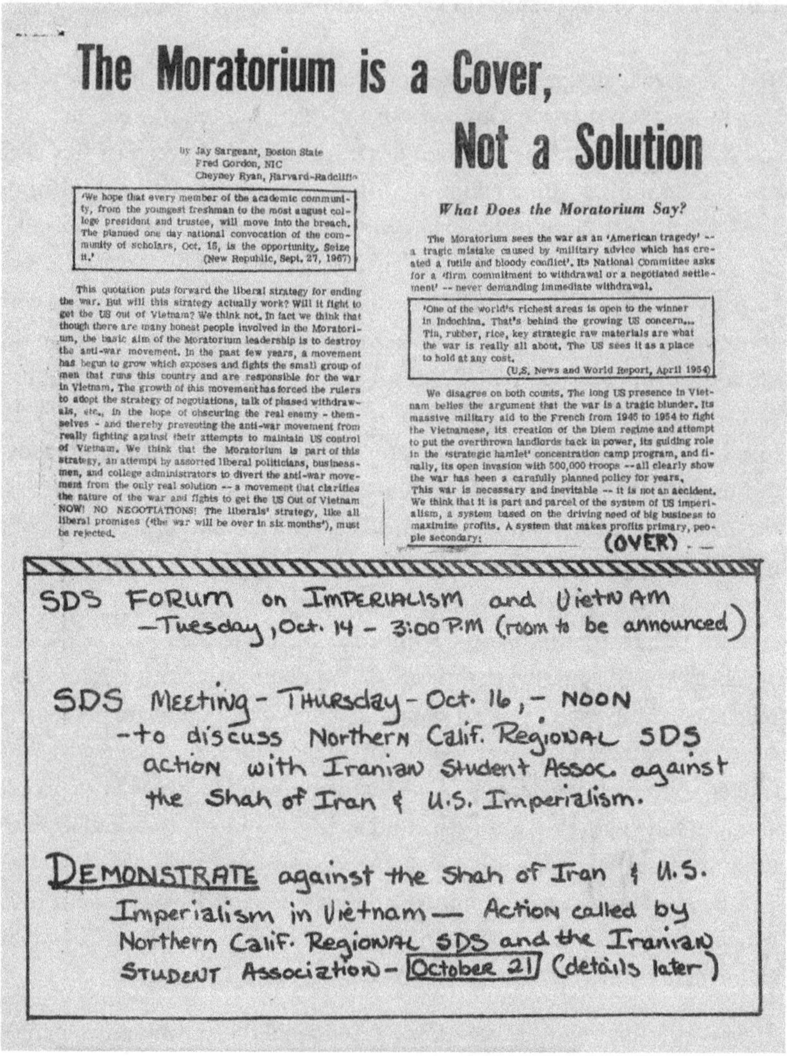

The Moratorium is a Cover,
Not a Solution

by Jay Sargeant, Boston State
Fred Gordon, NIC
Cheyney Ryan, Harvard-Radcliffe

'We hope that every member of the academic community, from the youngest freshman to the most august college president and trustee, will move into the breach. The planned one day national convocation of the community of scholars, Oct. 15, is the opportunity. Seize it.'
(New Republic, Sept. 27, 1967)

This quotation puts forward the liberal strategy for ending the war. But will this strategy actually work? Will it fight to get the US out of Vietnam? We think not. In fact we think that though there are many honest people involved in the Moratorium, the basic aim of the Moratorium leadership is to destroy the anti-war movement. In the past few years, a movement has begun to grow which exposes and fights the small group of men that runs this country and are responsible for the war in Vietnam. The growth of this movement has forced the rulers to adopt the strategy of negotiations, talk of phased withdrawals, etc., in the hope of obscuring the real enemy - themselves - and thereby preventing the anti-war movement from really fighting against their attempts to maintain US control of Vietnam. We think that the Moratorium is part of this strategy, an attempt by assorted liberal politicians, businessmen, and college administrators to divert the anti-war movement from the only real solution -- a movement that clarifies the nature of the war and fights to get the US Out of Vietnam NOW! NO NEGOTIATIONS! The liberals' strategy, like all liberal promises ('the war will be over in six months'), must be rejected.

What Does the Moratorium Say?

The Moratorium sees the war as an 'American tragedy' -- a tragic mistake caused by 'military advice which has created a futile and bloody conflict'. Its National Committee asks for a 'firm commitment to withdrawal or a negotiated settlement' -- never demanding immediate withdrawal.

'One of the world's richest areas is open to the winner in Indochina. That's behind the growing US concern... Tin, rubber, rice, key strategic raw materials are what the war is really all about. The US sees it as a place to hold at any cost.
(U.S. News and World Report, April 1954)

We disagree on both counts. The long US presence in Vietnam belies the argument that the war is a tragic blunder. Its massive military aid to the French from 1946 to 1954 to fight the Vietnamese, its creation or the Diem regime and attempt to put the overthrown landlords back in power, its guiding role in the 'strategic hamlet' concentration camp program, and finally, its open invasion with 500,000 troops --all clearly show the war has been a carefully planned policy for years. This war is necessary and inevitable -- it is not an accident. We think that it is part and parcel of the system of US imperialism, a system based on the driving need of big business to maximize profits. A system that makes profits primary, people secondary; (OVER) --

SDS FORUM on IMPERIALISM and VietNAM
—Tuesday, Oct. 14 - 3:00 P.M (room to be announced)

SDS Meeting - THursday - Oct. 16, - NOON
—to discuss Northern Calif. Regional SDS
action with Iranian Student Assoc. against
the Shah of Iran & U.S. Imperialism.

DEMONSTRATE against the Shah of Iran & U.S.
Imperialism in Vietnam — Action called by
Northern Calif. Regional SDS and the Iranian
Student Association - October 21 (details later)

Figure 4.8 ISA Flyer, Social Protest Collection. Bancroft Library, UC Berkeley.

This memory reveals a stark divergence in the affective attachments of Iranian and some American activists, a result of the fact that many US progressives did not view Israel as a colonial project but rather as a manifestation of national liberation for Jews. This incident also situates the ISA on the left flank of a heterogeneous antiwar movement, where anti-Zionism was an expression of revolutionary affects and orientations. It shows how affects of solidarity attach and move in disparate and uneven ways, and illustrates how affective dissonance, named here as "discomfort," can be the means through which political disagreements first emerge.

As the ISA grew in numbers and deepened its affective and political ties with like-minded students, it helped to create antiwar activities that reflected its own internationalist outlook. Vietnamese activists were invited guests at ISA-organized teach-ins and forums in Washington, DC, and Northern California. On October 24, 1973, the ISA cosponsored an event at UC Berkeley with the Union of the Vietnamese in the United States and the KPD (Union of Democratic Filipinos). The event was concerned with political prisoners and torture, and featured speakers from all three groups (figure 4.9).[87] An ISA leaflet written to promote the forum asks, "Do you know that there are some 200,000 political prisoners in more than 1,000 prisons in Thieu controlled South Vietnam?"[88] The leaflet goes into detail about who is being arrested, the conditions they suffer, and how political prisoners are being reclassified as "common criminals" in an effort to avoid censure. It then discusses the plight of political prisoners in the Philippines and in Iran, and argues that "the majority of the people" in all three countries are suffering and struggling against dictatorships backed by the US.[89]

The ISA shared with antiwar activists around the world a tremendous hope that the Vietnamese people would succeed in defeating the US and that this would tip the global balance in favor of Third World liberation movements elsewhere. In a leaflet written for the San Francisco Moratorium March against the war on November 15, 1969, the ISA argued, "The struggle of the heroic Vietnamese workers, peasants, and other revolutionary forces has brought US imperialism to its knees."[90]

As Iranians and Arabs faced off against heavily armed US proxy states in the Middle East, the ISA adapted its immanent critique of US imperialism to address the shifts in strategy and tactics implemented after the Tet Offensive in 1968, namely the "Vietnamization" of the conflict. An ISA leaflet calling for a demonstration in support of the revolution in Oman argues, "The Nixon Doctrine of using the troops of foreign puppet dictators to fight US battles has been used in Vietnam and the Middle East."[91] In 1975, the *Daily Californian* echoed the ISA's analysis: "The Vietnamese war exposed the nature of US imperialism worldwide, and politically isolated it, forcing it to formulate a new foreign policy: *the Nixon-Kissinger Doctrine*. In essence what the Nixon Doctrine says is: 'let the Asians fight the Asians,' or 'let the Iranians fight the Arabs.'"[92]

Members of the ISA argued that Nixon's "Vietnamization" of the war in Southeast Asia was not a regional anomaly but a new imperial modality.

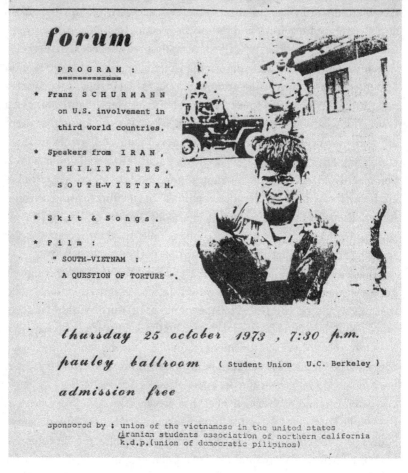

Figure 4.9 ISA Flyer, Social Protest Collection. Bancroft Library, UC Berkeley.

An ISA leaflet from 1973 summarized this analysis: "As the Thieu of the Persian Gulf, the Shah of Iran has been given great responsibilities to protect US and other Western interests there. As part of the Nixon Doctrine, Iran made a $2–3 billion arms deal with the US."[93] Citing a *New York Times* article from November 10, 1972, *Resistance* reported that "when the US was heavily building up Thieu's arsenal, the Shah's regime along with Taiwan and South Korea gave 116 F-5A aircrafts to the Saigon government."[94] The ISA organized protests against Nixon's 1972 trip to Iran and the Shah's 1973 visit to the US, linking them to both internal repression and the militarization of the Persian Gulf region.

The fear of "another Vietnam" was palpable for Iranian foreign student activists, who were haunted by the 1953 coup, outraged by the power of the US to thwart self-determination for Third World peoples, and active in the anti-war movement for over a decade. Indeed, there were over 1,000 American "advisers" stationed in Iran by 1973, and the ISA feared their presence could be the prelude to more direct military intervention, as had happened in Vietnam.[95] As an ISA leaflet calling a protest in defense of the revolution in Oman argues, "The potential is for another Vietnam-type conflict in the Middle East. Only this war would have US-trained Iranian pilots, instead of Americans, doing the dirty work."[96] A few paragraphs down, the same leaflet predicts that events could well spiral out of control, beyond the parameters of the Nixon Doctrine into all-out war.

This possibility led the ISA to issue direct pleas to Americans not to allow themselves to be used against the Iranian people's movement. An ISA-authored article in the *Daily Californian* argued: "*The American people have no interest in the oppression of other people and the stealing of their wealth. . . .* [A]s the struggle sharpens it is a certainty that the US will directly intervene. Americans may be sent to fight and die, to crush a people's revolution, in order to safeguard the profits of big US corporations. But the American people will never stand for this imperialist war!"[97] Fear and urgency pulsed through this emotionally charged appeal as did the presumption, or hope, that the affective map of solidarity connecting Americans to Vietnam could extend to include Iran and the Arab world among its legible coordinates.

Jaleh Pirnazar recalled how dire the situation felt at the time. "Iran could easily become another Vietnam. That's how we framed it because the president in Vietnam had asked for American support against his own people. This could easily happen to Iran. And this is Middle East, this is oil, this is so many ramifications way beyond Vietnam." Through the early to mid-1970s, the ISA held meetings and demonstrations across the country under the banner "Iran the Future Vietnam," and called for the US to "get out of Iran."[98] Such efforts constituted a campaign to preempt public support for this future war by arguing for a divergence of interests and identifications between people and states. "We felt compelled to disconnect ourselves from our government [in Iran]," Jaleh explained: "We would in fact demand that from our American friends as well. You are not your government; you are not representing your government. Neither am I. We are people to people, we have solidarity, we have interests that have been ignored by both of our governments. So that was the connection. That was the bonding." This bond allowed the ISA to work closely with Vietnam Veterans against the War, in addition to SDS, the Union of the Vietnamese in the United States, and the Friends of Indochina, among other antiwar groups.

When the war in Vietnam officially ended, the ISA joined in the celebration, but with an eye toward the implications for liberation movements across the Middle East:

> The victory of the Vietnamese people—the signing of the Peace Agreement on January 27, 1973—has forced Nixon to place all his hopes on the success of US imperialism in the Middle East, particularly in the Persian Gulf. But no amount of military "aid" or gifts of Phantom jets and Laser bombs and no amount of dealing and wheeling such as détente will be able to crush the soaring determination of the people's resistance. Inspired by the victorious struggle of the Indochinese, the people of Palestine, the Persian Gulf and Iran, together with their sisters and brothers in other parts of the Middle East, will continue their struggle against the new efforts of US imperialism and its puppets.[99]

Victory in Vietnam was thus proof that US imperialism could be defeated, but also signaled the need to prepare for an intensification of the Middle Eastern front of US Cold War domination. The ISA's strategy was to call for unity between Arabs and Iranians and to draw out the lessons of Vietnam for the next round of bloody confrontation with US empire. Attachment to revolution, to "the soaring determination of the people's resistance," was reaffirmed as the basis for sustaining and expanding the feelings and practices of solidarity the ISA had been part of for many years. As this passage makes clear, when it came right down to it, solidarity was all the diasporic student Left ever had to offer anticolonial movements in the Third World, and the lesson of Vietnam was that mass antiwar movements in the heart of empire were both possible and necessary.

Conclusion

Like Khosro smashing through the administration building's locked glass door at San Francisco State College, the ISA's involvement in movements against racism, colonization, and war shatters present-day assumptions about Iranian diasporic subjectivity in the US. Rather than ethnic nationalism or religion, ISA members united around a passion for fighting injustice expansive enough to embrace the "freedom dreams" of others.[100] For Iranian foreign student activists, memories of US-sponsored repression—and decades of resistance—in Iran mixed with the inspiration and influence of other radical activists in the US and around the world into powerful affects of solidarity. The melancholic and militant response of ISA members to the ongoing losses of imperialism and dictatorship resonated with the collective refusal of other racialized and colonized people to accept the conditions of their subjugation. Different but related experiences of victimization by the police and armed forces of the US government, by US-backed dictatorships, and by the US-Israel alliance made it possible for African Americans, Asian Americans, Latinx Americans, white Americans, Iranians, Arabs, and other foreign students from across Asia, Africa, and Latin America to imagine themselves working together on a joint project of human liberation. Opposition to state repression, campaigns to free political prisoners, and support for Third World self-determination became mutual sites for the accumulation of affective intensities and attachments, overlapping coordinates on the affective maps of revolutionaries with distinct histories and experiences.

Farid, who was active in Texas and Chicago, recalled with great pride how other activists responded to the ISA and how good it felt to be in a milieu of collective resistance: "The ISA itself was so strong that everybody else wanted to become part of it and have some relation. That's how we were. It was a mutual thing. You didn't have to go and beg someone like you do today and defend your cause. They would love to have their name next to your name, whether it was defending political prisoners or against US imperial policy in the Middle East or Vietnam or wherever. They would gladly do it." The wistfulness in Farid's words expressed a melancholic longing for a time when association with radical Iranians was an everyday practice. His words also remind us that solidarity often feels good, as people take pleasure in the giving and receiving of support and in a sense of personal connection to the power of mass movements.

Several non-Iranian activists confirmed Farid's feelings and commented on the ISA's strength and influence within the broader student movement. Ann Schneider, who was a student activist at the University of Wisconsin–Madison, viewed the ISA as crucial to a successful antiracist campaign on campus in 1979. "It was thanks to the Iranian Students Association that year that brought to power an African American president and vice president of the student government in an alliance we called United Progressives. They were highly organized and had cars, so they drove people to the polls." Mike

Haire met the ISA on his first day of college at the University of Texas–Austin, and continued to work with the ISA later in Houston. "I didn't attend one demonstration in the mid- to late seventies that didn't seem to have an ISA contingent," he said. "What I love about the ISA and what I learned from them more than anything was solidarity. They were (and are) among the best people I have known." Kate, who continued to organize with the ISA in Houston even after she and her Iranian activist boyfriend broke up, elaborated: "They launched a bunch of us as leftists. They really broadened the scope of things. They got people to think much deeper. They were here with a purpose, but they were true internationalists." This formulation, "here with a purpose but true internationalists," describes a way of thinking about the specificity of the Iranian anti-Shah movement's demands for national liberation and its investments in the liberation of others as mutually reinforcing. These memories, brimming with affection and admiration after so many years, recuperate affects of solidarity that could incorporate white, American leftists and Iranian foreign students into the same internationalist revolutionary worldview.

This chapter has centered on Iranian involvement in movements for Black liberation, Arab self-determination, and against the war in Vietnam, crucial locations for the coalescing of Third World internationalism as a feeling and practice of solidarity that mobilized people across multiple sites of difference. It is no coincidence that these three areas of struggle also became important locations for the development of Third World feminism and the circulation of affects of solidarity among Black and Brown women. Women were consistently drawn to the fight for large-scale social transformation. The particular experiences of different groups of women activists in the 1960s illuminated the ways that patriarchy, homophobia, racism, and imperialism were indeed "interlocking" and had to be challenged in comprehensive and dynamic ways this side of the revolution. Third World Women's Alliance was launched in 1968 by women who had been active in SNCC, and the Combahee River Collective was formed in 1974 by women who had been part of SNCC, the Black Panther Party, and the antiwar movement. The participation of Palestinian women in the anticolonial struggle was the context for Arab feminist organizing, including under the umbrella of the General Union of Palestinian Women founded in 1965, while the revolutionary movement in Dhofar was remarkable for its ambitious efforts to center women's liberation.[101] The US-based movement against the war in Vietnam also became a site from which American women of different racial backgrounds developed various iterations of revolutionary feminism.[102] As Rabab Abdulhadi argues, there is no single path to feminist consciousness, and for women involved in anticolonial movements, feminism often emerged from the desire to participate fully and equally in mass organizing and from the hope that revolution would upend all the forms of oppression that impacted their lives.[103]

Chapter 5 looks at how these desires played out within the diasporic Iranian student Left in the US. It is noteworthy that the US feminist movement, even its revolutionary Third Worldist iterations, did not become a site of affective attachment and solidarity for the anti-Shah movement as a whole or, with very few exceptions, for its individual members. The following chapter considers how revolutionary affects were mobilized toward gendered forms of belonging for women and men in the ISA. Rather than position the Iranian experience as exceptional, I take the ISA as a case study of the contradictory experiences of women involved in the making of Third World internationalism.

5

Political Cultures of Revolutionary Belonging

When Mina first encountered members of the ISA as a sociology undergraduate at UC Berkeley in 1971, she immediately stood out from the rest of the group. "I wasn't your typical Iranian when I arrived there, and I think everybody knew that. I had already become a hippie, so I was alternative already." While she shared an upper-class background with many other ISA members in Northern California, she had spent a few years during elementary school in the US, moved back to Iran, and then attended high school in Britain and the US. Not only was her English fluent, but she had been shaped by the Anglo-American counterculture in ways that did not align with the comportment and conduct of other women in the Iranian diasporic Left who had arrived straight from Iran. Whereas dating for male and female ISA members was usually done in private, Mina had a boyfriend whom she did not try to hide. This and her "hippie" style of dress were, for the leadership of the Berkeley ISA chapter, signs that she was politically unserious. "They thought I was too wishy-washy, so they had to put a bra on me," Mina said, laughing. "I was more like a radical American than some of the Iranians. Being a hippie was in conflict [with the ISA's politics] because they [hippies] weren't militants. It just didn't fit in with the culture of militancy of the ISA. There was peer pressure, collective pressure that you feel and you gradually change."

This chapter explores this "culture of militancy," which I understand to be a political culture of norms and practices derived from a feeling of political urgency, from the desire to hasten the coming revolution in Iran. Revolutionary affects attached to this transformative political goal, and also to the desire to belong to an organization of committed, like-minded activists. Revolutionary affects thus generated new forms of diasporic belonging in which the commitment to revolution became inseparable from the commitment to one's political organization and the adoption of its political culture. The prospect of devoting oneself to the cause of revolution proved compelling enough for Mina to transform herself from a "wishy-washy" hippie into a "serious" revolutionary. The fact that this required the upper-class Mina to wear a bra points to the extent to which gender, sexuality, and class were intersecting fault lines in the battle against the Western domination of Iran. Opposition to US imperialism and the Shah's dictatorship meant far more than just attending rallies and joining hunger strikes. It meant rejecting ways of being, habits of behavior, dress, and comportment associated with a decadent and corrupt regime and with a hypersexualized and exploitative West.

It also meant devoting a great deal of one's time, money, and labor to the internal activities necessary to build and sustain ISA chapters. To keep a movement going is no simple task. How would hundreds of young men and women, sometimes from different class, regional, religious, and ethnic backgrounds, manage to work together, trust each other, and support each other far from home? In many ways, this problem proved more challenging than building solidarity with other, non-Iranian movements because relations among Iranian student activists were a far more intimate affair. While the presence of women was generally celebrated as evidence of just how democratic and representative the ISA was, gender performance, class hierarchy, and sexual desire generated discomfort as potential sources of discord, disunity, and threat. Peer pressure to conform to new revolutionary sexual and gender norms was one common strategy for negotiating, and attempting to suppress, the tensions and differences among ISA members, and reveals the extent to which conflictual politics of class, gender, and sexuality converged on the bodies of Iranian women.

Revolutionary affects drew many Iranian students in the US away from the class privileges and career opportunities that characterized their imperial model minority status and trajectory. In this chapter, I explore what this profound reorientation looked and felt like in practice. The internal political cultures of ISA chapters were shaped predominantly by the politics of whichever Iranian leftist faction was most influential in a given location, rather than by any simplistic, static notion of Iranian or Muslim culture. Across all of these Marxist groups, it was not religion, ethnic nationalism, or blood ties that bound Iranian students together but the desire to overthrow the Shah and build a new, more just society. In the 1960s, Maoism became dominant among the Union of Iranian Communists (UIC) and the Revolutionary Organization (RO), while the National Front (NF) took a Third World Marxist turn. By the early 1970s, after China had established diplomatic relations with the Shah, CISNU became openly critical of Mao's foreign policy. The 1970s also saw the advent of armed struggle launched by both the Fadaiyan and the Mojahedin, which drew support across various student factions, including the RO and the NF. Some ISA members affiliated themselves directly with the Fadaiyan, which itself had Maoist and Stalinist tendencies toward dogmatism, hierarchy, and strict discipline. In the effort to bring about freedom, life could become rigidly circumscribed.

Below, I explore this contradiction and the affective dissonances it generated, analyzing the memories of former ISA members in order to make sense of the sacrifices, risks, pleasures, and disappointments that shaped the lived experience of Third World internationalism. This chapter argues that the ISA was a site of open contestation over the content and form of women's participation in revolutionary movements. First, I introduce the key conceptual terms that anchor my analysis of the ISA's political culture as a temporal and affective disruption of the imperial model minority mission. Then I look at how revolutionary affects expressed gendered forms of subjectivity both as a reaction to the gender and sexual politics of the alliance between the US and the Shah, and as a desire for equality. Finally, I work against exceptionalizing the Iranian leftist experience or reducing its oppressive aspects to Iranian or Muslim culture. I argue that the new forms of gender and sexual regulation carried out in the name of unity, discipline, and commitment to ending oppression were part of the broader, gendered expression of revolutionary affects of the era.

This chapter continues the case studies of the ISA in Northern California and Washington, DC, from the previous chapter, while also incorporating interviews with former ISA activists from the Texas-Oklahoma and Philadelphia ISA chapters. In this way, I delve deeply into lived experiences rooted in particular locations and also offer a perspective on regional and sectarian variations and continuities within the Iranian student movement in the US. Using a methodology of possibility to read these experiences, I argue that diasporic subjectivity and political orientation may emerge from a wellspring of alienation, rather than accommodation to the prevailing order. Ultimately, this chapter works against the erasure of failed gestures toward freedom, mining the diasporic leftist experiment for what it might teach us about the still unresolved tensions between national liberation, women's liberation, and the notion of freedom.

Revolutionary Time, Revolutionary Sociality, and "Gender Sameness"

For most former ISA activists I interviewed, commitment to the revolution became the singular priority that dominated every other aspect of life. This manifested as a deep and consuming commitment to one's organization. Ali Hojat, a leading member of the Northern California ISA chapter who was active with the RO, explained, "Going to school was just an excuse to get your visa. We really didn't care." He laughed. "We didn't think we were going to live that long because we were going back to Iran, to the underground—that was the plan." While some ISA members were encouraged to finish their studies so they could return to Iran openly, find jobs, and financially support the comrades working underground, many others never finished their degrees or completed them years later, after the revolution in Iran had taken place. Ali was working toward a master's degree in economics at San Jose State College when he left the US to conduct clandestine party work for the RO in Europe, India, and then Iran. Those students who were heading home to join the underground were fully aware of the risks involved. "We knew that the average life of someone doing political activity against the Shah [inside Iran] would be about two years, three years," Ali said in his jovial, matter-of-fact way. "They usually arrested you or killed you by then."

The logic embedded in this affective attachment to self-sacrifice—the willingness to die for the revolution—reconfigured the relationship to time for these erstwhile imperial model minorities.[1] Instead of orienting themselves toward future careers as neocolonial modernizers in Iran and the reproduction of the bourgeois patriarchal family, they rejected normative markers of stability and respectability along with the very notion of capitalist progress. Hundreds of ISA cadre existed instead in a revolutionary temporality, a fleeting present overshadowed by an imminent utopian future that they knew they might not live to see. Jila, active in the Northern California ISA from 1971 to 1979, described the internalization of the revolutionary imperative as follows: "There was this feeling that a revolution in Iran and the US was imminent, that in the US in twenty years everybody would be equal," she remembered. Or as Parviz, active in the same chapter from 1965 to 1979, put it: "We thought that we could really change the world, so any sacrifice was worth it."

Both Jila and Parviz described a temporal shift away from the forward march of capitalist development and toward a revolutionary temporality. By orienting themselves toward an alternative revolutionary future, diasporic

Iranian student leftists ruptured what Anne McClintock has called "national time," an evolutionary notion of time in which non-Western nations had to either catch up to Western standards of living or be left behind in a premodern era.[2] National time clings to an invented past to naturalize and "popularize the idea of linear national Progress."[3] While the Shah and the Islamist opposition mobilized competing, idealized notions of Iran's true and glorious past to bolster their arguments over what shape the modern nation-state should take, the leftist students of the ISA dispensed with the backward gaze of nationalism altogether. Their affective attachment was not to any longing for a lost world, nor was it to a particular plan for the postrevolutionary society, but rather to the overthrow itself. Revolutionary time did, however, share with national time a gendered notion of self-sacrifice. Whereas nationalism demands that women subordinate themselves to the needs of the new nation-state as transmitters of authentic culture and as reproducers of new national citizens, the revolutionary imperative demanded that women make themselves fit to join the movement by subsuming and remaking themselves within it.[4]

Through participation in new forms of social relations, Iranian foreign student activists remade themselves into revolutionary subjects. The collective refusal of imperial model minorities to gain mastery over the system as it was, or to embrace the temporal, productive, and reproductive requirements of capitalist-imperialist progress, manifested in alternative communities and social relations organized around what I call "revolutionary sociality." The gender and sexual politics that governed this sociality departed substantially, but not entirely, from the politics and practices of anticolonial nationalism. Women ISA members were not consigned to supporting roles as wives and mothers, or cooks and typists. They were not called upon to embody what McClintock calls "nationalism's conservative principle of continuity," but to model and prefigure a new Iranian revolutionary subjectivity that could only exist in revolutionary time.[5] Rather than invoking a glorious Iranian past, the ISA was firmly rooted in a future-oriented, Third World Marxism that managed to idealize the "masses" while remaining rather disconnected from the specificities of Iranian society.

The urgency and intensity of revolutionary time collapsed any distinctions between revolutionary sociality and revolutionary political goals, making the everyday actions of students feel charged with world historic significance. When Sina, who was active in the RO, looked back on his years in the movement he said, "Generally speaking, it did not appear at all bizarre that you belong so much to a cause that you are a part of a collective subject.

Things seemed natural and normal and obvious and legitimate that today appear like sacrifice." At the time, he said, "You didn't think twice. It was our age in a double sense: the age at which we were and the age in which we were." Sina thus offered another way of describing the revolutionary temporality that governed the lives of Iranian foreign student activists. His formulation invokes a connection between youthful optimism and energy and the historical moment in which these Iranian students happened to be young. At that age, and in that age, a "collective subject" was produced and reproduced through the quotidian and intimate details of daily life, including through negotiations of class, gender, and sexuality. Iranian women who came to study in the United States in the 1960s and 1970s were a small minority of the foreign student population, which was still 90 percent male in 1973.[6] The women who did go abroad were almost exclusively from the middle and upper classes of Iranian society, with far less class variation than among male foreign students.

In diaspora, women demanded and were sometimes encouraged to take their rightful place alongside men in the student movement, an egalitarian gesture that simultaneously facilitated the regulation of gender performance and sexual desire. Equality between men and women was imagined through "gender sameness," an ideology that offered an alternative to female sexual objectification and the normative roles of wife and mother. "Gender sameness" rested upon the fantasy that by transcending gender difference and abandoning the degraded category of the "feminine," women could also transcend gender-based oppression. Sexual oppression and compulsory heterosexuality were left untheorized and unchallenged, as was the gender binary itself. While I name the ideology "gender sameness" to emphasize the claims to egalitarian gender relations informing members' understanding of what was taking place and their willingness to participate, it was always and only women who were supposed to become the same as men, never the other way around. Parvin Paidar called this process "masculinization," highlighting the gap between ideology and practice.[7] I argue that gender sameness/masculinization expressed the revolutionary affects of Iranian women in the ISA—that is, their desire to participate equally in a revolutionary struggle. By adjusting their bodily comportment and keeping their sexual attractions and relations secret, Iranian women activists believed they could help to forge unity between men and women and increase the likelihood of the movement's success. Unity itself was masculinized, and this would have significant consequences for the Iranian Left during the 1978–79 revolution (see chapter 6).

In the late 1960s and 1970s, the ideals of gender sameness and practices of masculinization that came to dominate the Iranian Left in the US were markedly different from either Westernized or Islamist versions of femininity circulating in Iran. Yet all of these clashing ideas about how women should comport themselves were reactions to the alliance between imperialism and dictatorship, between Westernized modernity and the Shah's authoritarianism. This was just as true for the pro-Shah sections of Iranian society as for the anti-Shah sections, and goes some way toward accounting for similarities between secular and religious ideas about women's bodies, behaviors, and sexuality. Gender sameness/masculinization rested on logics that foreshadowed the gender politics of the religious forces that sought to construct a new, revolutionary Iranian identity in 1978–79. The leftist failure, in Haideh Moghissi's words, "to clarify any difference existing between socialist morality and patriarchal, religious-based morality on matters related to sexuality, personal autonomy and women's personal freedoms" facilitated acceptance or indifference toward the Islamist nationalist regulation of women in revolutionary Iran.[8] In other words, the gender politics of the Left colluded with those of anticolonial religious forces around a shared acceptance of females and femininity as degraded and, therefore, in need of revolutionary intervention and regulation.

The establishment of the Islamic Republic, with unequal terms of citizenship for men and women, has reinforced the association between women's oppression and Islam among many Iranians inside Iran as well as in the West. Haideh Moghissi and Minoo Moallem, feminist scholars who were both participants in the underground leftist opposition in Iran in the 1970s, complicate this reductionist analysis by exploring the complicity of the secular Iranian Left with Islamic populism in general, and particularly in relation to women's rights. Although through differing theoretical and political lenses, each considers the Iranian Revolution as emblematic of the wider phenomenon in which women's liberation was sidelined by the project of anticolonial nation-building. As Moallem argues, the Iranian Left's "revolutionary culture was a transnational production rooted in Third World revolutionary and anticolonial movements."[9] Interpreting the work of Moghissi and Moallem from the vantage point of diaspora makes salient the unique combination of Iranian and non-Iranian influences that impacted anti-Shah leftist political culture. These include polarizing conflicts over gender and sexuality within an Iranian society caught in the crosshairs of empire and dictatorship, classical Marxist formulations of "the woman question," and the influence of revolutionary Third World movements in the 1960s and 1970s.

The space of diaspora makes apparent how much the Iranian Left had in common with other non-Iranian revolutionary anti-imperialist movements. The shared revolutionary affects of Iranians, radicalized Americans, and other foreign student activists also generated a shared revolutionary temporality. From the Black Panthers to the Popular Front for the Liberation of Palestine, many movements developed internal political cultures and gender and sexual norms that subordinated individual needs and desires; these norms were based on the assumption that any individual might not live to see the better world to come. While particular racial, ethnic, and national backgrounds and histories structured the context in which leftist ideas were interpreted and applied in any organization, the decisive impact of the Chinese Cultural Revolution on an entire generation of young revolutionaries cannot be overstated, especially when it came to conceptions of women's participation in the revolutionary cause.[10] The primary agents of change Mao deputized to carry out this vast experiment in reshaping subjectivity were students. Like many student radicals in Europe, North America, and across the Third World, ISA members attempted no less than their own cultural revolution in order to purge bourgeois habits associated with the alliance between US empire and the Shah's dictatorship.

This mandate for changing individual and collective ways of being was sometimes leveraged to challenge "traditional" forms of male chauvinism within the ranks of the ISA. In the relatively less restrictive social and political space of US college campuses, there was more room to put into practice new "revolutionary" ideals of gender equality than there was for the leftists operating underground in Iran, where police state conditions and social/familial restrictions created additional obstacles to the flourishing of this pre-1979 cultural revolution of the Left. As Vida Samiian, a UCLA student who became a press spokesperson for the ISA in the late 1970s, explained, "I was always rebellious in Iran, but now in the US my rebellion could manifest openly." Below, I look at the conditions that generated this rebellion among a swath of Vida's generation and consider the gendered forms it took within a revolutionary diaspora.

Gender, Sexuality, and Revolutionary Affects

The Iranian women who came to the US to study in the 1960s and 1970s were, in the words of Minoo Moallem, "born into an uncompromising world of binaries in the middle of a culture war."[11] They had grown up during a period in which bourgeois, urban femininity was hyper-Westernized in the service of a patriarchal dictatorship that promoted modernization against tradition. Ever since the Constitutional Revolution at the beginning of the twentieth century, calls for women's rights were bound up with the push for modernization and secularization by intellectuals and Iranian feminists who saw feudalism and religion as barriers to Iran's advancement and its ability to resist colonial domination.[12] In 1935, during the reign of Reza Shah, the ministries of education and of the interior issued directives mandating the unveiling of women.[13] Despite the opposition of many women, who found their mobility and independence restricted as a result, women's bodies became a site of state-imposed modernization.[14] After 1953, religious opponents of the alliance between the US and the Shah criticized state policies that aimed to ameliorate the condition of women (on paper if not often in practice), attacking the extension of voting rights and changes in family laws as un-Islamic and a sign of Western erosion of Iranian sovereignty. In this polarized context, clandestine leftist political activity against the regime offered some women a way of rejecting both Westernization and religious appeals to "tradition" and "authenticity" as they searched instead for what Moallem has called "unattainable, outlawed and underground forms of knowing and feeling." For women like her: "The arena of social movements was also a space where we could distance ourselves from colonial and modernist civilizing models concerning femininity and seek refuge in a world where relations were less rigidly patriarchal and gender identities more ambiguous. Our need to participate in these social movements allowed for all kinds of imaginary and material transgressions and overruled the cultural pressures to conform to certain gender identities."[15] In diaspora, physically removed from the pressures of family and Iranian society, safe from the immediate threat of SAVAK torture chambers, Iranian women had the unprecedented opportunity to refashion themselves as revolutionary subjects. This was a highly contradictory process, enabling many women to experience new feelings of equality and empowerment as long as they adhered to certain conditions of belonging.

Iranian women in the ISA found themselves negotiating male domination as it manifested in the sexist behavior of male comrades *and* as it structured ideas about the meaning of women's liberation within the broader anti-imperialist vision of freedom popular at the time.[16] Women and men in the ISA did make efforts—however uneven, under-theorized, and inadequate—to implement a politics of women's equality. They openly grappled with ideas and practices about gender and sexuality they had absorbed from the Iranian context, as well as what they gleaned from Chinese and other Third World revolutionary experiments, and borrowed from the classics of Marxist literature. In addition, feminist analysis and criticism filtered into the ISA as the women's liberation movement influenced the activist milieu on and off college campuses in the 1970s.

"We had a tendency to dismiss American feminism as a bourgeois movement," said Zohreh Khayam, who was a master's student at Howard University, active in the Washington, DC, chapter of the ISA and a supporter of the Fadaiyan. However, she went on to add, "I think, even though we were not exactly in favor of American feminism, we were really impacted by it hugely." Jaleh Pirnazar, a UC Berkeley student active in the Northern California ISA and the RO, explained that, despite the distance she kept from feminist organizations, she nonetheless recognized similarities between the critique US feminists were making and her own experiences.[17] Iranian women in CISNU did not use the word *feminism* even as they adopted some of its analytical components. When I asked Jaleh if she and her comrades used terms like "patriarchy" or "chauvinism" to talk about gender relations in Iran and in the ISA, she answered, "Yes. Big time." It seemed quite obvious to talk in such terms, she said, "because Iranian culture is very much patriarchal. If a boy is born, oh, congratulations and so on. If a girl is born, not so much. So we were raising this awareness. Part of it came from the radical movement of women in this country [the US]."

At the same time, the language of feminism and women's rights put the ISA in an uncomfortable position. After all, the Shah's White Revolution incorporated this language into its modernizing rhetoric. "The Shah had launched a family protection law in which women were given rights to divorce," Jaleh said. "So we were at conflict [over] how to face this because after all he's taking some steps in the right directions. We would denounce the whole thing because we thought this is coming from above." The ISA criticized the Shah's package of reforms as little more than a propaganda effort to represent the dictatorship as progressive. While the Shah did raise the age of marriage and offer women rights to divorce and work outside the home, there were no enforcement mechanisms and many loopholes, leaving the majority of Iranian women unaffected by these policies.[18] When the Shah's government created the Women's Organization of Iran in 1966, the ISA viewed it as another attempt to obscure the true nature of the regime.[19] Because the ISA was opposed to Iranian state feminism, Iranian student activists in the US were unsure of how to relate to the grassroots women's movement springing up around them.

By the late 1960s, many women, and some men, began to speak up about the persistent problems they witnessed and experienced within the ISA. As more Iranian women than ever before were sent to study abroad in the mid-to-late 1970s, and their presence in the movement increased, women in the ISA were decisive in challenging what they identified as "traditional male chauvinism" among their comrades. For example, Zohreh, one of fifteen to twenty women active in the Washington, DC, ISA chapter that numbered 100 to 120 members, recalled, "My first presentation in the ISA was about chauvinism and the manifestations of chauvinism in our culture, in any culture, and I explained what that meant."[20]

The Northern California ISA chapter based in Berkeley had, according to Jaleh Behroozi and Ahmad Taghvai, approximately 300 active members at its height in the late 1970s, a third of whom were women.[21] This proportion of women activists, vastly disproportionate to their numbers in the overall foreign student population, resulted from conscious efforts to change what had been an overwhelmingly male-dominated organization. Indeed, the Berkeley chapter appears to have initiated institutional changes that spread to other chapters across the country. Under the auspices of the Organizational Committee, which was responsible for the daily running of the local ISA, several members formed a "committee against male chauvinism" to investigate the low levels of women's participation in the movement and propose solutions.[22] Along with chapters around the US, the Berkeley ISA held regular study groups on women's oppression that featured texts by Marx, Engels, Lenin, Alexandra Kollontai, and Clara Zetkin.[23] By studying this socialist canon, activists firmly established "the woman question" within the ISA's political and educational repertoire. But what it meant to apply a Marxist analysis of women's oppression to the social and cultural life of the group was far from clear. Jaleh, who was also active in the UIC, recalled:

When we started the conversation inside the organization it was very superficial. For example, [we told the men], you shouldn't open the door for women. But gradually the conversations became about the importance of women taking on leadership roles. The discussions helped. For instance, I became someone who would take responsibilities. I wasn't assertive at all in my own background, especially coming from a minority within Iran. I'm Jewish, so it was some sort of feeling about you are not a part of this group. But these discussions helped me to feel that I'm a part of this group, you are not a stranger, you feel a sense of family, you are equal, not a minority and they have accepted you as the leader of that task.

The desire to belong, then, was charged with other histories of marginalization and silence that had different affective registers, depending on the identities and experiences of each individual. As a Jewish woman, Jaleh found that recognition as a political leader brought feelings of equality that were deeply affectively rewarding.

When the Berkeley ISA committee against male chauvinism decided to launch an ongoing women's committee, Jaleh Behroozi and Jaleh Pirnazar, both Jewish women, joined. In the late 1960s, this women's committee produced a pamphlet in Persian titled "University Women Are Getting Organized," which was reproduced and distributed to ISA chapters across the US.[24] The pamphlet cited the SDS resolution against male chauvinism from 1967.[25] Many passages of the pamphlet focused on applying economistic Marxist formulations of women's oppression to the Iranian context, viewing gender inequality as a subset of labor exploitation that could only disappear after the revolution against feudalism, capitalism, and imperialism. However, the pamphlet also trespassed into feminist territory, arguing that male chauvinism permeated all social relations across classes and had to be fought resolutely in the here and now, including within the ISA.[26] While Moghissi has argued that "young educated women from the new and traditional middle classes" in Iran supported the revolution for reasons that "were, in most cases, no different from their male counterparts," the ISA women's committee in Northern California attempted to appeal to women *as women* with specifically gendered grievances, histories, and desires.[27]

By the mid-1970s, even as internal splits fractured the movement organizationally, many chapters had established women's committees, which held study groups on "the woman question," and annual celebrations of International Women's Day. This occasion often prompted ISA and CISNU publications to run articles on the plight of working class and peasant women in Iran. Women in the ISA represented the Iranian student movement at International Women's Day events sponsored by American organizations as well, including SDS. Eventually, quotas were adopted to ensure women's representation in leadership bodies of the ISA. For example, out of the five-person national secretariat, two places were reserved for women.[28]

Jaleh Pirnazar, who served as an elected member of the ISA's national secretariat in the 1970s, remembered feeling emboldened to openly challenge the actions of male comrades in ways that disrupted the traditional gendered division of labor: "I cannot say we were all feminist at that time because this was not quite [how it was] in the Iranian movement. But we demanded rights;

we wanted equality. If we were to break for lunch, it wasn't like, 'Okay girls get us some coffee' or 'Girls get us our sandwiches.' Especially, the group I was in, [which was composed of] leftists, these men are all for democracy and equality. So we would take them to task." Overall, Jaleh felt there was a limited attention span for the topic of women's oppression and liberation. "This was an ongoing problem in the American movement as well," she said. "I mean, there were hardly any men joining the women's cause. [Men in the ISA] were kind of like, 'Okay, it's a nice thing to have.' But if there was a time conflict with another committee, [they would say], 'Change that women's committee, come to this one. This is more important.'"

The men I interviewed, including Ali Hojat (the only man to join the women's committee in Berkeley), generally agreed with the assessment that the women's committee was not always taken seriously. "Other men, they sort of laughed at me," he remembered. Sina, active in Philadelphia, recalled a "genuine and honest attempt" to create gender equality. He felt that "compared with the baseline of who we were in Iran at the time," relations between the genders were quite advanced in the ISA. "Many chapters had female leaders, and females were among the leaders of the leftist organizations in Iran," he said. "But still, the girls of course constantly complained that we are still male chauvinist. But we couldn't see it. We'd say, 'You are my leader. I am accepting you. How can I be male chauvinist?'" Even while he tried to be self-critical, Sina expressed a lingering confusion over what exactly male domination looked like within the movement, evidence of the murkiness clouding the substance and meaning of women's equality. Like many male comrades, he hoped the "problem" could be solved through merely organizational adjustments, like leadership quotas, while the underlying assumptions about gender and sexual hierarchies that infused the movement's political culture remained unexamined. This meant there was a gap between even the institutionalized egalitarian intentions of Iranian diasporic activists and the ongoing enactment of male domination in practice.

Still, when compared with Moghissi's assessment of the leftist political culture in Iran, in which women "were neither gender-conscious nor committed to a feminist agenda" and "were confined to acting within an ideological framework set by male ideologues," the ISA became a place where gender consciousness emerged as women fought for autonomy and political influence within the movement, asserting their own equality in new ways. At the same time, enormous obstacles remained, ironically sustained by the same temporal and social forms that made revolutionary belonging so compelling.

Social Reproduction in Revolutionary Time(s)

Rejecting the normative markers of individual success and national progress, the ISA encouraged members to prioritize political work over everything else. Most of the Iranian diasporic leftist parties went even further,
demanding that members subordinate their personal lives to the needs of
their organizations and, in some cases, prepare to accept the personal risks of
returning to Iran to carry out illegal opposition activity. In the US South, Bijan
worked as an ISA organizer in Texas, Oklahoma, and Louisiana throughout
the 1970s, and also helped to recruit people to the UIC, the leftist party that
came to dominate the Iranian student movement in those states. "It was
very radical. It was massive," he said of the ISA membership in the region,
and he went on to summarize the revolutionary imperative that redirected
people's lives: "It basically got to a point [where the norm became] don't
go to school, which was different from other places. So you're not going to
school because you're not planning to do anything with your education.
Because you want to go [to Iran to] fight, you want to go organize. Why
do you need academic institutions?" This was not a general rule for all ISA
members. Rather, Bijan explained, "If you pass[ed] a level of activism in the
hierarchy in the organization, they were not expecting you to say, 'Oh, I have
to go finish my homework.' That's out of the question."

These high expectations had far-reaching implications for gender roles
and social reproduction. As Farid, who was a supporter of the Fadaiyan
and active in the ISA in Texas and Illinois, explained: "We didn't believe in
having kids; having kids was a burden to everything else you wanted to do.
I mean, you don't even know how long you're going to stay alive, why you
want to bring someone else? The life of a guerrilla in Iran was less than six
months. We knew that. That's the reason why it wasn't hard to make a decision about the other things, when you've already decided about your life."
This injunction against having children was in some ways the most direct
challenge to the reproductive futurity of nationalism, which assigns women
the politicized duty of producing future citizens. One ISA member, who
asked to remain anonymous, revealed that when she became pregnant, she
was "asked to abort" by the male leaders of the leftist organization to which
she belonged. As she spoke, tears gathered in her eyes. "I still remember.
I complied. I went ahead, but it's not easy. It was my first pregnancy. I was
really young, in my twenties. So I went ahead, but it's always been a major
issue with me, an injury. I never forgave them." The order "to abort" was
a far cry from the anticolonial and diasporic nationalist tendency to define

a woman's social function primarily through the institutions of the family and motherhood.²⁹ Yet, this order still denied her control over her own body. If national time depends on women's roles as wives and mothers, "revolutionary time" depends on a willingness to sacrifice oneself for the revolution. Both that willingness and the form that those sacrifices would take were thoroughly gendered.

Of course, sacrifice can sometimes feel good. Aside from a minimal amount of time spent studying and a few shifts a week doing working-class jobs off the books, members spent much of their time together cultivating what many referred to as an alternative form of kinship. Jila, one of only three people I interviewed who never joined a leftist party, worked in the international affairs section of the ISA as a journalist for its English-language newspaper, *Resistance*. She described the rhythm of her days: "We'd get up early, eat terrible food. We didn't sleep much. We'd spend all day going from one committee to another. Our parents were sending money expecting their children to become doctors and lawyers, but my heart was not in my education. It was a secondary thing." At the same time, "It was a lot of fun too," she recalled, "like living in a dorm. It was not a small group; there were hundreds of people." Nationally, there were thousands, a network of support that could be mobilized at a moment's notice. Wherever her activism took her—Oklahoma, Chicago, New York—Jila had "comrades, *rafigh*." "There was this pride," she said, "this sense of belonging."

This sense of belonging was often tested. "You were constantly criticized if you were not active," Jila said. The leadership encouraged "*enteghad* sessions" (criticism and self-criticism), what she called "a carbon copy of Marxism-Leninism." For example, "they would wait for me to criticize myself because I didn't go to a demonstration," she said, "because I went to class [instead], and I wouldn't do it." She suspected that this lack of total compliance accounts for why she was never recruited to join one of the underground leftist parties. "They never considered me top rank and file," she said. "There was no room for independent thinking."

Soosan came to the US in 1978 and quickly became immersed in the Iranian student left, both through the ISA and the UIC in Berkeley. "I actually went to adult school to learn English," she said. "But then I got so passionate about this work. My priority was that Iran has to be a democratic country and that's the only thing I was thinking." She said that the UIC "didn't value people to go to school or get [formally] educated. They wanted everybody to work full time as a full-time activist. I don't want to blame them; that was everybody's approach. I was accepting it, too. It was like a family, especially for me." With no work visa and no English skills, she worked as a dishwasher and shared a one-bedroom apartment with four or five other comrades. "We didn't care," she said. "We'd sleep on the floor. We'd eat a can of beans for a day. I remember some days I was so hungry!" She laughed and exclaimed, "We didn't have anything! But I never thought, just leave, go and live your life. I was a young woman. I could go to school. I could party. It wasn't like we were trapped. It wasn't like that. It was a family, our group. We were supporting each other 100 percent."

The bonds forged within this alternative family established a revolutionary kinship that often took priority over biological ties and obligations, sometimes resulting in painful conflicts with parents. Upper-middle-class Iranian parents often had difficulty understanding their children's refusal to take advantage of an American education and the lucrative career opportunities that awaited them back home. Jaleh Pirnazar and Ali Hojat both became alienated from their biological families as a result of their political activity in the US. Over tea and sandwiches in Ali's small print shop in Oakland, California, they told me their stories.

Both Jaleh and Ali were active members of the RO in addition to the Northern California ISA. The more active they became, the more pressure their families felt from the Iranian government. In 1970, after SAVAK questioned Jaleh's parents about their daughter's activities, her mother made a trip to Berkeley to find out what exactly was going on:

[My mother] was staying at my apartment, and my apartment was a *khune-e hezbi* [house used for political party activity]. Everybody was there. I mean some of these young students were working night shifts at a GM facility. They would come to the house at three o'clock in the morning. They would drop there, falling asleep before the next shift or waiting to go in the morning. They demanded nothing. Just a little blanket. My mom would wake up, and she'd have to tippy-toe over these bodies. "Who's this guy snoring? What's happening? Your apartment isn't even yours!" It was a shock. It had become a collective lifestyle, and of course my mom couldn't understand that. Then I introduced her to my future fiancé. Not Jewish. Radical. No money. "I wanted a better life for you," she said.

Although it pained Jaleh to disappoint her mother, her new life was so compelling that she never really considered abandoning it. For Jaleh, her inclusion in the ISA also countered her marginalization in Muslim-majority Iranian society. "As a Jewish woman who has always been on the fringes," she explained, "for a period in my life, I found this space and this recognition.

I excelled, and my potentials were being realized and met." Jaleh's vocal support for Palestine was also "a thorny issue"; she had "family members who left Iran to go to Israel because of anti-Semitism. So how do I reconcile all of these issues?" she asked, as if still grappling with the difficult subject position she had chosen. Disconnecting herself from her family and "stepping outside of tradition … wasn't easy," she said, "but we felt so strongly about our convictions and were so proud of our newly found identities as social activists, as political leaders trying to make change in the world."

When Ali's father traveled to Berkeley to check up on him, the consequences made headlines in Iran. "I became famous in the sense of my father disowning me because of my political activities," Ali said. In 1970, his father was a two-star general in the Shah's army and chief of staff at the Defense Ministry when Ali, along with Jaleh and thirty-nine other Iranian students, became part of the "ISA 41" who were arrested for occupying the Iranian consulate in San Francisco (as described in chapter 3). Ali faced criminal charges and deportation proceedings, prompting a four-star general to dispatch Ali's father to the US on a mission to "go and take care of your son." When his father returned to Iran, he was required to file a report that the Shah himself would read. "According to my father," Ali said, "SAVAK added the part that 'I disown my son.' This is what he said. Or he might have written that himself. I really don't know; either version could be true. Anyhow, they published this in the newspaper." Jaleh interjected: "This was a bombshell, okay? A high-ranking army official disowning his son because of political activity! This was front-page news. My parents read it. They talked about it for years." This incident did not dissuade Ali from pursuing the path he had chosen. By 1976 he was a full-time field organizer for the RO in Europe and India, recruiting and training Iranian students to join the underground opposition just as soon as they could find a safe passage home. These stories illustrate the deep affective attachment to revolutionary kinship and sociality that made even the very public loss of parental approval bearable. Yet Ali was also overcome with emotion when he talked about his estrangement from his father and had to leave the room. Such recollections overflow with unfinished pain, as losses that could not be mourned at the time still carry their affective charge decades later.

The ambivalence of this affective legacy of revolutionary sociality and time can also be seen in attachments to the ISA as a substitute for lost biological kinship ties—lost to distance but also to political disagreements and the secretive habits associated with preparing to go underground. The movement itself became a "family" capable of replacing the biological one.

In this iteration, family is synonymous with identification and belonging. However, given the central role of the family in perpetuating patriarchal gender and sexual relations, and, as McClintock has described, the use of the family as the controlling metaphor for nationalisms across the political spectrum, this repeated analogy of "family" cannot but carry contradictory meanings and implications.[30]

The notion of the movement as family gestures toward an alternative to normative, patriarchal configurations of kinship and social reproduction, with new options for how men and women could see themselves and relate to one another, especially since marriage and childbirth were discouraged. However, even while Iranian anti-Shah student activists rejected some forms of normativity, men continued to retain significant power in the movement through a retrenchment of certain unquestioned aspects of familial relations, including the generally accepted presumption that real (intellectual) authority resided with men, the social and organizational mandate to place the needs of the group ahead of those of the individual, and the personal desire to avoid any actions that might abrogate the terms of belonging. Below, I look in more detail at how the ISA's unconventional social structures mobilized these gendered family dynamics, in which those individuals who are expected to be the most self-abnegating are women. A focus on the affective investments of women themselves in new forms of revolutionary subjectivity can help illuminate the contradictions and tensions that attended the inclusion of women in anticolonial movements.

Gender, Sexuality, and the "Culture of the Proletariat"

The forms of Third World internationalism that flourished in the 1960s and 1970s had a decisive impact on the young people that joined the ISA. Cuba, Algeria, Palestine, Vietnam, along with other anticolonial movements, became objects of study and sources of inspiration; elements of each were incorporated into the political cultures of the ISA and their US contemporaries. However, the dramatic undertaking of the Chinese Cultural Revolution in 1966 meant that Maoism became the major conduit of Marxism to a generation of young activists from marginalized and colonized locations. In a seminal article, Robin D. G. Kelley and Betsy Esch argue that "China offered Black radicals a 'colored,' or Third World, Marxist model that enabled them to challenge a white and Western vision of class struggle [and] proved to Black folks the world over that they need not wait for 'objective conditions' to make a revolution."[31] This was just as true for the Iranian "new Left" that came of age after the 1953 coup during a period of mass disillusionment with traditional Iranian communism (the Tudeh Party). Like the Black Panthers, ISA members were attracted to the idea that racialized, colonized, and "semi-colonized" peoples could lead a revolutionary transformation that would remake their own subjectivities at the same time. When it came to the place of women, Kelley and Esch explain, simple references to "Mao's dictum 'women hold up half the sky' as well as his brief writings on women's equality and participation in the revolutionary process endowed women's liberation with some revolutionary legitimacy on the left."[32]

Considering the similarities in the dynamics surrounding gender and sexuality within the Black Panther Party, the most significant Black Maoist revolutionary organization in the US, and the ISA, helps decenter Islam as the sole explanation for the persistence of patriarchy among the Iranian Left and more clearly identify the weaknesses that marked secular Third World internationalism of that era. In a ground-breaking study, Robyn C. Spencer writes, "While [Black] Panther literature promoted internal revolution and provided both men and women with the tools to critique gender discrimination, sexist attitudes persisted and sometimes even thrived within the organization."[33] This literature included Black Panther cofounder Huey Newton's open letter, published in the party newspaper in 1970, theorizing support for gay and lesbian rights. Such stated commitments to gender and sexual equality encouraged many Panther women to argue that "male chauvinism and all its manifestations are bourgeois and . . . the success of the revolution depends upon the women."[34] However, Spencer observes, "these issues were not given priority within the organization. Conflicts about gender were subsumed under the larger category of potentially divisive criticism."[35] This summary also characterizes the experiences of Iranian women in the ISA and the response of the Iranian Left, especially during the upheavals of 1979–80.

Kelley and Esch end their article with a discussion of the affective and ideological links between Black Maoism and the biblical story of David and Goliath, in which the underdog fights back and wins against a much stronger enemy.[36] The desire for dignity, freedom, and self-determination connected old and new idioms of Black liberation on the affective maps of Black revolutionaries, expanding a cartography of Black radical thought that had long included Old Testament parables of emancipation. In the case of Iranian leftist students in the ISA, Maoism, Guevarism, and other Third World anticolonial models may certainly have connected to affective maps that already included the Shi'i story of Hussein surrounded at Karbala, what Farah Azari has called "an uprising by the forces of good seeking justice and a rebellion against the forces of tyranny ... all in the face of impossible odds and at a cost of martyrdom."[37] Unlike the victorious David, Hussein, along with virtually his entire family, is mercilessly slaughtered. The affective and political significance of martyrdom in Iranian Shi'ism resonated with the calls for self-sacrifice and discipline made under the sign of revolutionary commitment, which were perfectly encapsulated in Mao's "little red book" injunction that a communist should "at no time and in no circumstances ... place his personal interests first; he should subordinate them to the interests of the nation and of the masses."[38] Maoism, as an internationalist imaginary, was, in fact, also engaged in the pragmatic project of nation-building, where it was presumed that "the interests of the nation and of the masses" were the same. This set of contradictions plagued the Iranian diasporic Left and other revolutionary Marxist anticolonial formations around the world.

Chapters of the ISA often attempted to follow Mao's dictates directly. Jaleh Pirnazar, who used to accompany musical choruses of student activists on the piano at ISA events, was dismayed when she was told by some of the other leaders that she could no longer play Western composers. This directive was not relevant to her public performances, for which she already relied on her repertoire of political songs, but was rather an attempt to regulate her overall behavior as a pianist. "Chairman Mao banned Beethoven, and I had no logical reason to follow this," she said. "Why should I dismiss Beethoven as a person, as a musician?" And yet, rather than jeopardize her place in the movement, she went along with the new policy.

Nancy Hormachea, active in the Houston ISA, offers a unique insider/outsider perspective on the Iranian student opposition movement. She was a young, white American lawyer when she joined the ISA in Texas in 1976. During the revolution, she would risk her life as a member of the UIC and spend a year in detention in Iran. When I asked her why she was drawn to this movement, she replied without hesitation: "Their passion. It was very sincere. We had thousands of Iranians in Texas and Oklahoma. They were lower- to middle-class Iranians, working-class Iranians. It was really dedication. Lots of sacrifices were made. I adopted the same thing." Like her Iranian women peers, she found the ISA's revolutionary sociality and the new modes of gendered subjectivity available to her compelling enough to submit to new forms of discipline. "We did what we were told," she said. "Because you wanted to continue to be part of this big organization, this community, this movement."

As revolutionary affects attached to the movement itself, activists would discard those feelings, desires, and ways of being in the world that were not deemed, in Nancy's words, "consistent with the culture of the proletariat" or the Iranian "masses," an abstract, distant and, in fact, unstable and incoherent category. But this process was far from smooth and unfolded quite differently for men and women. "Because we were for the poor," Hamid Kowsari, who was active in Berkeley, explained, "everybody tried to show more sympathy. People would try to look poorer than they actually were. They wouldn't dress nicely. They wouldn't buy expensive things." This sometimes resulted in odd and rigid behaviors as second-hand knowledge tended toward caricature. "Someone would be called out for eating *chelo kebab*, as an insult," Parviz remembered, referring to an Iranian dish made with relatively expensive cuts of lamb. "They competed for being less bourgeois and more down with the struggle."

The emphasis on mimicking an imagined, homogenized "culture of the proletariat" was common among Marxist student movements, but these practices appear particularly incongruous in diaspora, quite far from the Iranian "masses." Unable to have any direct connection with workers and peasants in Iran, the ISA focused on preparing its own membership for the coming revolution by working to root out bourgeois habits. The desire to liberate the oppressed became bound up with the desire to *be like* "the oppressed," and this became a major rationale for conforming to a set of gendered "revolutionary" norms. Ironically, those norms had little to do with the culture of any proletariat, especially in Iran, and far more to do with the regulation of differences perceived as disruptive or threatening to the movement.

Gender sameness as an ideology and masculinization as a set of practices were crucial to this process of regulation because women were deemed especially vulnerable to bourgeois and other forms of corruption, a belief both Moallem and Moghissi have argued was common among Iranian anti-imperialists across the political spectrum, from the secular Marxists to the Islamists.[39] This belief informed the ISA's use of Marxism-Leninism to critique gender roles prescribed by the alliance between the US and the Shah. As Nancy explained:

> You've got to think of Iranian culture at that time. What we do know is that Shah had imposed a culture on people, and everyone was always talking about *mini jupe* [miniskirts]. Clothes were a sign of the bourgeoisie. That was totally Maoist. In China they did the same thing. Everybody had to wear a uniform and everything was very strict. I don't really know what

the culture of the proletariat was—looking back, I don't really know. But because of that perception, a certain culture was enforced. You've got to do it this way so that all of these proletariat over here don't lose respect for the organization. You don't want to offend them. Maoism also reinforced that, that this is the correct culture.

Nancy captures the seamless manner in which leftist critiques of Western cultural imperialism in Iran were integrated with the logics of Mao's Cultural Revolution. The *mini jupe* became a symbol of degraded, Westernized femininity, a metaphor for the penetration of foreign influence into the Iranian nation via the accessibility and visibility of women's bodies.

Women's clothing and gender performance became a major site for displaying "proletarian culture" and established the conditions of belonging for women in the diasporic anti-Shah movement. When it came to clothing, Nancy explained, "some people from a certain line, they would have blue jeans, but they might be from a brand name, it wouldn't be Sears, or [they would have] fancier shoes not from Sears.[40] The Fadaiyan dressed better. All the Third Line people [Revolutionary Organization] were shopping at the Goodwill and really dressing down to be proletariat."[41] Parviz also said he could correlate clothing with factional affiliation, despite the pretense of secrecy maintained by all of the leftist groups preparing to return to Iran. "*Sāzmān-e Enqelābi* [RO] dressed neat and clean, trying to look like normal students; our group [UIC] wore Chinese coats, peacoats, berets, a militaristic look; Tufan dressed lumpen; National Front [*Jebha-ye Mellī*] folks dressed classic Iranian, like the sons of the bazaari [bazaar merchants] that they were."[42] These uniforms, despite their variation, helped to minimize class as well as gender differences. "Fashion," Moallem has written, "was one of the most important tools of revolutionary imaginary. However, an analysis of the ramifications of such imaginary still needs to be articulated."[43] In the next section, I explore some of these ramifications.

Affective Dissonance and Embodied Critique

As women former ISA members recounted their memories of everyday life in the movement, resistant nostalgia for feelings of belonging and empowerment clashed with distressed feelings about the rigid terms on which that belonging was available. Shahnaz, an upper-class woman from Tehran who joined the ISA and the UIC in Northern California in 1975, rose quickly in the leadership and became the local secretary of culture in charge of the weekly forums at *Khane-e Iran* in Berkeley. She had fond memories of the efforts male activists made to educate themselves about equality between the sexes. "When we had discussions about women, I have a very good feeling of those days of having men be a part of it," she said. At the same time, and in virtually the same breath, Shahnaz described the form this imagined equality was supposed to take, and a visible affective shift occurred as she spoke. The affection and attachment she clearly felt toward her comrades and their collective political culture was abruptly ruptured by a sense of estrangement from the revolutionary subjectivity she herself had embodied: "When I go back to those days it was very—we had a very strange kind of behavior. It wasn't normal. Like, all of us decided to cut our hair. I came here with long hair and then after that it was cut so short. We were saying it's not important, the look of a woman is not important. The clothing that we had, all of a sudden became *goshad* [baggy]. You were not going to have skirts. Behaviors became like men's behavior." Westernized, bourgeois femininity had been internalized as "normal" by the middle- and upper-class women who joined the ISA; therefore, the experience of trying to look and act "like men" produced discomfort and even disorientation deriving from the replacement of a gender performance that felt "natural" with another that did not. The affective dissonance between identification with and alienation from these past practices registered in the body and became, several decades later, a source of critique. Shahnaz expressed dismay when she recalled that women had to change their deeply ingrained sense of themselves, of what it meant to be female. Nothing less than a feeling of self-estrangement overtook her when she confronted her acquiescence to a set of bodily regulations that did not feel "normal" to her. These feelings index an embodied, lived experience of the dogmatism and hierarchy that accompanied an expansive anti-imperialist vision of human liberation and solidarity.

Jila, who never joined a leftist group, nonetheless reported that she "wore jeans and simple tee-shirts. No makeup, no heels." She enjoyed working on the periodical *Resistance* and felt grateful to the ISA for the political education she received, for what she called "the light that has remained on, even today." At the same time, she said she "would underline in bold" that the organization was "very controlling, very undemocratic." There was little choice but to "comply with unspoken cultural norms" if she wanted to maintain the "sense of belonging" that she also craved and valued.

Soosan, who spent just over a year in the US before the revolution began, called her experience in the ISA "really one of my best times that I had in my life." As "news leader" of the Northern California chapter, she "gathered news from Iran or from other [ISA] branches in different states and gave talks in the *Khane-e Iran* for fifteen minutes every week." She considered herself "full-time," and smiled when she recalled "that passion of doing something" collectively. "We were so equal," she said. "I could be news leader or a man could be. As far as this kind of thing, we were okay."

However, despite the study groups and forums on women's oppression, she said she and the other women "mostly had to be like men." Soosan's entry into the movement was expedited by the fact that her brother was already involved. Therefore, when she arrived in the US, she went directly to the ISA's annual convention, held that year in Oklahoma.[44] It was there, among close to 2,000 other Iranian student activists, that she first encountered the new gender norms to which she would soon conform:

> When I came, I had my eyebrows fixed [threaded] and my hair long, and I wore a blouse. I remember, you could see through [it] kind of; [it was] very feminine, [like a] typical [middle-class] Iranian woman—they have to have their perfume and a little bit of makeup. Even though I was an activist [in Iran], and I didn't do makeup, I didn't have facial hair; I took care of it. My nails were pretty. My shoes were a little bit high heel, feminine. I came to that conference [thinking] I was very lefty in Iran. My friends were all into makeup and hair and dresses. I was very lefty compared with them. But when I came here [*laughs*] ... First thing, my brother took me to buy jeans and a tee-shirt, and I put my hair up. One of our leaders, the first thing he told me was, "Oh, if you want to be part of this organization, you should cut your hair."

As an activist coming from Iran, Soosan already accepted the idea that the category "feminine" was a problem for serious political activism. This notion was simply amplified in diaspora, as she was instructed to further adapt her gender performance to better serve the revolution. The disorientation she experienced in her first encounter with the ISA came from realizing she had not gone far enough in eschewing outward signs of femininity; the world she had just entered was even stricter in this regard than the one she had left behind. The nexus of class, gender, and the development of a Westernized bourgeoisie under the US-backed dictatorship was visible on Soosan's body: her sheer blouse, high heels, and threaded brows marked her as out of place, earning a reprimand from a male leader and an emergency shopping trip with her activist brother.

The speed with which Soosan was whisked off to be properly attired reveals the immediate identification of women's bodies with sex and sexuality, and both as an inherent problem.[45] If women's bodies were always inherently sexual, and always in danger of becoming sexualized, then they had to be concealed, prevented from becoming a distraction or threat to the sustainability of the revolutionary movement, which required a singular focus on making a revolution. Gender sameness ignores this hierarchal stigmatization and thus recapitulates the very gender binary it proposes to transcend. For male ISA members who had become sensitive to issues of women's oppression, the dress code was imagined as a step closer to gender equality. Masculine forms of dress would desexualize women, enabling men to respect women and women to respect themselves. If women had to choose between sexual objectification/traditional roles as wives and mothers and the promise of equality as revolutionary comrades, it is no surprise that the latter category held such appeal at the time. Gender sameness/masculinization was a strategic means of negotiating sexism in society as a whole as well as within the movement itself.

This logic maintains men as the normative gender and leaves male sexuality uninterrogated while female sexuality is understood as a threat to be managed, an inherently shameful and degraded category. Nancy remembered how she and the other women in the ISA would pin their button-down shirts to prevent any accidental display of cleavage. The problem, Nancy explained, was that "if women looked like women, it would distract the men, would show the group was morally loose." She quickly added that this was "the exact thinking of the Islamic Republic, the exact same thing."[46]

The notion of continuity between the uniform worn by Iranian leftist women in diaspora and the imposition of an Islamic dress code for women in Iran in 1981 might seem counterintuitive. After all, leftist attire, despite the variations among different parties described above, was intentionally androgynous, if not an explicit form of cross-dressing in which women attempted to look like men. The hijab, of course, has the exact opposite intention and effect as a visible marker of gender difference. And yet, Shahnaz also made an analogy between the two styles of gender comportment. The strictness of the dress code for women in the UIC in Northern California was, she said, "somehow like the way that this regime, [the Islamic Republic of Iran], says you have to have *rupush Islami* [Islamic covering for women]. Yeah, at that time we had that [a dress code]. We had to be so serious. We had to be militant; we had to act like our looks wasn't important. Behaviors became like men's behavior." Curious about this recurring comparison, I asked Soosan if she thought there was a link. "The connection is jeans and a tee-shirt and the veil," she said. "They don't want you to show your female body, your curves. They see this as sexual and feminine. They don't want this." Jeans and a tee-shirt were, of course, Western forms of dress, and offer another example of how the Iranian leftist opposition differed from pan-Africanist and other strains of anticolonial nationalism whose adherents donned "traditional" clothing as an expression of their political and cultural resistance. The low cost and ubiquity of "jeans and a tee-shirt" quickly made them a kind of global student uniform that was closely associated with the urban working class in the West. The leftist uniform and the hijab not only hid the female body, but were modes of reconstituting it outside of Westernized bourgeois forms of femininity and hypersexualization, promising different paths out of the degradations suffered at the intersection of dictatorship and imperialism.

Sex and Surveillance

Gender sameness/masculinization was thus intended to obscure the female body, minimize the perceived threat of female sexuality, and erase the existence of female sexual desire. To attract male attention was to express female desire for that attention, and this was not the behavior of serious revolutionaries. In fact, gender sameness was also a means of regulating men's sexuality, precisely by hiding the objects that would presumably incite male desire. Ironically, this attempt at sexual repression functioned as a mandate for some male leftists to become utterly preoccupied with the management of women's bodies.

While there was variation between chapters, largely depending on which leftist groups were dominant, women in the ISA were under surveillance by their peers, and some were explicitly told to cover up if they did not carefully hide "their curves," as Soosan put it. Jila remembered a wedding she attended in a borrowed dress that "had a little cleavage showing." Afterward, "one of the leadership came and said, 'We were told that you had cleavage showing and were wearing a dress.'" Nancy recalled an incident hiking with a group of comrades in Iran in 1979: because it was hot outside, she and another female activist "had taken our top shirts off, and we had on T-shirts. Later on we were called out on that, talked to separately."

With its hybrid Maoist and religious undertones, the ideology of gender sameness also instigated a preoccupation with regulating sexual relations within the ISA. While many of their American peers were engaging in a "sexual revolution," which was itself a complicated mix of oppressive and liberatory practices, Iranian student activists took advantage of the relatively permissive atmosphere to engage in nonreproductive sex outside marriage. Officially, sex and sexuality were considered "private" issues that should remain hidden and unspoken. Zohreh offered an overview of the Washington, DC, chapter: "Based on my information, people dated, but it wasn't really open. You know, people kept secrets because not many people married." Shahnaz offered a similar assessment: "It wasn't appropriate for girls to have a boyfriend and to announce it. So lots of things were hidden." Soosan explained this as a result of "the Muslim culture that we had, which affected us." While it may be true that a culture of privacy surrounding sexual relations in Iran led these activists to be less open about their sex lives than many of their American counterparts, the practices Soosan went on to describe had little in common with what was considered acceptable in Iran at the time, and were certainly not sanctioned by any religious doctrine. "In Iran you couldn't sleep with men and women in one room or go out with a man" in public, she said. At that time in Iran, men and women lived at home with their parents until they were married—unless they were studying abroad. The space of diaspora, however, made it possible for premarital sexual relations to flourish relatively unimpeded, and even for such relations to be conceivable as "private" rather than potential public and familial scandals. In the Berkeley ISA, Soosan recalled, "I don't think it was a taboo if you had sex; it wasn't about that. If you had sex, you had sex. It wasn't an issue. But you didn't advertise it. With sex I think this [fear] comes." Soosan then ventriloquized the leadership's concerns: "'You're going to be having fun and no, in revolution you don't have fun. You just go for being a revolutionary person and you put your life hundred percent for revolution and not for personal [gratification]. Sex is personal, having fun is personal.'" Soosan lamented the repressive atmosphere in the movement, saying, "I personally never thought of my own [sexual] feelings as a woman, my own needs. I had that feeling, but I suppressed it. I didn't let it come out because they didn't want that, and I accepted that."

Men were not subjected to the same scrutiny regarding their sex lives, and many openly dated American women. Of the sexual hierarchy between men and women in the ISA, Jila said, "The [male] leadership took care of themselves in every way. They would have their lovers, but they wanted to control" the sexual practices of Iranian women members. This control, encompassing dating as well as marriage, was justified as a way of shoring up party affiliations and loyalties. "You couldn't date outside the group,"

Jila said, an unofficial policy that became more challenging to enforce as the underground leftist parties fractured into what she called "a ridiculous number of splinter groups" and the ISA itself split in 1975. Regardless, in the Northern California ISA, Jila said, "You had to get the okay" to date someone and "you were not allowed go out with someone in a splinter group."

In Philadelphia, where Sina was active with the RO, there were also efforts to police personal behaviors and regulate dating in line with party interests. Although he was from a poor, rural background, "a genuine article," as he said wryly, "I could not tell people that I drink beer. One night I was caught coming out of a bar, and I had to make up a story because, 'while the proletariat is hungry and starving, why are you having a beer?'" The expectation was, he recalled, that "everything had to be done in the interests of the organization and the politics. You have to marry someone that was the right person for you, that was your comrade. You don't say. 'I love the guy, he looks good.' You do it in line with the interests. Even your marriage belongs to that; it's not something that you choose."

While marriage and reproduction were sometimes encouraged among Iranian leftists inside Iran, who needed a normative façade to avoid suspicion from family and neighbors, these constraints did not apply to college students living in the US. As I noted earlier, marriage and reproduction were discouraged altogether among some Iranian leftist groups outside Iran. Having a spouse or a child could be a liability, an incentive to prioritize safety over risk or to aspire to individual longevity independent of the party or even the revolution. Activists expected to face arrest, prison time, and even torture back home. They had to be willing to leave loved ones behind and to put party loyalty ahead of every other allegiance. In fact, these dramatic scenarios came true for many returning activists; among the thirty I interviewed, four went to jail in Iran and eight had to flee incognito without papers, escaping across the border into Pakistan, Turkey, or Iraq. In the process, many of them were separated from comrades they had married upon returning to Iran and from children born just after the revolution. The low numbers of arrests in Iran among my subject pool reflect the fact that the majority of leftists arrested after the revolution were executed. In this, the Iranian students were far from naive: there was indeed a conflict between the affective desire to give the self over to the cause of revolution and the normative practices of marriage and reproduction. However, there was also a competing impulse: the desire to use the institution of marriage to solidify political loyalties and channel sexuality into the service of the movement. At the intersection of these two tendencies, suppression and regulation, different ISA chapters addressed the ongoing "problem" of sexual desire among large numbers of young people living together far from home.

Experiments in communal living allowed for maximum control over young activists' personal lives. Financial and practical necessity, along with the pleasures of living among those who embodied the same political passions and priorities, often pushed members to share housing, particularly in regions with high concentrations of younger Iranian foreign student activists, such as Northern California and Texas-Oklahoma, rather than in places like New York City, where ISA members tended to be more integrated into the city rather than concentrated around campuses. As a small child in 1958, Leyli Shayegan had been exiled to the US along with her family because of her father's participation in the Mosaddeq government. Leyli was active in the New York City ISA from 1971 to 1979. She emphasized the fact that different ISA chapters had different political cultures and practices, and that the New York chapter was dominated by supporters of the Marxist wing of the NF (like herself) and those who still supported Tudeh:

> We weren't like the chapters in Washington and Baltimore or Houston and California. They were much younger and much more culturally revolutionary. We had more older people in New York, a lot of married people. There was a lot of freedom here. There was very little of that [regulation of personal life]. Although, even within our group, there was that stuff going on, but to a much lesser extent than with the Maoist groups. I think that the students who were here as students without their families and were really dependent on the group were really influenced by what was going on in the group as a whole.

The presence of an older generation of ISA members, who now held professional jobs and often had spouses and children, accounts for some of the variations in the demands placed on members of different chapters.

At the other end of the spectrum, the Texas-Oklahoma ISA created political communities that were less integrated into the broader society, which by the mid-1970s was increasingly hostile to their presence. According to Bijan, the children of oil industry personnel from southern Iran, who flocked to the ISA in the mid-to-late 1970s, "were all coming with $1,000, and the next day they were working in the gas station. It was a class issue. It wasn't like if you go there, your dad is going to send you money." To manage the influx of less affluent students with little knowledge of English and fewer financial resources, communal living became the norm. "We created in Texas a system," Bijan said: "Among these 200 to 300 [ISA members], we divided them into houses, [in groups of] five or six. It was a semi-professional activism. Other parts of the US, I don't think the ISA did that. But there, we went beyond just a student movement to another level. So, in a way, they isolated themselves from American society. So they were not part of American society anymore or [any] American movement. By [19]74, [19]75, there is no major American movement any longer. The idea was everyone was preparing to go back to join the underground." This short-term aspirational approach to time structured a revolutionary temporality in which the present was imbued with the urgent demands of the imminent revolutionary future. While communal living arrangements helped provide housing for cash-strapped, Persian-speaking foreign students, the fact that these "houses" were systematically organized as part of the work of a political movement made them sites where diasporic Iranian revolutionary sociality flourished in all of its contradictions.

The system of communal living was central to the management of gender difference and to efforts to control or suppress sexual desire. Bijan explained the larger context in which the numbers of Iranian women coming to the US for college increased:

A lot of women were involved [in the ISA in Texas-Oklahoma]. Out of 200, we had at least like twenty-five women involved. They were all recruited to become activists. The women that were coming were from more well-to-do middle-class families [than the men]. A few from Abadan and Khuzistan. Other cities like Shiraz, Esfahan, but more middle class. Most of the women who were coming, their families said "I'll pay for your education." They were not coming with $500 in their pockets. They don't send their daughters that way as they do with boys. Most of them were eighteen, nineteen, twenty. At the same time, we lived in a society [Iran] where there were people who wouldn't let their daughters go to another city or out to the movies. So they must have been from families that were open-minded enough that they could trust their daughters to go to another place.

While "boys" might be expected to fend for themselves, worries over the safety of "daughters" meant that only those with access to enough money to ensure a decent standard of living would be sent abroad. This contributed to the skewed class and gender dynamics, in which the women as a group tended to be more affluent than the men. Once women from upper- and middle-class backgrounds steeped in Westernized bourgeois norms of femininity arrived, the problem of how to integrate them into the movement became central. "We recruited a lot of these young women because it was a safe haven for them. It was a place where you feel there is a camaraderie. Your family is not here and you have a bunch of people around you. This in itself was a source of recruiting. It was like another family. You could live with the other women. The women lived separately from the men." Bijan openly grappled with the gender and sexual politics of a revolutionary political culture from which he now felt estranged:

> Then there was this puritan idea that you don't date as a revolutionary because this is corruption. Where did that come from, I don't know. How did I buy into that? I grew up with a family that dating is normal. Maybe not normal in all of Iran, but normal among my family. [In the ISA], if you date somebody, that means you love that person, and you're going to marry them. That was the concept. Very traditional for a bunch of radicals. I can't talk about other places, but men didn't like to see women mixed in that type of [i.e., a sexual] relationship. For me, I'm surprised at myself. I didn't care. My sister could go out. But there became this element of the puritan revolutionary. You even control your sexual desire for the higher cause of revolution.

When I suggested that, surely, with all these young people far from home, some of these activists must have dated or had sexual liaisons, Bijan replied:

> Yes, then we created a police to watch that. To watch who is going with who. I'm embarrassed myself. Why suddenly I got involved in that? It was not my background. It happened. We policed. Somebody would come and say, "I saw so and so sitting in a coffee shop." And we would go and ask them, "Any particular reason you were talking to this person. You are in a different committee so there is no reason for you to be talking." It became like very Stalinist. It was getting out of hand. Every aspect of your personal life should be subordinated to the party. But it was not the party decided from the top. It came from the bottom. I never saw any woman complain about why it was like that. I think the women of the group also liked it because it was some sort of safe haven for them. Our argument was exactly like the Muslims. Women are not sexual objects. So if they are not sexual objects, then you don't think about dating them. You think that dating equals sexual relationship and that equals being vulgar or corrupt. That was the downside of it. It was a double-edged sword. It was empowering, but it was not liberating.

Bijan's insight, "it was empowering, but it was not liberating," is an apt way of describing gender sameness as a leftist alternative to the sexual degradation of women that had occurred as a result of the Shah's importation of Western culture. While the hope was that masculine forms of dress would desexualize women and, therefore, enable men to respect women and women to respect themselves, this logic maintained female sexuality as a threat to be managed. Only by hiding their female bodies, eschewing the trappings of their upper- and middle-class backgrounds, and agreeing to the new forms of regulation and discipline could women hasten the end of their own oppression.

Again, it is useful to triangulate this analysis with the Chinese example. In both the ISA's and in Mao's Cultural Revolution, women were encouraged, if not forced, to erase qualities deemed "feminine." Hui Wu explains that Chinese women, "throughout their lives ... have been told that 'women are the same as men' and that 'women can do whatever men can do.'"[47] She goes on to argue, "Ironically, it was exactly the promotion of gender similarity that denied women 'the very language in which to express the gender inequality in their daily lives.'"[48] She could just as easily have been describing gender sameness in the ISA, incisively cutting to the quick of its inherent contradiction. Rather than simply dismiss gender sameness and the gender and sexual politics of the (Iranian) left *tout court*, I end this chapter by delving more deeply into the contradiction between empowerment and liberation to more fully understand the investments of the women involved.

The Appeal of Ultimate Sacrifice

When women reimagined themselves outside the preexisting models of femininity, whether Westernized or not, to what new ideal were they drawn? Frantz Fanon's *A Dying Colonialism* pays tribute to the presence of female guerrilla fighters in the Algerian National Liberation Front, a phenomenon that also loomed large in the Iranian diasporic leftist imaginary. For Fanon, Algerian women and girls lived in a state of domestic stupor and stagnation until awakened into full subjectivity by participation in revolutionary activity.[49] Feminist scholar Marnia Lazreg argues that this analysis erases women's gendered experiences of French colonialism, such as their instrumentalization by French civilizing discourses on gender and the veil and their vulnerability to state violence.[50] While the majority of Algerian women active in the struggle against French settler colonialism were based in rural areas, and many had no choice but to aid the opposition under siege, Lazreg emphasizes that many women did in fact choose to join the movement.[51] They had experienced injustice as much if not more than men and, therefore, "women's commitment to decolonization was no less intense than men's."[52] This was especially true for urban educated women, the imperial model minorities of Algeria, who had experienced Westernization in French lycées and who became infamous for their role in planting bombs in the French quarter of Algiers.[53]

In Algeria and elsewhere, the female guerrilla fighter became a role model for politically active women around the world. As the quintessential embodiment of revolutionary affects, her devotion to the revolution was absolute in her willingness to self-sacrifice and, at the same time, she enacted a key ideological pillar of gender sameness by proving that she could exhibit the same bravery and take on the same risks as men.[54] No longer available for the civilizing mission of Western imperial modernity, women's bodies were thus reimagined as instruments of anticolonial resistance. The female guerrilla was represented as always willing to adapt her physical appearance, comportment, and behavior to the needs of the revolution. She did not think of becoming the object of male sexual desire; her own sexual desire was unmentionable, presumably subsumed by her desire for national freedom.[55] Soosan's words, quoted earlier, express this sentiment: "I got so passionate about this work. My priority was that Iran has to be a democratic country and that's the only thing I was thinking . . . I never thought of my own feelings as a woman, my own needs."

The ISA helped to circulate these gendered affects of self-sacrifice and examples of women's revolutionary heroism in its own publications. Below, I analyze several examples, which were deemed affectively and politically important enough to be translated into English for an American audience in the pages of *Resistance*. The following poem by Marzieh Ahmadi Oskooi, a Fada'i fighter shot and killed on a Tehran street in 1974, reinforces Fanon's analysis of the relationship between women's agency and revolutionary activity. It appears in translation in an issue of *Resistance* from 1975:

> I used to be a cold, narrow brook
> Running in the forests, mountains
> and valleys.
> I knew that standing waters die
> from within.
> I knew that joining the waves of
> the seas
> Brings new life to the little brooks.
>
> Neither the long way
> Nor the dark craters

Nor the temptation to stop running
Prevented me from moving on.

Now I have joined the endless waves.
I exist in struggle,
And my rest is my death.[56]

The poem's simple metaphor casts the nonpolitical woman as stunted and lifeless, like a "cold, narrow brook" or "standing waters." This is much like the "narrow world" of the Algerian woman Fanon describes prior to becoming active in the Algerian Revolution.[57] Oskooi's poem follows the same trajectory as Fanon's sketch: just as the brook overcomes fear to "join … the endless waves," the Algerian woman "bursts the bounds" of her stultifying domestic existence by joining the underground.[58] Finally entering the flow of history, these women find a "new life" for themselves; the only force that can cause the narrator of the poem, or the brave Algerian "sister," to cease from struggle is death. Interestingly, the poem's narrator will die either way, whether of stagnation in the traditional, patriarchal home ("I knew that standing waters die from within"), or as a result of her political activities. Oskooi effectively gave voice to female revolutionary affects that circulated broadly in an age of Third World anticolonial movements. She expressed the genuine desire women had to transcend the confines of life as they knew it and to create a prefigurative subjectivity that could relentlessly pursue a better world, no matter what the obstacle. They also express what Lazreg has called "a deep-seated and widely held conception of women as creatures of sacrifice … [in which] suffering is also seen as inevitable, as part of the feminine condition."[59]

Oskooi's poem is just one example of the ongoing coverage the ISA gave to Fadaiyan women. Fadaiyan women were counterposed to the elite women in the Pahlavi family, who were routinely honored in the West as champions of women's rights, as evidence that Iran was indeed developing into a modern nation under US tutelage.[60] When Iran's Empress Farah made a solo trip to the US in 1977 and received an award for her work on "women's rights and equality in Iran," the ISA protested at every stop on her tour.[61] It produced posters and articles challenging the official narratives of progress crafted in Washington and Tehran and counterposed a revolutionary image of women's power (figure 5.1). A report on the entrenched patriarchal oppression and poverty faced by women agricultural and industrial laborers in Iran concludes with a list of female revolutionaries: "The true representatives of Iranian women are women like Ashraf Dehghani who heroically resisted the torture of SAVAK and later escaped; Marzieh Ahmadi Oskooi, who was martyred at the hands of the Shah's regime; Rafaat Afraz who was martyred in Oman while struggling with her Omani brothers and sisters; Mother Shayegan who at the age of 53 is resisting the Shah's brutal tortures; and Manizheh Ashraf Zadeh Kermani, the first woman freedom fighter executed by the Shah's dictatorial regime."[62] These women became heroes for the entire Iranian opposition movement, inside and outside Iran, and, by honoring them, the ISA condemned the Pahlavi regime's cynical posturing about the advancement of Iranian women.

Female guerrillas were invariably represented as superhuman in their abilities to withstand torture and they became symbols of perpetual defiance even in death. An affective attachment to this iconic figure and the power she seemed to possess helps explain the willingness of women in the ISA to conform to revolutionary regimes of discipline as an alternative to the degraded categories of the feminine, the bourgeois, and the Westernized. Zohreh Khayam explained the appeal of the female guerrilla for women attempting to resist male domination in the movement. "I don't think it's an exaggeration, because it wasn't just me," she said:

> We all wanted to prove that women could do anything that men can do. When it came to, say, armed struggle in Oman, we were automatically siding with women who took arms. Or with the Palestinian movement. Leila Khaled—she was one of the female symbols of Palestinian struggle, and she participated in hijackings and things like that, so she was really big for a lot of Iranian women. There was a woman who was involved in [the] Algerian independence movement by the name of Djamila Boupacha. She was a symbol of women's resistance. Really [there was] a window of opportunity for us to learn about other women and how they have participated in the struggle. So it was really inspiring for us.

Zohreh's reference to women guerrillas from across the Arab world reveals another transnational circuit of female solidarity, identification, and affective attachment not limited to the Iranian context.[63] It also shows that compliance with the political culture of gender sameness and self-sacrifice was not simply a matter of obeying the dictates of men in order to avoid exclusion from the group. As Minoo Moallem has pointed out, "The capacity of combative women to transcend traditional feminine responsibilities—marriage, motherhood, nurturance, protection of the family—gave rise to a new ethic of political responsibility."[64] Zohreh, among other leftist women in the ISA,

Figure 5.1 Courtesy of Shayegan Family Estate.

saw these heroic female figures as evidence of her own potential, as a visible assertion of the importance of women to the making of history.

This was especially true after the Fadaiyan launched a short-lived uprising in the northern Iranian city of Siahkal in 1971. Drawn to the guerrillas' audacity in the face of intense regime repression, a new generation of anti-Shah activists embraced the need for armed struggle. In the diasporic student movement, the influence of the Fadaiyan grew throughout the decade until it was a dominant organization. Whether or not Iranian diasporic leftists agreed with the Fadaiyan's strategy and tactics, they shared an affective map with these "freedom fighters." The discipline and sacrifice necessary to wage armed struggle were the ultimate expression of the revolutionary affects and temporality that shaped the ISA's political culture. Of course, if a man died in a guerrilla action, his martyrdom did not perpetuate a gendered system of subordination based on self-sacrifice. He was simply a hero devoted to the freedom of "the people." If a woman died as a result of taking up arms, her death might be lionized, but it also reinforced what Lazreg has called the "feminine condition" of endless and eternal suffering and sacrifice.

Women activists in the ISA found the female guerrilla's absolute refusal to accept defeat to be a great source of hope and inspiration, a lesson in how to fortify oneself for the battles ahead. Nancy Hormachea remembered that "there was a lot of romanticizing" of women guerrilla fighters. This romantic attachment helped sustain her during her eleven-month detention in Iran in 1981. "When I went to jail [in Iran], I knew, oh, this is the jail that Ashraf was in, and she managed to escape." Ashraf Dehghani was a legendary Fadaiyan fighter who had escaped from prison in 1973. According to a report in *Resistance*, she "was subjected to barbarous tortures by the hated regime but with determination and fortitude endured it all and revealed nothing."[65] After her escape, Dehghani published a memoir titled *Torture and Resistance in Iran*, which was translated into English and excerpted in *Resistance* for an American audience. The editors selected the most harrowing scene in the entire book as if they intended to present a narrative so awe-inspiring the reader could not help but respond with devotion to the anti-Shah cause. In this scene, Dehghani describes her moral victory over her torturer, named Niktab, who attempts to extract information from her about other Fadaiyan members. Here I reproduce the excerpt exactly as it appeared:

> with every stroke of the whip, Niktab howled "address, address." The pain grew more excruciating, more and more difficult to endure. There were moments when I really wanted the whipping to stop. . . . There was no way out of the agony. I really felt there was nothing I could do. I was like a mother delivering a baby. The pain is there and goes on. Nothing can be done but wait for the birth of the child. And in that situation, the birth of the child was the arrival of death. I had to wait for that.
>
> Gradually their repulsive faces filled with dismay. Looking at them, my confidence soared. They looked more and more bereaved. What else were the poor, feeble beasts to do? The worst and most important thing they had to offer was torture, and they had seen it fail miserably. The whipping stopped. They picked up a pair of tongs, gripping and twisting my flesh. They began compressing my fingers in a vice. They said they were going to pull out my nails, but they did not do that. Perhaps they did not want to leave any permanent proof of their crimes. They were helpless, frustrated, infuriated. They seemed to be exerting more pressure on their teeth than on my fingers. Other tortures were painful but not as painful as the whipping. In between other barbarities, they would also whip me. They had lost their rhythm, seemed to have forgotten the order. Their hateful and cretin faces were covered with despair.[66]

This memoir was written, translated, and distributed by the ISA as evidence of torture practices in Iran *and* as a testimonial to the moral righteousness of the opposition. Dehghani represents her body in pain as a symbol of the inevitable success of the revolution. This is not simply a self-mythologizing move, but one that elevates the revolutionary cause itself to mythic status. Trapped in the most subordinate and disempowered position imaginable, Dehghani could not be degraded or defeated. No matter what tortures and injustices she endured, she kept her dignity through her fealty to her comrades and to the revolution. It is her torturers, and not Dehghani, who become abject and dehumanized, turning into "feeble beasts" as a result of the violence they enact on her body. It is they, and not she, who are "helpless, frustrated, infuriated." She compares torture at the hands of SAVAK with childbirth, illustrating the vast distance between the version of female heroism she narrated and the nationalist romanticization of the woman as mother of the nation. Childbirth is equated with death, and not with a brighter future.

The refusal of abjection and the feelings of empowerment expressed in Dehghani's memoir and Oskooi's poem were deeply compelling and enabling for women in the ISA, elevating the revolutionary affects and actions of women to a level of heroism equal to that of men.[67] Attachments to the figure of the female guerrilla manifested both the feminist desire to transcend gender subordination and the patriarchal mandate to sacrifice the self for the greater good as it was defined by men. This combination of liberatory and oppressive impulses was not unique to the Iranian opposition movement. On the contrary, this mode of revolutionary belonging for women became the basis of feminist critique by Third Worldist feminists such as Francis Beale, who pointed out in her 1968 manifesto, "To die for the revolution is a one-shot deal; to live for the revolution means taking on the more difficult commitment of changing our day-to-day life patterns."[68] This shift in the expression of revolutionary affects, from the willingness to die for the revolution to the desire to live and make the revolution a vehicle for Iranian women's freedom, is the subject of the next chapter.

Conclusion

The experiences of the women and men I interviewed illustrate that the manner in which the Iranian diasporic Left attempted to discipline and regulate female sexuality and the female body, even including the womb, was quite distinct from the typical role prescribed for women as reproducers of *both* postcolonial *and* diasporic citizenship.[69] The agency and value of women in the diasporic Left was not based on their ability to maintain traditional culture and gender roles, or to reproduce ideal citizens. Instead, as I have shown, women in the ISA lived and worked as active members of a revolutionary movement and remade themselves within a revolutionary sociality.

Moghissi summarizes the mixture of aspirations for equality and acceptance of subordination that characterized women's revolutionary affects of the era: "Only within the revolutionary struggle could women prove their worthiness and demonstrate that they had the same potential, talents and capabilities as their male comrades."[70] Especially for upper- and middle-class women, there was tremendous peer pressure to shed a Westernized bourgeois femininity deemed complicit with imperialism and dictatorship. While Iranian women in the movement sometimes experienced the new "revolutionary" norms as a welcome change from the forms of gender and sexual regulation that had previously governed their lives, the affective dissonances that emerged in my interviews index more than just negative feelings generated in hindsight. They recall moments of bodily unease and estrangement from the self that were neglected at the time but that can become sources of feminist critique today. For the men who look back with a mixture of shame and bewilderment at the role they played in enforcing gender and sexual regulations, there is the potential for a reckoning with deeply internalized patterns of male domination that reproduced women's oppression in a new form. For the women I interviewed, the surprise, upset, and dismay many of them exhibited when recounting actions taken voluntarily constitute evidence of what Anne McClintock has called a "designated agency," one granted by the male comrades who invite women to join the resistance on certain, narrowly prescribed terms.[71] If women's agency begins at the invitation of men and as an appendage to the movement for national liberation, then women can be (and were) disinvited in country after country, their demands subordinated to the patriarchal priorities of the postcolonial nation-state. The consequences of this "designated agency" would not become clear to diasporic Iranian student activists until they finally encountered the revolution head on.

6

Intersectional Anti-Imperialism
Alternative Genealogies of Revolution and Diaspora

Iranian anti-Shah activists, like their American leftist peers, called for revolution from US college campuses throughout the 1970s. "We lived as if the revolution would happen in Iran any day now, and then we were proven right," Jila remarked, reflecting on the years she spent organizing with the ISA in Berkeley, California. Unlike their American counterparts, however, Iranian student activists had the chance to experience a revolution first hand. In 1978, demonstrations and strikes in Iran unleashed massive popular opposition that succeeded in overthrowing a brutal dictatorship backed by a global superpower. It was as if the future that ISA members had been longing for from diaspora had finally arrived, as if the sacrifices of the imprisoned, the tortured, and the martyred would soon be redeemed. The sacrifices of imperial model minorities—their neglect of their studies and willingness to become targets of state repression in the US and in Iran—also appeared worthwhile. When Jila arrived in Tehran after seven years abroad, she encountered a radically changed society. "The first six months in Iran were amazing," she remembered. "It was a kind of utopia. You felt some kind of total freedom in a despotic land." Almost all of the former ISA members I interviewed could still recall with wonder the feeling of that initial encounter with the revolution, what might simply be called the feeling of freedom.

Jila was one of approximately five to six thousand CISNU activists who made the reverse migration from the US and Europe.[1] Of the thirty former

ISA members I interviewed, twenty-six traveled to Iran at some point during the upheaval from 1978 to 1980 (two were already in Iran and two remained in the US). While a shared affective experience of victory as a kind of euphoria was a common refrain, it was also the preface to diverging accounts of what went wrong, what caused the revolution to turn against many of its own supporters. For some of the people I interviewed, the first sign that political developments were not proceeding the way they had hoped came very quickly, just six weeks after the Shah left, in the form of government pronouncements that targeted women for particular forms of restriction and control. This chapter argues that gender and sexuality were not only central to the discourses of a revolution against Western imperialism and to the mobilization of masses of women, but were also central to the shift from revolutionary possibilities to new forms of authoritarianism.

I make this argument mindful of the ways that discrimination against women and, to a lesser extent, sexual minorities in Iran has been weaponized by the US government and used to justify persistent imperial aggression. In the West, the hyper-visibility of the mandatory wearing of the hijab in Iran not only affirms the Orientalism and Islamophobia that fuel the current "war on terror," but also triggers visceral, negative emotions among many diasporic Iranians who fled the revolution and its aftermath. In this context, it is extremely difficult to address gender and sexual oppression in Iran without reproducing a cascading set of rigid, categorial oppositions: US/secularism/democracy/women's liberation versus Iran/Islam/dictatorship/extreme misogyny. An intersectional anti-imperialist framework can disrupt this binary way of thinking and acting, and reconfigure the geopolitical and affective terrain on which we understand Iranian and US societies. While both governments have made it their official policy to perpetuate a narrative of polar opposites, with each side promoting itself as morally superior, it is more accurate to view the US and Iran as locations riven with distinct manifestations of oppression and resistance. Although these nations are far from equal in terms of their global power and reach, they are both sites of militarism, mass incarceration, mass poverty, corruption, and incompetence at the highest political levels. Racism, gender and sexual discrimination, religious intolerance, and anti-immigrant nationalism exist in different forms in both the US and Iran. While it would be a mistake, for example, to apply the same critique of racism or patriarchy in the US to conditions in Iran, my argument is that freedom remains an ongoing aspiration for millions of people in both countries.

It is from this diasporic feminist perspective that my reading of the Iranian Revolution focuses on a refusal of imperialism and dictatorship in all their forms. The need to contend with the intersection of multiple, interrelated structures and causes of state violence and injustice defines the lives of Iranians today, *and* was also present in 1979. Nowhere was this need more apparent than in the Iranian women's uprising that took the nation by surprise in the immediate aftermath of the revolution, during a spring still remembered for its unprecedented feeling of freedom. This chapter combines memories of former ISA members with close readings of movement ephemera in order to center events that have been marginalized over decades of historiography on the Iranian revolution.[2] One of the most important documents of the uprising is *Mouvement de Libération des Femmes Iraniennes: Année Zéro*, a short film made by French feminists visiting Iran during the height of the women's demonstrations in early March. By reading this film against the grain of its own narrative and against the mistranslation of the Persian audio, I center the voices of the Iranian women interviewed. My counter-reading of the film, along with other documents by Iranian women activists, offers a glimpse of an intersectional anti-imperialism that was illegible within the hierarchical anti-imperialism that held sway over an otherwise heterogeneous revolutionary movement.

The women's uprising of March 1979 opened up an arena of struggle in which revolutionary affects diverged and clashed, and the meaning of freedom and self-determination were publicly contested. It represented nothing less than a turning point in the direction of the post-Shah society. I read these events both within the Iranian social and political context, but also as part of a transnational and diasporic reimagining of feminism. When confronting the choice between inequality under the US-backed dictatorship and inequality in a revolutionary Iran, tens of thousands of women were compelled to fight for an alternative future in which they could be free.

This chapter situates the March 1979 women's uprising as part of a genealogy of anti-imperialist or Third World feminism arising in many parts of the world throughout the era of decolonization. These events also constitute an inheritance for the Iranian diaspora, offering a profound illustration of the rejection of the rigid binaries between West and East, secular and religious, that continue to constrain our political horizons. Not unlike the revolutionary Third World feminism that arose out of antiracist movements in the US during the late 1960s and 1970s to insist that patriarchy was central to the operation of racism and capitalism, participants in the Iranian women's uprising believed their revolution should uproot all of the sources and systems of oppression they faced. It is this conceptual and analytical synergy that inspires my use of "intersectional anti-imperialism" as a transnational adaptation of the term *intersectionality* first coined by Black feminist legal scholar Kimberlé Crenshaw."[3] As this book has argued, the oppression of Iranian women cannot be fully understood without considering how gendered legacies of imperialism and dictatorship intersect to produce "*new* measures of oppression and inequality."[4]

The fact that the notion of intersecting forms of oppression, rather than a series of binary oppositions, proves so generative for the Iranian context complicates the meaning of "Western influence," which is often considered automatic grounds for disqualification of any movement in the Global South as inauthentic or a tool of the West. Instead of understanding "western influence" only as the purview of western governments or of nongovernmental agencies that aim to spread western hegemonic notions of freedom, we might consider that there are alternative models of the transnational circulation of radical ideas and traditions. The March women's uprising in Tehran began on International Women's Day, a socialist holiday originating with working women's struggles in the United States, which was also understood to be a significant day for Iranian women who had just carried out a revolution against US imperialism. Revolutionary affects attached to an internationalist legacy of women's collective organizing against patriarchy and capitalism— one as relevant for Iranian women as it was for Western women, who were also not yet free. This sensibility would ring out in the slogans of the uprising itself.

Using what I call a "methodology of possibility," I read the revolutionary affects that manifested in the women's movement as an archive of potentialities that did not come to pass but that, nonetheless, open up space for reconceiving the diasporic relationship to the 1979 revolution for current and future generations. How might the revolutionary affects from the women's uprising live on in diaspora as a counter to the polarized gender politics that pit "Western values" against a monolithic version of Islam? How might an understanding of the revolutionary roads imagined yet not taken inform an intersectional anti-imperialist politics today?

This chapter follows the journey of some ISA members who returned home and joined the women's movement. First, I explain the position of the different leftist parties and the conditions that produced the uprising. Then, I offer close readings of the words of Iranian women who appear in the French documentary in order to challenge several misrepresentations of the movement. The final sections of this chapter analyze how various actors responded to this movement and to the attacks on it, and show how a prevailing consensus across religious and party lines undermined the set of possibilities the uprising brought into being. Despite this, several women's groups continued trying to organize in extremely difficult conditions, insisting that their vision of women's equality was not a threat to the goals of the revolution as they understood them.

The Left after the Revolution

When the Shah left Iran on January 17, 1979, CISNU's major goal, the focus of almost twenty years of tireless effort, had suddenly been accomplished. Once in Iran, most CISNU members devoted themselves to political work under the auspices of the leftist parties to which they belonged, joined the main Tehran University student organization, or simply joined mass demonstrations as individuals. No longer part of a diasporic student movement, the revolutionary affects of former ISA members merged with those of student activists who had never left Iran. Thus, when I refer to the Iranian "Left" in this chapter, I do not always distinguish between those who spent time abroad and those who did not. The experience of diaspora was not insignificant, as I argue below; however, there was no causal or simple relationship between having been part of the ISA or CISNU and how one situated oneself within the political landscape of the revolution.

Like all revolutions, the Iranian events proved far messier and more difficult to navigate then any Marxist could have known, despite many years of preparation and debate over strategy and tactics, such as whether the Chinese or Cuban or Bolshevik model was most appropriate for Iranian conditions. In fact, none of these models or debates helped orient the Iranian Left, which faced a totally new question of what position to take toward the religious makeup of the revolutionary leadership and the implementation of an utterly new concept: an "Islamic republic." The revolutionary internationalism that had animated the opposition movement in diaspora collided head on with the project of constructing a new nation-state in a hostile world dominated by Soviet and American superpower.

Ayatollah Khomeini was the only figure able to mobilize millions of people to demonstrate against the monarchy. While in exile in Iraq and then Paris, he had adopted some of the rhetoric of the Left and reframed it within a version of Shi'ism akin to Third World populism in Latin America.[5]

The revolutionary affects of millions of Iranians found expression in a religious ideology that championed the *mostazafin* (oppressed) against the *mostakberin* (oppressors)—that is, the Iranian people against the alliance between imperialism and dictatorship.[6] Before the revolution, Khomeini promised an Islamic republic that would end poverty, exploitation, and corruption and establish a society based on social justice, including full equality for women.[7] Thus, a broad coalition of forces, including Marxists, the traditional middle class, liberal democrats, and different sections of the clergy, united behind him as the leader of the revolution. After Khomeini's return to Iran on February 1, 1979, he appointed Mehdi Bazargan, a liberal democrat educated in France, as prime minister. The provisional government held a referendum on the establishment of an Islamic republic at the end of March, in which the concept was undefined, and the only choices were to vote either "yes" or "no."[8] While the Mojahedin, the Tudeh Party, and the National Front called for a "yes" vote, the Fadaiyan was the major leftist organization to boycott the referendum. At the time, there was little agreement on the meaning of an "Islamic republic" even among the clerics who made up the Assembly of Experts tasked with writing the new constitution, a fractious process that lasted seven months.[9] When the new constitution went into effect in December 1979, Bazargan had already resigned in protest over the US embassy occupation that started that November. This occupation bolstered Khomeini's supporters, who ultimately prevailed in establishing a form of government that subordinated democratic institutions, such as parliament, to the new office of "Supreme Leader."[10] However, in early March, the form the new government would take had yet to be determined.

Instead of pushing for democracy during this period of flux, the Tudeh Party positioned itself as a "loyal opposition" to the newly emerging religious state, ultimately defending its most conservative and repressive policies in an effort to maintain a united front against imperialism.[11] The Fadaiyan were critical but not openly confrontational at first. However, as different sectors of Iranian society, including urban women, Kurds, and Turkman peasants protested the lack of democracy, the Fadaiyan came under tremendous pressure to choose sides. In June 1980, a minority formally broke away to oppose the Islamic Republic, while the majority maintained support for the anti-imperialist clerics.[12] Among the leftist groups that were primarily based in diaspora before the revolution, activists from the National Front Abroad in Europe, the US, and the Middle East launched the Organization of Communist Unity (Sāzman-i vahdat-i kumūnisti) in Iran in 1979 to openly oppose the liberal and conservative religious factions that were in the process of forming a new state.[13] Of the two main diasporic Maoist groups, the RO supported the Islamic liberals and Khomeini, while UIC split into pro-government and anti-government factions.[14]

The repressive measures of the revolutionary Iranian government were certainly exacerbated by external factors. Chief among these was the threat of another CIA coup, and the expectation of foreign intervention was used to enforce national unity against a common enemy. While concerns over foreign intervention were justified, the fact that the Iranian Revolution did not create a society with equal rights for all its citizens was largely an internal calamity, one in which the Left played a minor, supporting role. As Behrooz Ghamari-Tabrizi has shown, support for certain forms of state repression, like calling for executions of opponents, was shared by liberals, conservatives, and leftists, even while the Left had no institutional power.[15] Maziar Behrooz argues that the Left behaved in such a way because it also "lack[ed] respect for democratic rights" as a result of its Stalinist training and the impact of generations of repression under dictatorship.[16] In a similar vein, Haideh Moghissi has argued that patriarchy was so deeply entrenched in society that the male-dominated Iranian Left actively perpetuated unequal gender relations. Given a context in which feminism was tainted by association with the West, she maintains that the majority of leftist women were not able to cultivate a robust gender consciousness under such conditions. According to Moghissi, the Marxism-Leninism of the Iranian Left, across an array of parties, tendencies, and factions, stipulated a hierarchy of oppressions, and patriarchy was never the top priority.[17]

Embracing all of these insights, I argue against the conclusion that the repressive outcomes of the revolution expressed something inherent to Islam, a perspective dominant among the Iranian diaspora today. This chapter also resists another common narrative: that the revolution was on a path toward a liberal, secular democracy until it was hijacked by reactionary clerics.[18] Instead, I emphasize that there was a struggle over the meaning of the revolution immediately after it occurred and that this struggle mattered—and matters still. In the course of political struggle, the potential exists for human beings to be transformed, for old ideas and attachments to give way to new ways of imagining social and political relations, and for many possible futures to present themselves.

I dwell on the 1979 women's uprising and the movement that it launched because these events generated new revolutionary subjectivities and new visions of the post-Shah future. Just after the revolution had succeeded, the most urgent and immediate debates over the status of women in the new society were not primarily articulated as a conflict between religion and secularism. Minoo Moallem makes a similar point when she writes, "despite the hegemony of Khomeini's vision, in the postrevolutionary era, Iranian civil society continued to be a battleground for proponents of various ideologies, with most of them claiming their own interpretations of Islam."[19] Within this battleground, movements for equal rights for women, workers' control over production, and Kurdish autonomy became part of the terrain of struggle, often waged by people of faith who expressed support for the revolution even as they sought to redefine its practical implications. All of these movements were seen as sites of "disorder" by those who occupied the seats of power and were met with different degrees and forms of violent suppression.[20]

The women's movement *did* create disorder; it was a deliberate attempt to disrupt the gendered revolutionary logics that threatened to become a newly oppressive order. It lasted in different forms from March 1979 until early 1981, when state and para-state repression became too severe to hold public meetings or continue producing women's publications. While the majority of the organized Left dismissed, denounced, or attempted to control women's political activity, some women leftists, including some returning students from the ISA, participated in the marches, sit-ins, meetings, and publications that constituted the movement.[21] Rather than understand these events as a struggle of secularism against religion, or women against men, I argue that the women's movement was an expression of revolutionary affects that put pressure on all existing ideologies, including Marxism, liberalism, Shi'i liberation theology, and feminism, to respond to the substantive demands of women for equal power in determining the shape of their lives in the postrevolutionary society. It is to these fleeting events, and their lasting import, that I now turn.

A New Kind of Uprising

Taking stock of the mobilizations of Iranian women that occurred so soon after the moment of national liberation from a US-allied dictatorship, Negar Mottahedeh writes, "No other revolution had produced a radicalized women's movement of this magnitude."[22] The conditions of possibility for such a movement did not include the presence of explicitly feminist politics or organization, nor did they include support from secular leftist or liberal parties. Instead, what appeared to be a largely spontaneous outpouring of militancy on the part of tens of thousands of urban women can best be understood as a continuation of the revolutionary affects that had toppled the old order. As Moallem notes, "women participated in all aspects of the revolution, from demonstrations to acts of political belligerence."[23] These revolutionary women came from all socioeconomic classes, with varying degrees of education and religiosity. From upper-class women affiliated with the Shah-sponsored Women's Organization of Iran, some of whom turned against the monarchy, to the daughters of the traditional bazaar merchant class, to university students, teachers, nurses, and the urban poor, women entered the political/historical stage in unprecedented numbers.[24] However, there was a sharp divergence among the ways in which women's participation was narrated and solicited by the religious mainstream of the movement and by the various Marxist groups. For the former, Shiʻi mythology was repackaged into a contemporary revolutionary ideology, most famously by Ali Shariati in his text *Fatima Is Fatima*. Shariati offered Fatima, the prophet's long-suffering and dutiful daughter and the wife of Imam Ali, as a role model for a new "authentically Iranian" female political subjectivity.[25] As Minoo Moallem has argued, Zeinab, Imam Ali's daughter and Imam Hussein's sister, who defied the oppressive ruler Yazid and died in the massacre at Karbala, was also mobilized as a figure of courageous militancy, thereby facilitating Iranian women's participation in the revolution.[26]

On the surface, this overtly gendered way of encouraging and representing women's revolutionary activity clashed with the gender sameness/masculinization of the Iranian Left discussed in chapter 5. Yet, as that chapter showed, there were implicit similarities that often registered affectively in the body— as discomfort, disorientation, and self-estrangement—years before they were expressed as open challenges to leftist orthodoxies. The most obvious similarity was that the female body and female sexuality were treated as sites of corruption and decadence that must be covered up, a legacy of the association of bourgeois femininity with capitalist consumer culture and the Shah's Westernizing dictatorship. Gender sameness/masculinization reinforced gender hierarchy by privileging masculinist forms of power and agency and rendered the Left theoretically unequipped to understand, let alone oppose, specifically gendered forms of oppression.[27] The Left's desire to suppress gender difference in the name of unity would, ironically, facilitate a dismissive attitude toward the gendering of citizenship proposed by different religious elements within the fractious postrevolutionary state. It would also result in feelings of alienation and betrayal on the part of some leftist women, a painful rupture with their own political ideologies that would generate new affective attachments to feminist politics.

From March 8, International Women's Day, until March 13, tens of thousands of women took part in a series of meetings, demonstrations, and sit-ins to demand full legal equality and to support a host of other democratic demands. As Heidi Moghissi has argued, these events unfolded in a moment when many possible futures for postrevolutionary Iran were still imaginable.[28] With their chants, banners, manifestos, resolutions, and speeches, these women challenged the meaning of populist watchwords presumed to be axiomatic and universal, such as "freedom," "revolution," and "anti-imperialism." The revolutionary affects that had drawn people from different sociopolitical perspectives together in opposition to the Shah had begun to fragment and move in different directions.[29] Women protesters expressed their feelings of sovereignty over the revolutionary process of which they had been a part, and the tensions between their willingness to sacrifice themselves for the revolution and the desire to live free and equal in its aftermath exploded into view.

As Mottahedeh has noted, celebrations of International Women's Day were banned under the Shah, turning the very possibility of publicly marking the occasion into a victory for the revolution.[30] In the immediate aftermath of the revolution, virtually every leftist group launched a women's organization with corresponding weekly or monthly publications. In practice, this meant that many women stepped into new roles as leaders and organizers specifically around women's rights. Azar Tabari, a participant and former student in the US, notes that "a large number of these women had spent some time as students in Europe and the United States in the 1960s and 1970s. Invariably they had been affected, in some cases quite deeply, by the rise of the women's movement in these countries."[31] Several of the women I interviewed were among them. Returning ISA members Vida Samiian and Leyli Shayegan participated in Emancipation of Women (EW), which was affiliated with Communist Unity. Leyli, whose father had been a minister in Mossadeq's cabinet, was a student at Barnard College and active in the women's movement there as well as in the New York City ISA chapter. Vida had been active in CISNU in Los Angeles until she was elected head of publications on its five-member secretariat based in Europe. Once she returned to Iran, she worked on EW's publication, *Rahai-e Zan* ("Women's Emancipation"), which adopted a confrontational approach toward the new government.[32]

According to Jaleh Behroozi, who arrived in Iran from Berkeley in January on the same day that the Shah left: "We started it actually. Three weeks after

I got to Iran, [women from the UIC faction critical of Khomeini] formed a committee, the Society for the Awakening of Women (Jam'iat-e bidāri-e zanān). We decided we want to have a demonstration on March 8."[33] Jaleh and her comrades wanted to continue the CISNU tradition of celebrating International Women's Day, which situated Iranian revolutionary women alongside other Third World women (figure 6.1). As she explained in an interview she gave to Nasser Mojaher and Mahnaz Matin, many of the women who immediately got involved in organizing for March 8 "had been activists with a major role in the formation of women's committees" in CISNU. In fact, the selection of their new group's name was inspired by an Iranian women's organization with a similar name from the 1920s, which Jaleh and others learned about in a women's committee study group in Northern California.[34] The Society for the Awakening of Women (SAW) quickly got together with a handful of other groups and individuals to call a planning meeting. "A hundred and twenty people showed up to help organize," she remembered.

When Zohreh Khayam returned to Iran from Washington, DC, in February—on the same day as Khomeini—she helped to form the National Union of Women (NUW) along with Moghissi and other Fadaiyan members and supporters. As Moghissi has documented, Fadaiyan efforts to control the NUW and limit the scope of its critique of the new government would become a major obstacle to its development as a vehicle for women's liberation.[35] Nonetheless, the NUW attracted many unaffiliated women and became the largest of the women's organizations that existed in the immediate aftermath of the revolution.[36] Many women got involved in order to apply what they had learned in the anti-Shah movement to the struggles of women. This was true for returning students as well. "Because [the] ISA was such a huge, wonderful, and successful experience," Zohreh said, "I thought that we owed it to women to repeat that experience in terms of organizational structure, but with a concentration on women."

While these relatively small groups of leftist women were busy organizing for March 8, a series of provocations from Khomeini moved concerns over gender equality to center stage. On February 26, he issued an order suspending the 1967 family laws until they could be brought in line with sharia.[37] These laws had been part of the Shah's reforms, which the ISA had dismissed as top-down, inadequate, and unenforceable (see chapter 2). On March 3, women were banned from serving as judges, and on March 6 Khomeini called for the hijab to be mandatory for women who worked in government offices.[38] Gender segregation in schools was also announced for the fall term, igniting resistance from female high-school students.[39]

Figure 6.1 The Black Mountain Press Iranian Revolutionary Posters Collection. Published as *In Search of Lost Causes; Fragmented Allegories of an Iranian Revolution*, by Hamid Dabashi.

Apparently aware that plans to commemorate March 8 were underway, state television aired a denunciation of International Women's Day as a Western tradition.[40] What happened next would surprise everyone, not least the women activists at the center of the March 8 organizing efforts. Jaleh Behroozi recalled:

> The night before the demonstration, we thought maybe four to five hundred people would come and we only made banners and signs for a few people. We decided first we were going to have a seminar before the demonstration in Polytechnic Hall. As I was getting closer to Tehran University, I saw masses of women are going, moving, and I thought, "Where the hell are these people going?" We had only made a few announcements on radios and in newspapers. When I got to the hall, I was the speaker, and I couldn't even get to the stage. There were people inside the hall, there were people outside the hall. Thousands were there. In the middle of my talk, they said, "Let's go!" They didn't want to listen.

Eliz Sanasarian's account also supports the notion that the turnout for March 8 swelled spontaneously in response to Khomeini's announcement that women government employees should wear the hijab: "The news traveled fast from house to house in Tehran. ... Women who went to work early the next morning were told to don a *hejab* [*sic*] before entering their workplaces. Many refused to go to work and staged demonstrations."[41] Two thousand showed up to a hastily organized meeting at a high school.[42] When hundreds of women students meeting on the Tehran University campus found they had been locked in by Khomeini's supporters, they scaled the gates to join the thousands of women marching toward government offices.[43]

The March 8 demonstration turned into six days of mass marches and sit-ins that offered an alternative vision of what the revolution could become. None of these actions were officially supported by a political party, a fact that highlights the relative spontaneity and autonomy of the uprising, but which also made it difficult to sustain against a multisided counteroffensive.[44] Some leftist women who were members and supporters of groups like the Fadaiyan, which did not mobilize for the protests, showed up anyway and took part as individuals. Zohreh was among them. "What I remember about those demonstrations, which lasted a few days, was this huge, and I'm telling you, this *huge* number of people," she said. "Women from high-school age, like ninth grade, to older women had come to this. It was packed. You couldn't really move around very much. I'm talking about hundreds of thousands of women." This memory, while it might exaggerate the actual numbers of protesters, is entirely accurate in another, perhaps more important, sense: it captures the shock Zohreh, Jaleh, and other organizers experienced when they realized that the numbers of women who had come into the streets far exceeded anything they could have imagined. As Zohreh and Jaleh describe their memories, they bring the affective intensity of the protests into the present, as they try to convey the overwhelming feeling of power and possibility generated by large-scale collective struggle.

By March 10, the protests had taken the form of a mass sit-in outside the Ministry of Justice, despite violent attacks from religious vigilantes. Women protesters linked their opposition to mandatory wearing of the hijab to demands for freedom of the press and assembly and a host of other rights related to employment, family law, and legal standing. According to Moghissi's account, "many declarations and letters of support from various professional associations and political organizations were read and an eight-point manifesto was issued."[45] The manifesto, which was later published in a popular newspaper, covered a wide range of demands, including that decisions about "women's clothing must be left to them according to tradition, customs, and the needs of the environment" rather than imposed by the state, that "political, social and economic rights of women must be maintained and guaranteed without prejudice," that "true access to ... freedom of the pen, freedom of expression, freedom of opinion, freedom of employment, and social freedoms must be guaranteed for men and women of the nation."[46]

Nowhere in this manifesto is Islam or Khomeini attacked. Instead, the preamble to the list of demands invokes "women's selfless participation in the opposition to imperialism and despotism" and calls on Khomeini to make good on his "messages, interviews and statements" in which "women were promised freedom, equality, and inclusion in all social and political rights, and were explicitly promised that they will not be forced back fourteen hundred years."[47] The fear that doctrinaire applications of Islam would undermine women's standing was not expressed as a desire for secular government or as opposition to Islam. By insisting that Khomeini fulfill his own promises to women, the manifesto tried to leverage women's support for the revolution and its leader. Nuanced analyses of the relationship between religion, revolution, and the state, and the role of women in negotiating the shifting terms of this relationship, came from the voices of women protesters, some of which were captured on film.

Contested Interpretations of "Year Zero"

The collective effort of many thousands of Iranian women to create an affective and discursive space in which to express their support for the revolution *and* their criticism of the gender subordination that was being carried out in its name emerges as the central theme of the short documentary film *Mouvement de Libération des Femmes Iraniennes: Année Zéro* [Iranian Women's Liberation Movement: Year Zero], often despite the efforts of the filmmakers to impose a more simplistic anti-hijab narrative on the events.[48] This nearly twelve-minute film, made by visiting French feminists from the group Practice, Politics, and Psychoanalysis, includes footage from the mass sit-ins on March 10 outside the Ministry of Justice and on March 12 outside the Ministry of Television and Radio, which was followed by an enormous march to Freedom Square. It offers sensorial evidence of a brief historical opening, perhaps an even more daring "leap into the open air" than the overthrow of the Shah, when an Iranian revolutionary feminist sensibility was forged on the streets of the capital.[49]

The film opens with scenes of women marching with their fists raised, chanting, "Freedom is planetary, it's not Eastern or Western" (Azadi jahanist, na sharghist, na gharbist!).[50] The first part of this slogan expressed a capacious vision of freedom that was not reducible to any single ideology or national context. The second part of this slogan expressed a long-standing position on Iranian sovereignty, dating back at least to the pro-Mosaddeq movement, that rejected both Eastern (Soviet) and Western intervention in Iran. It was especially important that the women locate themselves within this anti-imperialist political tradition and assert their independence from any outside force. As Nima Naghibi has argued, women protesters were all too aware of how easily they could be labeled "West-toxified" (gharbzadeh) and discredited.[51] The association of women's rights and feminism with the West was further complicated by the fact that the Shah had paid lip service to these concepts and established the state-controlled Women's Organization of Iran. It would not be easy, under these circumstances, to assert a feminist vision of a revolutionary future. Indeed, the word *feminist* could not be used. Instead, the discourses of independence and freedom—which were shared by secular Marxists, liberals, and Islamists alike—would have to expand and change to accommodate the revolutionary affects of a heterogenous movement of women. Feminism, too, would have to be reimagined outside its associations with the secular West and with single-issue politics in order to build on the affective bonds forged by men and women as they fought against imperialism and the Shah.[52] One of the major slogans of the revolution—"Independence, Freedom, Islamic Republic!"—was thus revised by women protesters: "Independence, Freedom, Equal Rights!"[53] Perhaps most damning was the slogan "At the dawn of freedom, we have no freedom," because it questioned the very core of the revolutionary promise. The chants and interviews captured in the documentary reveal nuanced efforts to rearticulate the popular demand for national sovereignty with demands for women's independence from patriarchal state regulations and discrimination. I read these efforts as an expression and extension of revolutionary affects, now channeled toward a possible future in which women's freedom was necessary for the freedom of society as a whole.[54]

As the camera pans across the massive crowd, women with headscarves or chadors stand out among the majority of uncovered heads. In fact, the protesters were overwhelmingly made up of the urban middle and working classes, including nurses, teachers, students (from middle school to graduate school), government employees, women lawyers, and leftist and liberal women marching without the permission of their political parties. Reports attest to the presence of some women who had been active with the Pahlavi-run Women's Organization of Iran. Their presence, as well as that of a handful of Western feminists, was used by the religious right to slander the women as "counterrevolutionary insurgents."[55] In fact, these few Western women could not speak Persian, had very few connections to Iranian women organizers, and exercised no political influence over events. While the French women who made *Mouvement de Libération des Femmes Iraniennes* created an invaluable document of an almost-forgotten movement, I have chosen to decenter them in favor of the voices of Iranian women.

This was not a simple task, for the voices of Iranian women in the film are often drowned out by the French voice-over. However, efforts to discern the original Persian audio yielded important insights, such as the role of violence in the process of radicalization. This aspect of the motivation of women to protest emerges in the very first interview shown in the film, yet it is submerged in mistranslation and almost missed completely by the French woman holding the mic who appears more interested in asking questions about the chador.[56] The footage appears to have been taken at the March 12 sit-in organized in response to the state media's failure to report on the previous day's demonstrations and to condemn the violent response from pro-government men. Two older women wearing chadors, whose body language, clothing, and accents suggest a lack of formal education and affluence, explain why they have come. They are visibly upset and communicate with a sense of life-and-death urgency, practically shouting in Persian to the uncomprehending French filmmakers. They embody both the revolutionary affects that toppled the monarch and also an affective dissonance generated by recent events. "We fought for freedom," the first woman says, her black chador draped loosely over her head and wrapped around her waist. "Women were martyred alongside men. Now we are here for our own freedom." Mobilizing the revolutionary affects of self-sacrifice shared by men and women before the overthrow, she is outraged by what she perceives as an abuse of women and an abuse of Islam. "If Khomeini continues as he does, I will—as a religious Muslim woman—turn my back and leave my religion!" she threatens. Here she rejects Khomeini's authority to use her beliefs in order to justify the violent suppression of dissent. As she speaks, her open hand slices the air, rests on her heart, and, then, with her open palm forward, moves toward the camera as if pushing something intolerable away. There is no room for her affects, gestures, threats, or religious provocations in the leftist caricature of the women protesters as "West-toxified" and bourgeois.

The French woman moves on to ask a young, French-speaking Iranian woman her thoughts on the chador, but the two older women are not finished and demand to be heard. Now the second older woman speaks. She pulls her chador, dotted with white flowers, tightly around her face, and declares, "We want to be equal with men! My children studied! They want to be free!" Here the Persian audio, barely discernible under the French voice-over, differs drastically from the English subtitles. While the English translation tells viewers that this woman is speaking about her complicated relationship to the chador, and her desire to keep her daughters from being forced to wear it, I only hear one sentence on the topic from the woman, "Chador is religion!"[57] It is unclear if she is simply asserting a fact she considers banal to satisfy her questioner or if she intends some critique. In either case, she immediately returns to the topic that has brought her to the protest, which is the use of religion in the service of oppression: "If they [the religious factions] continue in this way, we'll become unbelievers! Being an unbeliever is better than the life [*inaudible*] by the likes of this garbage (ashghal)![58] My children are not free! What kind of freedom is this?! [*Inaudible*.] What kind of freedom is this?!" Then the first woman interjects, shifting the conversation to the immediate cause of her outrage. "Right now, my child is in the hospital! They hit her on the head!" The women speak at the same time about the violence their daughters experienced at the hands of religious forces, most likely for joining the protest on March 8. The second woman says, "They hit my daughter!" She shouts, "Madam! Madam!" at the French interviewer, who remains off camera, as if appealing to her to understand the full injustice of the situation. "They hit her on the head! They hit her on the face, on the nose! She's in the hospital!" As she speaks, she puts her hand on her nose, then opens it flat and pushes down, as if she is miming the act of violence meted out against her daughter. None of what these women say is translated in the French voice-over or in the English subtitles that appear on screen.

The affects, feelings, and political demands of these two women may have been deemed insignificant by the filmmakers, but they were also illegible to the majority of the leftist and liberal forces. As religious women, wearing their chadors in the most conservative manner, they demand freedom of expression without violence for their children. It is hard to imagine a more compelling democratic demand, and yet the Left could not recognize it in their eagerness to support the new regime against the ever-present imperialist threat. The presence, speech, gestures, and affects of both of these older, observant women prevent a reductive reading of the women's marches as "secular" or as singularly focused on opposition to wearing the hijab, though this was certainly a central concern. Donning the chador did not stop these women from occupying public space and demanding a different kind of freedom and equality than that which they feared the government had in mind. Thus, in the very first interview, we are confronted with female revolutionary subjectivities and affects radically out of sync with those of the established leaders—secular and religious—and with those women who were uncritical supporters of the new government.

The camera then cuts to a multistory hospital, panning across the outdoor balconies lined with female nurses in white uniforms who cheer, fists in the air, to show their support. "Salute to the nurses!" the crowd chants, "Salute to the nurses!" This shot reveals yet another group of women who, because they were educated at a time when illiteracy rates were upward of 80 percent, did not register with the Left as the "true proletariat." Next to the nurses stand two older women (perhaps patients?) in headscarves, smiling. A nursing student gives an interview, sitting outside among her colleagues, the snow-capped Alborz Mountains north of Tehran visible in the distance. She summarizes the role she and her friends played in the revolution and positions their protest as an extension and reinterpretation of its stated goals:

> When our revolution started, the whole nation struggled for freedom against dictatorship, against American imperialism. Men and women protested together to support the political claims in unity. We studied at the same time we worked in the hospital. During the revolution, we helped injured protesters. Voluntarily, for free. When the army capitulated, and the revolution triumphed, we all were on the streets. Then Khomeini said: "Stop protesting! Leave the streets!" So we went back to school. But since last Thursday, the religious people are making waves. For days we are protesting in the streets and proclaim that we do not want to wear the veil. If they want to do this, they should have said that before the revolution. They should have told us that they don't want equality of men and women. We are fighting for our rights. We want equality. If we do not speak out now, if we wait until the constitution is written, they will not make any allowances.

This is the most extensive counternarrative of the revolution offered in the documentary. The nursing student's sense of identification with "*our* revolution" (emphasis added) is proportionate to her dismay over the fractured unity of the early days ("men and women protested together"). The fact that she and her classmates participated in overthrowing the Shah has empowered her with the expectation that they should continue to play a role in shaping the course of the new society. In her interview, this nursing student posits the women's movement as the legitimate expression of what she and the other women thought they were fighting for all along. If this is not the case, she argues, "They should have said that *before* the revolution [emphasis added]. They should have told us that they don't want equality of men and women." The current moment, she maintains, is vital and pivotal, for there is still time to redefine the direction of the postrevolutionary society. A new constitution had not yet been written and the revolution's potential was still unfolding in the streets. Before ending the interview, she goes on to say, "We are not only protesting because of the veil. We are protesting because of all these things, which are even much more important." With great prescience, she views the state imposition of the veil as one example of a broader erosion of the democratic rights the revolution was supposed to deliver.

The film offers expansive shots of women marching toward Freedom Square on March 12, with no end to the crowds in sight. A line of men holding hands along the perimeter of the march is occasionally visible, moving in and out of the camera's frame. Several men from CISNU joined this ad hoc solidarity contingent organized by the main student organization at Tehran Polytechnic University and placed their bodies between the women and religious vigilantes.[59] "It was very interesting," Jaleh Behroozi said. Men "from [CISNU], they were holding hands protecting the demonstration." She argued that these men were acting on a "sense of solidarity," based on practices forged in diaspora. Ahmad Taghvai, who had returned from Berkeley a few months before Jaleh, and Nicky Nodjoumi, who had come back from New York City in 1978, both participated. "Actually," Nicky recalled, "I was one of the guys who held hands, and they attacked, they viciously attacked. Amazing. Other members of [CISNU] were there. I joined them. They did defend the women. It was a huge demonstration with a lot of men holding hands." The documentary does not include any of the violence that occurred.

From crowd shots of women marching, participating in a sit-in, and chanting, the films cuts to one final interview, this time with a young Iranian woman whose fluent French suggests an elite class background. She expresses her fury at the efforts of religious forces to subordinate women in the name of the revolution. "A free government has no right to dictate to us what we are allowed to do or not. We want to decide for ourselves. We— the women—are deciding our rights." She does not bother establishing her revolutionary credentials and does not use the language of self-sacrifice. Instead, she denounces media censorship and state television disinformation campaigns that reported a band of women with knives instead of a demonstration ten to fifteen thousand strong. While she speaks, just next to her, only partially visible in the camera's frame, stands a woman covered in a chador. This juxtaposition underscores the heterogeneity of the movement and the fact that it was not against the hijab in general; rather it was against the state-mandated regulation of women's bodies, a move that was understood, correctly, to be intrinsic to a broader authoritarian turn. At the end of the film, the camera cuts away from the footage to the credits while the audio from the protests continues. Thousands of women can be heard chanting over and over, "We didn't make a revolution to go backward!" Their voices linger beyond their visual presence, like a haunting invocation of a future that might have emerged from the collective imagination and will assembled at those demonstrations.

Response and Retreat

The demonstrations led to an immediate, partial victory, and on March 11, the interim government withdrew the plan to impose the veil. Yet this would prove to be a temporary concession, evidence of the power of the women's mobilizations to impact government policy in the short term—that is, when there was a movement occupying public space. The government, however, was not about to let this issue go. As Anne McClintock has argued, "because, for male nationalists, women serve as the visible markers of national homogeneity, they become subjected to especially vigilant and violent discipline. Hence the intense emotive politics of dress."[60] Islamists, without organized liberal or leftist dissent, would continue to press for the hijab, eventually succeeding in imposing it *de facto* for all women, not just government employees, in 1981, and *de jure* in 1983. Just as the women protestors warned, this was part of a sweeping legislative initiative, which resulted in "forty-six articles embedded in Iran's Civil Code, twenty-two in the Penal Code, and one Constitutional article used to ban women from seeking the office of the president."[61] These laws, some of which were continuations of Shah-era policy and some of which represented new forms of state discrimination, effectively turned women into second-class citizens. It is important, however, not to see this outcome as inevitable, or as the natural progression of an "Islamic" revolution. It is also crucial to state that Iranian women were not set back fourteen hundred years, as some had feared. Although it is beyond the scope of this chapter, many Iranian feminist scholars have written about the unprecedented gains in education and employment made by women after the revolution, as well as about the many new forms of women's and feminist organizing that have persisted in Iranian society over several decades.[62]

Remembering the 1979 women's uprising and claiming it as part of a diasporic Iranian feminist inheritance disrupts essentializing and totalizing versions of the revolution. The fact that the women's uprising met with initial success illustrates that the process of regendering citizenship after the fall of the Shah was far from smooth and that there was no guarantee of success for the revolution's conservative forces. As Behrooz Ghamari-Tabrizi has argued, it was not only the most rigid interpreters of Islam, but revolutionaries from across the political spectrum who intervened to undermine the uprising.[63] While some leftist groups, such as the Fadaiyan, condemned vigilante violence against the women, the leftist consensus was that the women's marches were a side issue, a distraction from the primary fight against imperialism. Speaking in the name of poor and laboring women and the "toiling masses" in general, the Left dismissed a movement they disqualified as middle class and, therefore, irrelevant to the idealized subjects they had constructed.

This way of defining the proper subjects of the revolution, shared by leftists, liberal nationalists, and Islamists alike, exemplifies what Gayatri Spivak has called "catachresis." In her words, there "are no literal referents, no 'true' examples of the 'true worker,' the 'true woman,' the 'true proletarian' who would actually stand for the ideals in terms of which you've mobilized."[64] Spivak notes that it is when movements are "*succeeding* in political mobilizations based on the sanctity of those masterwords, then it begins to seem as if these narratives, these characteristics, really existed."[65] She warns, "That's when all kinds of guilt tripping, card-naming, arrogance, self-aggrandizement and so on, begin to spell the beginning of an end."[66] Speaking to the frequency with which this dynamic occurs in the course of anticolonial movements, Spivak argues for the necessity of decentering the subject of change, not as the starting point for a political program but as a way of preventing the rise of "fundamentalisms and totalitarianisms of various kinds, however seemingly benevolent."[67] In this vein, the women's uprising of 1979 can be seen as an intervention into what Spivak has called "a critical moment" in national liberation movements, "when a deconstructive vigilance would not allow a movement toward orthodox nationalism."[68] In the footage from *Mouvement de Libération des Femmes Iraniennes*, we see and hear from women who defy the rigid categories of male-dominated revolutionary forces across the political spectrum and remind us that there is no "true woman," but rather tens of thousands of women with a multiplicity of histories and reasons for marching.

The rhetorical act of catachresis, the misuse of terms such as *the toiling classes* as an idealized category to wield against the mass mobilizations of women, proved effective largely because revolutionary affective attachments to Iranian freedom and independence were shared by the women protesting *and* by those who wanted them to stop. During the mass sit-in in front of the Ministry of Justice, speakers with leftist-liberal credentials tried to dissuade the women from continuing their nascent movement, sowing uncertainty and doubt. Homa Nateq, a professor and prominent intellectual who had initially been "horrified" by the sight of "all women in black chadors" marching in "the early stages of the revolution," now told women protesters: "Revolutionary struggle is gender blind. In recent years, many women, from the [Fadaiyan] or [Mojahedin] organizations, have been jailed and endured torture. They did not fight or lose their lives because of women's issues. They struggled on behalf of the Iranian people. We have no separate demands from those of the toiling classes; at least I don't. ... We believe that women's emancipation cannot be achieved independently from the emancipation of all the toiling masses, and Imam Khomeini is a defender of the toiling classes."[69] In the name of a gender-blind revolution, Nateq asserts that the heroic sacrifices of female guerrillas can only be honored by new acts of female sacrifice. The women's demands are, for no stated reason, presumed to be counterposed to and separate from those of "the toiling masses." Why it would harm the "toiling masses" for women to choose their own clothing, serve as judges, or have the same rights to divorce and child custody as men is never explained. And yet, the need to defend against this repeated charge of putting forward "separate demands" is evidenced in the manifestos and statements of the NUW, SAW, and EW, all of which use virtually identical phrases in their literature to assure readers that there is no separation between the struggles of women and those of the "toiling masses."

This knee-jerk association of women's issues with a separatism that colonized groups can ill afford has been widespread across various liberation movements. It is an argument that resonates in the diasporic context of the US as a common refrain among antiracist movements, where unity among racially targeted men and women is understood to be necessary for any hope of freedom. During the 1960s and 1970s, this demand for unity too often manifested in a male-dominated agenda in which "women's issues" were viewed as divisive. Just as feminism was defamed by association with the Shah and the West in Iran, feminism in the US has historically been rejected by many people of color as the purview of white, middle-class women that cannot speak to the shared experience of racism among men and women and that actively participates in maintaining a racial hierarchy among women.[70] Privileging the struggle against racism and/or imperialism over and above gender and sexual equality correlated with Marxist arguments that positioned class oppression as primary and race, gender, and sexual oppression as secondary side effects of capitalist exploitation. Both the Left and secular liberals in Iran shared hierarchical, theoretical, and political frameworks of "primary" and "secondary" struggles with many other liberation movements in the West and around the world.

These arguments were, of course, explicitly challenged by radical Black, Chicana, Indigenous, and Asian-American feminists in the US from at least the late 1960s on, but have only recently entered the mainstream of US society, largely through the concept of intersectionality and the Black Lives Matter movement. These antiracist, anti-capitalist, and anti-imperialist versions of feminism, just as much a product of life in the West as the most Orientalist forms of white, middle-class feminism, were never engaged with directly by Iranian opposition groups and have yet to become a reference point for Iranian diasporic scholars of the Iranian revolutionary women's movement. And yet it is striking that the Iranian Revolution produced an uprising of women who, much like their racialized counterparts in anticolonial and antiracist movements elsewhere, mobilized an embodied knowledge of multiple, intersecting forms of oppression afflicting Iranian society. They refused to separate the struggles against feudalism, imperialism, and dictatorship from demands for the emancipation of women. Their revolutionary affects fueled the fight for gender equality as a constitutive element in the radical transformation of society. Against ceaseless charges of separatism, they demanded that men join their fight.

Speakers at the rally in Tehran on March 10, 1979, however, appeared to take for granted the incompatibility between the women's demands and the integrity of the revolution. Speeches by Nateq and other respected figures, such as Mossadeq's grandson and revered anti-Shah activist, Hedayat Matin-Daftari, demoralized and disoriented the women's movement, made up as it was of supporters of the revolution. According to Nasser Mohajer—who, along with Mahnaz Matin, coauthored a major Persian-language study of the protests—the state media's deliberate misreporting of the women's movement caused "apprehension and hesitation ... to set in. Many of the students asked themselves: 'Could it be true that we may have become the unsuspecting vehicle of monarchist machinations?'"[71] Fearful that the

US might attempt another 1953-style coup, and wary of the fact that women's rights discourse had previously been deployed by the Shah's government, many women were unsure how to proceed. This hesitation became especially pronounced when it appeared that the government was walking back the enforcement of the mandatory wearing of the hijab. "It is understandable," Mohajer said. "A people who only three weeks previously freed themselves from the yoke of the Shah's regime, did not wish to be perceived as the pawns of the monarchy. . . . The Islamist forces which had just reached power were well aware of this ambivalence and ably capitalised on it to the detriment of this emancipatory movement."[72]

Yet many women's groups continued to organize and publish for months after the mass uprising had been driven off the streets. Members of SAW led an effort to launch a united national women's organization that could merge many of the smaller organizations into a more powerful force. This project was stymied by political disagreements over how to relate to the newly forming Islamic Republic and by the intensification of violent repression. When the SAW called an open demonstration against the cancellation of the 1967 family laws, the NUW did not support them, and the few hundred women who showed up were attacked by a mob of Khomeini supporters. Nonetheless, the SAW initiated a Committee for Unity that organized a solidarity conference in November 1979, the goal of which was to organize "the struggle of progressive women of Iran against oppression, inequality and exploitation."[73] The conference passed a resolution that tried again to respond to accusations discrediting women's desires for equality:

> Iranian women are well aware that world imperialism and the internal reaction try to mislead the rightful demands of women in order to serve their own interests. We condemn and denounce this well-worn trick. We shall not allow our struggle against discrimination and inequality to be identified as separate from that of Iranian toilers. But, at the same time, we must also denounce all the open and hidden violations of women's rights that have been taking place, not only around legislation passed or abolished but in the discriminatory attitudes towards women that have been present from the beginning of the victory of our uprising.[74]

"Trust us," this resolution seems to implore. "We are not the weak link or third column you fear." By rejecting the notion that women must either subordinate themselves to a patriarchal vision of the revolution or stand accused as tools of imperialism, the resolution quoted above pushes in another direction: toward a revolutionary anti-imperialist feminism that

I call intersectional because it recognized and contended with multiple, overlapping sources and forms of oppression. It is precisely the politics of the "But, at the same time" in the quotation above that are so instructive. Claiming the revolution as theirs and critiquing it at the same time, women's rights activists of this era imagined another possible Iran and developed a methodology crucial for feminist politics today.

Fragmentation and Decline

The refusal of the organized Left to mobilize behind the women's protests caused major conflicts to erupt among its ranks, splitting organizations and, ultimately, leading many women, and some men, to leave their party affiliations behind. Ahmad Taghvai, Jaleh Behroozi, Parviz Shokat, Hamid Kowsari, and a handful of like-minded leftists quit the UIC because of the group's backing of Khomeini, and formed another, even smaller, group that supported the women's demands.[75] Ahmad attributed his alienation from the majority of the Left to the time he spent abroad: "The thing that is important here is the impact of the US movements on us. Those of us who were members of [CISNU] and grew up politically in the US—yes, they made a lot of mistakes and sided with Khomeini—but when it came to issues like women, when the activists who were in Iran said this is not important, the majority of [CISNU] members were sensitive to this. When the women protested, we went to support them. We had this tradition of showing support." According to Ahmad, the efforts made to grapple with women's equality in ISA chapters and the ISA's practice of solidarity with other liberation movements enabled him to support the women's mobilizations when the majority of the Left did not. The problem, as Ahmad saw it, was that the Left "started following the Islamic movement" hoping "to cause change within that discourse instead of making their own." While Ahmad found himself in fundamental disagreement with the dominant leftist argument that "women or religious issues were not the main issues of the day," he was in a distinct minority. Most CISNU members rigidly followed party lines and suppressed criticism of Khomeini, just like their counterparts who had never left Iran.

Jaleh Pirnazar recalled her departure from the Revolutionary Organization after the March 1979 events: "That was my breaking point with my organization. Because they were not supporting the movement, they were supporting Khomeini." The affective shift from belonging to alienation was extremely painful and disorienting for her. "Come March 8, we are stepping on our own ideology," she said. "The women's movement, we should have embraced it. But my organization didn't. So I finally started putting the dots together. I don't belong! I'm in the wrong train! There are so many things going against my grain . . . and I can't reconcile this anymore."

Zohreh Khayam remembered the refrain that would greet anyone who "had some concerns about a religious takeover. People would stop them with the slogan '*bas bad az marg-e Shah*,' 'discussion after the death of the Shah,' so they would abort any substantive conversation around political issues." This strategy did not go uncontested. As a founding member of the NUW, Zohreh engaged in political battles with the Fadaiyan leadership, who "wanted to mobilize women for themselves [to recruit women to the party]. They wanted to even influence the internal democratic processes in terms of elections and things inside our group, and we said no." The Fadaiyan attempted to control the NUW through women "who were part of them and thought exactly the same," Zohreh said.[76] The Fadaiyan argument was that women had to "wait until we reach socialism in our country and then we would get to issues of minorities and women."

Zohreh, along with many other women, fought for the autonomy of the NUW. One year after the women's uprising, on March 8, 1980, the NUW organized an event marking the occasion at a university. Much to Zohreh's dismay, the Fadaiyan "opted to have a [separate] demonstration to go and support the hostage takers" at the US embassy at the exact same time. This was the breaking point for her and for many other women. "That's where we started really splitting ourselves from their thought process because we knew [the Fadaiyan socialist strategy] didn't work in other places and it's not going to work [in Iran]." She argued that: "just participating in economic production was not enough and was not liberating. Even in the Soviet Union, the motto that people had at the time was that women should contribute to social production, so women became productive members of society in every possible profession. And yet they would go home, their husbands would get drunk and they would get beat up. So obviously that wasn't our goal. Women are half of the population. How can you say hold off and not to ask for your rights?" While Zohreh was developing a feminist critique of Fadaiyan socialist politics, some leftist women were wearing the chador to show their support for Khomeini, something Zohreh was "very much against."

During the official governmental process of writing a new constitution, the NUW was invited to a forum to present their proposals. Zohreh was charged with editing the group's report, which had been researched and compiled by lawyers, and with presenting it at what she recalled was a "huge gathering": "We were asking for equality in pay, equality before the eyes of the law at all levels, in family law and civic law ... the question of custody, equality in divorce proceedings, and things like that. Everything that sharia law has brought, everything against that. We weren't against any person who voluntarily wanted to wear the chador, because when we were kids it was convenient. A lot of women who didn't work outside of the home, they would just put the chador on and go to the store and come back. That was their choice." Yet the question of whether or not to oppose the legal imposition of the hijab split the NUW, while the regime turned its attention to persecuting its erstwhile leftist supporters. Nonetheless, some women persisted in organizing until it became too dangerous even to hold a meeting. "Towards the end of our open activities, one of the very last major works that [the NUW] did was a lot of education about the law of retribution," Zohreh said, referring to a law that defined the life of a woman as worth half the life of man and assigned unequal monetary amounts for death payments on this basis. "How backward is that?" she said. "And you know what? We didn't have any support from the leftist men." What moved Zohreh to action simply failed to move the male Fadaiyan leadership, as well as many Fadaiyan women who were devoted to carrying out the party line. The "huge reluctance, if not refusal" by Fadaiyan men and women to consider women's liberation as anything other than a by-product of socialism finally led Zohreh to quit the organization. She believed "that they were a good group against the Shah's regime. They had fought very hard, they had made a lot of sacrifices, but they are not thinking the way I do, and they don't give equal value to women."

These memories reveal the extended struggle of some Iranian women, months after the March uprising was suppressed, to advocate for gender equality. Vida Samiian, who had been part of the CISNU five-person international secretariat, arrived in Iran in May of 1979 and organized with the Organization of Communist Unity, a revolutionary coalition formed by returning members of the Marxist wing of the National Front.[77] She also helped to found the EW, and was one of the organizers of a women's conference in February 1980 at Tehran University, among the last efforts by women to participate in open democratic opposition to the government. "The *Basij* [internal security forces] surrounded the conference and cut off the electricity before anyone could start to speak," she recalled. "I was going to speak and say that we had to continue the struggle against hijab and for women's equality. But instead, we led some chants and marched out."

Of the former ISA members I interviewed, Soosan, Shahnaz, and Nancy remained stalwarts of party discipline in the UIC, following orders that landed each of them in jail. None of them were in Iran for the March 1979 women's uprising, but when they did arrive in the months that followed, they did not join any women's organizations. The ideology of gender sameness was so entrenched for some women that the notion of state-imposed hijab seemed incidental rather than oppressive. "We saw women as men," Soosan said. "We thought, 'So what? You wear this [scarf] on your head.'" For her, and many other leftist women, a piece of cloth did not undermine the notion that men and women had already achieved equality in the process of carrying out revolutionary activity. Even from abroad, the women's protests did not appeal to Soosan in either an affective or a political register. "I was completely for Khomeini," she remembered, "and I couldn't believe that he would force women to be [covered] like that. He said he's going to come, and he's going to go to Qom, and the government will govern, and it's going to be democratic. I hundred percent believed him."

Nancy remembered that "when [the government] started imposing hijab and Islamic dress, the [UIC] said, 'Let's just do it.' We were already in that framework. We had already adopted a culture that was very stifling." Her organization was so pro-Khomeini that they sent a delegation to the occupied US embassy to hold a press conference with the Students in the Line of the Imam, the group holding Americans hostage. "Looking back on it, the tactic was wrong," she said. The embassy takeover "was one of the things the regime used to consolidate their power. Until that time, things were very much in flux, not that the Left would have come out the winner, but there could have been a more leveling of the playing field to avoid a takeover by the religious extremists."

Several of the men I interviewed shared the perspective that the women's movement marked a turning point for the fate of the revolution—and of the Left. Ali Hojjat remembered that the Revolutionary Organization held a separate celebration of March 8, 1979, instead of joining the mass marches. "That was the biggest mistake," he said. When some women came from the protest to the meeting to ask for support, a debate ensued. Ali, now highly critical of his role at the time, responded then by calling the women's movement petty bourgeois. "They [the women] were from upper- to middle-class people. We were also from [the] upper middle class and middle class, but we dressed down. Our attitude towards them was polite, but we did not agree with them." At the meeting, the women's concerns did not register affectively or politically with Ali and his comrades, who remained unmoved. Gender, class, and Westernization had been sutured together during the reign of the Shah so profoundly that the Left could disqualify women's rights activists with Marxist rhetoric against imperialism and the bourgeoisie. Of course, the bourgeois class backgrounds of many leftist men were never grounds for disqualification of their political ideas.

Like Ali, Bijan, who returned to Iran from Texas in 1978 and stayed until 1982, was filled with regret over the role he and his comrades in the UIC had played:

> I think this is one of the most unfortunate things because most of the Left, including us, decided that these are a bunch of prostitutes and bunch of Westernized people; they are not concerned about poverty or imperialism. That's how we treated them. People change their minds, including me, when they look retrospectively, based on where they are now, they change their stories. I try to stay as honest to who I was at that time as possible. I try my best. It's very difficult to be that way. Some of my friends that I talk to, including when it comes to the issue of women at that time, they say, "Oh, we were backward, we were reactionary. Monarchists were more progressive." They go to the other extreme.

Bijan spoke haltingly, struggling under the weight of history to find the right words with which to hold himself, and his peers, accountable for the mistakes he believes they made. There is sorrow in this deliberation, yet he insists on facing the past as he lived it, rather than absolving himself or renouncing the entire revolutionary project by going "to the other extreme" of rehabilitating the monarchy. Bijan also recalls the practice shared by leftists and religious revolutionaries alike of slandering and discrediting unruly women by calling them prostitutes. The association of prostitution with Westernization, immorality, and corruption led to horrendous acts of violence against women working in the sex industry, and even some executions, as the gendered logics of masculinist anti-imperialism crystalized in the attempt to obliterate this quintessential figure of debased, sexualized femininity.[78]

Conclusion

The memories of former ISA members and the documentary footage of the March 1979 events in Tehran work against romanticizing the revolutionary affects that underpinned the diasporic student movement, revealing the ways these affects mapped along existing gender hierarchies, even to the extent that many women sided with the male-dominated leftist leadership against women's social and legal equality.[79] The revolutionary affects that enabled thousands of Iranian foreign students to repudiate the good life of the imperial model minority and to reject the normative temporality of social reproduction brought new dissident diasporic subjectivities into being that were nonetheless embedded in unequal social relations. We are left to reckon with the expectation of the majority of the Iranian Left—men and women—that women should not have objected to the new forms of state regulation to which they were being subjected. I read this as a stark illustration of how an enduring and heartfelt commitment to freedom in the form of national sovereignty was channeled primarily through masculinist forms of revolutionary subjectivity, in which a hierarchal model of oppression reigned and the demand for self-sacrifice as the dominant mode of liberation could be especially applied to women. As the previous chapter showed, affective attachments to gender sameness/masculinization in the ISA and among the diasporic Iranian Left were underpinned by demands for female self-abnegation. This combination facilitated the diasporic Left's slide into an embrace of Islamist forms of gender regulation back in Iran, where the measure of revolutionary belonging became a willingness to exchange the androgynous, curve-covering uniforms of the Marxist-Leninist student milieu for the hijab. The state imposition of the mandatory wearing of the hijab was part of a host of other forms of gender discrimination, and yet it became the most visible reminder that women's bodies were viewed as suspect, corruptible, and in need of legally binding forms of control.

The fleeting appearance of a women's movement that was both in favor of the revolution—composed of participants active in the overthrow of the Shah—and that redefined self-determination to include women's liberation in the new society gestured toward another possible future. It was at this moment that women rejected the "designated agency" available to them through self-sacrifice to the male-dominated movement and attempted to renegotiate the terms of their revolutionary subjectivity.[80] Foucault's observation, made during his stint as a reporter in Iran covering the revolution in 1978, seems even more appropriate for those few days in March 1979 when tens of thousands of Iranian women stood, to borrow his words, "at the threshold of a novelty," rejecting the patriarchal politics of the modernizing pro-Western regime and those of the leftist-liberal-Islamist coalition. Foucault coined this phrase after witnessing earlier mass marches against the Shah, during which support for Khomeini was ubiquitous on the streets and millions of people donned the white burial shrouds of Shi'i mourning practices to display their willingness to die for the revolution. As moving and unprecedented as this affective and political force was, the teleological religious vision of a transnational Islamic community advocated by Khomeini was hardly novel, even while it drew on a contemporary populist amalgam of religious and leftist ideas.[81]

The contrast with the March uprising is worth emphasizing. The revolutionary affects of Iranian women protesters manifested as a fierce, immediate rejection of their own subordination as a necessary part of Iran's "emancipation." This embodied refusal positioned Iranian women protesters on the threshold of something so novel—a new revolutionary feminist sensibility—that it was both illegible and impermissible within the dominant paradigms of the revolution. Thus, these women were attacked from all sides with charges of separatism and complicity with imperialism, for which no evidence was ever produced. Despite its brevity, the women's movement that emerged on the streets in 1979 constitutes a vital diasporic inheritance for Iranians in the West negotiating alienation and discrimination in multiple locations. As a heterogeneous movement, Iranian women protesters insisted that their demands for gender equality were unaligned, "neither Eastern nor Western," and irreducible to any existing party or ideology. Their demands emerged instead from the lived experience of US-backed dictatorship and, crucially, from within the revolutionary process itself.

This chapter has sought to expand a transnational genealogy of revolutionary anti-imperialist feminism, allowing us to understand the post-revolutionary interventions of Iranian women in relation to other feminist challenges to unjust state power. The expression of revolutionary affects as a commitment to ending multiple, overlapping forms of socioeconomic and cultural oppression was a shared experience among women in the Black Power movement and other Third Worldist movements in the US and around the world.[82] While Third World solidarity between the anti-Shah and other liberation movements has been acknowledged and even celebrated by previous scholars, the connection between the Iranian women's uprising and Third World/women-of-color feminisms has not received attention as part of the same global phenomenon. However, for women revolutionaries around the world, the experience of revolutionary activity created the possibility of reimagining social relations, including gender relations.[83]

The revolutionary affects that fueled the women's uprising in March 1979 might live on in diaspora as a reminder that patriarchy is embedded in both religious and secular ideologies, and, furthermore, that there is no single ideology that will guarantee the formation of a non-hierarchical society. Marxism, Islamism, and liberal secularism (as the ideology of US imperialism) have each been mobilized to repressive ends that were not inevitable but the outcome of struggles over what these ideas would mean in practice and over which organization of socioeconomic power relations they would support. We might have had an Iranian revolution in which religious and secular women's demands for equality were seen as the legitimate extension of the desire for freedom. This desire has not gone away but lives on in the efforts of contemporary Iranian feminists to challenge patriarchy and imperialism using a variety of ideas and strategies.

Rather than viewing the oppression of Iranian women as the inevitable outcome of the revolution, and the disparate gender politics of Iran and the West as singular evidence of their polarized opposition, an intersectional anti-imperialist framework allows us to critique gender and sexual regulations associated with Western intervention and with religious dictatorship. The feminist anti-imperialism of 1979 might yet circulate in diaspora as an affective attachment to a capacious vision of freedom that is not circumscribed by the mandate to align with either the US or Iranian states. It might open up new possibilities for affinities among feminists in Iran and in the US and the West more broadly who oppose the multiple, overlapping forms of gender, sexual, racial, and class inequality that structure their lives. Recalling this marginalized history of women and revolution can reroute the circuits of diasporic subjectivity and solidarity today and transgress the ideological borders drawn by dictatorships and empires.

Conclusion
Revolutionary Affects
and the Remaking of Diaspora

In this concluding chapter, I consider how the affective legacy of the ISA might intervene in dominant constructions of Iranian diasporic subjectivity since 1979. In the postrevolutionary period, the waves of migration from Iran to the US, Canada, and Europe have constituted a much larger, permanent diaspora, largely understood as a response to a theocratic revolution against modernity that sent Iran backward in time. How might a reckoning with the unpredictability of the Iranian Revolution alter this narrative? This chapter works through an archive of memories that render the lived experience of revolution as an affective encounter with possibility, risk, and disorientation. Much of what former ISA activists feel and remember has been erased or discredited amidst the shaming and blaming of the Left for supporting many aspects of the Islamic Republic's emerging authoritarianism (see chapter 6). Marginalized among Iranian immigrant narratives about the difficulties of making a life in a new country is the story of what it means to live with the deadly consequences of one's mistakes while striving to sustain revolutionary hope for the future. What are the political implications of those revolutionary affects that linger in diaspora? How might attachments to revolutionary futures that did not come to pass make new forms of Iranian diasporic revolutionary subjectivity possible today?

Loss among the Iranian diaspora is deeply politicized. While loss is foundational to diaspora, not all members of a displaced population are grieving the same losses. Examinations of how loss shapes diasporic politics have primarily focused on politically conservative manifestations. Nostalgia for lifestyles of wealth and elite social status under the Shah has been institutionalized in Iranian exilic media, literature, and even architecture since the 1980s.[1] However, as the memories and affects of former ISA members illustrate, exilic nostalgia is not always or inherently a politically conservative phenomenon.[2] To engage with the heterogeneity of loss and the discredited sites of diasporic nostalgia is to confront the contingency of historical events and to abandon teleologies of victory or defeat. Reckoning with contingency is not the same as ignoring the historical and material context in which events occur. It is not true that *anything* was possible in 1978–79, in an Iranian society in which class and gender formations had been shaped by the vicissitudes of dictatorship and imperialism over the preceding century, and where opposition activities had been severely repressed for decades. The near liquidation of the older generation of leftists after the 1953 CIA-backed coup and the persecution of the subsequent Marxist-Leninist generation prevented leftist parties from establishing roots and building significant bases beyond college campuses. In contrast, established networks of seminaries and mosques proved capable of coordinating and sustaining a popular revolution. From Shariati to Khomeini, a Shi'i liberation theology provided the most compelling ideological framework through which to mobilize the revolutionary affects of millions of people.[3]

Taking these conditions into account does not mean settling for the inevitability of things as they happened. While it is not true that the Left had enough influence to lead the revolution, it is also not the case that Khomeini was all powerful and in total control of events, as the initial success of the March 1979 women's mobilizations in pushing back mandatory wearing of the hijab shows (see chapter 6). Avoiding both idealism and determinism, I offer a methodology of possibility that not only "brushes history against the grain," as Walter Benjamin described the work of historical materialism, but sifts among the wreckage of the past for lost futures.[4] Analyzing the revolutionary affects of former ISA members allows us to recuperate the lived experience of "feeling revolutionary," as José Muñoz put it, a feeling that takes on new meaning and urgency in the current global context of rapacious, authoritarian capitalism.[5] While the previous chapter focused on the 1979 women's uprising as a turning point in the direction of the revolution, this chapter considers other flashes of danger and hope that retain their affective charge decades later. The memories discussed in this chapter brim with affects that sustain revolutionary hope as well as those that recall the rapid unfolding of tumultuous events beyond one's control, something akin to the feeling of free fall. This chapter thus assembles an archive of what Avery Gordon has called "fugitive" knowledges, which were smuggled across borders as Iranian leftists, hunted and stateless, ran for their lives.[6]

Using a methodology of possibility to read memories of revolution highlights the political potential embedded in Hirsch and Spitzer's concept of "resistant nostalgia," discussed in chapter 1, as an open engagement with the past that intervenes in the present. While Wendy Brown has been very critical of what she calls "left melancholia," which she defines as a conservative attachment to the states and parties that ruled in the name of socialism or communism, I argue that the melancholic attachments of the former ISA members I interviewed function differently.[7] The men and women whose affects and memories I have been tracing throughout this book are not nostalgic for any political party or state, or even for a particular ideology; since the destruction of the organizations they built as students and the invalidation of their theoretical frameworks by actual events, they have been improvising and surviving, staring into the face of defeat and trying to untangle their political desires from the doctrines and parties that once defined their lives. If attachments to the past are affective rather than programmatic, then they retain the potential for reinterpretation and the energy to fuel new transformative agendas. My argument thus aligns with Enzo Traverso's efforts to de-pathologize left melancholia. "Rather than a regime or an ideology, the lost object can be the struggle for emancipation as a historical experience that deserves recollection and attention in spite of its fragile, precarious, and ephemeral duration," he writes.[8] Crucially for this study of leftist alienation from a revolution many activists experienced as having turned against them, "melancholy means . . . a fidelity to the emancipatory promises of revolution, not to its consequences."[9] It is this fidelity to the promise of emancipation that can disrupt an acceptance of the finality of capitalist triumph over socialism, or of US imperialism as the lesser evil to an Islamic republic. Left melancholia can emerge as what Traverso has called "an obstinate refusal of any compromise with domination."[10]

One common expression of resistant nostalgia that occurred during my interviews with former ISA members about the Iranian Revolution was the assertion, as Afshin Matin-asgari puts it, that "people who say we should have predicted were wrong. It was not predictable. It could have gone different ways."[11] Rather than argue for or against the truth of this sentiment, I consider it part of the affective afterlife of the revolution, evidence of a sustained longing for a future that never arrived, or one that might have been. Such sentiments can disrupt the widespread nostalgia for the Shah that has constituted normative Iranian American identity since 1979. Resistant nostalgia, or left melancholia, can bring revolutionary affects of hope and possibility into the present as part of an unflinching look at the hidden losses that have constituted our contemporary diaspora.

In the months that followed the women's marches, the new government began to attack leftist and liberal media outlets, organizations, and individuals. Returning ISA members often found themselves blindsided by events, scrambling to understand, adapt, and survive. While many activists continued trying to organize for months, and sometimes years, almost every former ISA member I interviewed recalled a turning point when escape into exile became the best-case scenario. At the same time, moments of resistant nostalgia also emerged as affective formations, in the words of David Eng and David Kazanjian, "full of volatile potentiality and future militancies rather than … pathologically bereft and politically reactive."[12] This form of nostalgia has enabled the former ISA members I interviewed to resist identification with the dominant narratives of the revolution, those propagated by the Iranian state and by the mainstream of the Iranian diaspora. Though for different reasons, these two narratives share a condemnation of the Left and the leftist project in its entirety. In contrast, my interview subjects are decades into a reckoning with loss that can inform efforts to imagine a way out of the current standoff between US imperialism and dictatorship in Iran.

This chapter looks first at memories of freedom and collective transformation, before turning to consider how former ISA members narrate lived experiences of the revolution's authoritarian turn. I then offer close readings of the stories of five ISA members who became political prisoners of the revolutionary government they had supported. Finally, the chapter concludes by drawing the narrative arc of the book together around a culminating argument: by following the movement of revolutionary affects, an unexpected and subversive diasporic legacy emerges to reinterpret the standard narrative of leftist disappointment, failure, and betrayal.[13] This reinterpretation enables new understandings of the relationship between revolution, migration, and diaspora that might lead away from assimilation and an embrace of US global dominance.[14] A melancholic attachment to the long Iranian freedom struggle discussed in chapter 1 places the revolutionary affects of former ISA members discussed below within a longer genealogy of opposition to both imperialism and dictatorship.

The relationship between melancholia and nostalgia traverses the intimate and historical registers that I weave together throughout this book. As Svetlana Boym argues, melancholia "confines itself to the planes of individual consciousness," while nostalgia mediates "the relationship between individual biography and the biography of groups or nations, between personal and collective memory."[15] Resistant nostalgia carries what remains of the affects, feelings, dreams, and violent ruptures that attended the lived experience of the revolutionary process for former ISA members. As Marianne Hirsch and Leo Spitzer write, "A past reconstructed through the animating vision of nostalgia can serve as a creative inspiration ... 'called upon to provide what the present lacks.'"[16] Emotions, affects, and memories tied to that other possible Iran can, this chapter argues, enact a "resistant relationship to the present, a 'critical utopianism' that imagines a better future."[17]

Remembering Another Possible Iran

Sina's reflections on his experiences of the Iranian revolution emerged as those of a collective subject, a mode of revolutionary subject formation marginalized by our neoliberal present. Sina could not speak only of himself, for the affective power of his memories derives from the notion that they were widely shared. At the end of 1978, he placed his studies in the US on hold and traveled to Iran in time to witness the enormous demonstrations and strikes that gave the revolution its mass character, with as much as 10 percent of the population actively participating.[18] Sina spoke of a moment frozen in time, one that does not exist according to official (US and Iranian) state histories or within the foundational exilic narrative of the majority of the diaspora. His memories emerged like a reverie: "We glimpsed something. We really did. We as an organization and as members of the period, we glimpsed something. We are like Sufis, there was an apparition. In that revolution, we glimpsed the possibility of a world that is neither Shah nor Islamic Republic." That apparition has remained an outcast among the many ghosts haunting the Iranian diaspora.[19] Yet Sina insists on remembering: "There is no way as an individual for you to deny or reject your past. Your health will come if you acknowledge it, if you work through it. But it's always there. It's a wound; it's there. We cannot restart the world afresh."

For Sina, a melancholic relationship to revolutionary politics has allowed him to "retain [Marxism], but not in its original form." He is still searching for what he glimpsed in Iran in 1978, for a way out of the impasse of our times, so dramatically illustrated in the contemporary Middle East, between secular and religious forms of authoritarian capitalism. Rather than becoming disillusioned with the entire project of revolutionary transformation, he is concerned with whether and how there might be a chance to try again, differently. "I really wish we could find the word for revolution in Iran that is no longer tainted [by association with the state]," he said. The fact that this wish remains, despite the many losses he suffered is an expression of the revolutionary affects and beliefs he still carries. "There is no way to act politically correctly without being communist," Sina continued. "No matter what you say, we may not have the name for it. This name may be disqualified. But the idea ... the intersection of justice and politics and the commons, there is no other way." Far from a romance with an idealized past, resistant nostalgia makes it possible to hold on to radical notions of justice and human liberation even while disaffiliating from states linked to the words *revolution* and *communism*. The affective experience of revolutionary hope and triumph—however short-lived or misapprehended—thus becomes a conduit to other possible futures and a bulwark against cynicism and despair.

Rather than functioning as a warning against, or condemnation of, youthful revolutionary activity as mistaken or naive, memories of the flourishing of democratic practices and collectivities in Iran can affirm the initial impulse to throw oneself into revolutionary activity. Nicky Nodjoumi, a painter who was active in the ISA in New York City, returned to Iran in time to join the mass demonstrations in 1978. At Tehran University, he helped to spearhead an artistic initiative designed to capture and spread the revolutionary spirit. "Our poster organization had the symbol of a red star and fist. We organized a huge workshop of silk-screening and cartooning in Tehran University. We occupied a whole section of the Faculty of Fine Arts. Thirty students and teachers worked days and nights to make all of these posters." Nicky and his fellow artists tried to maintain a nonsectarian openness to the movement that was unfolding around them. "We had everybody involved," he explained. "For every session, we would collect slogans and ideas and decide what posters to do." The artists' organization maintained independence from existing leftist parties, working alongside various groups without joining them. "We were more like democracy in action. We had exhibitions of our posters. We counted and every day more than 5,000 people would visit our exhibition, and on the top floor we had all the materials ready for whoever wants to make a poster." This period of open, collective artistic production was short-lived. "On the other side of campus," he continued, "there was this hardline Muslim organization and, one year later, they burned the whole floor, the space we occupied. But we had printed and sent out many of our posters to the schools and the factories in Tehran."

Universities were the site of major battles between leftist and Islamist students after the revolution, and the shift from leftist to Islamist domination over the campuses, especially in Tehran, was a critical part of the suppression of the Left overall. And yet it is worth recalling the passion and vision of this revolutionary artistic collective, and the many thousands of visitors to their exhibits, evidence of the revolution's creative, democratic, and liberatory potential.

Ali Hojat, active in the Northern California ISA, described the overwhelming feeling he shared with other returning ISA members when he first encountered the revolution. "We were euphoric," he said, his eyes watering, an irrepressible smile spreading across his face. "We didn't think in our wildest dreams, comparing to two years ago, that this regime would crumble." By "two years ago" he meant two years before the overthrow of the Shah. It was as if the emotional charge of his memory had transported him back in time. "I mean, imagine what's happening in Iran," he said, continuing to speak of the past in the present tense, "and then in six months, one year, you go to Tehran and everything is free! You become so euphoric!" Ali's affective attachment to this feeling also led him to couch his criticisms of what went wrong within the context of the period. "We thought it was very important to support this revolution. We were under the impression that there is always a danger for the *ancien regime* to come back. So we sort of didn't care much about women's issues in the sense of marching and everything. And later on we supported Khomeini for a few months more. That was a mistake. But it's like Monday morning quarterback[ing]. At that time, it was hard." At the end of the interview, Ali asked me for a transcript, explaining, "This is the first time in my life I've sat down to go over what I have done."

Jaleh Pirnazar, who had served on the ISA's national secretariat in the 1970s, offered her own attempt to balance her contradictory feelings about her activity. Insisting that people need to understand this history "with all the nuances," she went on to say, "It's not rosy. It has its rosy moments, yes. When Vietnam won, it was our victory. We just were ecstatic! [The] US failed in Vietnam and had to pull out. There were great moments." Then she went on to say: "What has been difficult for us is having our very close comrades killed by this present regime. These were very, very lovely human beings, comrades in arms with us who went to Iran, and they didn't make it, and we made it." Carrying this history with her "has been, personally, a very difficult journey," Jaleh said, "because of the entanglement of so many issues. And you don't even have time to sit down and sort them out. You're in it. You are inside this river and it's taking you. I think finally it [the magnitude of loss] hits you one day, and then you have to try not to be negative."

One way to avoid renouncing her past is to articulate her personal losses with those of the era as a whole. In the following passage, she recounts how her return to Northern California after the revolution, to the place where she began her activist life in the ISA, has been haunted by the ghosts of those "who didn't make it" and then situates this experience within a broader context: "There's this house down here on [a street in Berkeley]. Three of our friends lived there together and all three have been killed. So for me to come back and see the International House [where the ISA held many of its events] and drive past these apartment houses and all that, it's really difficult. It's a reminder of failure, disappointment. I miss them. And at the same time, it was part of the era. Nineteen sixty-eight was an eruption of movements, student movements, so we were just part of that. We were lucky to be part of that." Jaleh's memories of victory, failure, and disappointment are tied together with the threads that bound her to these "very lovely human beings." Her sense of loss moves from the personal to the global scale, allowing her to also remember the ecstatic feelings attached to the high points of Third World liberation. Revolutionary affects live on in diaspora as euphoria mixed with grief, and resistant nostalgia makes it possible to hold on to what might have been while continuing to mourn the casualties of what was. Carving out space in diaspora to recall revolutionary feelings of collective power, including affects of solidarity that made the victory in Vietnam feel like a victory for Iranians, is not easy given that any positive feelings about the revolution can be misinterpreted as support for the current Iranian government. It is, therefore, crucial to note that affective attachments to the high points of revolution were, as Jaleh's quote above illustrates, always bound up with painful memories of devastating loss. The following section reckons with the affects of disorientation and dissonance that are as much the legacy of the Iranian Left as the euphoria described above.

Things Fall Apart

From the end of March 1979, when the national referendum establishing the Islamic Republic was held, until the official banning of all political parties besides the Islamic Republic Party in the summer of 1981, each of the organizations to which ISA members belonged were eviscerated, their offices shuttered, their members arrested or driven underground. If thousands of women were among the first to feel the brunt of the postrevolutionary consolidation of state power, aggressive censorship of the press signaled the curtailment of the revolution's democratic potential to an even broader swath of the population.[20] For many of the former ISA members I interviewed, the closing of the most popular national newspaper, *Ayandegan*, on August 7, 1979, made the new balance of power apparent. As Parvin Paidar has argued, this event was part of Khomeini's efforts to eliminate both his Islamist rivals and his secular critics.[21] More than any other newspaper, *Ayandegan* had become a symbol of the new democratic opening, giving voice to an expansive range of revolutionary opinions. Its name meant "the future people," or posterity, and derived from the root *ayandeh*, meaning both future and futurity. The shuttering of *Ayandegan* by government decree precipitated a major confrontation between Khomeini's supporters, known as the hezbollai, and supporters of the leftist-liberal National Democratic Front (NDF), in what became a symbolically and physically violent foreclosure of other revolutionary futures.

Several of the ISA members I interviewed participated in the demonstration. Afshin recalled a critical moment:

> That infamous truck came loaded with rocks that *hezbollai* people were throwing at us. I felt something hit my head. I touched it, and it was all bloody. I had three stitches in my head from that day. I also indulged in a little bit of violence. There was this guy who had a young woman pinned down on the ground and just by her hair was banging her head down on the asphalt. I had a bar, and I hit the guy with it, and he fell down. We got sucked into the violence, so we beat them back. Then we went to the office of the prime minister, Bazargan, and nothing much happened, and they closed *Ayandegan* anyway.

Rahim Bajoughli, who had been active in the ISA chapter in Washington, DC, also attended the NDF protest. He still remembered "the brutality of the followers of Khomeini. I realized this is not the way it should go. If they cannot accept that [liberal] type of newspaper, there is no way that they can tolerate other opposition." The NDF was banned the day after the protest. By the end of August, sixty-three newspapers were shut down, and the Fadaiyan headquarters was ransacked by government forces.[22]

While the closing of *Ayandegan* was a turning point for some leftists, others were still hoping that the liberal nationalist elements in the government would rally against the conservative factions. Then came the taking of hostages at the American embassy in Tehran in November 1979, which was justified as a preemptive move against a repeat of the 1953 coup. This action had a polarizing impact on society, helping to consolidate power for Khomeini and those who supported the incorporation of a "supreme leader" into the new structure of governance.[23] Several of my interviewees cited this event as the decisive turning point on the road to authoritarianism. US-imposed sanctions and the onset of war with Iraq in 1980 created new conditions of deprivation, threat, and fear, in which the government further cracked down on dissent.[24] In June 1981, the first elected president of the postrevolutionary government, Abolhassan Bani Sadr, went into hiding and then exile.[25]

A new campaign of violence against the Left followed. The Muslim-Marxist Mojahedin held a mass demonstration against the government in June 1981, the brutal repression of which was witnessed by several returning ISA members. After this, many leftists went into hiding, including Ali Hojat, who spent three years underground in Tehran, moving from house to house. "Mostly I was trying to save people from getting arrested. To get them some [forged travel] documents to send them to Kurdistan or outside the country. We were basically licking our wounds." The shift from triumph to retreat was dizzying, as Jaleh Pirnazar pointed out during the joint interview with Ali. "He [Ali] was the one who used to be recruiting people to join the movement and go be bold and courageous," she said. "This time around he was collecting them to survive." Without a valid passport, Ali would eventually sneak into Iraq through Kurdistan, where he was protected by Kurdish movements resisting central governments on both sides of the border.

Bijan, who had organized with the UIC in the Texas-Oklahoma ISA, was also in Iran working hard to mitigate the damage to members of his organization. He described the process of confronting the UIC's lack of support among the Iranian population and the inability to hold the organization together in the face of extreme repression:

> People are going and voting for Khomeini; they don't vote for me [or my organization]. Maybe we should work among the masses long term, twenty years, thirty years, was what was coming to my mind. And this coincided with the arrests. And life becomes difficult. I became homeless. Then, meanwhile, if you are arrested with a piece of paper [leftist literature], you are executed. Meanwhile we are trying to discuss the masses and if what Stalin said is correct or what Lenin said is correct, and taking this paper to another home you can get arrested and get killed, and for what? Are we going to kill ourselves over just having a piece of paper?

This is not an academic discussion. It wasn't worth it. We were running on empty. I argued, "Let's dismantle the whole thing." We were the first group that did that. So to cut the damage, you eliminate all the connections. Find a safe haven for yourself. If you want to leave the country, just leave. Nobody is going to say you are liberal. It's okay. Just leave.

Bijan and his wife were eventually smuggled through Iran to the Turkish border where they walked fifteen hours through the mountains until they reached a small village. Turkey was under martial law at the time. As they made their way to Istanbul by bus, they were searched several times, along with the other passengers. With only expired Iranian passports marked by the dubious smugglers' stamp, they were simply lucky that the Turkish airport official allowed them to board a plane for Barcelona, Spain, which did not then require Iranians to have entry visas.

Even as former ISA members reckon with their mistakes and failures, some also remember painstaking efforts carried out under incredibly unfavorable conditions to connect Marxist politics with Iranian workers. When Hamid returned from Berkeley to Iran in 1978 to participate in the massive demonstrations that overthrew the Shah, he was already deeply concerned by what he saw. As a founding member of the UIC in Berkeley, he was not euphoric but "disappointed, very much. Initially, yes. See, I had been outside the country for sixteen years. I loved to go back there, and I loved to be part of the revolution. I even went back there illegally to take part." Hamid was on SAVAK's wanted list; he risked arrest simply by returning home and was careful to avoid contact with other leftists lest he endanger them. He joined demonstrations alone and was dismayed by "all these religious slogans." They "were so bad that I just couldn't take it. I would get out of the line." Although he said the Left sometimes tried to raise different slogans, they did not want to be accused of sowing divisions at a time when Islamist ideas, idioms, and organization "had already dominated the movement."

After the Shah was overthrown, Hamid went to Tabriz for seven or eight months to try to build influence among the factory councils (shoras) that had sprung up around the country in the preceding months.[26] "We already had a member of ours who was one of the leaders of the shoras in the milk industry, pasteurization. I had meetings with workers from the tractor factory, auto factory, different industries. We were trying to organize these little cells within the factories. I would study Marxist literature with them. I had meetings with some workers from the railroad." It might have taken years, if not decades, for this slow work to result in any significant base of leftist workers in Tabriz. However, even these small inroads were soon blocked by government repression. "I left Iran in 1983," Hamid said, "because they arrested all of my friends, and they killed them. I was in hiding."

Of the thirty people I interviewed, nine, including Hamid, were smuggled out of Iran without valid passports via smugglers' routes through Turkey, Iraq, or Pakistan. Fourteen left legally, most during the first year after the revolution, many expecting to return. Two were asked by their organizations to stay outside Iran and act as spokespeople for the revolution. Mohammed Eghtedari was sent by the Revolutionary Organization (RO) from Iran to Lebanon at the request of the Palestinian Liberation Organization (PLO), a move based on relationships built between the PLO and RO in diaspora, as well as the long-standing importance of Palestine to Iranian leftists overall. At the home of a PLO leader in Beirut, Mohammed addressed representatives from the Palestinian movement as well as from the Iraqi Communist Party and the Turkish Communist Party:

> They had come there for a meeting to know what is going on in Iran. They were all concerned. They took me to the American University of Beirut and I made a speech there. They took me to the Palestinian camps close to Israel, just about one kilometer from Israel. And there I explained to the leadership what was happening in Iran. You could see Katyushas [Soviet-made rockets] going off. Right on the border. I even went close to the Syrian border. There was some high official over there. We stayed there in the mountains and we talked and it was a great discussion.

Such memories offer glimpses into the hopeful possibilities the Iranian revolution held for the region as a whole by removing a major ally of the US and Israel from power. It brings into the present those affects of solidarity that circulated among Iranian and Arab revolutionaries, an important counter to the anti-Arab Persian imperial identity that dominates the diaspora today.

Political Prisoners of the Revolution

Throughout its twenty years as an opposition formation, the ISA had spent a great deal of its organizational capacity exposing the conditions in the Shah's prisons and campaigning to spare the lives of political prisoners (see chapter 3). The Iranian Revolution was in many ways a revolution against the torture chambers of SAVAK, and succeeded in freeing thousands of political prisoners.[27] These prisoners emerged into throngs of joyous demonstrators, who held them aloft and celebrated them as heroes.[28] Yet the prisons rapidly filled up again, and not just with pro-Shah stalwarts, but with a wide range of secular and religious dissidents. The reproduction of a carceral state stands as one of the greatest indictments of the postrevolutionary government and one of the greatest sources of heartbreak for the leftists who managed to survive when many of their comrades did not.[29] It also necessitates an honest reckoning with the role played by various communist groups in demanding swifter and more extreme punishment for former SAVAK agents and other pro-Shah individuals. As Ghamari-Tabrizi has shown, leftists and radical Islamists pressured the provisional government to use more, not less, state violence to silence opponents.[30] The Left was not in power, of course, and not in control of the courts and prisons. Its zeal for persecution of those it deemed enemies of the people and its disdain for the concept of human rights, tainted by association with the imperialist West and the Shah's empty rhetoric, would ultimately prove suicidal; government suppression of even those Marxist groups that had supported Khomeini was eventually deemed necessary for the defense of the revolution.

Five of the former ISA members I interviewed were detained after the revolution for varying periods as a result of their political activities. Nicky Nodjoumi was picked up one day at a demonstration where the government had deployed its security forces, the Revolutionary Guards, against protesters. "This was the first demonstration where several people died by Revolutionary Guards. It was bloody," Nicky recalled. "When Revolutionary Guards were after us, I went into an alley and I ran and ran and ran. I can't run very much. I had open-heart surgery [years earlier]. So at one point, I stopped. And there was the Revolutionary Guard with the bayonet on my chest. So he got me, and [then] a couple of other Revolutionary Guards beat me up. Then there was a truck with a lot of other people. They took us to Qasr Prison." Qasr Prison, the oldest political prison in Iran, had been the site of executions of the Shah's top officials immediately following the overthrow of his regime and was now bursting with leftists.[31] Nicky estimates he was one of 170 people picked up that day, all of whom were stuffed into one cell with "no room to sit or sleep until morning." The next day, Nicky and his cellmates were led into the prison courtyard where Ayatollah Khalkhali, nicknamed "the hanging judge" for his role in numerous executions, gave a short lecture, which Nicky summarized as follows: "We arrested you. We arrested your leadership. But we can let you go after 100 lashes, and you have to promise that you're not going to be on any demonstrations, and you sign a letter, and you go home."

After shaving all of the prisoners' heads, guards lined the men up in the courtyard with a bench at one end and commenced issuing the punishment of 100 lashes. "I thought to myself, I have to get out of this situation," Nicky recalled. He tried to appeal to Khalkhali, insisting he had not been part of the demonstrations and was merely on his way home. The Ayatollah demanded to see the contents of Nicky's pockets. "In my pockets were my [US] green card and two [US] dollars," Nicky remembered. This evidence of his life in the US could only seal his fate. Keeping his wallet closed in his hands, he insisted again that he was not involved in any political activity. Khalkhali replied, "We don't care. You've been part of this. You've been arrested. Your face screams communist. We will beat you so hard here until you're finished." Nicky then said, "I have heart problem" and showed the scar from his surgery. But this had no effect, and he was ordered back into the line.

The line moved slowly. "Each [prisoner's beating] would take like half an hour, more than half an hour," Nicky said. "I am number forty-something [in line]. I saw a bunch of people, how they were beaten so bad. Now it's becoming like five o'clock. We are getting close to the bench." Growing increasingly desperate, Nicky tried appealing to one of the young guards, telling him the prisoners had learned their lesson. The guard slapped him a few times and sent him back to the line. There was nothing left to do but prepare for the beating to come. By that time, it was at least seven o'clock and darkness surrounded the dimly lit courtyard. There was no food, and everyone was exhausted, including the guards who were carrying out the lashings. Then, a general appeared and announced that Khalkhali had left for the day, so he would let the prisoners go after they signed a letter. The irony of this demand struck Nicky to his core. Years earlier, detained and under interrogation by SAVAK in an empty house in Tehran, he had been forced to sign another letter promising to abstain from participation in any political organization opposed to the Shah. This new letter was even more categorical, promising not to participate in any political demonstration and acknowledging that if he were arrested again, he would be executed. "I signed the letter," Nicky said, "and with my shaved head, I came out."

Nicky left Iran and returned to New York to see if his wife, Nahid, also a prominent Iranian artist, was ready to go back to Iran with him. "She didn't think things were heading in a democratic direction, so she said, 'No, not now.'" Based on what turned out to be a false promise that he would be hired to teach art at Tehran University, Nicky returned to Iran alone. "When I got there in September 1979, before the hostage taking, they said, 'You're not going to be hired.' I said, 'Why?' They said, 'Because you are a leftist. Your file is here, and it shows your activity was not Islamic.' Nahid was right." Nicky stayed in Iran another year until he was nearly run out of the country. The occasion was a retrospective of his work put on by Tehran's Museum of Contemporary Art, which wanted to feature him as an anti-Shah artist. The museum had closed for one year following the revolution, and Nicky's show went up shortly after it reopened in September 1980. The exhibition included works critical of the postrevolutionary government as well as of the Shah, and, the day after the opening, it was condemned in the government's official newspaper. Nicky described what happened:

> The chief editor was Mir-Hossein Mossavi, who later on became prime minister and is now under house arrest for leading a pro-democracy movement in 2009. There was a huge article about my show. Anti-revolution, anti-Islam, anti-Khomeini. This is Thursday. Thursday night someone calls the museum to warn that after the Friday prayer, they are going to attack the museum. After the prayer, a large group of people dressed in black came to attack the museum with knives. There was a committee of guards who sent them away. But that weekend, when the public came to see the show, all the images depicting mullahs, which they said were against the Islamic Republic, were turned backwards facing the walls.

Nicky viewed this as an attack on the revolution he had supported. "We fought for democracy. This is our fight," he said. He penned a harsh letter to a newspaper, in which he "attacked the Islamic Republic and said this is worse than SAVAK, but we are fighting it." The museum director told him not to publish the letter for it would only place both the museum and Nicky in more danger. Regardless, it was no longer safe for Nicky to stay in Iran. "I left all the paintings in the museum. One hundred and twenty-five of them. And the day I left, it was one o'clock in the morning. By noon that same day, Saddam Hussein bombed the airport. That was the first day of the war. The twenty-first of September, 1981. I got out. Amazing. After the incident I had with the museum, they branded me as anti-revolutionary."

After two narrow escapes—from lashings in prison and from persecution because of his exhibit—Nicky was reeling back in the US, "depressed, traumatized." Having left his paintings, and the dream of a democratic Iran, behind, Nicky struggled to make a life in a hostile land he had never called home. "I didn't connect to any Iranians. It was such a difficult time. Iran was everywhere now. Contrary to that first time when no one knew what it was, now they hated it. It was a tough, tough time." The losses he mourned in exile differed so dramatically from those of the majority of Iranians who came to the US at that time that he could not relate to his compatriots. He had not rejected the revolution, but rather it had rejected him and the freedom of artistic expression for which he stood.

Farid, who had been organizing with the ISA and the Fadaiyan in Chicago, returned to Iran in 1978. He became a student organizer for the Fadaiyan majority faction in Tehran, which had approximately 20,000 members by the time it was banned in 1983.[32] He helped organize demonstrations at the universities, but his main job was to develop a new cadre, "the secret nucleus that can be the core of the small engine" that could pull the revolution to the left, he explained, self-consciously adopting the language of those days. Having been abroad for six years, he was overwhelmed by the popular support for the Fadaiyan, by the reputation they had earned through daring acts of armed opposition to the Shah. He found it easy to recruit new members. "If you would have told them who you are, they would have loved to come and just associate with you. That's how it was. The name was so big it wouldn't take too much … the blood was already spilt in the society for many years. People knew of the sacrifices. So—" Suddenly, overcome by emotion, Farid could not continue the interview. He left the room, and when he returned, shifted the discussion back to the nuances of the Fadaiyan political line. Perhaps he had not expected to share his memories of the love and gratitude thousands of people had felt toward the organization to which he had once devoted his life. Or perhaps such feelings were generally unwelcome in diaspora, and this was a rare moment in which they could surface. These memories brought into the present powerful revolutionary affects that had once moved and transformed the people around him. For Farid, the confrontation between what might have been and what came to pass was profoundly painful. His resistant nostalgia for the love and support he could still feel surrounding him as a young Fadaiyan organizer has been deemed impermissible, and his losses have thus been unmournable in the conservative political climate of the post-1979 Iranian diaspora.

In 1981, Farid was arrested and held for six months, at a time when the Mojahedin continued to engage in armed resistance and government repression was on the rise. "The situation was really bad," he said. "I had a sixteen-year-old cousin who was Mojahedin and he got arrested and executed the next day. They caught him distributing leaflets in the street, and he just went right from there in front of the firing squad. Those days, they used to every night call in the names [of those executed] on the eight o'clock news on radio and TV, just call in the names, and you would just sit down and listen to the names, tens of names, hundreds, every night." His father, a former policeman, used whatever connections he had to secure Farid's release. "I don't know how much that helped," Farid said. "It probably did." He views his survival as "one of the ironies and the dichotomies of the whole thing. For me to be here is just accidental, it's just luck." That luck must have followed him on his flight into exile, as he used a fake passport to travel through Kurdistan into Turkey and then, eight months later, when he was granted political asylum, to France.

The arbitrariness of his survival can only be fully appreciated in context. Farid sketched the timetable and scale on which the liquidation of the opposition took place: "We know that almost 90 percent of the [Fadaiyan members] got arrested after the breakdown of the organization started in eighty-one and eighty-two; eighty-three was the highest point of arrests. After that, the organization went completely underground and still continued until eighty-four and eighty-five, and then it went through the mass execution of political prisoners. Of all these people who were in jail, a lot of my very close friends, 90 percent of them were executed. The highest number we have is 4,500 in 1988. The majority [of those executed were] Mojahedin."[33] In addition to Mojahedin and Fadaiyan, Tudeh Party members, UIC members, and other dissidents also perished in the periodic purges that reached their height at the end of the Iran-Iraq War.[34] Farid spoke slowly and softly as he recited these numbers, which have haunted him for decades, but his affect was flat. It was the earlier memory of joy and hope amidst throngs of Fadaiyan supporters, not the talk of executions, that caused his emotions to overtake him.

As Ella Shohat has argued, "Memories that endanger the hegemonic narrative are forbidden, expelled, proscribed. Their marking as 'taboo' ends up being internalized, even if only unconsciously, by the scarred bodies and souls who might have desired to tell history in a different way, from an alternative angle or perspective."[35] Although Farid is critical of the "one-sided" support the Fadaiyan Majority gave to Khomeini, the revolutionary affects that propelled him toward a different future in 1979 still resonate, stirring up nostalgia—not for an idealized pre-1979 homeland, but for the collective joy that came from standing on the cusp of freedom. The loss of this possibility runs counter to hegemonic exilic accounts of what was lost and what can be grieved, marking Farid's affects, emotions, and memories as taboo.

In 1981, at the start of the Iran-Iraq War, Soosan was arrested while working with UIC activists to bring food and medicine to disabled and elderly people unable to evacuate the border town of Abadan, home to Iran's largest oil refinery and a strategic target for the Iraqi army. "We didn't understand the situation," Soosan said. Even though she knew Islamist vigilantes had attacked students at university rallies and meetings in Tehran, and even though she had been threatened with arrest if she did not leave Abadan, she "was hoping that inside the government the people would still have the energy to bring change, especially young people. I never thought they [the Islamists] would win, that they are going to stay and win," she said. After eight months in jail under threat of a death warrant, Soosan and another female activist were released. It was the end of April 1981, about a month before what she called "the coup d'état that took Bani Sadr away." After Bani Sadr was ousted, "that's when they killed everybody in the jails, all of the political prisoners, most of them," she said quietly. "Thirty days is nothing in history, but it was the difference between life and death for us." Despite this harrowing experience, Soosan did not hesitate to describe her years of revolutionary activity as "really one of the best times I've had in my life." As I discuss further below, this assessment was far from unique among those I interviewed and impinges directly on the political implications of diasporic nostalgia.

When Nancy looked back on the year she spent imprisoned in Tehran, she began with an analysis similar to Soosan's, focusing on the lack of clarity among the UIC and their mistaken assessment of the political situation. In the summer of 1981, despite the crackdown against the Mojahedin and other leftist groups that was underway, Nancy was ordered by the UIC leadership to return to Tehran from Shiraz, a provincial city where she was staying with a friend. "Even though I was told to come back, I shouldn't have been," she said. "I could have fled the country from Shiraz, but I didn't. We were a highly disciplined organization, and you did what you were told. They [the authorities] were looking for somebody, and my arrest gave her time to leave. I brought myself to where they were waiting for me," Nancy remembers. Enacting the ethos of self-sacrifice that was so central to leftist political culture, she willingly turned herself in to allow an Iranian woman the chance to escape. "I had read all these books and there was a lot of romanticizing," Nancy said, explaining how she thought of her arrest at the time. "When I went to jail, I knew, oh, this is the jail that Ashraf [Deghani] was in and she managed to escape and blah, blah, blah." As discussed in chapter 5, going to jail was widely understood and embraced as a probable result of revolutionary activity, and Nancy was already prepared to accept the risk. After eleven months in Qasr Prison, she was released and escorted by a Swiss envoy to the airport.

I asked Nancy if she felt angry or bitter about her time in jail, which she could have avoided simply by ignoring the leadership's orders. She responded not by talking about her own sacrifices, but by lamenting the far worse fate of so many people who were not allowed to leave. "A lot of people got executed about a year after I was back [in the US]. So that was a big blow. Just trying to understand what we had done, where we'd been," she said. "I didn't see it as a waste of time [or think] I'd been used. I said, 'Okay, I went into this pretty much knowing what I was doing.' I'm real sorry I didn't stand up at all and say, 'I think this is wrong.' I went along with it. But I never resented it. I never felt bitter about the experience." Instead of blaming any individual or her organization as a whole, she said she realized in hindsight that the leadership of the UIC "was just as naive" as she was. "What I came back understanding was that the leadership didn't know much more than me. Unfortunately, unfortunately. A lot of people got killed; some people became informants. I don't judge anybody because I feel like it was a very young movement." The sadness and grief she expressed was not about her time in prison. "I just felt bad about the people who died [and] the people who became passive for the rest of their lives."

To be involved, of course, is to risk failure and loss—an inescapable part of any effort at social transformation. Memories of loss, for my informants, thus become archives of those efforts, many of which were also personally transformative. In 1980, Shahnaz went to prison in Tabriz where she'd been sent by the UIC to teach women and children rug-weavers a combination of literacy skills and socialist politics. The police initially rounded her up in a crackdown on prostitution; then they found the communist pamphlets tucked under her chador. Of her three months in jail, she said: "That experience is one of the [she breathed a deep sigh] greatest experiences I had in my life! I had a chance—because they didn't have political prisons—I lived with women who were murderers, prostitutes, drug dealers, and it was amazing! Amazing! In the beginning these people didn't want to talk to us about their lives. But then they opened up, they trusted us. They knew that we were political, and they were begging us not to talk about politics because they [the prison officials] could kill us." The feeling of elation Shahnaz expressed when she remembered her relationships with women whose lives were so different from hers—her joy at earning their trust and becoming a recipient of their concern—indexes another set of revolutionary affects that might otherwise disappear from history. The space of the women's prison became one in which women who engaged in different forms of rebellion, different forms of nonnormative behavior for which they were punished, formed a community.[36] At the same time, Shahnaz's evident nostalgia for this period of her life was not based on naivete. In 1981, her brother and her sister were arrested, and in 1983 her brother was executed. Despite her grief, she continues to embrace her experience of the women's prison as part and parcel of the revolutionary life she had chosen, one which opened her up to new relationships with working-class and poor women, experiences she was still unwilling to disavow. On the verge of turning sixty years old, she explained that when she looked back on her life:

> One of the things that I'm very happy about is that my life is different from the majority of people who were born at the same time that I was born in Iran. I really don't want to change it. If I lived again, I would repeat it again. One of the places that I learned a lot, I always say, university was a place that I learned a lot, but after that was [CISNU]. It was day and night, reading and discussing and researching and everything. Learning, as my father said, is not always learning from positives and good things. You have to learn from negatives also.

Indeed, she was quick to sum up those negatives, calling CISNU "a dictatorship" because of the rigid demands for total dedication, "twenty-four hours, seven days a week." Rather than encouraging individuals to choose their own level of involvement, "It was saying, you're doing your life this way, this way and there was no other way. It was peer pressure and it was regulation that there was just one way of life." At the same time, Shahnaz's political experience built her confidence as a leader and allowed her to develop the organizing skills she uses today as the head of a nonprofit organization. "That's the comfort that [CISNU] has given me," she said. "I learned possibilities."

While UIC members Soosan, Nancy, and Shahnaz went to jail, a handful of people in the organization who had been active in the Berkeley ISA and who had returned to Iran, including Hamid, Jaleh Behroozi, and Ahmad, argued against supporting Khomeini. When the UIC backed the takeover of the US embassy in Tehran, they split from it and formed an even smaller group. In 1982, the remaining UIC members realized that they had made a mistake in following the Islamist factions. Some "went to the other extreme and said we should start an armed revolution" against Khomeini's government, Hamid explained. Hamid, Jaleh, and Ahmad were adamantly opposed to this course of action. Hamid argued that the only hope was to unite with as many opposition groups as possible and form one large organization. "Don't start it yourself, you will be killed," Hamid begged his dear friend,

Siamak Zaim, who was a leading UIC theoretician and a major proponent of armed resistance to the Islamic Republic. Hamid, Siamak, Parviz, Jaleh Behroozi, and Ahmad had spent their formative political years together in the ISA's Northern California chapter and were now facing a life-and-death decision about how to respond to the repression that followed the revolution.

One night in particular haunts Ahmad to this day—a long, heated argument he could not win. Siamak came to the house where Jaleh and Ahmad were staying and tried to convince them to participate in an armed act of resistance his group was planning. Unable to persuade Siamak to call off the mission, Ahmad stayed behind, helpless, as some of his dearest friends embarked on a suicidal revolt (later known as the Amol Struggle, after the town on the Caspian Sea where it occurred). The small band of rebels failed to garner support from the local population and was no match for government forces. "Almost thirty of the people of Northern California, the best and most important leaders of the ISA, were there [in Amol]," Ahmad said, "and they were all executed there. Out of the sixty people in the core of the group between 1969 and 1972, most of them got executed. Only ten or fifteen survived this period." As Ahmad tallies his losses, he offers this explanation of what went wrong: "Their main mistake was that they followed Khomeini before the revolution, and their second mistake was that they decided to use guns." This episode has stayed with Ahmad ever since and informs his current conviction that any future movement for progressive change in Iran should be a nonviolent one.

After the disaster at Amol, Hamid, Jaleh, and Ahmad all made plans to leave the country. "We got news that they were coming for us," Ahmad said. "We were hiding in Iran for a while, and then I went to [UAE] and Jaleh went undercover to Pakistan." Jaleh added, "Since I was a Jew, I couldn't go to [UAE]." Eventually, they ended up in Israel for six months, waiting to get green cards to the US. "We had nothing," Jaleh remembered. Bereft and heartbroken when they arrived back in the US, they did not feel relieved or rescued. "We came back to the place that we didn't want to go to at all because our hope was to live in Iran after the revolution," Ahmad said. "I was so, so sad, but we couldn't go back. We never went back." Their reluctant journey back to the US revises the standard immigrant trope, in which the old country is left behind for the promise of a better life. In fact, it was the promise of a better life that had to be abandoned in Iran. Ahmad and Jaleh's sadness is the remainder of that radical vision, the affective state in which they encounter the ghosts of Amol.

Conclusion: Other Possible Diasporas

"While the longing is universal," Boym writes of the condition of diaspora, "nostalgia can be divisive."[37] Returning to the US in the early 1980s, this time as a permanent exile rather than as a foreign student planning to go home, Zohreh Khayam felt marginalized by the affective responses to the revolution that structured the new post-1979 diaspora: "Maybe this is exaggerated, but that's how I felt, that the former members of [CISNU] were treated like Vietnam vets who came back to the United States. Because now things were going wrong, so everything was our fault. Especially from the rightist [monarchist] factions, you hear that everything that happened in Iran and went wrong was our problem because we were the opposition [to the Shah]." While Zohreh's analogy may be politically problematic—for it invokes a narrative created by the US right to try to discredit antiwar protesters for the supposed mistreatment of returning veterans—she endeavored to describe what it felt like to be condemned by and alienated from other Iranians.[38]

In this context, it has been socially and politically unacceptable to feel nostalgia for the fleeting moments of freedom and democracy that preceded the onset of state repression under the Islamic Republic. If, as the "common sense" diasporic narrative goes, the revolution inevitably led to a new form of dictatorship, then any nostalgia for the collective upheavals of 1978–79 can be construed as an unconscionable justification of the mass persecutions that followed. When former ISA members remember loved ones who were killed, their words—and the grief and horror they embody—might seem to corroborate precisely that well-trod anti-revolutionary narrative. But in the interviews I conducted, memories of loss and the affective states they evoked diverged in important ways from the standard script, revealing impermissible feelings of pride and joy painfully out of sync with the present mood. "For whatever it might be worth," Zohreh said, "the first six months of revolution was the most beautiful social experience of my life because people were so good to each other." Given the hostility toward the Islamic Republic among the diaspora and in US society since 1979, former ISA members have had few collective or individual opportunities to grieve for these aspects of the revolution, let alone for the lost future they desperately hoped to build. Indeed, for some of the people I interviewed, their conversations with me were a first attempt to explain, out loud to a stranger, how they have tried to make sense of what they did more than forty years ago.

The process of working through "taboo memories" of another possible Iran also suggests another possible diaspora oriented in ways that defy the

US versus Iran script. In our current impasse, in which the forces of dictatorship and imperialism work to narrow political horizons, the memories of former ISA members that have shaped this study suggest alternatives to the dominant ways of being Iranian in the US. Rather than viewing the Islamic Republic as the singular antithesis to Western liberal values, we might learn from the ISA activists who refused alignment with both the Iranian and the US states and pointed to the hypocrisies embedded in each ruling ideology. This approach, as I have argued throughout this book, is foundational to an intersectional anti-imperialist framework and illustrates the significance of engaging with the legacy of the pre-1979 Iranian student diaspora.

In the 1960s and 1970s, it was undeniably easier to simultaneously oppose both the internal and external sources of injustice in Iran because they worked in alliance. Since 1979, the Islamic Republic and US imperialism have been in a dangerous, protracted conflict, one that exerts continual pressure on Iranians to pick a side. But neither "side" offers peace, freedom, equality, or justice to the majority of people who live within the borders of either the US or Iran. Despite dramatically differing geographic and economic reach, both Iran and the US pursue foreign policies driven by geopolitical rivalries that destroy the lives and futures of people in other nations as well. Iran's interventions are limited to its regional neighbors, while the US continues to try to dominate the world. Yet when Iraqis protested against foreign interference in their country in the winter of 2019–20, the crowds in Baghdad's Tahrir Square chanted "No to Iran, no to America."[39] Today, Iranian diasporic affects of solidarity must find expression as a critique of the atrocities carried out by both sides, whether in the name of Islam and anti-imperialism or in the name of secularism, anti-terrorism, and human/women's rights.

This Flame Within has followed the movement of affect, emotion and memory along with the transnational journeys of Iranian foreign students. By tracing the formative impact of growing up under the US-backed Pahlavi dictatorship and the influence of social movements in the US and across the Third World, this book has argued that affective encounters with repression and resistance made it possible for revolutionary subjectivities to emerge in unexpected places, from among the ranks of imperial model minorities. Not only is the study of affect crucial to understanding the willingness of privileged foreign students to go against the entire world order that they were charged with spreading, but the power of revolutionary affects is also a central part of the story of how political movements sustain themselves and discipline their members, creating new political cultures of belonging that can be deeply rewarding. Affective attachments to making a revolution render the risks and sacrifices of revolutionary activity worthwhile. They can also remain embedded within existing social hierarchies, such as those of gender, sexuality, and class, which profoundly shape how revolutionary subjectivities are embodied and compel forms of self-sacrifice that can maintain those very hierarchies.

The revolt of imperial model minorities described in this book must be understood as an expression of the latent affective potential emanating from the long, and often suppressed, modern Iranian freedom struggle *and* as the visceral response of a new generation to the era of decolonization and global student uprisings. It is a reminder that empires and dictatorships are not all powerful and often produce unintended consequences. Among these were the displacement and scattering of young Iranian men and women outside Iran's borders, and, consequently, the circulation and convergence of revolutionary affects among heterogeneous populations that embodied a militant response to oppression. The emergence of affects of solidarity as a transformative force generating new affiliations between the ISA and other freedom movements is one of the most important legacies of the pre-1979 diaspora. Traversing the borders of race, nation, religion, and language, affects of solidarity made it possible for Iranians, racialized Americans, and white American leftists to understand their struggles and futures as intimately linked. The feeling and practice of solidarity described in this book can assist in the project of rerouting contemporary Iranian diasporic subjectivity outside and against a Persian imperial identity and toward affective attachments to the liberation of others.

This book's emphasis on solidarity as something lived and felt among Iranian and non-Iranian activists committed to Third World liberation contributes to recent scholarly efforts to situate the Iranian revolution in a global context. I have built on existing scholarship that focuses on particular connections between Iranian leftists and other revolutionary movements and stretched the frame of Afro-Asian studies to include foreign students from West Asia. At the same time, this study has also worked to expand our understanding of the central political dynamics of the era of Third World internationalism beyond just solidarity and affiliation across different racial, national, religious, and language groups. One of the most important political developments of the era, I argue, was the emergence of Third World revolutionary feminism, a new form of feminism that fought for liberation from the entangled forces of patriarchy, racism, and colonialization as part of the overall transformation of society.

Throughout this book, I have worked to expand the genealogy of revolutionary feminism to make the Iranian experience legible and to foreground its unique contributions. This has involved shifting the conceptual framework from a "primary" focus on imperialism to one attuned to the complex relationship between imperialism and dictatorship as a key source of gender and sexual oppression. As I have shown, the lived experience of the intersection of foreign and domestic sources of oppression in Iran generated revolutionary affects no less for women than for men, both as a reaction to state repression and in response to the particular ways women were targeted for modernization under a Westernizing, patriarchal regime. The opportunity to join a mass student movement in the United States provided Iranian women studying abroad with the chance to express their grievances and their hopes for a better world. The imperial model minority revolt was not just a class rebellion; for many of the women involved, it was a clear rejection of traditional *and* Westernized gender roles.

Not unlike their peers in other Third Worldist student movements, Iranian women in the ISA were incorporated into a masculinist form of revolutionary subjectivity that was simultaneously empowering and oppressive. Through the ideology of gender sameness and the practices of masculinization, Iranian women activists embraced a new form of revolutionary subjectivity. In the course of building and sustaining their movement, ISA members challenged sexism and male domination, albeit in ways that often reinforced the stigma against femininity as Westernized, bourgeois, and, therefore, uniquely corruptible. Still, it must be noted that by the late 1960s, ISA women's committees were formed and eventually instituted policy changes, such as leadership gender quotas, while also circulating an analysis of the interconnections between patriarchy, feudalism, dictatorship, and empire. Like so many others involved in anticolonial struggles, Iranian revolutionaries rejected feminism as separatism and attached their hopes for freedom to the versions of Marxism-Leninism that were dominant among the Left at the time.

Yet, in the immediate aftermath of the revolution, the desire to extend revolutionary activity to issues of gender and sexual oppression became urgent and necessary for many Iranian leftist women, including some in the ISA, who were part of the March 1979 women's uprising in Tehran. Without the backing of any political party, the revolutionary affects of thousands of women were mobilized around specific demands for full gender equality and bodily autonomy. These demands were understood by those on the streets as intrinsic to the success of the revolution as a whole and entirely compatible with the anti-imperialist politics that had been the basis for unity against the

Shah. We will never know what might have happened if the major leftist and liberal parties rallied behind these women instead of disparaging and undermining them. The hierarchical forms of revolutionary politics that dominated across the political spectrum, and to which many women subscribed as well, foreclosed the further development of the revolutionary anti-imperialist feminism that began to take shape in the mass demonstrations, meetings, and publications put out by newly established women's organizations.

As the new government began to consolidate power and persecute dissent, there was little time to fully parse the intersections between patriarchy, dictatorship, feudalism, capitalism, religion, secularism, and imperialism, let alone to win over existing leftist parties to a capacious and nuanced analysis of gender and sexual oppression. And yet there were women who tried to integrate women's liberation into the anti-imperialist revolutionary project and resist the new iterations of authoritarian patriarchy forming in post-revolutionary Iran. They argued for the need to oppose the interlocking oppressions that structured their lives and challenged the hierarchical thinking that dominated the Left. Their efforts, however fleeting and faltering, must be recognized as part of a feminist genealogy that includes anticolonial feminisms from across the Global South, as well as Black, Indigenous, and women-of-color feminisms developed in the US context. It is on the basis of this genealogy that we might forge an intersectional anti-imperialism critical of patriarchy, state repression, and the lack of democracy in both the US and Iran.

My reading of the significance of the Iranian women's uprising for the direction of the revolution and for a genealogy of anti-imperialist feminism emerges from the methodology of possibility that has guided this study. The work of this book, therefore, is not purely restorative; it is not only concerned with filling in gaps in scholarship on 1960s and 1970s social movements, especially in the US, and making the Iranian student leftist experience legible within Afro-Asian studies and ethnic studies. *This Flame Within* has offered a critical reappraisal of the Iranian student diaspora and of the internationalist revolutionary Left in which the ISA and CISNU as a whole participated. My close readings of archival documents and interviews—of affects, emotions, and memories—are intended to open up new possibilities and potentialities for Iranian diasporic politics and subject formation today. The diasporic reorientation called for in this book requires a reengagement with the complexity of the Iranian revolutionary experience as more than just trauma and failure. It requires that we expand our notion of the losses that structure the melancholic longings of diaspora. Resistant nostalgia for fleeting moments of victory, for lost comrades, and a lost socialist future live on in diaspora as attachments to a revolutionary possibility that was both lived and imagined. From this tangle of grief and hope, revolutionary affects continue to circulate, this time without ideological certainties and party lines. Revolutionary affects emanating from the long Iranian freedom struggle find new forms of expression as they move across generations and borders, haunting the diaspora from the margins.

This extended mourning for the lost futures of the Iranian Revolution may prove far more hopeful and healing than efforts to organize a tidy narrative of what went wrong. As Avery Gordon has written, "to be haunted in the name of a will to heal" is to allow history's ghosts to offer their "utopian grace: to encourage a steely sorrow laced with delight for what we lost that we never had; to long for the insight of that moment in which we recognize, as in Benjamin's profane illumination, that it could have been and can be otherwise."[40] It is in this sense that the affective attachments discussed in this book—to that "possibility of a world that is neither Shah nor Islamic Republic" and to the possibility of a revolutionary feminist alternative to dictatorship and imperialism—can help wrest from the unbearable present new momentum toward a radically just future.

NOTES

Introduction: Before We Were "Terrorists"

1 "Iranian and American Students," *Resistance*, February 1977.

2 Qtd. in Vietnam Veterans against the War, "Support Iranian Struggle," April 1977, 14.

3 "Iranian and American Students," *Resistance*, February 1977, 4.

4 "Iranian and American Students," *Resistance*, February 1977, 4.

5 "Iranian and American Students," *Resistance*, February 1977, 4.

6 "Iranian and American Students," *Resistance*, February 1977, 4.

7 I define "revolutionaries" as people who have decided to organize their lives around the project of making a revolution.

8 Gopinath, *Unruly Visions*, 129–30.

9 Gopinath, *Unruly Visions*, 125–26.

10 Cvetkovich, *Archive of Feelings*, 13.

11 Cvetkovich, *Archive of Feelings*, 14.

12 Flatley, *Affective Mapping*, 21–22.

13 Gould quoting Williams, in "On Affect and Protest," 32.

14 See Flatley, *Affective Mapping*; Eng and Kazanjian, *Loss*.

15 Gould, "On Affect and Protest," 32.

16 Gould, "On Affect and Protest," 27.

17 Gould, *Moving Politics*, 31.

18 Ahmed, *Living a Feminist Life*, 27–28.

19 Gould, *Moving Politics*, 28.

20 Gould, *Moving Politics*, 3.

21 Hardt, "Foreword," ix.

22 Massumi, *Parables for the Virtual*, 4–5.

23 Gould, *Moving Politics*, 27.

24 Flatley, *Affective Mapping*, 79.

25 Cvetkovich, *Archive of Feelings*, 167.

26 Based on interview with Jaleh Behroozi, June 23, 2012.

27 All quotes from former ISA members are from interviews with the author unless otherwise noted.

28 Featherstone, *Solidarity*, 5.

29 Featherstone, *Solidarity*, 5.

30 Matin-asgari, *Iranian Student Opposition*, 13.

31 Young, *Soul Power*, 4.

32 See Reddy and Sudhakar, "Introduction."

33 Alexander and Mohanty, *Feminist Genealogies*, xxiv.

34 Paidar, *Women and the Political Process*, 149–50.

35 See Najmabadi, "Hazards of Modernity and Morality," 48–76. See also Moallem on Ali Shari'ati's denunciations of *zan-e hich va pouch* in *Between Warrior Brother and Veiled Sister*, 92–93.

36 Moallem, *Between Warrior Brother and Veiled Sister*, 3.

37 Moghissi, *Populism and Feminism*, 2–3.

38 Paidar, *Women and the Political Process*, 171.

39 Flatley, *Affective Mapping*, 79.

40 See Collins, *Intersectionality*.

41 Elahi and Karim, "Introduction," 383, 387.

42 Elahi and Karim, "Introduction," 384.

43 For an overview of the concept of "intersectionality" and its multiple genealogies, see Collins and Bilge, *Intersectionality*.

44 See Ghamari-Tabrizi on the "myth of the stolen revolution" in *Foucault in Iran*, 19–53.

45 See Ghamari-Tabrizi, *Islam and Dissent*; Abrahamian, *Khomeinism*.

46 See, e.g., Abayomi Azikiwe, "US Activists Meet with Iranian President," *Worker's World*, September 30, 2010, https://www.workers.org/2010/us/iran_1007/.

47 See, e.g., Herb London, "The Iranian People Are Pro-American, Unlike Their Government," *Fox News*, January 5, 2018, https://www.foxnews.com/opinion/the-iranian-people-are-pro-american-unlike-their-government.

48 I am indebted to the scholarship and activism of women of color, transnational, and queer diasporic feminist criticism for my approach. See, e.g., Nadine Naber's analysis of Arab diasporic activism against US-Israeli imperialism and Islamophobia in *Arab America*, 159–246.

49 The difficulty of addressing sexism and homophobia within groups targeted by racism and imperialism has been at the center of women-of-color feminism. See, e.g., Combahee River Collective, "Statement," in Taylor, *How We Get Free*; Moraga

and Anzaldúa, *This Bridge Called My Back*; Hernández and Rehman, *Colonize This!*; Abdulhadi et al., *Arab and Arab American Feminisms*.

50 See Narayan, *Dislocating Cultures*.

51 The formulation that the major systems of oppression are interlocking comes from the Combahee River Collective Statement. See *How We Get Free*, 15. Critical race scholar Kimberlé Crenshaw coined the term *intersectionality* to describe oppression that occurred at the intersection of race, gender, sexuality, and class. See Crenshaw, "Demarginalizing the Intersection."

52 See Abu-Lughod, *Remaking Women*; Ahmed, *Women and Gender*; Kandiyoti, *Gendering the Middle East*.

53 See Moallem, *Between Warrior Brother and Veiled Sister*.

54 See Bacchetta et al., "Transnational Feminist Practices," 302–8.

55 See Abu-Lughod, "Do Muslim Women Really Need Saving?," 783–90; Rostami-Povey, *Afghan Women*.

56 See, e.g., Mohanty, Russo, and Torres, *Third World Women and the Politics of Feminism*; Shohat, *Talking Visions*; and Grewal and Kaplan, *Scattered Hegemonies*.

57 See, e.g., Osanloo, *Politics of Women's Rights*; Sameh, *Axis of Hope*.

58 See, e.g., Tabari and Yeganeh, *In the Shadow of Islam*; Najmabadi, "Hazards of Modernity and Morality"; Sanasarian, *Women's Rights Movement*; Paidar, *Women and the Political Process*; Najmabadi, "Crafting an Educated Housewife"; Moghissi, *Populism and Feminism*; Hoodfar, "The Veil."

59 On the dominance of a developmentalist notion of progress among colonial and anti-colonial forces, see Saldaña-Portillo, *Revolutionary Imagination*, 7.

60 Here I build on Nadine Naber's concept of "diasporic feminist anti-imperialism" and adapt it to encompass the changing iterations of dictatorship in Iran. See Naber, *Arab America*, 203–46. Because Iran was not directly colonized, and has not been governed by a pro-Western state for over forty years, repression in Iran has its own dynamics not entirely reducible to Western domination.

61 In 2003, sociologist Nilu Mostofi defined *diaspora* as "the mass migrations of peoples to various locations around the world." Thus, the term is aptly applied despite the temporary status of student migration, which, in many cases, became permanent after 1979. Mostofi, quoted in Elahi and Karim, "Introduction," 384.

62 Naber, *Arab America*, 27.

63 Shannon, *Losing Hearts and Minds*, 3 and 155.

64 Matin-asgari, *Iranian Student Opposition*, 131.

65 Matin-asgari wrote the first book-length study, *Iranian Student Opposition to the Shah*, without which my book would not have been possible. Shannon's *Losing Hearts and Minds* looks at the presence of Iranian foreign students from the perspective of US-Iran diplomatic and policy relations. There are no other monographs in English focusing on the pre-1979 Iranian population in the US.

66 See, e.g., Naficy, *Making of Exile Cultures*.

67 For statistics on educational levels and occupation trends among the post-1979 wave of Iranian immigrants, see Sabagh and Bozorgmehr, "Are the Characteristics of Exiles Different?"

68 My approach to different forms of diasporic nationalism (across the political spectrum) is indebted to Gayatri Gopinath's queer diasporic feminist critique in *Impossible Desires*. For an analysis of Iranian American racial identity, see Maghbouleh, *Limits of Whiteness*, in which she argues that first-generation Iranian immigrants have largely embraced a "white" identity. On the roots of the "Aryan myth," see Zia-Ebrahimi, "Self-Orientalization and Dislocation," 445–72.

69 For a range of examples of the diversity of experience within Iranian American and Iranian diasporic literature, see Karim and Khorrami, *World Between*; Karim, *Let Me Tell You Where I've Been*; Amirrezvani and Karim, *Tremors*.

70 Maghbouleh, *Limits of Whiteness*, 171–73.

71 See Maghbouleh, *Limits of Whiteness*, 135–61; Maira, *The 9/11 Generation*.

72 I am indebted to José Muñoz's formulation of queer concrete utopianism as "a backward glance that enacts a future vision" and his insistence that hope rests on the ability to "pull from the past the no-longer-conscious ... to push beyond the impasse of the present." Muñoz, *Cruising Utopia*, 4 and 31.

73 Muñoz, *Cruising Utopia*, 12.

74 See Ghameri-Tabrizi's discussion of leftist support for Khomeini in *Foucault in Iran*, 19–53.

75 For an account of the Left's attitude toward women's rights immediately after the revolution, see Ghamari-Tabrizi, *Foucault in Iran*, 113–58.

76 Examples include Behrooz, *Rebels with a Cause*; Moghissi, *Populism and Feminism*; Ghamari-Tabrizi, *Foucault in Iran*; Tabari and Yeganeh, *In the Shadow of Islam*.

77 I take the term *resistant nostalgia* from Hirsch and Spitzer, "'We Would Not Have Come without You.'" The notion of the "good life" as the reproduction of a normativity that produces unsustainable crisis comes from Berlant, *Cruel Optimism*, 2.

78 See Mottadeh, *Whisper Tapes*.

79 Merrit Kennedy, "A Look at Egypt's Uprising, 5 Years Later," NPR, January 25, 2016, https://www.npr.org/sections/thetwo-way/2016/01/25/464290769/a-look-at-egypts-uprising-5-years-later.

80 For the concept of "revolutionary time" I take inspiration from the definition of "queer time" in Halberstam's *In a Queer Time and Place*, 6.

81 My attempts to interview additional former ISA members living in Iran proved unsuccessful, perhaps because of ongoing fears of government repression.

82 Butler, *Giving an Account of Oneself*, 10–12.

83 Halbwachs, *On Collective Memory*, 51.

84 Halbwachs, *On Collective Memory*, 31.

Chapter One: Revolutionary Affects and the Archive of Memory

1   Creet, "Introduction."

2   Canefe, "Home in Exile," 170.

3   Creet, "Introduction." See also Gopinath, *Unruly Visions*, 83.

4   Creet, "Introduction," 6.

5   See discussion of Ricoeur in Creet, "Introduction," 7.

6   See Creet, "Introduction," 9.

7   Canefe, "Home in Exile," 172.

8   Canefe, "Home in Exile," 172.

9   Hirsch and Spitzer, "'We Would Not Have Come without You,'" 253–67.

10 Freud, "Mourning and Melancholia," 158–59.

11 For an incisive discussion of how mourning without end can become a politically subversive mode of contesting ongoing systems of dispossession and imagining alternative futures, see Eng and Kazanjian, *Loss*, 1–25.

12 Eng and Kazanjian, *Loss*, 11. See also Ahmed, *Promise of Happiness*, 121–59.

13 Clough, *Affective Turn*, 2.

14 Ricoeur, *Memory*, 87.

15 Ricoeur, *Memory*, 88.

16 Abrahamian, *Iran*, 321.

17 Abrahamian, *Iran*, 325. See also Abrahamian, *Coup*, 190–91.

18 Cronin, "Iran's Forgotten Revolutionary," 123.

19 Abrahamian, *Iran*, 119.

20 Jones and Singh, "Guest Editors' Introduction," 6.

21 Cronin, "Iran's Forgotten Revolutionary," 141.

22 Matin-asgari, *Iranian Student Opposition*, 42.

23 Abrahamian, *Iran*, 460.

24 William Arthur Cram, "Unseen Images of the 1953 Iran Coup—In Pictures," *Guardian*, December 16, 2015, https://www.theguardian.com/world/iran-blog/gallery/2015/dec/16/unseen-images-of-the-1953-iran-coup-in-pictures.

25 Cram, "Unseen Images," *Guardian*, December 16, 2015.

26 For an account of the theory of combined and uneven development, see Löwey, *Politics of Combined and Uneven Development*.

27 Abrahamian, *Iran*, 426.

28 Abrahamian, *Iranian Mojahedin*, 21.

29 Abrahamian, *Iran*, 480.

30 Abrahamian, *Iran*, 480–81.

31 Abrahamian, *Iran*, 480.

32 For more on this perspective on Tudeh, see Behrooz, *Rebels with a Cause*, 15–16.

33 Coles, *Political Life of Children*, 49.

34 Canefe, "Home in Exile," 173.

Chapter Two: Revolt in the Metropole

1 "Sina" is a pseudonym. This interviewee requested that his actual name be with-held because he continues to travel to Iran.

2 Shannon, *Losing Hearts and Minds*, 17–34.

3 On the term *special relationship*, see Oelsner and Koschut, *Friendship and International Relations*, 16.

4 Bargetz, "Distribution of Emotions," 581.

5 Bargetz, "Distribution of Emotions," 584.

6 I am referencing Gayatri Spivak's canonical essay "Can the Subaltern Speak?"

7 Matin-asgari, *Iranian Student Opposition*, 36. See also Shannon, *Losing Hearts and Minds*, 34–39.

8 Shannon, *Losing Hearts and Minds*, 40.

9 Matin-asgari, *Iranian Student Opposition*, 36. See also Shannon, *Losing Hearts and Minds*, 35.

10 Behdjou, "Economic and Trade Relations," *Los Angeles Times*, January 25, 1976.

11 Kramer, "Is the World Our Campus?," 783, 781.

12 Lippman quoted in Kramer, "Is the World Our Campus?," 799.

13 The first published use of the term *model minority* was by sociologist William Petersen in the *New York Times* in 1966. He used it to describe the apparent success of Japanese Americans. The term was then used to refer to the "successful" assimilation of various Asian American populations.

14 See, e.g., Kim, "Racial Triangulation," 119.

15 Victor Bascara has shown how Asian model minority citizenship was also predicated on acceptance of and, often, participation in US interventions abroad, describing a "model minority imperialism" in which Asian Americans are deployed to "civilize" Third World peoples. See Bascara, *Model Minority Imperialism*.

16 "Reception to Be Held for Foreign Student," *Los Angeles Times*, February 14, 1954.

17 Rogers, "US Learns from Exchange Students," *Washington Post*, November 15, 1953.

18 Rogers, "US Learns from Exchange Students," *Washington Post*, November 15, 1953.

19 Rogers, "US Learns from Exchange Students," *Washington Post*, November 15, 1953.

20 See McAlister, *Epic Encounters*, 2.

21 Klein, *Cold War Orientalism*, 7 and 24–25.

22 Klein, *Cold War Orientalism*, 13.

23 Klein, *Cold War Orientalism*, 12.

24 Klein, *Cold War Orientalism*, 16.

25 Martin and McLenden, "Iran Envoy Abruptly Recalled," *Washington Post*, February 24, 1962. See also Donihi, "Foreign Students Are Parties' 'Lions,'" *Washington Post*, March 30, 1960.

26 The pages of mainstream newspapers from this era featured multiple articles celebrating the ornate style of Iranian "Oriental" culture that was on display at various diplomatic venues in Washington, as well as ads for Persian rugs and fashion designers. See, e.g., "Mid-East Modes," *Washington Post*, October 12, 1959. The article is about an Iranian designer's fashion show at Middle East House in Washington sponsored by the CIA-front group American Friends of the Middle East, held in order to raise money for scholarships for Iranian foreign students.

27 Dudziak, *Cold War Civil Rights*, 6–8.

28 Kramer, "Is the World Our Campus?," 782.

29 Ahmed, *Promise of Happiness*, 121–59.

30 Quoted in Shadman, "Iran's False Image," *Daneshjoo*, March 1964, 10.

31 Ahmed, *Promise of Happiness*, 158.

32 Ahmed, *Promise of Happiness*, 159.

33 Ahmed, *Promise of Happiness*, 159.

34 Matin-asgari, *Iranian Student Opposition*, 38.

35 Matin-asgari, *Iranian Student Opposition*, 38.

36 Matin-asgari, *Iranian Student Opposition*, 38.

37 Matin-asgari, *Iranian Student Opposition*, 38.

38 Matin-asgari, *Iranian Student Opposition*, 38.

39 Matin-asgari, *Iranian Student Opposition*, 39.

40 Matin-asgari, *Iranian Student Opposition*, 39.

41 While the ISA moved in a secular leftist direction, Qotbzadeh was religiously devout and would soon shift his focus from the ISA to Muslim student associations in Europe, the US, and the Middle East. He was with Khomeini in exile in Paris in 1978 and became foreign minister in the first postrevolutionary government. He was executed by the Iranian government in 1982. See Chehabi, *Iranian Politics*, 192–93.

42 Matin-asgari, *Iranian Student Opposition*, 39.

43 Rancière, *Politics of Aesthetics*, 7.

44 Bargetz, "Distribution of Emotions," 589.

45 Bargetz, "Distribution of Emotions," 585.

46 Bargetz, "Distribution of Emotions," 592.

47 Bargetz, "Distribution of Emotions," 592.

48 Matin-asgari, *Iranian Student Opposition*, 35.

49 Matin-asgari, *Iranian Student Opposition*, 50, 57.

50 Matin-asgari, *Iranian Student Opposition*, 90, 130.

51 Matin-asgari, *Iranian Student Opposition*, 53, 59.

52 "*Payam-e daneshjoo*," *Shanzdah-e azar*, April 5, 1962, 1.

53 Matin-asgari, *Iranian Student Opposition*, 55.

54 Parsa, *States*, 100.

55 Matin-asgari, *Iranian Student Opposition*, 57.

56 Matin-asgari, *Iranian Student Opposition*, 57.

57 "Political Repression in Iran," March 1971, Parviz Shokat Collection, Hoover Institute, Stanford University (hereafter PSC), 17.

58 "Iran's Kent State and Baton Rouge," 1973, PSC.

59 Bargetz, "Distribution of Emotions," 593.

60 Matin-asgari, *Iranian Student Opposition*, 1.

61 Matin-asgari, *Iranian Student Opposition*, 123.

62 The amount given is in historic dollars. See USAID, *Overseas Loans and Grants*.

63 Mobasher, *Iranians in Texas*, 26, 28.

64 Matin-asgari, *Iranian Student Opposition*, 131.

65 Matin-asgari, *Iranian Student Opposition*, 58.

66 Matin-asgari, *Iranian Student Opposition*, 91.

67 "21st Convention of ISAUS," *Resistance*, November 1973.

68 "In a Spirit of Solidarity," *Resistance*, March 1978.

69 "International Students Give Point of View," *Commerce Journal*, April 29, 1971.

70 Matin-asgari, *Iranian Student Opposition*, 89.

71 Matin-asgari, *Iranian Student Opposition*, 85.

72 Malkiel, *"Keep the Damned Women Out,"* 18–19.

73 The report on the ISA's 1964 congress, published in *Daneshjoo*, includes a thank you note to the US National Students Association for providing financial assistance in the fight to return Iranian student activists' passports that had been canceled by the Iranian government. See "Messages of 11th Annual Congress of ISAUS," *Daneshjoo*, November 1964. Members of the ISA were unaware that this organization received funding from the CIA. Even before these revelations were made, however, the ISA had severed its ties based on political differences. See Matin-asgari, *Iranian Student Opposition*, 49, 91, 94.

74 "Restless Youth," report, 1970, LBJ Library, University of Texas, 6.

75 On the Revolutionary Organization, see Abrahamian, *Iran*, 454.

76 See Abrahamian, *The Iranian Mojahedin*.

77 Matin-asgari, *Iranian Student Opposition*, 147.

78 Interview with Behzad Golemohammadi, May 31, 2015.

79 "On the Question of Splits," *Iran Report*, March 1976.

80 See Benab, *One Hundred Year History*.

81 At the time, the ambassador was married to the Shah's daughter, Princess Shahnaz.

82 Ahmed, *Cultural Politics of Emotions*, 25.

83 "Iranian Students Picketing," news footage, 1961, Bay Area Television Archive.

84 Scheutte, "Iranians Stage 3-Hour Sit-In," *Washington Post*, January 24, 1962.

85 Ehrman, "Striker Ousted from Embassy," *Los Angeles Times*, January 23, 1963.

86 Ehrman, "Striker Ousted from Embassy," *Los Angeles Times*, January 23, 1963.

87 "Iranians See R. Kennedy," *Washington Post*, January 27, 1962.

88 Martin and McLenden, "Iran Envoy Abruptly Recalled," *Washington Post*, February 24, 1962.

89 "Iranian Students Picket Shah Arrival," *Washington Post*, April 12, 1962.

90 Shannon, *Losing Hearts and Minds*, 62–68.

91 The White Revolution refers to a set of policies the Shah adopted at the behest of the Kennedy administration that were designed to industrialize the Iranian economy, including land reform and major infrastructure projects to be carried out through partnerships with US companies. The reforms also included certain initiatives that stemmed from liberal and leftist demands and that had been part of CISNU's platform since 1962, such as granting women the right to vote and promoting mass literacy.

92 Shadman, "Iran's False Image," *Daneshjoo*, March 1964, 12.

93 "Shah Praised by Kennedy," *Washington Post and Times-Herald*, February 14, 1963.

94 "President Emphasizes Aid Values," *Washington Post and Times-Herald*, April 3, 1963.

95 "What Are US Imperialist Interests in Iran?," May 1971, ISA file, Social Protest Collection, Bancroft Library, UC Berkeley (hereafter ISA/SPC). The leaflet, issued by the ISA Northern California chapter, says that there were 30,000 advisers, but a later article in the ISA's quarterly journal, *Iran Report*, explains that there were 30,000 US personnel in Iran by 1976, 12,000 of which were military advisers. See "Shah's Heightened Dependence on U.S. Imperialism," *Iran Report*, September, October, and November Issue, 1976.

96 Abrahamian, *Iran*, 425.

97 Abrahamian, *Iran*, 425.

98 "Political Repression in Iran," World Confederation of Iranian Students (National Union), PSC.

99 "Fifty Years of Pahlavi Dynasty Rule," ISA, 1976, ISA/SPC.

100 "Iranian Women," *Resistance*, June 1973.

101 Abrahamian, *Khomeinism*, 21.

102 Matin-asgari, *Iranian Student Opposition*, 85, 90.

103 The erosion of this position for different individuals and organizations is discussed in chapter 7.

104 Untitled ISA flyer, ca. 1970/71, ISA/SPC.

105 See Behrooz, *Rebels with a Cause*, 51, 69; Matin-asgari, *Iranian Student Opposition*, 127–28; Parsa, *States*, 100.

106 "Iranian Student Demonstration," film footage, 1967, YouTube.

107 "Iranian Student Demonstration," YouTube.

108 "Four Iranian Students Arrested," *Washington Post*, August 24, 1967, A15.

109 "Four Iranian Students Arrested," *Washington Post*, August 24, 1967, A15.

110 Policy guideline of CISNU, quoted in Matin-asgari, *Iranian Student Opposition*, 104.

111 "Free the 12 Iranian Artists," photograph, 1973, Flickr.

112 "People's Living Conditions," 1972, ISA/SPC.

113 "People's Living Conditions," ISA/SPC.

114 "What Are US Imperialist Interests in Iran?," ISA/SPC.

115 "Shah of Iran Visits His US Imperialist Bosses!," 1969, ISA/SPC.

116 "What Are US Imperialist Interests in Iran?," ISA/SPC.

Chapter Three: Making the Most of An American Education

1 "To All Fair-Minded People," leaflet, 1964, Library Special Collections, UCLA Library, University of California–Los Angeles (hereafter LSC/UCLA).

2 "To All Fair-Minded People."

3 "Why the Shah Should Not Be Invited to UCLA," 1964, LSC/UCLA.

4 Matin-asgari, *Iranian Student Opposition*, 75–76.

5 In Lisa Lowe's seminal work, *Immigrant Acts*, she argues that the contradiction between legal citizenship for Asian Americans and ongoing forms of racism emerges within Asian American cultural production as an *immanent critique* of the class, race, and gender formations of liberal multiculturalism. Here, I adapt her term to describe a critique of US foreign policy emerging from the tension between the official embrace of Iranian imperial model minorities by the US government and the forms of exploitation and political repression the US sponsored in Iran.

6 SAVAK was established with the help of the CIA and the FBI: see Abrahamian, *Iran*, 219.

7 "Restless Youth," LBJL, 6.

8 Chatterjee and Maira, *Imperial University*, 6.

9 Chatterjee and Maira, *Imperial University*, 7.

10 Chatterjee and Maira, *Imperial University*, 7.

11 See, e.g., Biondi, *Black Revolution*; Erlich and Erlich, *Student Power*.

12 Victoria Wong, email correspondence with the author, July 23, 2020.

13 "Penn around the World," online exhibit, 2007, Penn University Archives and Record Center.

14 Ahmed, *Cultural Politics of Emotions*, 45.

15 Boggs and Mitchell, "Critical University Studies," 436.

16 Boggs and Mitchell, "Critical University Studies," 441.

17 Ferguson, *Reorder of Things*, 8.

18 Ferguson, *Reorder of Things*, 12.

19 Ferguson, *Reorder of Things*, 13.

20 Boggs and Mitchell, "Critical University Studies," 442.

21 See, e.g., Miyoshi and Harootunian, *Learning Places*, 2.

22 On the chair in petroleum engineering, see Larry Gordon, "John R. Hubbard Dies at 92; USC President, Historian, and Diplomat," *Los Angeles Times*, August 23, 2011. Closing quote from "Americanization of Iranian Education," *Resistance*, February 1977.

23 "US Universities Hustle Iran Contracts," *Daily Californian*, March 6, 1975.

24 Quoted in "American Universities," *Resistance*, April 1977.

25 "American Universities," *Resistance*, April 1977.

26 "American Universities," *Resistance*, April 1977.

27 "Iranian Recruiters Skip Campus Visit," *Daily Californian*, February 9, 1976.

28 "Iranian Recruiters Skip Campus Visit," *Daily Californian*, February 9, 1976.

29 McGraw, "US Iranian Students Criticize Shah," *Daily Californian*, April 9, 1976.

30 *Iranian Students Association v. Sawyer.*

31 *Adibi-Sadeh v. Bee County College.*

32 "Texas College Asked to Reinstate Iranian Students," *Odessa American*, April 14, 1979.

33 Blum, "Save the Beeville 103," *Texas Monthly*, June 1978, 86.

34 Blum, "Save the Beeville 103," *Texas Monthly*, June 1978, 84.

35 Blum, "Save the Beeville 103," *Texas Monthly*, June 1978, 86.

36 Matin-asgari, *Iranian Student Opposition*, 148.

37 Matin-asgari, *Iranian Student Opposition*, 152–53.

38 Abrahamian, *Iranian Mojahedin*, 29.

39 The Amnesty report explained that the numbers it gave were unverifiable. See Amnesty International, *Annual Report 1974/75*, 128–29. See also Matin-asgari, *Iranian Student Opposition*, 154.

40 See, e.g., the list of names of professors and students "standing trial in military courts" in Iran in "Letter of the ISAUS to [United Nations] Secretary-General," *Daneshjoo*, March 1964.

41 See, e.g., the Ansari torture memoir in "Notes from Evin Prison," *Resistance*, June 1974.

42 For an in-depth look at the campaign against torture in Iran, including the role of CISNU, see Nikpour, "Claiming Human Rights."

43 "Shah of Iran Visits His US Imperialist Bosses!," 1969, ISA/SPC.

44 "Shah of Iran Visits His US Imperialist Bosses!," ISA/SPC.

45 "Shah of Iran Visits His US Imperialist Bosses!," ISA/SPC.

46 See Lusinchi, "Torture and Denials of Rights," *New York Times*, May 29, 1976; Matin-asgari, *Iranian Student Opposition*, 151; "Iranian Revolution," John Thorne Papers, University of California–Santa Cruz Special Collections and Archives, which includes an article from the *San Jose Mercury*, January 3, 1980, on John Thorne's multiple trips to Iran at the behest of the Confederation of Iranian Studies and the National Lawyers Guild.

47 For example, the *Guardian* reported that Dr. Hans Heinz Heldmann, a German lawyer, had been sent on behalf of Amnesty International to conduct an investi-

gation into human rights abuses in Iran. He was deported within ten days of his arrival, and his Iranian interpreter was jailed. See "Amnesty Says 1,000 Arrests in Iran," *Guardian*, November 26, 1970. Subsequently, Heldman published a scathing report about the torture of political prisoners in Iranian jails and the harassment of their family members. See Shannon, *Losing Hearts and Minds*, 125.

48 For example, *Resistance* republished an Amnesty International news release from 1975 quoting American observer Betty Assheton's dismay at the "ludicrously inadequate" case an Iranian prosecutor made against seven dissidents who were then executed. See "Amnesty International News Release," *Resistance*, May 1977. See also Lusinchi, "Torture and Denials of Rights," *New York Times*, May 29, 1976.

49 "Shah Spies," *Der Spiegel*, September 6, 1976.

50 "SAVAK Activities," pamphlet, n.d., ISA/SPC; "SAVAK's Reactionary Collaboration," leaflet, n.d., ISA/SPC.

51 See "SAVAK Exposed," *Resistance*, January 1977.

52 "SAVAK Exposed," *Resistance*, January 1977, 36.

53 "Shah of Iran on the Issue of Torture," television interview, YouTube.

54 "Shah of Iran on the Issue of Torture," YouTube.

55 "Shah of Iran on the Issue of Torture," YouTube.

56 "Shah of Iran on the Issue of Torture," YouTube.

57 See Anderson and Whitten, "CIA Seen Abetting Foreign Agents," *Washington Post*, October 26, 1976; Anderson and Whitten, "Iranian Secret Police Dirty Tricks," *Washington Post*, October 29, 1976; Anderson and Whitten, "CIA Trained Iranian Secret Police," *Washington Post*, November 4, 1976.

58 The first quotation is from "US Queries Iran," *Washington Post*, October 29, 1976; the second is from Marro, "Intelligence Panel," *New York Times*, December 17, 1976.

59 "Foreign Agents," *US News and World Report*, July 4, 1977.

60 "Foreign Agents," *US News and World Report*, July 4, 1977.

61 "Foreign Agents," *US News and World Report*, July 4, 1977.

62 "SAVAK's Attacks," *Defense Bulletin of the ISAUS*.

63 Herron and Lewis, "The Nation," *New York Times*, August 12, 1979.

64 Anderson and Whitten, "Iranian Secret Police Dirty Tricks," *Washington Post*, October 29, 1976.

65 "Political Repression in Iran," 1971, PSC, 27.

66 "Chicago Police Charged," *New York Times*, March 10, 1977; Thompson, "200 Organizations," *Los Angeles Times*, July 19, 1978.

67 "SAVAK Activities," ISA/SPC, 8.

68 "SAVAK Activities," ISA/SPC, 8.

69 "SAVAK Activities," ISA/SPC, 8.

70 Matin-asgari, *Iranian Student Opposition*, 98.

71 See Schrader, *Badges without Borders*.

72 Purnell, "Iranian Students Protest," *Daily Californian*, January 15, 1976.

73 Untitled standalone photograph 6 by Cal Montney, *Los Angeles Times*, January 28, 1976, D8.

74 "Political Repression in Iran," PSC, 43.

75 "41 Iranians Face Deportation," June 1970, ISA/SPC.

76 "41 Iranians Face Deportation," June 1970, ISA/SPC.

77 ISA flyer for Eisenstein film screening, 1970, ISA/SPC.

78 "Iranian Students Claim Harassment," *Daily Californian*, April 11, 1973.

79 "Iranian Students Claim Harassment," *Daily Californian*, April 11, 1973.

80 Walsh, "Carter Asserts Human Rights," *Washington Post*, December 7, 1978.

81 Oberdorfer, "12 Groups Press Carter," *Washington Post*, January 17, 1977.

82 Quoted in "In Appreciation," *Resistance*, December 1977.

83 Valentine, "Shah's Visit Stirs Worry," *Washington Post*, November 5, 1977.

84 Valentine, "Shah's Visit Stirs Worry," *Washington Post*, November 5, 1977.

85 Valentine, "Shah of Iran's Friends," *Washington Post*, November 13, 1977.

86 Valentine, "2 Iranian Factions Clash," *Washington Post*, November 16, 1977.

87 Valentine, "2 Iranian Factions Clash," *Washington Post*, November 16, 1977.

88 Valentine, "2 Iranian Factions Clash," *Washington Post*, November 16, 1977.

89 Valentine, "2 Iranian Factions Clash," *Washington Post*, November 16, 1977.

90 Valentine, "2 Iranian Factions Clash," *Washington Post*, November 16, 1977.

91 "Mr. 'Human Rights' Meets King Torture," *Resistance*, December 1977, original in italics.

92 "Mr. 'Human Rights' Meets King Torture," *Resistance*, December 1977.

93 "Crocodile Tears," *Resistance*, December 1977.

94 Lynton and Milloy, "Shah Violence Sporadic," *Washington Post*, November 17, 1977.

95 Lynton and Milloy, "Shah Violence Sporadic," *Washington Post*, November 17, 1977.

96 Lynton and Milloy, "Shah Violence Sporadic," *Washington Post*, November 17, 1977.

97 Forsyth, "Letters to the Editor," *Washington Post*, November 19, 1977.

98 See, e.g., Robinson, "Letters to the Editor," *Washington* Post, November 19, 1977.

99 Charlton, "Shah's Visit," *New York Times*, November 21, 1977.

100 Furgurson, "Do the Iranian 'Students' Ever Study?," *Los Angeles Times*, November 22, 1977.

101 Furgurson, "Do the Iranian 'Students' Ever Study?," *Los Angeles Times*, November 22, 1977.

102 Kneeland, "182 Iranians Face Hearings," *New York Times*, May 19, 1978.

103 Matin-asgari, *Iranian Student Opposition*, 162.

104 Hazlett and Coutu, "30 Hurt," *Los Angeles Times*, September 2, 1978.

105 Keats, "Letter to the Times," *Los Angeles Times*, September 2, 1978.

106   Keats, "Letter to the Times," *Los Angeles Times*, September 8, 1978.

107   Matin-asgari, *Iranian Student Opposition*, 162. See also Lindsey, "Iranian Students Riot," *New York Times*, January 3, 1979.

108   Lindsey, "Iranian Students Riot," *New York Times*, January 3, 1979.

109   Lindsey, "Iranian Students Riot," *New York Times*, January 3, 1979.

110   "Iranian Students Storm Shah's Mother's Home," *Washington Post*, January 3, 1979.

111   "Iranian Deportations," *Washington Post*, January 4, 1979.

112   "Bell Says US Will Deport Iranians," *Washington Post*, January 5, 1979.

113   "Bell Says US Will Deport Iranians," *Washington Post*, January 5, 1979.

114   Dorman and Farhang, *US Press and Iran*, 153.

115   Mobasher, *Iranians in Texas*, 37.

116   The sentiments and statements cited here come from Kaplis, "Letters to the Editor," *Washington Post*, January 7, 1979; Cantrell, "Letters to the Editor," *Washington Post*, November 14, 1979; Finney, "Letters to The Times," *Los Angeles Times*, December 21, 1979.

117   "Deportation Threat," *Daily Californian*, January 8, 1979.

118   "Student Visa Violations," *Washington Post*, January 30, 1979.

119   "Bell Will Shake Up Immigration Unit," *New York Times*, January 29, 1979.

120   "Report on Alien Agency," *New York Times*, February 12, 1979.

121   "US Taking Steps," *Los Angeles Times*, February 26, 1979.

122   "Computer Will Help," *Los Angeles Times*, June 6, 1979.

123   "Computer Will Help," *Los Angeles Times*, June 6, 1979.

124   Omang and Bonner, "Aliens Invading America's Campuses," *Washington Post*, April 22, 1979.

125   Rosenzweig, "Directive on Foreign Students," *Los Angeles Times*, March 18, 1979.

126   Rosenzweig, "Directive on Foreign Students," *Los Angeles Times*, March 18, 1979.

127   Rosenzweig, "Directive on Foreign Students," *Los Angeles Times*, March 18, 1979.

128   Rosenzweig, "Directive on Foreign Students," *Los Angeles Times*, March 18, 1979; Maxwell, "UCLA Joins USC," *Los Angeles Times*, November 21, 1979.

129   "The State," *Los Angeles Times*, March 27, 1979.

130   See, e.g., Zuckerman, "Police Break Up Disturbance," *Los Angeles Times*, October 8, 1979, in which police are called to intervene when a group of anti-Khomeini protesters disrupted a meeting of pro-Khomeini students at the Museum of Science and Industry in Los Angeles.

131   Nunes, "SC State School," *Washington Post*, November 22, 1979.

132   Maxwell, "'We Are the Hostages,'" *Los Angeles Times*, November 16, 1979; Sulzberger, "Federal Order," *New York Times*, November 13, 1979.

133   Dickey and Babcock, "Student Visa Reviews," *Washington Post*, November 13, 1979.

134   Babcock, "Carter's Visa Crackdown," *Washington Post*, April 9, 1980.

135 Mobasher, *Iranians in Texas*, 36.

136 Ramos, "Iranian Attending College," *Los Angeles Times*, November 9, 1979.

137 Sulzberger, "Americans Assail Iranians," *New York Times*, November 10, 1979.

138 See "Protesters Jeer," *Los Angeles Times*, November 9, 1979; "Angry Americans," *Los Angeles Times*, November 8, 1979.

139 Kaiser, "Iranians in US," *New York Times*, November 22, 1979.

140 Kaiser, "Iranians in US," *New York Times*, November 22, 1979.

141 Meyer, "Screaming Americans," *Los Angeles Times*, November 10, 1979.

142 Meyer, "Screaming Americans," *Los Angeles Times*, November 10, 1979.

143 Morrison, "Many in County Upset," *Los Angeles Times*, November 9, 1979.

144 Quotes from "Angry Americans," *Los Angeles Times*, November 8, 1979; "White House in Plea for Calm," *New York Times*, November 9, 1979.

145 "Iranian Marchers," *Los Angeles Times*, November 9, 1979.

146 Kaiser, "Iranian Flags," *New York Times*, November 21, 1979.

147 "San Antonio," *Los Angeles Times*, December 9, 1979.

148 Whitaker and Harris, "US Appeals Court," *Washington Post*, December 28, 1979; "Iranians Won't Be Deported," *Los Angeles Times*, November 8, 1979.

149 Mobasher, *Iranians in Texas*, 38.

150 "Only 19 Iran Students Sent Home," *Los Angeles Times*, April 2, 1980.

151 Mobasher, *Iranians in Texas*, 39.

152 "Protesters Jeer," *Los Angeles Times*, November 9, 1979.

153 Mobasher, *Iranians in Texas*, 57.

Chapter Four: The Feeling and Practice of Solidarity

1 "Anti-Suspension Demonstrations," 1967, Bay Area Television Archive (hereafter BATA).

2 For more on this incident, see Biondi, *Black Revolution*, 52–53.

3 "Anti-Suspension Demonstrations," BATA.

4 "Wanted," San Francisco State Strike file, Social Protest Collection, Bancroft Library, University of California–Berkeley.

5 All quotes from interview with Margaret Leahy, March 6, 2013.

6 A report from David Carliner, Khosro's lawyer in this case, was published in a special English-language pamphlet "Political Repression in Iran," 1971, PSC.

7 For more on Margaret Leahy's role, see Biondi, *Black Revolution*, 61.

8 See Elbaum, *Revolution in the Air*; Kelley and Esch, "Black Like Mao"; Young, *Soul Power*.

9 Young, *Soul Power*, 4.

10 Gopinath, "Archive," 168.

11 Reddy and Sudhakar, "Introduction."

12 See Takriti, *Monsoon Revolutions*, 236.

13 The Non-Aligned Movement was launched in 1961 by the leaders of India, Indo-nesia, Egypt, Ghana, and Yugoslavia, and still exists as an official grouping of 120 "developing nations" within the United Nations. See Young, *Post-Colonialism*, 192.

14 Reddy and Sudhakar, "Introduction."

15 The authors of this statement were veterans of the civil rights, antiwar, and socialist movements. See Taylor, *How We Get Free*, 23.

16 Combahee, *How We Get Free*, 15.

17 Hong and Ferguson, *Strange Affinities*, 2.

18 Hong and Ferguson, *Strange Affinities*, 3.

19 To view the original documents listing the five TWLF strike demands, see Third World Liberation Front, "Notice of Demands," SF State College Strike Collec-tion. For the ten BSU strike demands, see Whitson, "STRIKE!" The reference to tools for dismantling the master's house comes from Audre Lorde's seminal essay "The Master's Tool Will Never Dismantle the Master's House," in *Sister Outsider*, 110–13.

20 See Young, *Soul Power*, for an analysis of the impact of Third World liberation movements on the development of a radical American Left.

21 Flatley, *Affective Mapping*, 19–20.

22 Flatley, *Affective Mapping*, 20.

23 Crimp, "Mourning and Militancy," 9.

24 Eng and Kazanjian, *Loss*, 2, 5, 6.

25 Freud, "Mourning and Melancholia," 153.

26 Mohammed could not recall whether this meeting occurred in 1971 or 1972.

27 Flatley, *Affective Mapping*, 4.

28 Flatley, *Affective Mapping*, 4.

29 Flatley, *Affective Mapping*, 4.

30 Freud, "Mourning and Melancholia," 165.

31 Fanon, "On Violence," in *Wretched of the Earth*, 122.

32 Quoted in Gould, "On Affect and Protest," 35. Gould is quoting Durkheim's *The Elementary Forms of Religious Life*.

33 Eng and Kazanjian, *Loss*, 5.

34 For more on Iranian-Chicano joint organizing, see Aquilina, "Common Ground," 321–34.

35 Fanon, "On Violence," in *Wretched of the Earth*, 1.

36 For more on the issues involved in, and the significance of, this campaign, see Carl Nolte, "SF Palace Hotel Sit-In Helped Start Revolution 50 Years Ago," *SFGATE*, February 28, 2014, http://www.sfgate.com/bayarea/article/S-F-Palace -Hotel-sit-in-helped-start-revolution-5279160.php.

37 "Plea for Humanity in Iran," 1965, LSC/UCLA.

38 Bloom and Martin, *Black against Empire*, 135.

39 "From the Iranian Students Association," *Black Panther*, January 1970.

40 "From the Iranian Students Association," *Black Panther*, January 1970.

41 "Stop all Political Repression in Iran!!," 1970, ISA/SPC.

42 "Stop all Political Repression in Iran!!," ISA/SPC.

43 "Stop all Political Repression in Iran!!," ISA/SPC.

44 "Copy of Telegram sent to Iranian Consulate," 1970, ISA/SPC.

45 "US Public Protests," *Defense Bulletin of the ISAUS*, February 1972.

46 "US Public Protests," *Defense Bulletin of the ISAUS*, February 1972.

47 "623 Foreign Students," *The Hilltop*, February 8, 1960.

48 "Student Movement," *Daneshjoo*, May 1968.

49 Ubani, "Iranian Students," *The Hilltop*, March 5, 1976.

50 Ubani, "Iranian Students," *The Hilltop*, March 5, 1976.

51 Ekpo, "Shah of Iran," *The Hilltop*, March 17, 1978.

52 Ekpo, "Shah of Iran," *The Hilltop*, March 17, 1978.

53 "Contrary to 'Human Rights,'" *The Hilltop*, November 18, 1977.

54 "Contrary to 'Human Rights,'" *The Hilltop*, November 18, 1977.

55 Adeboye, "Iranian People," *The Hilltop*, March 2, 1979.

56 Adeboye, "Iranian People," *The Hilltop*, March 2, 1979.

57 Iranian Students Association, "Iranian Struggle," *The Hilltop*, November 11, 1977.

58 Flatley, *Affective Mapping*, 4.

59 "Iranian-Israeli Ties," pamphlet, ca. 1973, Iranian Leftist Opposition Collection, Library of Congress, Washington, DC.

60 "Defend the Heroic Struggles," *Iran Report*, September 1976.

61 "Confederation of Iranian Students Report," PSC, 124.

62 "Young Iranians Stage March," *The Hilltop*, January 15, 1971.

63 "Young Iranians Stage March," *The Hilltop*, January 15, 1971.

64 All quotes from interview with Camelia Odeah, March 29, 2015.

65 "Imperialism in the Middle East," April 22, 1970, ISA/SPC.

66 "Protest Israeli Terrorism!!," 1973, ISA/SPC.

67 "War in the Middle East,"1973, ISA/SPC.

68 Paknejad, "'Palestine Group,'" December 1970, PSC, 20.

69 Paknejad, "'Palestine Group,'" PSC, 11.

70 Sohrabi, "Remembering the Palestine Group," 288.

71 "The Creed," *Daneshjoo*, March 1964, 18.

72 "Struggle in Oman," *Daily Californian*, December 10, 1975.

73 "Struggle in Oman," *Daily Californian*, December 10, 1975.

74 "Oppose the Shah's US-Backed Invasion," leaflet, 1974, ISA/SPC.

75 "Revolution in Oman," *Resistance*, December 1975, 17.

76 Takriti, *Monsoon Revolutions*, 292–93.

77 "Revolution in Oman," *Resistance*, December 1975, 18.

78 "Revolution in Oman," *Resistance*, December 1975, 18.

79   "Revolution in Oman," *Resistance*, December 1975, 18.

80   Behrooz, *Rebels with a Cause*, 63.

81   "International Appeal," leaflet, 1975, PSC.

82   "Letter from Information Committee," *Iran Report*, September 1976.

83   "Revolution in Oman," *Resistance*, December 1975, 20.

84   "Moratorium Is a Cover," October 1969, ISA/SPC.

85   "Moratorium Is a Cover," ISA/SPC.

86   "Rally Rally," October 1972, ISA/SPC.

87   "Question of Political Prisoners," October 24, 1973, ISA/SPC.

88   "Question of Political Prisoners," ISA/SPC.

89   "Question of Political Prisoners," ISA/SPC.

90   "US Imperialism," November 15, 1969, ISA/SPC.

91   "Oppose the Shah's US-Backed Invasion," ISA/SPC, 2.

92   "Struggle in Oman," *Daily Californian*, December 10, 1975.

93   "Iran: Persian Gulf and Energy Crisis," leaflet, 1973, PSC.

94   "Shah 'Supervises' Peace in Vietnam," *Resistance*, n.d.

95   "US Sends More Military Advisors," *Resistance*, July 1973, 13–14.

96   "Oppose the Shah's US-Backed Invasion," ISA/SPC, 2.

97   "Struggle in Oman," *Daily Californian*, December 10, 1975.

98   "Iran, the Future Vietnam," May 1971, ISA/SPC.

99   "Why Is Nixon Going to Iran?," May 31, 1972, ISA/SPC, 8.

100 Kelley, *Freedom Dreams*, 6–7.

101 Takriti, *Monsoon Revolution*, 241–44.

102 Wu, *Radicals on the Road*, 194.

103 Abdulhadi, "Whose 1960s?"

Chapter Five: Political Cultures of Revolutionary Belonging

1   My analysis of the imperial model minority's temporal break from the forward march of capitalist progress shares an affinity with Jack Halberstam's notion of "queer time," which he describes as "liv[ing] outside the logics of reproductive and familial time as well as on the edges of employment and production ... outside the organizations of time and space that have been established for the purposes of protecting the rich few from everyone else." Halberstam, *In a Queer Time and Place*, 10.

2   McClintock, *Imperial Leather*, 259.

3   McClintock, *Imperial Leather*, 359.

4   McClintock, *Imperial Leather*, 359.

5   McClintock, *Imperial Leather*, 359.

6   Matin-asgari, *Iranian Student Opposition*, 131.

7   Paidar, *Women and the Political Process*, 172.

8   Moghissi, *Populism and Feminism*, 101–2.

9   Moallem, *Between Warrior Brother and Veiled Sister*, 84.

10 See Pulido, *Black, Brown, Yellow, and Left*; Elbaum, *Revolution in the Air*; Kelley and Esch, "Black Like Mao."

11 Moallem, *Between Warrior Brother and Veiled Sister*, 2.

12 Moghissi, *Populism and Feminism*, 31.

13 See Rostam-Kolayi and Matin-asgari, "Unveiling Ambiguities."

14 Hoodfar, "The Veil."

15 Moallem, *Between Warrior Brother and Veiled Sister*, 3.

16 Moghissi argues that the Iranian Left's "theories of women's oppression and emancipation, on the one hand, and its anti-imperialist and populist tendencies on the other ... compounded and maintained the force of patriarchal culture." Moghissi, *Populism and Feminism*, 88.

17 See Ella Shohat's analysis of the ambivalent relationship of colonized women to feminism. Shohat, *Talking Visions*, 11.

18 "Iranian Women," *Resistance*, June 1973.

19 "Farah's Trip Exposed," *Resistance*, July 1977.

20 These numbers cannot be verified. It is possible that there was more than one ISA formation operating at the time that these membership numbers applied.

21 Again, these numbers cannot be verified and are in reference to the wing of the ISA dominated by the UIC.

22 Interview with Parviz Shokat, May 14, 2015.

23 Interviews with Jaleh Behroozi, June 23, 2012, and Leyli Shayegan, May 19, 2017.

24 "University Women," ISA pamphlet, ca. 1968, PSC.

25 "University Women," PSC, 13.

26 See Moradian, "Iranian Diasporic Possibilities."

27 Moghissi, *Populism and Feminism*, 57–58.

28 Interview with Jaleh Behroozi and Ahmad Taghvai, June 23, 2012.

29 McClintock, *Imperial Leather*, 357; Gopinath, *Impossible Desires*, 6.

30 McClintock, *Imperial Leather*, 357.

31 Kelley and Esch, "Black Like Mao," 8.

32 Kelley and Esch, "Black Like Mao," 24–25.

33 Spencer, *Revolution Has Come*, 95.

34 Quoted in Spencer, *Revolution Has Come*, 96.

35 Spencer, *Revolution Has Come*, 96.

36 Kelley and Esch, "Black Like Mao," 25.

37 Azari, "Islam's Appeal," 25.

38 "Quotations from Chairman Mao," quoted in Kelley and Esch, "Black Like Mao," 18.

39 See Moallem, *Between Warrior Brother and Veiled Sister*, 82; Moghissi, *Populism and Feminism*, 83.

40 Sears is a national chain of American discount department stores founded in 1892.

41 "Third Line" refers to a split from the ISA after 1975 that was neither "rightist," meaning against armed struggle, nor "leftist," meaning uncritically supportive of the Fadaiyan, but in between. Goodwill refers to a nonprofit organization that runs a national network of stores selling second-hand clothing and household goods.

42 Tufan, meaning "tempest," was the name of a small Maoist group that split from the RO. See Behrooz, *Rebels with a Cause*, 42.

43 Moallem, *Between Warrior Brother and Veiled Sister*, 78.

44 It is likely that this memory refers to the December 1977 ISA convention in Oklahoma.

45 Moghissi notes that women could only participate in the Fadaiyan in Iran if they "rejected their sexuality." Moghissi, *Populism* and *Feminism*, 118.

46 Afsaneh Najmabadi argues that "Islamic traditionalists and the radical secular left" in Iran shared "common ground" when it came to legitimizing community control over the personal lives of individuals and to maintaining women's modesty. Najmabadi, "Hazards of Modernity and Morality," 65.

47 Wu, *Once Iron Girls*, 4.

48 Wu, quoting Gail Hershatter, *Once Iron Girls*, 4.

49 Fanon, *Dying Colonialism*, 107–8.

50 Lazreg, *Eloquence of Silence*, 127.

51 Lazreg, *Eloquence of Silence*, 113.

52 Lazreg, *Eloquence of Silence*, 117.

53 These events are depicted in Gillo Pontecorvo's famous film *The Battle of Algiers* (1966) and in Zohra Driff's memoir, *Inside the Battle of Algiers*.

54 Unlike CISNU, the Algerian National Liberation Front deployed an explicitly gendered discourse ascribing "feminine" qualities to women that predisposed them toward certain tasks and not others in the service of the revolution. See Lazreg, *Eloquence of Silence*, 121–23.

55 Lazreg shows how female sexuality was considered a problem to be regulated, either through marriage or extreme punishment, even capital punishment of sexual liaisons. Lazreg, *Eloquence of Silence*, 124.

56 "Farah's Trip Exposed," *Resistance*, July 1977, 27.

57 Fanon, *Dying Colonialism*, 107–8.

58 Fanon, *Dying Colonialism*, 107–8.

59 Lazreg, *Eloquence of Silence*, 122.

60 "Farah's Trip Exposed," *Resistance*, July 1977.

61 Quote from Appeal of Conscience Foundation president Rabbi Arthur Schneier in his speech at the awards ceremony. "Queen Farah's Visit," *Resistance*, August 1977, 2.

62 "Farah's Trip Exposed," *Resistance*, July 1977, 26.

63 Moallem argues that "Stories of revolutionary women, Layla Khaled and Jamila Buhrayd in the Middle East, were essential in encouraging women to join the guerilla movement." Moallem, *Between Warrior Brother and Veiled Sister*, 78.

64　Moallem, *Between Warrior Brother and Veiled Sister*, 78.

65　Explanatory note accompanying excerpt from Dehghani, *Torture and Resistance in Iran, Resistance*, June 1977, 19.

66　Dehghani, *Torture and Resistance in Iran, Resistance*, June 1977, 19.

67　Moghissi is quite critical of Dehghani for apparently accepting the notion that women constitute a weak, reactionary force unless they join the revolutionary struggle. Moghissi, *Populism and Feminism*, 116–18.

68　Beale, "Double Jeopardy."

69　Gopinath has argued that heteronormative gender roles are crucial both to post-colonial and diasporic forms of nationalism. Gopinath, *Impossible Desires*, 9–10.

70　Moghissi, *Populism and Feminism*, 117.

71　McClintock, *Imperial Leather*, 366.

Chapter 6: Intersectional Anti-Imperialism

1　Matin-asgari, *Iranian Student Opposition*, 161.

2　Important exceptions to this marginalization, on which this study builds, include Tabari and Yeganeh, *In the Shadow of Islam*; Moghissi, *Populism and Feminism*; Naghibi, *Rethinking Global Sisterhood*, 74–107; Ghamari-Tabrizi, *Foucault in Iran*, 113–58; Mottahedeh, *Whisper Tapes*; and Mottahedeh, "Planetarity: The Anti-disciplinary Object of Iranian Studies," in *Global 1979*, 389–410.

3　My conceptualization of "intersectional" anti-imperialism is informed by the work of Kimberlé Crenshaw and Patricia Hill Collins, who draw on the insights of the Third World Women's Alliance and the Combahee River Collective, among other radical Black and women-of-color feminist formations.

4　Taylor, *How We Get Free*, 4.

5　Abrahamian, *Khomeinism*, 17.

6　Abrahamian, *Khomeinism*, 17.

7　On Khomeini's populist promises, see Abrahamian, *Khomeinism*, 32. On Khomeini's promises regarding women's equality, see Mottahdeh, *Whisper Tapes*, 10, 174.

8　Official tallies show over 99 percent of the more than 20 million votes cast were "yes" votes, although the concept of an "Islamic Republic" was not explained on the ballot. See Nohlen, Grotz, and Hartmann, *Elections*, 72.

9　Ghamari-Tabrizi, *Islam and Dissent*, 40–42.

10　Ghamari-Tabrizi, *Islam and Dissent*, 106.

11　Behrooz, *Rebels with a Cause*, 126.

12　Behrooz, *Rebels with a Cause*, 105–15.

13　Tabari and Yeganeh, *In the Shadow of Islam*, 209; Behrooz, *Rebels with a Cause*, 132.

14　Tabari and Yeganeh, *In the Shadow of Islam*, 209; Behrooz, *Rebels with a Cause*, 133. For more on Communist Unity, see Sadeghi-Boroujerdi, "Origins of Communist Unity."

15　Ghamari-Tabrizi, *Foucault in Iran*, 118–20.

16 Behrooz, *Rebels with a Cause*, 161.

17 Moghissi, *Populism and Feminism*, 102, 118–19, 151.

18 For a critique of this position, see Ghamari-Tabrizi, *Foucault in Iran*, 81–82.

19 Moallem, *Between Warrior Brother and Veiled Sister*, 6.

20 Ghamari-Tabrizi, *Islam and Dissent*, 52–53.

21 Tabari and Yeganeh, *In the Shadow of Islam*, 9.

22 Mottahedeh, *Whisper Tapes*, 31.

23 Moallem, *Between Warrior Brother and Veiled Sister*, 93.

24 Sanasarian, *Women's Rights Movement*, 117–19.

25 See Moallem, *Between Warrior Brother and Veiled Sister*, 91–94.

26 Moallem, *Between Warrior Brother and Veiled Sister*, 93.

27 Moghissi writes of the "theoretical vacuum" from which the Fadaiyan attempted to respond to Khomeini's attacks on equal citizenship for women. Moghissi, *Populism and Feminism*, 119.

28 Moghissi, "Troubled Relationships," 210–11.

29 It is important to note that in the Iranian context, the term *revolutionary* refers to all those who, across the political spectrum and with varying degrees of religiosity, supported overthrowing the Shah.

30 Mottahdeh, *Whisper Tapes*, 1.

31 Tabari and Yeganeh, *In the Shadow of Islam*, 9.

32 Tabari and Yeganeh, *In the Shadow of Islam*, 209.

33 The Society for the Awakening of Women was the first of the new revolutionary women's organizations to form. It was run by women who were part of the UIC, which existed primarily in the US Iranian student diaspora.

34 Mohajer and Matin, *Uprising of Iranian Women*, vol. 1, 350.

35 Moghissi, *Populism and Feminism*, 150–51.

36 Tabari and Yeganeh, *In the Shadow of Islam*, 203.

37 Moghissi, *Populism and Feminism*, 140.

38 Tabari and Yeganeh, *In the Shadow of Islam*, 233.

39 Mottahedeh, *Whisper Tapes*, 77.

40 Moghissi, *Populism and Feminism*, 140.

41 Sanasarian, *Women's Rights Movement*, 125.

42 Mottahedeh, *Whisper Tapes*, 15.

43 Mottahedeh, *Whisper Tapes*, 17.

44 Moghissi, *Populism and Feminism*, 142.

45 Moghissi, *Populism and Feminism*, 141.

46 "Statement by Iranian Women's Protesters," in Afary and Anderson, *Foucault and the Iranian Revolution*, 245–46.

47 "Statement by Iranian Women's Protesters," in Afary and Anderson, *Foucault and the Iranian Revolution*, 245. See also excerpts of Khomeini's speeches on women's rights in Tabari and Yeganeh, *In the Shadow of Islam*, 98–103.

48 *Mouvement de Libération des Femmes Iraniennes: Année Zéro*, short film, 1979, YouTube.

49 Benjamin, "Theses," 261.

50 I am using Negar Mottahedeh's translation, in which she substitutes "planetary" for the more common "global" or "universal" in order to connote a move "toward a quality of social justice that cannot be satisfied by the selective logics of consumption." Mottahedeh, *Whisper Tapes*, 115.

51 Naghibi, *Rethinking Global Sisterhood*, 96. The terms *West-toxified* and *West-toxification* entered the lexicon of the revolution and the discourse of the Islamic Republic largely via the writings of Jalal Al-e Ahmad, although he did not coin the term. For a thorough discussion of the genealogy and political power behind this concept, see Boroujerdi, "*Gharbzadehgi*."

52 See Mottahedeh's *Whisper Tapes* for an illustration of how difficult it was for Western feminists to comprehend the affects, emotions, and politics of the Iranian women's movement, the depth of the solidarity women felt with men, and the desire to have men with them in this new phase of struggle.

53 Mottahedeh, *Whisper Tapes*, 27.

54 This formulation is inspired by the Combahee River Collective Statement. See *How We Get Free*, 22–23.

55 Naghibi, *Rethinking Global Sisterhood*, 96.

56 The chador is a traditional form of clothing for females in Iran, which has carried different meanings at different times in history. Over the course of 1978, it became an expression of both religious devotion and revolutionary fervor.

57 The English subtitles read as follows: "I have been wearing the chador for years but in a chador, I am not able to move. I am not at this protest rally to stop wearing the chador. I am the mother of six daughters and I am protesting because I don't want that they are forced to wear the chador, because I don't want the men to force them to wear the chador. I am here to defend my daughters against the chador."

58 The interviewee uses the Persian word *ashghal* ("garbage") to refer to the religious people in power.

59 The presence of male CISNU members, who had recently returned from the US and Europe, as a line of defense for women protesters is noted in several first-hand accounts collected in Mohajer and Matin, *Uprising of Iranian Women*, vol. 1, 282, 291.

60 McClintock, *Imperial Leather*, 365.

61 See Sameh, *Axis of Hope*, 36–37.

62 Iranian women were not sent "backwards fourteen hundred years" after the Iranian Revolution, but in fact were incorporated unequally into the Islamic Republic through an uneven process that resulted in some gains (in education and employment opportunities) simultaneous with ongoing forms of legal discrimination, especially in family law. See Najmabadi, "(Un)veiling Feminism"; Moghadam, *Modernizing Women*, 193–226; Osanloo, *Politics of Women's Rights*; Hoodfar, "The Veil"; Sameh, *Axis of Hope*; Shahrokhni, *Women in Place*.

63 Ghamari-Tabrizi, *Foucault in Iran*, 126–35.

64 Spivak, *Post-Colonial Critic*, 104.

65 Spivak, *Post-Colonial Critic*, 104.

66 Spivak, *Post-Colonial Critic*, 104.

67 Spivak, *Post-Colonial Critic*, 104.

68 Spivak, *Post-Colonial Critic*, 104.

69 Quoted in Ghamari-Tabrizi, *Foucault in Iran*, 131–32.

70 For a critique of this approach, see Collins, "What's in a Name?"

71 Eskandar Sadeghi-Boroujerdi, "The Post-Revolutionary Women's Uprising of March 1979: An Interview with Nasser Mohajer and Mahnaz Matin," *IranWire*, June 11, 2013, https://iranwire.com/en/features/24.

72 Sadeghi-Boroujerdi, "Post-Revolutionary Women's Uprising," *IranWire*, June 11, 2013.

73 Tabari and Yeganeh, *In the Shadow of Islam*, 212.

74 Tabari and Yeganeh, *In the Shadow of Islam*, 213.

75 Tabari and Yeganeh, *In the Shadow of Islam*, 207–10.

76 Zohreh's assessment is corroborated by Moghissi's account. See Moghissi, *Populism and Feminism*, 174–77.

77 See Sadeghi-Boroujerdi, "Origins of Communist Unity."

78 Najmabadi, "Hazards of Modernity and Morality."

79 For a discussion of the lack of feminist consciousness among leftist Iranian women, see Moghissi, *Populism and Feminism*, 88–104.

80 See my discussion of Anne McClintock's concept of "designated agency" in chapter 5.

81 I am indebted to Golnar Nikpour for this insight about Foucault's inability to recognize the religious teleology governing the dominant Islamist idiom of the revolution.

82 See Mohanty, "Cartographies of Struggle," 1–40.

83 See Springer, *Living for the Revolution*, 1–44.

Conclusion: Revolutionary Affects and the Remaking of Diaspora

1 See Naficy, *Making of Exile Cultures*; Maghbouleh, *Limits of Whiteness*.

2 Feminist and queer scholars of diaspora have challenged the notion that the "backward glance" of nostalgia is always a politically reactionary one by interrogating the political stakes of what is remembered and what is forgotten. See Shohat, *Taboo Memories*, 201–32; Gopinath, *Impossible Desires*, 21.

3 Abrahamian, *Khomeinism*, 23.

4 Benjamin, "Theses," 255.

5 Duggan and Muñoz, "Hope and Hopelessness," 278.

6 Gordon, *Ghostly Matters*, xviii.

7 Brown, "Resisting Left Melancholia," 25.

8   Traverso, *Left-Wing Melancholia*, 51.

9   Traverso, *Left-Wing Melancholia*, 51.

10   Traverso, *Left-Wing Melancholia*, 45.

11   Interview with author, November 17, 2016.

12   Eng and Kazanjian, *Loss*, 5.

13   Rather than an account of "what really happened" in Iran, the memories described below contribute to what sociologist Charles Kurzman has called an "anti-explanation" of the revolution, which demands that we "abandon ... the project of retroactive prediction in favor of recognizing and reconstructing the lived experience of the moment." Kurzman, *Unthinkable Revolution*, viii.

14   See Shakhsari, *Politics of Rightful Killing*, a study of neoliberal assimilation and diasporic entrepreneurship in the Persian-language blogosphere.

15   Boym, *Future of Nostalgia*, xvii.

16   Hirsch and Spitzer, "'We Would Not Have Come without You,'" 258–59.

17   Hirsch and Spitzer, "'We Would Not Have Come without You,'" 258.

18   For a sense of scale, contrast this with the French Revolution, in which participation is estimated at 2 percent. See Kurzman, *Unthinkable Revolution*, 121.

19   I borrow this notion of "haunting" from Grace Cho, *Haunting the Korean Diaspora*.

20   See Shahidi, *Journalism in Iran*, 41.

21   Paidar called this closure "the first opportunity [that] presented itself to the [Islamic Republic Party] and its grassroots supporters to attack the oppositional left." Paidar, *Women and the Political Process*, 228.

22   Shahidi, *Journalism in Iran*, 42. See also Paidar, *Women and the Political Process*, 228–29.

23   Ghamari-Tabrizi, *Islam and Dissent*, 82–83.

24   Ghamari-Tabrizi, *Islam and Dissent*, 124.

25   Bani Sadr had been an active member of CISNU in Paris during his student days at the Sorbonne. He was a leading figure of the revolution, helping to facilitate leftist support for Khomeini by promoting an Islamic anti-imperialism and by accompanying Khomeini on his return to Iran. Bani Sadr held several positions in the postrevolutionary government, and was elected president of the Islamic Republic on January 25, 1980, with 78 percent of the vote. His four-year term was cut short, however; he was impeached in retaliation for his efforts to limit Khomeini's political power.

26   See Bayat, *Workers and Revolution*; Jafari, "Showras."

27   Darius Rejali, author of two major books on torture, called the 1979 Iranian revolution "the revolution against torture" and argued that opposition to torture played a major role in uniting Iranians against the Shah and the US, which helped to establish and train SAVAK. See Scott Hornton, "Six Questions for Darius Rejali, Author of *Torture and Democracy*," *Harper's Magazine*, February 13, 2008, https://harpers.org/2008/02/six-questions-for-darius-rejali-author-of-torture-and-democracy/.

28 Talebi, *Ghosts of Revolution*, 20–21.

29 This analysis of Iran, before and after the revolution, as a carceral state is indebted to Golnar Nikpour. See Nikpour, "The Criminal Is the Patient."

30 Ghamari-Tabrizi, *Foucault in Iran*, 119.

31 Ghamari-Tabrizi, *Foucault in Iran*, 119.

32 The Fadaiyan Majority supported Khomeini in the name of national unity—even while facing repression from the new government—in order both to defend the revolution from imperialism and support the war effort against Iraq. This caused a split, with the Fadaiyan Minority turning to armed struggle against the new government. See Behrooz, *Rebels with a Cause*, 105–20.

33 Amnesty International recently estimated that 5,000 men and women were executed in the 1988 executions. See Amnesty International, *Iran*, 11.

34 See Mohajer, *Voices of a Massacre*.

35 Shohat, *Taboo Memories*, xviii–xix.

36 For vivid descriptions of the communal life of women in prison in Iran after the revolution, see Talebi, *Ghosts of Revolution*.

37 Boym, *Future of Nostalgia*, xiii.

38 On the lack of evidence for, and the right-wing creation of, stories of anti-war protesters disparaging Vietnam veterans, see Neale, *The American War*, 184.

39 "Thousands of Iraqis Rally against Government, US, and Iran," *Globe Post*, January 10, 2020, https://theglobepost.com/2020/01/10/iraq-protests-us-iran/.

40 Gordon, *Ghostly Matters*, 57.

BIBLIOGRAPHY

Interviews

Amini, Mohammed. Plano, TX, July 2, 2012.

Ashkan, Farid. New York, NY, December 14, 2012.

Bajoughli, Javad. New York, NY, May 24, 2012.

Bajoughli, Rahim. Tyson's Corner, VA, June 24, 2012.

Behroozi, Jaleh. Vienna, VA, June 23, 2012.

Benab, Younes Parsa. Washington, DC, June 22, 2012.

Eghtedari, Mohammed. Tyson's Corner, VA, June 24, 2012.

Golemohammadi, Behzad. Berkeley, CA, May 31, 2015.

Haire, Mike. Phone interview, March 17, 2017.

Hojat, Ali. Oakland, CA, July 12, 2012, and April 8, 2015.

Hormachea, Nancy. Berkeley, CA, July 22, 2012, and April 3, 2015.

Jila. Skype interview, January 20, 2013, and in-person interview, San Francisco, CA, December 13, 2014.

Khayam, Zohreh. Vienna, VA, June 23, 2012.

Kowsari, Hamid. Plano, TX, July 2, 2012, and follow-up phone interviews, September 7, 2012, and January 12, 2013.

Leahy, Margaret. San Francisco, CA, March 6, 2013.

Lombardi, Kate. Phone interview, March 17, 2017.

Matin-asgari, Afshin. Skype interview, November 17, 2016.

Mazandarani, Shahnaz. Berkeley, CA, July 20, 2012.

Mina. Amherst, MA, August 10, 2015.

Mirsepassi, Ali. New York, NY, October 24, 2016.

Moradian, K. Sunnyside, NY, March 15, 2012.

Mostashari, Jalil. New York, NY, October 27, 2011.

Nayeri, Kamran. Phone interview, April 20, 2017.

Nodjoumi, Nicky. Brooklyn, NY, May 25, 2017.

Odeah, Camelia. Phone interview, March 29, 2015.

Pirnazar, Jaleh. Oakland, CA, July 12, 2012, and April 8, 2015.

Royanian, Simin. Skype interview, June 21, 2013.

Samiian, Vida. New York, NY, May 4, 2017.

Schneider, Ann. Email interview, March 12, 2017.

Shayegan, Leyli. New York, NY, May 19, 2017.

Shokat, Parviz. Berkeley, CA, July 14, 2012, and May 14, 2015.

Sina. Berkeley, CA, July 23, 2012.

Soosan. Oakland, CA, May 31, 2013.

Soudabeh. Oakland, CA, May 2, 2015.

Tabrizi, Bijan. San Francisco, CA, April 19, 2015.

Taghvai, Ahmad. Vienna, VA, June 23, 2012.

Weiner, Stephanie. Phone interview, April 17, 2017.

Wong, Victoria. Zoom interview, August 31, 2020.

Archives

HC   Howardiana Collections, Moorland-Spingarn Research Center, Howard University

ILOC   Iranian Leftist Opposition Collection, Library of Congress, Washington, DC

PSP   Parviz Shokat Papers, Hoover Institute, Stanford University, Stanford, CA

SC   Special Collections, UCLA

SPC   Social Protest Collection, Bancroft Library, University of California–Berkeley

UA   University Archives, Bancroft Library, University of California–Berkeley

YPB   Younes Parsa Benab Private Collection

Works Cited

"21st Convention of ISAUS." *Resistance* 2, no. 2 (November 1973), np. ILOC.

"41 Iranians Face Deportation." Iranian Students Association flyer, June 1970. SPC.

"623 Foreign Students." *Hilltop*, February 8, 1960, 1. HC.

"639 F2d 1160 Iranian Students Association v. M Sawyer | OpenJurist." Accessed April 16, 2015. http://openjurist.org/639/f2d/1160/iranian-students-association-v-m-sawyer#fn3_ref.

"A Deportation Threat." *Daily Californian*, January 8, 1979, 5. UA.

"A Plea for Humanity in Iran," ISA leaflet. June 1965, RS#259, Student Activism, box 4, folder 2. SC.

"A Question of Political Prisoners." Leaflet. October 24, 1973. SPC.

Abdulhadi, Rabab Ibrahim. "Whose 1960s? Gender, Resistance, and Liberation in Palestine." In *New World Coming: The Sixties and the Shaping of Global Consciousness*, ed. Karen Dubinsky, Catherine Krull, Susan Lord, Sean Mills, and Scott Rutherford, 13–23. Toronto: Between the Lines, 2009.

Abdulhadi, Rabab, Evelyn Alsultany, and Nadine Naber, eds. *Arab and Arab American Feminisms: Gender, Violence, and Belonging*. Syracuse, NY: Syracuse University Press, 2010.

Abrahamian, Ervand. "Ali Shariati: Ideologue of the Iranian Revolution." *MERIP Reports* (January 1982): 25–28.

Abrahamian, Ervand. *The Coup: 1953, the CIA Coup, and the Roots of Modern US-Iranian Relations.* New York: New Press, 2013.

Abrahamian, Ervand. *Iran between Two Revolutions.* Princeton, NJ: Princeton University Press, 1982.

Abrahamian, Ervand. *The Iranian Mojahedin.* New Haven, CT: Yale University Press, 1989.

Abrahamian, Ervand. *Khomeinism.* Berkeley: University of California Press, 1993.

Abu-Lughod, Lila. "Do Muslim Women Really Need Saving? Anthropological Reflections on Cultural Relativism and Its Others." *American Anthropologist* 104, no. 3 (2002): 783–90.

Abu-Lughod, Lila, ed. *Remaking Women: Feminism and Modernity in the Middle East.* Cairo: American University in Cairo Press, 1998.

Adeboye, Sam. "Iranian People Should Be an Example for All." *The Hilltop,* March 2, 1979, 5. HC.

"Adibi-Sadeh v. Bee County College, 454 F. Supp. 552 (S.D. Tex. 1978):: Justia." Accessed April 16, 2015. http://law.justia.com/cases/federal/district-courts/FSupp /454/552/2135674/.

Afary, Janet, and Kevin B. Anderson. *Foucault and the Iranian Revolution: Gender and the Seductions of Islamism.* Chicago: University of Chicago Press, 2005.

Ahmed, Leila. *Women and Gender in Islam: Historical Roots of a Modern Debate.* New Haven, CT: Yale University Press, 1992.

Ahmed, Sara. *The Cultural Politics of Emotions.* New York: Routledge, 2004.

Ahmed, Sara. *Living a Feminist Life.* Durham, NC: Duke University Press, 2017.

Ahmed, Sara. *The Promise of Happiness.* Durham, NC: Duke University Press, 2010.

Alexander, M. Jacqui, and Chandra Talpade Mohanty, eds. *Feminist Genealogies, Colonial Legacies, Democratic Futures.* New York: Routledge, 1997.

"The Americanization of Iranian Education." *Resistance* 4, Supplement 2, February 1977, 5. ILOC.

"American Universities at the Service of U.S. Neocolonialism." *Resistance* 4, no. 5 (April 1977): 1. ILOC.

Amirrezvani, Anita, and Persis Karim, eds. *Tremors: New Fiction by Iranian American Writers.* Fayetteville: University of Arkansas Press, 2013.

Amnesty International. *Annual Report 1974/75.* https://www.amnesty.org/en /documents/pol10/001/1975/en/.

Amnesty International. *Iran: Blood-Soaked Secrets: Why Iran's 1988 Prison Massacres Are Ongoing Crime against Humanity.* Report, 2018. https://www.amnesty.org/en /documents/mde13/9421/2018/en/.

"Amnesty International News Release." *Resistance* (May 1977): np. ILOC.

"Amnesty Says 1,000 Arrests in Iran." *Guardian,* November 26, 1970, 4.

Anderson, Jack, and Les Whitten. "CIA Seen Abetting Foreign Agents." *Washington Post,* October 26, 1976, B15.

Anderson, Jack, and Les Whitten. "C.I.A. Trained Iranian Secret Police." *Washington Post,* November 4, 1976, DC11.

Anderson, Jack, and Les Whitten. "Iranian Secret Police Dirty Tricks." *Washington Post*, October 29, 1976, D15.

"Angry Americans Speak and March in Iran Protests." *Los Angeles Times*, November 8, 1979, A1.

"Anti-Suspension Demonstrations at SF." KTVU news report, December 4, 1967. Bay Area Television Archive. https://diva.sfsu.edu/collections/sfbatv/bundles/187219.

Aquilina, Susannah. "Common Ground: Iranian Student Opposition to the Shah on the US/Mexico Border." *Journal of Intercultural Studies* 32, no. 4 (2011): 321–34.

"Around the Nation." *New York Times*, May 20, 1979, 26.

Azari, Farah. "Islam's Appeal to Women in Iran: Illusions and Reality." In *Women in Iran: The Conflict with Fundamentalist Islam*, ed. Farah Azari, 1–71. London: Ithaca Press, 1983.

Azikiwe, Abayomi. "U.S. Activists Meet with Iranian President." Accessed July 29, 2019. https://www.workers.org/2010/us/iran_1007/.

Babcock, Charles R. "Carter's Visa Crackdown Won't Hurt Immediately." *Washington Post*, April 9, 1980, A16.

Bacchetta, Paola, Tina Campt, Inderpal Grewal, Caren Kaplan, Minoo Moallem, and Jennifer Terry. "Transnational Feminist Practices against War: A Statement." *Meridians* 2, no. 2 (2002): 302–8.

Bald, Vivek. *Bengali Harlem and the Lost Histories of South Asian America*. Cambridge, MA: Harvard University Press, 2013.

Bargetz, Brigitte. "The Distribution of Emotions: Affective Politics of Emancipation." *Hypatia* 30, no. 3 (2015): 580–96.

Bascara, Victor. *Model Minority Imperialism*. Minneapolis: University of Minnesota Press, 2006.

Bayat, Asef. *Workers and Revolution in Iran: A Third World Experience of Workers' Control*. London: Zed Books, 1987.

Beale, Frances M. "Double Jeopardy: To Be Black and Female." *Meridians* 8, no. 2 (2008): 166–76. First published 1969.

Behdjou, J. H. "Economic and Trade Relations between the United States and Iran Flourish." *Los Angeles Times*, January 25, 1976, N8.

Behrooz, Maziar. *Rebels with a Cause: The Failure of the Iranian Left*. London: I. B. Tauris, 2004.

"Bell Says U.S. Will Deport Iranians Guilty of Violence." *Washington Post*, January 5, 1979, A15.

"Bell Will Shake Up Immigration Unit." *New York Times*, January 29, 1979, A15.

Benab, Younes Parsa. *A One Hundred Year History of Political Parties and Organizations of Iran (1904–2004)*. Washington, DC: Ravandi Publishing House, 2004.

Bender, Thomas, ed. *Rethinking American History in a Global Age*. Berkeley: University of California Press, 2002.

Benjamin, Walter. "Theses on the Philosophy of History." In *Illuminations*, ed. Hannah Arendt, trans. Harry Zohn, 196–209. New York: Schocken Books, 1969.

Berger, Dan, ed. *The Hidden 1970s: Histories of Radicalism*. New Brunswick, NJ: Rutgers University Press, 2010.

Berlant, Lauren. *Cruel Optimism*. Durham, NC: Duke University Press, 2011.

Bhatia, Sunil. *American Karma: Race, Culture, and Identity in the Indian Diaspora*. New York: New York University Press, 2007.

Biondi, Martha. *The Black Revolution on Campus*. Berkeley: University of California Press. 2012.

Bloom, Joshua, and Waldo E. Martin Jr. *Black against Empire: The History and Politics of the Black Panther Party*. Berkeley: University of California Press, 2013.

Blum, John. "Save the Beeville 103." *Texas Monthly*, June 1978, 84–88.

Boggs, Abigail, and Nick Mitchell. "Critical University Studies and the Crisis Consensus." *Feminist Studies* 44, no. 2 (2018): 432–63.

Boroujerdi, Mehrzad. *"Gharbzadehgi:* The Dominant Intellectual Discourse of Pre- and Post-Revolutionary Iran." In *Iran: Political Culture in the Islamic Republic*, ed. Samih K. Farsoun and Mehrdad Mashayekhi, 30–56. New York: Columbia University Press, 1992.

Boroujerdi, Mehrzad. *Iranian Intellectuals and the West: The Tormented Triumph of Nativism*. Syracuse, NY: Syracuse University Press, 1996.

Boym, Svetlana. *The Future of Nostalgia*. New York: Basic Books, 2002.

Bozorgmehr, Mehdi. "Does Host Hostility Create Ethnic Solidarity? The Experience of Iranians in the United States." *Bulletin of the Royal Institute for Inter-Faith Studies* 2, no. 1 (2000): 159–78.

Bozorgmehr, Mehdi. "High Status Immigrants: A Statistical Profile of Iranians in the United States." *Iranian Studies* 21, nos. 3/4 (1988): 5–36.

Bozorgmehr, Mehdi. "Internal Ethnicity: Iranians in Los Angeles." *Sociological Perspectives* 4, no. 3 (1997): 387–408.

Bozorgmehr, Mehdi. "Iranians." In *Refugees in America in the 1990s*, ed. David W. Haines, 213–31. Westport, CT: Greenwood Press, 1996.

Bozorgmehr, Mehdi. "Middle Easterners: A New Kind of Immigrant." In *Ethnic Los Angeles*, ed. Roger David Waldinger and Mehdi Bozorgmehr, 345–78. New York: Russell Sage Foundation, 1997.

Bozorgmehr, Mehdi, and Alison Feldman, eds. *Middle Eastern Diaspora Communities in America: Proceedings of the 17th Annual Summer Institute of the Joint Center for Near Eastern Studies of New York University and Princeton University*. New York: Hagop Kevorkian Center for Near Eastern Studies at New York University, 1996.

Brown, Wendy. "Resisting Left Melancholia." *Boundary 2* 26, no. 3 (1999): 19–27.

Butler, Judith. *Giving an Account of Oneself*. New York: Fordham University Press, 2005.

Butler, Judith. *Undoing Gender*. New York: Routledge, 2004.

Canefe, Nergis. "Home in Exile: Politics of Refugehood in the Canadian Muslim Diaspora." In *Memory and Migration: Multidisciplinary Approaches to Memory Studies*, ed. Julia Creet and Andreas Kitzmann, 156–80. Toronto: University of Toronto Press, 2011.

Cantrell, Kathlyn D., "Letters to the Editor: More on the Crisis in Iran." *Washington Post*, November 14, 1979, A26.

Charlton, Linda. "Shah's Visit Underscored Large Number of Iranian Students in U.S." *New York Times*, November 21, 1977, 10.

Chatterjee, Piya, and Sunaina Maira. *The Imperial University: Academic Repression and Scholarly Dissent*. Minneapolis: University of Minnesota Press, 2014.

Chehabi, H. E. *Iranian Politics and Religious Modernism: The Liberation Movement of Iran under the Shah and Khomeini*. London: I. B. Tauris, 1990.

"Chicago Police Charged with Spying on Iranians." *New York Times*, March 10, 1977, 18.

Cho, Grace M. *Haunting the Korean Diaspora: Shame, Secrecy, and the Forgotten War*. Minneapolis: University of Minnesota Press, 2008.

Clough, Patricia Ticineto, ed. *The Affective Turn: Theorizing the Social*. Durham, NC: Duke University Press, 2007.

Cohen, Robert, and Reginald E. Zelnik, eds. *The Free Speech Movement: Reflections on Berkeley in the 1960s*. Berkeley: University of California Press, 2002.

Coles, Robert. *The Political Life of Children*. New York: Atlantic Monthly Press, 1986.

Collins, Patricia Hill. *Intersectionality as Critical Social Theory*. Durham, NC: Duke University Press, 2019.

Collins, Patricia Hill. "What's in a Name?" *Black Scholar* 26, no. 1 (1996): 9–17.

Committee for National Liberation in the Middle East. "War in the Middle East." Leaflet, October 24, 1973. SPC.

"Computer Will Help Catch Illegal Aliens, Bell Says." *Los Angeles Times*, June 6, 1979, A2.

"Confederation of Iranian Students Report on the 17th Congress." Pamphlet 1, no. 1 (March 1977): 1–124. PSP.

"Contrary to 'Human Rights.'" *Hilltop*, November 18, 1977, 4. HC.

"Copy of Telegram sent to Iranian Consulate by Black Student Union," 1970. SPC.

Cram, William Arthur. "Unseen Images of the 1953 Iran Coup-in Pictures." *Guardian*, December 16, 2015, sec. Iran Blog. Accessed August 8, 2018. https://www.the guardian.com/world/iran-blog/gallery/2015/dec/16/unseen-images-of-the-1953 -iran-coup-in-pictures.

"The Creed." *Daneshjoo*, March 1964, 18. YPB.

Creet, Julia. "Introduction: The Migration of Memory and Memories of Migration." In *Memory and Migration: Multidisciplinary Approaches to Memory Studies*, ed. Julia Creet and Andreas Kitzmann, 1–29. Toronto: University of Toronto Press, 2011.

Crenshaw, Kimberlé, "Demarginalizing the Intersection of Race and Sex: A Black Feminist Critique of Antidiscrimination Doctrine, Feminist Theory and Antiracist Politics." *University of Chicago Legal Forum* 1989, Issue 1, Article 8, 139–67.

Crenshaw, Kimberlé, "Mapping the Margins: Intersectionality, Identity Politics and Violence Against Women of Color," *Stanford Law Review* 43, no. 6 (July 1991): 1241–99.

Crimp, Douglas. "Mourning and Militancy." *October* 51 (1989): 3–18.

"Crocodile Tears." *Resistance* 5, no. 1 (December 1977): 2. ILOC.

Cronin, Stephanie. "Iran's Forgotten Revolutionary." In *Reformers and Revolutionaries in Modern Iran: New Perspectives on the Iranian Left*, ed. Stephanie Cronin, 118–46. London: Routledge Curzon, 2004.

Cvetkovich, Ann. *An Archive of Feelings: Trauma, Sexuality, and Lesbian Public Cultures*. Durham, NC: Duke University Press, 2003.

Dailami, Pezhmann. "The First Congress of the Peoples of the East and the Soviet Republic of Gilan 1920–21." In *Reformers and Revolutionaries in Modern Iran: New*

Perspectives on the Iranian Left, ed. Stephanie Cronin, 86–87. London: Routledge Curzon, 2004.

Das Gupta, Monisha. *Unruly Immigrants: Rights, Activism, and Transnational South Asian Politics in the United States*. Durham, NC: Duke University Press, 2006.

Daulatzai, Sohail. *Black Star, Crescent Moon: The Muslim International and Black Freedom beyond America*. Minneapolis: University of Minnesota Press, 2012.

"Defend the Heroic Struggles of the Palestinian People." *Iran Report: Quarterly Journal of I.S.A.U.S.* Series 24, no. 1 (September, October, and November 1976): np. PSP.

Dehghani, Ashraf. "Torture and Resistance in Iran." *Resistance* (June 1977): 19.

Dickey, Christopher, and Charles R. Babcock. "Student Visa Reviews under Way," *Washington Post*, November 13, 1979, A1.

Donihi, Rosemary. "Foreign Students are Parties' 'Lions.'" *Washington Post*, March 30, 1960, D7.

Dorman, William A., and Mansour Farhang. *The US Press and Iran*. Berkeley: University of California Press, 1987.

Driff, Zohra. *Inside the Battle of Algiers: Memoir of a Woman Freedom Fighter*. Charlottesville, VA: Just World Books, 2017.

Dudziak, Mary. *Cold War Civil Rights: Race and the Image of American Democracy*. Princeton, NJ: Princeton University Press, 2002.

Duggan, Lisa, and José Esteban Muñoz. "Hope and Hopelessness: A Dialogue." *Women and Performance* 19, no. 2 (2009): 275–83.

Edwards, Brent Hayes. *The Practice of Diaspora: Literature, Translation, and the Rise of Black Internationalism*. Cambridge, MA: Harvard University Press, 2003.

Ehrman, Anita. "Striker Ousted from Embassy." *Los Angeles Times*, January 23, 1963, 3.

Ekpo, Akpan. "Shah of Iran—Enemy to Africa." *Hilltop*, March 17, 1978, 5. HC.

Elahi, Babak, and Persis M. Karim. "Introduction: Iranian Diaspora." In "Iranian Diaspora," ed. Babak Elahi and Persis M. Karim. Special issue, *Comparative Studies of South Asia, Africa and the Middle East* 31, no. 2 (2011): 381–87.

Elbaum, Max. *Revolution in the Air: Sixties Radicals Turn to Lenin, Mao and Che*. New York: Verso, 2002.

Eng, David, and David Kazanjian, eds. *Loss: The Politics of Mourning*. Berkeley: University of California Press, 2003.

Erlich, John, and Susan Erlich, eds. *Student Power, Participation, and Revolution*. New York: Association Press, 1971.

Falk, Richard. "Was It Wrong to Support the Iranian Revolution in 1978 (Because It Turned Out Badly)." *Foreign Policy Journal*, October 12, 2012.

Fanon, Frantz. *Black Skin, White Masks*. New York: Grove Press, 1967.

Fanon, Frantz. *A Dying Colonialism*. New York: Grove Press, 1965.

Fanon, Frantz. *The Wretched of the Earth*. New York: Grove Press, 1963.

"Farah's Trip Exposed." *Resistance*, Special Pamphlet 5, no. 4 (July 1977). ILOC.

Featherstone, David. *Solidarity: Hidden Histories and Geographies of Internationalism*. London: Zed Books, 2012.

Ferguson, Roderick. *The Reorder of Things: The University and Its Pedagogies of Minority Difference*. Minneapolis: University of Minnesota Press, 2012.

"Fifty Years of Pahlavi Dynasty Rule: Benevolence or Betrayal?" Leaflet, 1976. SPC.

Finney, Paul. "Letters to the Times." *Los Angeles Times*, December 21, 1979, C6.

Flatley, Jonathan. *Affective Mapping: Melancholia and the Politics of Modernism*. Cambridge, MA: Harvard University Press, 2008.

Foltz, Richard. *Religions of Iran: From Prehistory to the Present*. London: Oneworld Publications, 2013.

Foran, John. "Discursive Subversions: *Time* Magazine, the CIA Overthrow of Musaddiq, and the Installation of the Shah." In *Cold War Constructions: The Political Culture of United States Imperialism, 1945–1966*, ed. Christian G. Appy, 157–82. Amherst: University of Massachusetts Press, 2000.

"Foreign Agents in America: Shady Tactics and Worse." *U.S. News and World Report*, July 4, 1977, 23.

Forsyth, Lawrence. "Letters to the Editor: The Shah and the Demonstrators." *Washington Post*, November 19, 1977, A18.

Foucault, Michel. *History of Sexuality*, vol. 1: *An Introduction*. New York: Random House, 1978.

Foucault, Michel. *Society Must Be Defended: Lectures at the Collège de France 1975–1976*. New York: Picador, 1997.

"Four Iranian Students Arrested in a Protest." *Washington Post*, August 24, 1967, A15.

"Free the 12 Iranian Artists 1973 # 03 | Flickr—Photo Sharing!" Accessed November 1, 2012. http://www.flickr.com/photos/washington_area_spark/5536255754/.

Freud, Sigmund. "Mourning and Melancholia." In *Collected Papers*, vol. 4, ed. Ernest Jones, 152–70. London: Hogarth Press and the Institute of Psycho-Analysis, 1948. Essay first published 1917.

"From the Iranian Students Association in the United States." *The Black Panther*, no. 24 (January 1970): 5. Accessed June 20, 2012 at Moorland-Spingarn Research Center, Howard University, Washington, DC.

Furgurson, Ernest B. "Do the Iranian 'Students' Ever Study?" *Los Angeles Times*, November 22, 1977, D7.

Gandhi, Leela. *Affective Communities: Anticolonial Thought, Fin-de Siècle Radicalism, and the Politics of Friendship*. Durham, NC: Duke University Press, 2006.

Ghamari-Tabrizi, Behrooz. *Foucault in Iran: Islamic Revolution after the Enlightenment*. Minneapolis: University of Minnesota Press, 2016.

Ghamari-Tabrizi, Behrooz. *Islam and Dissent in Postrevolutionary Iran*. London: I. B. Tauris, 2008.

Ghamari-Tabrizi, Behrooz, Mansour Bonakdarian, Nasrin Rahimieh, Ahmad Sadri, and Ervand Abrahamian, eds. "The Iranian Revolution Turns Thirty." Special issue, *Radical History Review* 105 (2009).

Gopinath, Gayatri. "Archive, Affect, and the Everyday." In *Political Emotions: New Agendas in Communication*, ed. Janet Staiger, Ann Cvetkovich, and Ann Reynolds, 165–92. New York: Routledge, 2010.

Gopinath, Gayatri. *Impossible Desires: Queer Diasporas and South Asian Public Cultures*. Durham, NC: Duke University Press, 2005.

Gopinath, Gayatri. *Unruly Visions: The Aesthetic Practices of Queer Diaspora*. Durham, NC: Duke University Press, 2018.

Gordon, Avery. *Ghostly Matters: Haunting and the Sociological Imagination*. Minneapolis: University of Minnesota Press, 2008.

Gordon, Larry. "John R. Hubbard Dies at 92; USC President, Historian, and Diplomat." *Los Angeles Times*, August 23, 2011, AA5.

Gould, Deborah. *Moving Politics: Emotion and ACT UP's Fight against AIDS*. Chicago: University of Chicago Press, 2009.

Gould, Deborah. "On Affect and Protest." In *Political Emotions: New Agendas in Communication*, ed. Janet Staiger, Ann Cvetkovich, and Ann Reynolds, 18–44. New York: Routledge, 2010.

Grewal, Inderpal. *Transnational America: Feminisms, Diasporas, Neoliberalisms*. Durham, NC: Duke University Press, 2005.

Grewal, Inderpal, and Caren Kaplan. "Global Identities: Theorizing Transnational Studies of Sexuality." *GLQ* 7, no. 4 (2001): 663–79.

Grewal, Inderpal, and Caren Kaplan, eds. *Scattered Hegemonies: Postmodernity and Transnational Feminist Practice*. Minneapolis: University of Minnesota Press, 1994.

Gualtieri, Sarah. *Between Arab and White: Race and Ethnicity in the Early Syrian American Diaspora*. Berkeley: University of California Press, 2009.

Halberstam, Judith. *In a Queer Time and Place: Transgender Bodies, Subcultural Lives*. New York: New York University Press, 2005.

Halbwachs, Maurice. *On Collective Memory*. Chicago: University of Chicago Press, 1992.

Hall, Stuart, and Paul Du Gay, eds. *Questions of Cultural Identity*. London: SAGE Publications, 1996.

Hardt, Michael. "Foreword: What Affects Are Good For." In *The Affective Turn*, ed. Patricia Clough, ix–xiii. Durham, NC: Duke University Press, 2007.

Hazlett, Bill, and Diane Coutu. "30 Hurt as Iranians, L.A. Police Clash: 171 Arrested after Protest against Shah Erupts into Melee." *Los Angeles Times*, September 2, 1978, A13.

Hernández, Daisy, and Bushra Rehman, eds. *Colonize This! Young Women of Color on Today's Feminism*. 2nd ed. New York: Seal Press, 2019.

Herron, Caroline Rand, and Daniel Lewis. "The Nation: A Catalogue of Foreign Spies in Our Midst." *New York Times*, August 12, 1979, E2.

Hirsch, Marianne, and Leo Spitzer. "'We Would Not Have Come without You': Generations of Nostalgia." *American Imago* 59, no. 3 (2002): 253–76.

Hong, Grace Kyungwon, and Roderick A. Ferguson, eds. *Strange Affinities: The Gender and Sexual Politics of Comparative Racialization*. Durham, NC: Duke University Press, 2011.

Hoodfar, Homa. "The Veil in Their Minds and on Our Heads." *Resources for Feminist Research* 22, nos. 3/4 (1993): 5–18.

Hornton, Scott. "Six Questions for Darius Rejali, Author of *Torture and Democracy*." *Harper's Magazine*, February 13, 2008. https://harpers.org/2008/02/six-questions -for-darius-rejali-author-of-torture-and-democracy/.

"Imperialism in the Middle East and the Struggle of the Palestinian People." Leaflet, April 22, 1970. SPC.

"In a spirit of solidarity …" *Resistance* 5, no. 2 (March 1978): 7. ILOC.

"In Appreciation." *Resistance* 5, no. 1, December 1977. ILOC.

"International Appeal." From the Omani Red Crescent, Aden, People's Democratic Republic of Yemen, January 1, 1975. PSP.

"International Students Give Point of View." *Commerce Journal*, April 29, 1971, 34. Accessed July 12, 2021. *Newspaper Archive*, access-newspaperarchive-com.ezproxy.cul.columbia.edu/us/texas/commerce/commerce-journal/1971/04-29/page-34/.

"Iran, the Future Vietnam: U.S. Get Out of Iran." Leaflet. Iranian Student Association of Chicago, May 1971. SPC.

"Iran: Persian Gulf and Energy Crisis." Committee to Defend the Iranian Students, May 16, 1973. PSP.

"Iranian and American Students Seize Statue of Liberty in Support of 18 Iranian Patriots." *Resistance* 4, no. 2 (1977): 1. ILOC.

"Iranian Deportations Asked." *Washington Post*, January 4, 1979, A9.

"Iranian-Israeli Ties Strengthen." ISA pamphlet, circa 1973. ILOC.

"Iranian Marchers Met by Jeers, Taunts Across U.S." *Los Angeles Times*, November 9, 1979, A2.

"Iranian Recruiters Skip Campus Visit." *Daily Californian*, February 9, 1976. UA.

"Iranian Revolution" entry in *Activism in the Archives*, UC Santa Cruz Digital Exhibits. Accessed January 28, 2020. https://exhibits.library.ucsc.edu/exhibits/show/activism-in-the-archives/john-thorne-collection/iran.

"Iranians See R. Kennedy." *The Washington Post*, January 27, 1962, B18.

Iranian Student Association of Northern California. "What Are U.S. Imperialist Interests in Iran?" May 1971. SPC.

"Iranian Student Demonstration at the White House." Film footage, 1967. https://www.youtube.com/watch?v=9HVhPiaSIZk.

Iranian Students Association. "Iranian Struggle Against Injustice." *Hilltop*, November 11, 1977, 5. HC.

"Iranian Students Claim Harassment." *Daily Californian*, April 11, 1973, 4. UA.

"Iranian Students Criticize Shah." *Daily Californian*, April 9, 1976, 3. UA.

"Iranian Students Picketing (1961)." KPIX news footage, September 6, 1961. Bay Area Television Archive. https://diva.sfsu.edu/collections/sfbatv/bundles/232530.

"Iranian Students Picket Shah Arrival Here." *Washington Post*, April 12, 1962, 12.

"Iranian Students Storm Shah's Mother's Home." *Washington Post*, January 3, 1979, A1.

"Iranian Women: Oppression and Struggle." *Resistance* 1, no. 4 (June 1973), 8. SPC.

"Iranians Won't Be Deported, U.S. States." *Los Angeles Times*, November 8, 1979, A1.

"Iran's Kent State and Baton Rouge." 1973. Box 1. PSP.

"Iran Students Picket, Fast at Consulate." *Daily Californian*, August 1, 1961, 12. UA.

ISA flyer for Eisenstein film screening at UC Berkeley, July 21, 1970. SPC.

Jafari, Peyman. "The Showras in the Iranian Revolution: Labor Relations and the State in the Iranian Oil Industry 1979–1982." In *Worlds of Labor Turned Upside Down*, ed. Pepijn Brandon, Peyman Jafari, and Stefan Müller, 252–85. Leiden: Brill, 2020.

Jamal, Amaney, and Nadine Naber. *Race and Arab Americans before and after 9/11: From Invisible Citizens to Visible Subjects*. Syracuse, NY: Syracuse University Press, 2008.

Jayawardena, Kumari. *Feminism and Nationalism in the Third World*. London: Zed Books, 1986.

Jones, Andrew F., and Nikhil Pal Singh. "Guest Editors' Introduction." In "The Afro-Asian Century," ed. Andrew F. Jones and Nikhil Pal Singh. Special issue, *Positions* 11, no. 1 (2003): 1–9.

Kaiser, Robert Blair. "Iranian Flags Sell Fast in the U.S.; Buyers Burn Them at Protests." *New York Times*, November 21, 1979, A12.

Kaiser, Robert Blair. "Iranians in U.S. Fear Retaliation on Two Fronts." *New York Times*, November 22, 1979, A18.

Kandiyoti, Deniz, ed. *Gendering the Middle East: Emerging Perspectives*. Syracuse, NY: Syracuse University Press, 1996.

Kaplan, Amy, and Donald E. Pease, eds. *Cultures of United States Imperialism*. Durham, NC: Duke University Press, 1993.

Kaplan, Caren, Norma Alarcón, and Minoo Moallem, eds. *Between Woman and Nation: Nationalisms, Transnational Feminisms, and the State*. Durham, NC: Duke University Press, 1999.

Kaplis, Hilda. "Letters to the Editor." *Washington Post*, January 7, 1979, C6.

Karim, Persis, ed. *Let Me Tell You Where I've Been: New Writing by Women of the Iranian Diaspora*. Fayetteville: University of Arkansas Press, 2006.

Karim, Persis M., and Mehdi Khorrami, eds. *A World Between: Poems, Short Stories and Essays by Iranian Americans*. New York: George Braziller, 1999.

Karim, Persis M., and Nasrin Rahimieh, eds. "Multi-Ethnic Literatures of the United States." Special issue, *Iranian American Literature* 33, no. 2 (2008).

Keats, Mark. "Letter to the Times." *Los Angeles Times*, September 8, 1978, D6.

Keddie, Nikki R., and Mark J. Gasiorowski, eds. *Neither East nor West Iran, the United States, and the Soviet Union*. New Haven, CT: Yale University Press, 1990.

Kelley, Robin D. G. *Freedom Dreams: The Black Radical Imagination*. Boston: Beacon Press, 2002.

Kelley, Robin D. G., and Betsy Esch. "Black Like Mao: Red China and Black Revolution." *Souls: A Critical Journal of Black Politics, Culture, and Society* 1, no. 4 (1999): 6–41.

Kennedy, Merrit. "A Look at Egypt's Uprising, 5 Years Later," January 25, 2016. Accessed July 24, 2019. https://www.npr.org/sections/thetwo-way/2016/01/25/464290769/a-look-at-egypts-uprising-5-years-later.

Khalidi, Rashid. *Sowing Crisis: The Cold War and American Dominance in the Middle East*. Boston: Beacon Press, 2009.

Kim, Claire Jean. "The Racial Triangulation of Asian Americans." *Politics and Society* 27, no. 1 (1999): 105–38.

King, Anthony D., ed. *Culture, Globalization and the World-System: Contemporary Conditions for the Representation of Identity*. Binghamton, NY: Department of Art and Art History, State University of New York–Binghamton, 1991.

Kinzer, Stephen. *All the Shah's Men: An American Coup and the Roots of Middle East Terror*. Hoboken, NJ: Wiley, 2003.

Klein, Christina. *Cold War Orientalism: Asia in the Middlebrow Imagination, 1945–1961*. Berkeley: University of California Press, 2003.

Kneeland, Douglas E. "182 Iranian Face Hearings on Visa Status after Protest." *New York Times*, May 19, 1978, A12.

Kramer, Paul A. "Is the World Our Campus? International Students and US Global Power in the Long Twentieth Century." *Diplomatic History* 33, no. 5 (2009): 775–806.

Kurzman, Charles. *The Unthinkable Revolution in Iran*. Cambridge, MA: Harvard University Press, 2004.

Latham, Michael E. *Modernization as Ideology: American Social Science and "Nation Building" in the Kennedy Era*. Chapel Hill: University of North Carolina Press, 2000.

Lazreg, Marnia. *The Eloquence of Silence: Algerian Women in Question*. London: Routledge, 2018.

"Letter from Information Committee of the People's Front for the Liberation of Oman." *Iran Report: Quarterly Journal of I.S.A.U.S.* Series 24, no. 1 (September, October, and November 1976): 5. Younes Parsa Benab private collection.

"Letter of the ISAUS to [United Nations] Secretary-General." *Daneshjoo* 12, no. 6 (March 1964) [English-language section].

Lindsey, Robert. "Iranian Students Riot in California As Shah's Mother Visits His Sister." *New York Times*, January 3, 1979, A8.

Lockman, Zachary. *Contending Visions of the Middle East: The History and Politics of Orientalism*. New York: Cambridge University Press, 2010.

London, Herb. "The Iranian People Are Pro-American, Unlike Their Government." Accessed July 29, 2007. https://www.foxnews.com/opinion/the-iranian-people -are-pro-american-unlike-their-government.

Lorde, Audre. *Sister Outsider*. Berkeley, CA: Crossing Press, 2007.

Lowe, Lisa. *Immigrant Acts: On Asian American Cultural Politics*. Durham, NC: Duke University Press, 1996.

Löwey, Michael. *The Politics of Combined and Uneven Development: The Theory of Permanent Revolution*. London: New Left Books, 1981.

Lubin, Alex. *Geographies of Liberation: The Making of an Afro-Arab Political Imaginary*. Chapel Hill: University of North Carolina Press, 2014.

Lusinchi, Victor A. "Torture and Denials of Rights Laid to Iran by Jurists' Group." *New York Times*, May 29, 1976, 51.

Lynton, Stephen J., and Courtland Milloy. "Shah Violence Sporadic." *Washington Post*, November 17, 1977, A1.

Maghbouleh, Neda. *The Limits of Whiteness: Iranian Americans and the Everyday Politics of Race*. Stanford, CA: Stanford University Press, 2017.

Maira, Sunaina Marr. *Missing: Youth, Citizenship, and Empire after 9/11*. Durham, NC: Duke University Press, 2009.

Maira, Sunaina Marr. *The 9/11 Generation: Youth, Rights, and Solidarity in the War on Terror*. New York: New York University Press, 2016.

Maira, Sunaina, and Magid Shihade. "Meeting Asian/Arab American Studies: Thinking Race, Empire, and Zionism in the US." *Journal of Asian American Studies* 9, no. 2 (2006): 117–40.

Malkiel, Nancy Weiss. *"Keep the Damned Women Out": The Struggle for Coeducation*. Princeton, NJ: Princeton University Press, 2016.

Marro, Anthony. "Intelligence Panel Is Investigating Friendly Governments' Acts in U.S." *New York Times*, December 17, 1976, 1.

Martin, Judith, and Winzola McLenden. "Iran Envoy Abruptly Recalled." *Washington Post*, February 24, 1962, A1.

Massumi, Brian. *Parables for the Virtual*. Durham, NC: Duke University Press, 2002.

Matin-asgari, Afshin. *Iranian Student Opposition to the Shah*. Costa Mesa, CA: Mazda Publishers, 2002.

Maxwell, Evan. "UCLA Joins USC in Banning Campus Checks of Iranians." *Los Angeles Times*, November 21, 1979, 18.

Maxwell, Evan. "'We Are the Hostages Here': Iranian Students Worried by Crackdown." *Los Angeles Times*, November 16, 1979, 2.

McAlister, Melani. *Epic Encounters: Culture, Media, and US Interests in the Middle East, 1945–2000*. Berkeley: University of California Press, 2001.

McClintock, Anne. *Imperial Leather: Race, Gender, and Sexuality in the Colonial Context*. New York: Routledge, 1995.

McGraw, Bill. "U.S. Iranian Students Criticize Shah." *Daily Californian*, April 9, 1976, 3. UA.

"Messages of 11th Annual Congress of ISAUS to: The United States National Students Association." *Daneshjoo* 13, no. 1 (November 1964): 9–10.

Meyer, Richard E. "Iranian Protest March Routed in Beverly Hills: Screaming Americans Slug, Kick Khomaini Backers; 150 Arrested." *Los Angeles Times*, November 10, 1979, SD1.

"Mid-East Modes." *Washington Post*, October 12, 1959, B3.

Millspaugh, Arthur C. *Americans in Persia*. Washington, DC: Brookings Institute, 1946.

Mirsepassi, Ali, Amrita Basu, and Frederick Weaver, eds. *Localizing Knowledge in a Globalizing World: Recasting the Area Studies Debate*. Syracuse, NY: Syracuse University Press, 2003.

Miyoshi, Masao, and Harry Harootunian, eds. *Learning Places: The Afterlives of Area Studies*. Durham, NC: Duke University Press, 2002.

Moallem, Minoo. *Between Warrior Brother and Veiled Sister: Islamic Fundamentalism and the Politics of Patriarchy in Iran*. Berkeley: University of California Press, 2005.

Mobasher, Mohsen M. *Iranian in Texas: Migration, Politics, and Ethnic Identity*. Austin: University of Texas Press, 2012.

Moghadam, Valentine. *Modernizing Women: Gender and Social Change in the Middle East*. Boulder, CO: Lynne Rienner, 1993.

Moghissi, Haideh. *Populism and Feminism in Iran: Women's Struggle in a Male-Defined Revolutionary Movement*. New York: St. Martin's Press, 1994.

Moghissi, Haideh. "Troubled Relationships: Women, Nationalism, and the Left Movement in Iran." In *Reformers and Revolutionaries in Modern Iran: New Perspectives on the Iranian Left*, ed. Stephanie Cronin, 209–28. London: Routledge Curzon, 2004.

Mohajer, Nasser. *Voices of a Massacre: Untold Stories of Life and Death in Iran, 1988*. London: Oneworld Publications, 2020.

Mohajer, Nasser, and Mahnaz Matin. *The Uprising of Iranian Women, March 1979*. In Persian. Berkeley, CA: Noghteh Books, 2013.

Mohanty, Chandra Talpade. "Cartographies of Struggle: Third World Women and the Politics of Feminism." In *Third World Women and the Politics of Feminism*, ed. Chandra Talpade Mohanty, Ann Russo, and Lourdes Torres, 1–47. Bloomington: Indiana University Press, 1991.

Mohanty, Chandra Talpade. *Feminism without Borders: Decolonizing Theory, Practicing Solidarity*. Durham, NC: Duke University Press, 2003.

Mohanty, Chandra Talpade, Ann Russo, and Lourdes Torres, eds. *Third World Women and the Politics of Feminism*. Bloomington: Indiana University Press, 1991.

Moradian, Manijeh. "Iranian Diasporic Possibilities: Tracing Transnational Feminist Genealogies from the Revolutionary Margins." In *Global 1979: Geographies and Histories of the Iranian Revolution*, ed. Arang Keshavarzian and Ali Mirsepassi, 104–38. Cambridge: Cambridge University Press, 2021.

Moraga, Cherríe, and Gloria Anzaldúa, eds. *This Bridge Called My Back: Writings by Radical Women of Color*, 4th ed. Albany: State University of New York Press, 2015.

"The Moratorium Is a Cover, Not a Solution." Leaflet, October 1969. SPC.

Morrison, Patt. "Many in County Upset: Iranian Flag Lowered but Tensions Still Run High." *Los Angeles Times*, November 9, 1979, A1.

Mottahedeh, Negar. "Planetarity: The Anti-disciplinary Object of Iranian Studies." In *Global 1979: Geographies and Histories of the Iranian Revolution*, ed. Arang Keshavarzian and Ali Mirsepassi, 389–410. Cambridge: Cambridge University, 2021.

Mottahedeh, Negar. *Whisper Tapes: Kate Millet in Iran*. Stanford, CA: Stanford University Press, 2019.

Mouvement de Libération des Femmes Iraniennes: Année Zéro, dir. Sylvina Boissonnas, Claudine Mulard, Sylviane Rey, and Michelle Muller. Short film, 1979. https://www.youtube.com/watch?v=ulJwXHji6f4&list=PLUHWAB4-eoaQmWxQxaE2U5YgtOWR9fb_n.

"Mr. 'Human Rights' Meets King Torture." *Resistance* 5, no. 1 (December 1977). ILOC.

Muñoz, José. *Cruising Utopia: The Then and There of Queer Futurity*. New York: New York University Press, 2009.

Muñoz, José. *Disidentifications: Queers of Color and the Performance of Politics*. Minneapolis: University of Minnesota Press, 1999.

Muñoz, José. "Feeling Brown, Feeling Down: Latina Affect, the Performativity of Race, and the Depressive Position." *Signs* 31, no. 3 (2006): 675–88.

Naber, Nadine. *Arab America: Gender, Cultural Politics, and Activism*. New York: New York University Press, 2012.

Naber, Nadine. "Arab American Femininities: Beyond Arab Virgin/American(ized) Whore." *Feminist Studies* 32, no. 1 (2006): 87–111.

Naficy, Hamid. *The Making of Exile Cultures: Iranian Television in Los Angeles*. Minneapolis: University of Minnesota Press, 1993.

Naghibi, Nima. *Rethinking Global Sisterhood: Western Feminism and Iran*. Minneapolis: University of Minnesota Press, 2007.

Najmabadi, Afsaneh. "Crafting an Educated Housewife." In *Remaking Women: Feminism and Modernity in the Middle East*, ed. Lila Abu-Lughod, 91–125. Princeton: Princeton University Press, 1998.

Najmabadi, Afsaneh. "Hazards of Modernity and Morality: Women, State, and Ideology in Contemporary Iran." In *Women, Islam and the State*, ed. Deniz Kandiyoti, 48–76. Philadelphia: Temple University Press, 1991.

Najmabadi, Afsaneh. "(Un)veiling Feminism." In *Secularisms*, ed. Janet R. Jakobsen and Ann Pellegrini, 39–57. Durham, NC: Duke University Press, 2008.

Narayan, Uma. *Dislocating Cultures: Identities, Traditions, and Third World Feminism.* New York: Routledge, 1997.

Neale, Jonathan. *The American War: Vietnam 1960–1975.* London: Bookmarks, 2001.

Ngai, Sianne. *Ugly Feelings.* Cambridge, MA: Harvard University Press, 2005.

Nikpour, Golnar. "Claiming Human Rights: Iranian Political Prisoners and the Making of a Transnational Movement, 1963–1979." *Humanity: An International Journal of Human Rights, Humanitarianism, and Development* 9, no. 3 (2018): 363–88.

Nikpour, Golnar. "The Criminal Is the Patient, the Prison Will Be the Cure: Building the Carceral Imagination in Pahlavi Iran." In *Global 1979: Geographies and Histories of the Iranian Revolution*, ed. Arang Keshavarzian and Ali Mirsepassi, 293–327. Cambridge: Cambridge University Press, 2021.

Nohlen, Dieter, Florian Grotz, and Christof Hartmann. *Elections in Asia and the Pacific: A Data Handbook*, vol. 1: *Middle East, Central Asia, and South Asia.* Oxford: Oxford University Press, 2002.

Nolte, Carl. "S.F. Palace Hotel Sit-in Helped Start Revolution 50 Years Ago." Accessed December 7, 2014. http://www.sfgate.com/bayarea/article/S-F-Palace-Hotel-sit -in-helped-start-revolution-5279160.php.

Notes from Evin Prison. Resistance 2, no. 4, special pamphlet (June 1974). ILOC.

Nunes, Donnel. "S.C. State School Suspends All Its Iranian Students." *Washington Post*, November 22, 1979, A10.

Oberdorfer, Don. "12 Groups Press Carter on Human Rights Overseas." *Washington Post*, January 17, 1977, A2.

Oelsner, Andrea, and Simon Koschut, eds. *Friendship and International Relations.* New York: Palgrave Macmillan, 2014.

Omang, Joanne, and Alice Bonner. "Aliens Invading America's Campuses." *Washington Post*, April 22, 1979, A2.

"Only 19 Iran Students Sent Home, U.S. Says." *Los Angeles Times*, April 2, 1980, A1.

"On the Question of Splits in the Iranian Students Association." *Iran Report Special Issue*, March 8, 1976. Box 2. PSP.

"Oppose the Shah's U.S.-backed Invasion of Oman." Leaflet, March 12, 1974, 1–2. SPC.

Osanloo, Arzoo. *The Politics of Women's Rights in Iran.* Princeton, NJ: Princeton University Press, 2009.

Paidar, Parvin. *Women and the Political Process in Twentieth Century Iran.* New York: Cambridge University Press, 1995.

Paknejad, Shakrollah. "The 'Palestine Group' Defends Itself in Military Tribunal." December 1970, 1–33. Parviz Shokat Papers, Hoover Institute, Stanford University, Stanford, CA. PSP.

Parrenas, Rachel S., and Lok C. D. Siu, eds. *Asian Diasporas: New Formations, New Conceptions.* Stanford, CA: Stanford University Press, 2007.

Parsa, Misagh. *States, Ideologies and Social Revolutions: A Comparative Analysis of Iran, Nicaragua and the Philippines.* Cambridge: Cambridge University Press, 2000.

"*Payam-e daneshjoo.*" In *Shanzdah-e azar,* no. 7 (April 5, 1962). Published by the Confederation of Iranian Students. ILOC.

"Penn around the World: A History of Penn's Engagement with Specific Regions and Countries: The Middle East." Online exhibit, Penn University Archives and Record Center, 2007. https://archives.upenn.edu/exhibits/penn-history/global -engagement/specific-regions/middle-east.

"People's Living Conditions, Reason for Struggle." Leaflet, *ca.* 1972. SPC.

"Political Repression in Iran." World Confederation of Iranian Students (National Union), March 1971, 1–49. Box 1, Parviz Shokat Collection, Hoover Institute, Stanford University, Stanford, CA. PSP.

Pontecorvo, Gillo, dir. *The Battle of Algiers.* 1966.

Prashad, Vijay. *The Darker Nations: A People's History of the Third World.* New York: New Press, 2008.

Prashad, Vijay. *Everybody Was Kung Fu Fighting: Afro-Asian Connections and the Myth of Cultural Purity.* Boston: Beacon Press, 2001.

"President Emphasizes Aid Values in Message: TO THE CONGRESS OF THE UNITED STATES: Record of History Present Needs Objectives for Improvement of Private Investment Alliance for Progress Authorizing Legislation Conclusion." *Washington Post* and *Times-Herald,* April 3, 1963. https://www.presidency.ucsb.edu/documents /special-message-the-congress-free-world-defense-and-assistance-programs.

"Protesters Jeer and Burn Flags in Oregon, Texas, California as U.S. Backlash Flares." *Los Angeles Times,* November 9, 1979, 7.

"Protest Israeli Terrorism!!!" Leaflet, March 1, 1973. SPC.

Pulido, Laura. *Black, Brown, Yellow, and Left: Radical Activism in Los Angeles.* Berkeley: University of California Press, 2006.

Purnell, Daniel. "A Deportation Threat." *Daily Californian,* January 8, 1979, 5. UA.

Purnell, Daniel. "Iranian Students Protest, Hunger Strike Ends." *Daily Californian,* January 15, 1976, 16. UA.

"Queen Farah's Visit: Can the Rule of Torture Be Prettified?" *Resistance* 4, no. 7 (August 1977). ILOC.

Rajan, Rajeswari Sunder. *Real and Imagined Women: Gender, Culture, and Postcolonialism.* New York: Routledge, 1993.

"Rally Rally." Leaflet. SPC.

Ramos, George. "Iranian Attending College at Riverside Found Shot to Death." *Los Angeles Times,* November 9, 1979, B20.

Rancière, Jacques. *The Politics of Aesthetics: The Distribution of the Sensible.* Trans. Gabriel Rockhill. London: Bloomsbury, 2013.

"Reception to Be Held for Foreign Students." *Los Angeles Times,* February 14, 1954.

Reddy, Vanita, and Anantha Sudhakar. "Introduction: Feminist and Queer Afro-Asian Formations." In *Feminist and Queer Afro-Asian Formations,* ed. Vanita Reddy and Anantha Sudhakar. Special issue, *Scholar and Feminist Online* 14, no. 3 (2018). http://sfonline.barnard.edu/feminist-and-queer-afro-asian-formations /introduction-feminist-and-queer-afro-asian-formations/.

Rejali, Darius. *Torture and Democracy*. Princeton, NJ: Princeton University Press, 2007.

Rejali, Darius. *Torture and Modernity: Self, Society, and State in Modern Iran*. Boulder, CO: Westview Press, 1994.

"Report on Alien Agency Expected Within Month." *New York Times*, February 12, 1979, B10.

"Reprisals by SAVAK: Fear Strikes Iranian Students." *Daily Californian*, April 19, 1975, 10. UA.

"Restless Youth." Report on Student Protest in 1968. C.I.A. Intelligence File, National Security File, box 3, LBJ Library, Austin, TX. Published June 1970.

"Revolution in Oman and Shah's Invasion." *Resistance* 3, no. 1 (December 1975): 17–20. PSP.

Ricoeur, Paul. *Memory, History, Forgetting*. Chicago: University of Chicago Press, 2004.

Riley, Robin L., Chandra Talpade Mohanty, and Minnie Bruce Pratt, eds. *Feminism and War: Confronting US Imperialism*. London: Zed Books, 2008.

Robinson, Cedric. *Black Marxism: The Making of the Black Radical Tradition*. Chapel Hill: University of North Carolina Press, 2000.

Robinson, J. L. "Letters to the Editor." *Washington Post*, November 19, 1977, A18.

Rogers, Jeanne. "U.S. Learns from Exchange Students: A 'Live' Lesson in Foreign Relations." *Washington Post*, November 15, 1953.

Rosenzweig, David. "Directive on Foreign Students Criticized." *Los Angeles Times*, March 18, 1979, A3.

Rostam-Kolayi, Jasamin, and Afshin Matin-asgari. "Unveiling Ambiguities: Revisiting 1930s Iran's *Kashf-i Hijab* Campaign." In *Anti-Veiling Campaigns in the Muslim World: Gender, Modernism and the Politics of Dress*, ed. Stephanie Cronin, 121–48. London: Routledge, 2014.

Rostami-Povey, Elaheh. *Afghan Women: Identity and Invasion*. London: Zed Books, 2007.

Sabagh, Georges, and Mehdi Bozorgmehr. "Are the Characteristics of Exiles Different from Immigrants? The Case of Iranians in Los Angeles." Working Papers 2, no. 5 (1986). Institute for Social Science Research, University of California–Los Angeles. https://escholarship.org/uc/item/54d5s0q5.

Sadeghi-Boroujerdi, Eskandar. "The Origins of Communist Unity: Anticolonialism and Revolution in Iran's Tri-Continental Moment." *British Journal of Middle Eastern Studies* 45, no. 5 (2018): 796–822.

Sadeghi-Boroujerdi, Eskandar. "The Post-Revolutionary Women's Uprising of March 1979: An Interview with Nasser Mohajer and Mahnaz Matin." https://iranwire.com/en/features/24. June 11, 2013.

Said, Edward. *Culture and Imperialism*. New York: Vintage Books, 1994.

Said, Edward. *Orientalism*. New York: Vintage Books, 1978.

Saldaña, María Josefina. *The Revolutionary Imagination in the Americas and the Age of Development*. Durham, NC: Duke University Press, 2003.

Sameh, Catherine. *Axis of Hope: Iranian Women's Rights Activism across Borders*. Seattle: University of Washington Press, 2019.

"San Antonio Bars Anti-Shah March." *Los Angeles Times*, December 5, 1979, 28.

Sanasarian, Eliz. *The Women's Rights Movement in Iran: Mutiny, Appeasement, and Repression from 1900 to Khomeini.* Greenwood, NY: Praeger, 1982.

"SAVAK Activities Outside Iran." *Resistance* pamphlet, n.d. SPC.

"SAVAK Exposed." *Resistance* 5, no. 2 (January 1977): 19–22. SPC.

"SAVAK's Attacks on ISA (DC)." *Defense Bulletin of the ISAUS* 2, nos. 2/3 (February–April, 1972): 10. PSP.

"SAVAK's Reactionary Collaboration against Iranian Students." *Resistance* leaflet, n.d. SPC.

Sayres, Sohnya, Anders Stephanson, Stanley Aronowitz, and Fredric Jameson, eds. *The Sixties without Apology.* Minneapolis: University of Minnesota Press, 1984.

Scheutte, Paul A. "Iranians Stage 3-Hour Sit-In at Their Country's Embassy Here." *Washington Post,* January 24, 1962, A15.

Schrader, Stuart. *Badges without Borders: How Global Counterinsurgency Transformed American Policing.* Berkeley: University of California Press, 2019.

"Senate Says No to Shah." *Daily Californian,* May 13, 1964, 1. UA.

Shadman, Dariush. "Iran's False Image." *Daneshjoo* 12, no. 6 (March 1964): 10–17. YPB.

Shahidi, Hossein. *Journalism in Iran: From Mission to Profession.* New York: Routledge, 2007.

"Shah of Iran on the Issue of Torture." Mike Wallace interview with the Shah of Iran, *60 Minutes,* October 24, 1976. https://www.youtube.com/watch?v=u8u2UKWCHtM.

"The Shah of Iran Visits His U.S. Imperialist Bosses!" Leaflet, October 1969. SPC.

"Shah Praised by Kennedy on Reforms." *Washington Post and Times Herald* (1959–1973), February 14, 1963, A12.

Shahrokhni, Nazanin. *Women in Place: The Politics of Gender Segregation in Iran.* Berkeley: University of California Press, 2020.

"Shah's Heightened Dependence on U.S. Imperialism." *Iran Report.* Series 24, no. 1 and (September, October, and November 1976), np. SPC.

"Shah Spies: 'Beans' and 'Clean Finger.'" *Der Spiegel,* September 5, 1976. https://www.spiegel.de/politik/schah-spitzel-bohnen-und-sauberfinger-a-f970e0cb-0002-0001-0000-000041147022.

"Shah 'Supervises' Peace in Vietnam." *Resistance,* n.d. SPC.

Shakhsari, Sima. *The Politics of Rightful Killing: Civil Society, Gender, and Sexuality in Weblogistan.* Durham, NC: Duke University Press, 2020.

Shams, Alex. "Are Iranians People of Color? Persian, Muslim, and Model Minority Race Politics." December 3, 2013. http://ajammc.com/2013/12/03/are-iranians-people-of-color/.

Shannon, Matthew. "Contacts with the Opposition: American Foreign Relations, the Iranian Student Movement, and the Global Sixties." *The Sixties: A Journal of History, Politics and Culture* 4, no. 1 (2011): 1–29.

Shannon, Matthew. *Losing Hearts and Minds: American-Iranian Relations and International Education during the Cold War.* Ithaca, NY: Cornell University Press, 2017.

Shariati, Ali. *Fatima Is Fatima.* Translated by Laleh Bakhtiar. Tehran: Shariati Foundation, 1981.

Shawkat, Hamid. 1999. *Kunfidirasiyun-i Jahani-i Muhassalin va Danishjuyan-i Irani* [World Confederation of Iranian Students]. Tehran: 'Aṭā'ī, 1999.

Shohat, Ella. *Race in Translation: Culture Wars around the Postcolonial Atlantic*. New York: New York University Press, 2012.

Shohat, Ella. *Taboo Memories, Diasporic Voices*. Durham, NC: Duke University Press, 2006.

Shohat, Ella, ed. *Talking Visions: Multicultural Feminism in a Transnational Age*. Cambridge, MA: MIT Press, 1998.

Shohat, Ella, and Evelyn Alsultany, eds. *Between the Middle East and the Americas: The Cultural Politics of Diaspora*. Ann Arbor: University of Michigan Press, 2013.

Sohi, Seema. *Echoes of Mutiny: Race, Surveillance, and Indian Anticolonialism in North America*. Oxford: Oxford University Press, 2014.

Sohrabi, Naghmeh. "The 'Problem Space' of the Historiography of the 1979 Iranian Revolution." *History Compass* 16, no. 11 (2018): e12500. https://doi-org.ezproxy.cul.columbia.edu/10.1111/hic3.12500.

Sohrabi, Naghmeh. "Remembering the Palestine Group: Global Activism, Friendship and the Iranian Revolution." *International Journal of Middle East Studies* 51 (2019): 281–300.

Spencer, Robyn C. *The Revolution Has Come: Black Power, Gender, and the Black Panther Party in Oakland*. Durham, NC: Duke University Press, 2016.

Spivak, Gayatri Chakravorty. "Can the Subaltern Speak?" In *Colonial Discourse and Post-Colonial Theory: A Reader*, ed. Patrick Williams and Laura Crisman, 66–111. New York: Columbia University, 1994.

Spivak, Gayatri Chakravorty. *The Post-Colonial Critic: Interviews, Strategies, Dialogue*, ed. Sarah Harasym. New York: Routledge, 1990.

Springer, Kimberly. *Living for the Revolution: Black Feminist Organizations 1968–1980*. Durham, NC: Duke University Press, 2005.

"The State." *Los Angeles Times*, March 27, 1979, B2.

"Stop All Political Repression in Iran!!!" Iranian Students Association in Northern California, December 9, 1970. SPC.

"Struggle in Oman." *Daily Californian*, December 10, 1975, 5. UA.

"The Student Movement in the West." *Daneshjoo*, no. 3 (1347 Ordibehesht [May 1968]), np. ILOC.

"Student Visa Violations May Total 42,000." *Washington Post*, January 30, 1979, A7.

Sullivan, Zohreh T. *Exiled Memories: Stories of Iranian Diaspora*. Philadelphia: Temple University Press, 2001.

Sulzberger, A. O., Jr. "Americans Assail Iranians Rallying in Washington." *New York Times*, November 10, 1979, 6.

Sulzberger, A. O., Jr. "Federal Order Expected Today on Iranian Students in the U.S." *New York Times*, November 13, 1979, 8.

Suny, Ronald Grigor. "Don't Paint Nationalism Red! National Revolution and Socialist Anti-Imperialism." In *Decolonization: Perspectives from Now and Then*, ed. Prasenjit Duara, 176–98. New York: Routledge, 2004.

Szanton, David, ed. *The Politics of Knowledge: Area Studies and the Disciplines*. Berkeley: University of California Press, 2004.

Tabari, Azar, and Nahid Yeganeh, eds. *In the Shadow of Islam: The Women's Movement in Iran*. London: Zed Press, 1982.

Takriti, Abdel. *Monsoon Revolutions: Republicans, Sultans and Empires in Oman, 1965–1976*. Oxford: Oxford University Press, 2013.

Talebi, Shahla. *Ghosts of Revolution: Rekindled Memories of Imprisonment in Iran*. Stanford, CA: Stanford University Press, 2011.

Tavakoli-Targhi, Mohammad. *Refashioning Iran: Orientalism, Occidentalism, and Historiography*. New York: Palgrave, 2001.

Taylor, Keeanga-Yamahtta. *How We Get Free: Black Feminism and the Combahee River Collective*. Chicago: Haymarket Books, 2017.

"Texas College Asked to Reinstate Iranian Students." *Odessa American*, April 14, 1979.

"Third World Liberation Front: Notice of Demands." SF State College Strike Collection. https://diva.sfsu.edu/collections/strike/bundles/187994.

Thompson, Elizabeth. "200 Organizations Purported to be Surveillance Targets." *Los Angeles Times*, July 19, 1978, D1.

"Thousands of Iraqis Rally Against Government, US, and Iran." *Globe Post*, January 10, 2020. https://theglobepost.com/2020/01/10/iraq-protests-us-iran/.

"To All Fair-minded People. . . ." ISA Southern California Chapter. Leaflet, May 8, 1964. SC.

Traverso, Enzo. *Left-Wing Melancholia: Marxism, History, and Memory*. New York: Columbia University Press, 2017.

Ubani, Marazere. "Iranian Students Blast CIA-Backed Shah." *Hilltop*, March 5, 1976, 2–3. HC.

"University Women are Getting Organized." ISA, ca. 1968, 1–13. English translation by Atefeh Akbari. PSP.

Untitled ISA flyer, ca. 1970/71. SPC.

USAID. *US Overseas Loans and Grants: Obligations and Loan Authorizations, July 1, 1945–September 30, 2019*. Report. https://pdf.usaid.gov/pdf_docs/PBAAJ833.pdf.

"U.S. Imperialism Must Be Defeated." November 15, 1969. SPC.

"US Public Protests." *Defense Bulletin of the ISAUS* 2, nos. 2/3 (February–April 1972): 1. PSP.

"U.S. Queries Iran on Snooping Here." *Washington Post*, October 29, 1976, C11.

"U.S. Sends More Military Advisors to Iran." *Resistance* 1, no. 5 (July 1973): 13. SPC.

"U.S. Taking Steps for Deportation of 38 Iranian Students." *Los Angeles Times*, February 26, 1979, A1.

"U.S. Universities Hustle Iran Contracts." *Daily Californian*, March 6, 1975, 1. UA.

Valentine, Paul W. "Shah of Iran's Friends, Foes Mobilize for His Visit." *Washington Post*, November 13, 1977, B1.

Valentine, Paul W. "Shah's Visit Stirs Worry Over Clash." *Washington Post*, November 5, 1977, C1.

Valentine, Paul W. "2 Iranian Factions Clash: 124 Hurt at White House." *Washington Post*, November 16, 1977, A1.

Vietnam Veterans against the War. "Support Iranian Struggle." Leaflet reprinted in *The Veteran* 7, no. 2 (April 1977): 14.

Walsh, Edward. "Carter Asserts Human Rights Is 'Soul of Our Foreign Policy.'" *Washington Post*, December 7, 1978, A2.

"Wanted." Leaflet. San Francisco State Strike file, SPC.

Whitaker, Joseph D., and Art Harris. "U.S. Appeals Court Approves Iranian Student Deportation." *Washington Post*, December 28, 1979, A1.

"White House in a Plea for Calm Over Iranians in U.S." *New York Times*, November 9, 1979, A12.

Whitson, Helene. "STRIKE . . . Concerning the 1968–69 Strike at San Francisco State College: Historical Essay." *Found SF*, n.d. https://www.foundsf.org/index.php ?title=STRIKE!. . . _Concerning_the_1968-69_Strike_at_San_Francisco_State _College.

"Why Is Nixon Going to Iran?" ISA Northern California leaflet, May 31, 1972, 8. SPC.

"Why the Shah Should Not Be Invited to UCLA." ISA leaflet, May 19, 1964. SC.

Williams, Raymond. *Marxism and Literature*. New York: Oxford University Press, 1977.

Williams, William Appleman. *Empire as a Way of Life*. Oxford: Oxford University Press, 1980.

Wolin, Richard. *The Wind from the East: French Intellectuals, the Cultural Revolution, and the Legacy of the 1960s*. Princeton, NJ: Princeton University Press, 2010.

Wu, Hui, ed. *Once Iron Girls: Essays by Post-Mao Chinese Literary Women*. Lanham, MD: Lexington Books, 2010.

Wu, Judy Tzu-Chun. *Radicals on the Road: Internationalism, Orientalism, and Feminism during the Vietnam Era*. Ithaca, NY: Cornell University Press, 2013.

Young, Cynthia A. *Soul Power: Culture, Radicalism, and the Making of a US Third World Left*. Durham, NC: Duke University Press, 2006.

Young, Robert J. C. *Post-Colonialism: An Historical Introduction*. Chichester: Wiley, 2016.

"Young Iranians Stage March." *Hilltop*, January 15, 1971, 2. HC.

Zia-Ebrahimi, Reza. "Self-Orientalization and Dislocation: The Uses and Abuses of the 'Aryan' Discourse in Iran." *Iranian Studies* 44, no. 4 (2011): 445–72.

Zuckerman, Steven. "Police Break Up Disturbance by Iranian Students." *Los Angeles Times*, October 8, 1979.

INDEX

Page numbers followed by *f* indicate figures.

anti-imperialism, 4, 13, 15, 23; in early years of Russian Revolution, 40; feminism, genealogy of, 217–18, 245, 271–72; intersectional, 215–46; and solidarity with Palestine, 156–62. *See also* imperialism

antiracism, 139, 145, 173, 217, 236–37

antiwar movement, 29, 45, 51, 84, 98, 113, 135, 142; anti-Zionism, 168; San Francisco Moratorium March, 169; solidarity with Vietnam, 167–72; and women's movements, 174–75. *See also* Vietnam

apartheid regimes, 152

Arab-Israeli War (1973), 157

Arab self-determination, 154–66

Arab Students Association, 134, 158

area studies programs, Orientalism of, 100

art, political, 147, 252–53, 260–61

Aryan myth, 23, 157–58, 278n68

Asheton, Betty, 286n48

Ashkan, Farid (student activist), 10, 58–63, 109, 173, 189; as political prisoner, 262–63

Ashraf (Shah's sister), 96, 120

Asian American Political Alliance, 98

Asian Americans, 74, 98, 280nn13,15, 284n5

Assembly of Experts, 220

Ayandegan (newspaper), 255

Azari, Farah, 195

Azerbaijan, 40–41

backlash against Iranian students, 96, 114–26; and Beverly Hills march (1979), 120–22; dehumanization of students, 117–18

Bajoughli, Rahim, 41, 255

Baku, Iran, oil field workers, 10, 40

Bandung conference (1955), 135

Bani Sadr, Abolhassan, 222, 256, 264, 299n25

Bargetz, Brigitte, 71, 79–80

Bazargan, Mehdi, 220, 255

Beale, Francis, 213

Bee County College (East Texas), 102–3

Behdjou, J. H., 73

Behrooz, Maziar, 221

Behroozi, Jaleh (student activist), 9–10, 45–48, 85, 162, 186; activism in Iran, 224–25, 226, 233, 239–40

Bell, Griffin, 121, 122

belonging, revolutionary, 175, 176–214, 269–70; affective dissonance and embodied critique, 197–201; appeal of ultimate sacrifice, 207–13; and fashion, 196–97; gender, sexuality, and revolutionary affects, 183–88, 223; kinship, alternative, 83, 190–93; revolutionary sociality, 179–83, 192, 195, 214; sex and surveillance, 201–7; social reproduction

in revolutionary time(s), 189–93. *See also* gender

Benab, Younes Parsa, 88, 151, 160

Benjamin, Walter, 248, 273

Bentsen, Lloyd, 121

Beverly Hills march (1979), 120–22

Bijan (ISA organizer), 107–8, 189, 204–6, 243, 256–57

binaries: East/West, 18–19, 41, 75; Global South/Global North, 20; indigenous and foreign, 41

Black Lives Matter, 237

Black Panther, 149

Black Panther Party for Self-Defense, 135, 146–49, 194

Black politics, 11, 14, 45, 110; Afro-Iranian connections, 12–13, 29, 136, 143–54, 157, 169; on college campuses, 128–29; and Maoism, 193–94; Palestine, support for, 156

Black Student Union (BSU) (San Francisco State College), 128–29, 138, 145, 150

body: affective capacity of, 6; affective dissonance and embodied critique, 197–201; "attitude toward capitalism," 144–45; firsthand knowledge of injustice, 144; history mapped onto, 35; impact of moral hurt on, 56–57; revolutionary affects felt in, 2, 4, 7–9, 36–37, 41–42, 56–57, 58, 68, 71, 81, 144–45, 160, 197–201, 216, 237, 270; self-immolation, 56; as site of militancy, 139–40

Boggs, Abigail, 99

Bolsheviks, 40, 63, 66

Boupacha, Djamila, 210

Boym, Svetlana, 250–51, 268

Britain, 17, 37, 40, 165, 166

"brotherhood of nations," 136, 145

Brown, Wendy, 249

Brzezinski, Zbigniew, 122

Buhrayd, Jamila, 294n63

California State Assembly, 123

Cambodia, US bombing of, 47

Campos Torres, José, 143

Canefe, Nergis, 35

capitalism: African American "attitude about," 144–45; anti-capitalism, 135, 138, 154, 187; authoritarian, 24, 248, 251; colonialist and racist logics of, 138; critiques of, 17–19; global, 97; patriarchy as central to, 217–18; "there is no alternative" (TINA), 24; "US interests," 17–18, 22, 81, 134, 170

Carmichael, Stokely, 145, 152

Carter, Jimmy, 114, 116, 117f, 123, 153

diasporic subjectivity, 4, 17–19, 22–23, 27, 76, 141, 172, 178, 244–47, 270

dictatorship, intersection of imperialism with, 15–17, 21, 26, 28, 36, 81, 218, 271

"distribution of emotions," 79

"distribution of the sensible," 79

Dudziak, Mary, 76

Durkheim, Émile, 142

A Dying Colonialism (Fanon), 207

economy, affective, 99–100, 126

Eghtedari, Mohammed, 78–79, 87, 101, 140–41, 152; as spokesperson outside Iran, 258; on support for Palestine, 156–57

Egypt, popular uprising (2011), 24

"the 18," 1, 2*f*

Ekpo, Akpan, 153

Elahi, Babak, 18

"emancipation," 79; affective politics of, 80, 81

Emancipation of Women (EW), 41, 224–25

Eng, David, 36, 140, 250

"*enteghad* sessions" (criticism and self-criticism), 190

Esch, Betsy, 193–94

executions, 203, 257–59, 262–65, 286n48; names read on radio and TV, 262–63; students saved from, by campaign, 105; of women by Shah, 210

factory councils (shoras), 257–58

fadaiyan ("self-sacrificers"), 60

Fadaiyan (Organization of Iranian People's Fadā'i Guerrillas) (Marxist), 60, 87, 178, 300n32; efforts to control NUW, 225, 238, 240–41; executions of members, 263; offices ransacked after revolution, 255; and Omani resistance, 165; opposition to religious state, 220; protests on Iranian campuses, 104; recruitment in Iran, 262; Siahkal guerrilla assault (Gilan province), 60, 91–92, 211; women in, 209, 240, 294n45

families: alienation from, 48, 62, 191–92; alternative kinship, 83, 190–93; contradictory meanings of, 193; orientation of, 37–38, 42–54, 58, 62–66; SAVAK pressure on, 108, 191, 192; Shah, connections with, 48–52. *See also* belonging, revolutionary

Fanon, Frantz, 142, 145, 207–9

Fatemi, Ali, 89

Fatima Is Fatima (Shariati), 223

FBI, 110, 156

Featherstone, David, 11–12

feminism, 13, 137, 194; affect and gender, 14–17; contemporary Iranian, 245–46; French, 228; genealogy of, 217–18, 245, 271–72; Iranian, first-generation, 14–15, 26; and modernizing rhetoric in Iran, 185; reimagined outside Western associations, 229; Shah's co-optation of, 14, 238; and solidarity with other groups, 174–75; state-sponsored, 185; texts used in study groups, 186; Third World, 19–20, 136–37, 174, 217–18, 245, 270; transnational, 20; US, dismissal of, by people of color, 236–37; women-of-color, 14, 19–20, 136–37, 235, 272, 276n49

Ferguson, Roderick, 99, 137

First Amendment rights, 102

First Congress of the Peoples of the East, 40

Flatley, Jonathan, 7, 9, 16, 139, 141

Fleishell, J. L., 3

Foucault, Michel, 244

freedom, 215–17; as aspiration for people in Iran and US, 216; Iranian women's views, 229; memories of, 250, 253, 254, 263; as "planetary," 229, 297n50; Western notions of, 18–19, 44, 74, 110, 218

French colonialism, 207

French feminists, 228

Freud, Sigmund, 36, 142

fugitive knowledges, 249

gender: and CISNU, 83–84, 185, 233, 235, 239; "feminine" as problematic, 181–82, 197–201; Left politics of, 15–16, 19, 29, 182; masculinist forms of revolutionary subjectivity, 10, 14–16, 198, 244, 247, 271; and modernization, 14, 53–54, 76, 184, 185, 196–97, 206–7, 223; oppression, 17, 19–21, 136, 178, 181–82, 186–88, 199–200, 207, 209–10, 214, 216–18, 223, 231, 237–39, 244–48, 271–72; and revolutionary affects, 183–88, 223; self-sacrifice expected, 180, 189–90, 193–97, 207–9, 244; used to justify oppression, 19–21; and "Western values," 14–15, 177, 182, 184, 198, 223, 229, 243, 271; women's sexuality seen as threat, 200–201. *See also* belonging, revolutionary; patriarchy; women

"gender sameness," 15–16, 29, 179–83, 200–202; as alternative to Shah's modernization, 206–7, 223

genealogy, leftist, 10, 28, 30, 62, 66, 135, 137, 250; Benab's publication, 88; roots of, 39–40; women's, 217–18, 245, 271–72

General Union of Palestinian Women, 174

Germany, ISA women members, 84

Ghamari-Tabrizi, Behrooz, 221, 235, 259

Iran (continued)
presidential office, 234; living conditions, 92–93; monarchy, 62, 75; nostalgia for pre-revolutionary, 23, 27, 30, 249–50; observers sent to, 105–7; oil nationalization movement, 37; Oman and Yemen invaded by, 163–66, 164f, 165f; as one-party state, 104, 254; Pahlavi dynasty (1925–79), 21; postrevolutionary repression, 20–21, 30, 218; Qajar dynasty (1785–1925), 48; state repression across borders, 104–14; student activists in, 82, 94–96, 104–5, 120–21, 161, 219; suppression (1961–63), 44, 47, 50; Tabriz uprising, 41; Tehran bus workers' strike (1967), 57, 59; Tehran taxi workers' strike, 50–51; underground in, 42, 60, 179, 182–84, 192, 203, 205; White Revolution, 90, 91, 93, 283n91. *See also* coup of 1953 (Iran); hostage crisis (1979); Iranian Revolution (1979); Islamic Republic of Iran; political prisoners; US-Iran relations; women's movement in Iran
Iran-American Chamber of Industry and Commerce, 73
"Iranian Anti-Communist Organization" (SAVAK letter), 108
Iranian Communist Party (Tudeh Party), 37–40, 42–43, 46, 60–64; attacks on members after coup, 43; banned (1922), 41, 60; formation of, 10, 40; Leftist critiques of, 61–62, 194; as "loyal opposition" to religious state, 220; Palestine, support for, 160–61
Iranian embassy. *See* hostage crisis (1979)
Iranian Eviction Petition, 124
Iranian Helicopter Company, 101
Iranian Navy, plans to train at US universities, 101
"Iranian People Should Be an Example for All" (Adeboye), 154, 155f
Iranian Revolution (1979), 5, 6, 18–19, 22, 61, 237; "anti-explanation" of, 299n13; Black responses to, 153–54; Left after, 219–22; Left organizations eviscerated, 254–58; and masculinized unity, 181; political prisoners of, 258–67; provisional government, 220; and refusal of imperialism and dictatorship, 217, 269; religious makeup of leaders, 219; struggle over meaning of, 221–22. *See also* Tehran women's uprising (March 1979)
Iranian Students Association (ISA), 1–7, 2f; Berkeley chapter, 6, 36, 45–47, 82, 85, 106f, 186; Beverly Hills march (1979), 120–22; break with Iranian regime, 77–80;

campus crackdowns on, 102–4; CIA funding for, 72–73; congresses, 77–78, 80, 82–83; differences subordinated to larger project, 87–88; exile as best option for, 250; financial independence of, 84; formation of, 28, 71–73; gender and sexual politics of, 15, 84, 183–88, 271; generations of, 41–42, 63; hunger strikes, 89, 91, 111f, 111–12, 157; International Relations Committee, 142, 152; *Iran Report*, 156, 165; *Khane-e Iran* (Iran House), 47, 84–85, 87, 108, 131, 156; labeled "counterrevolutionaries," 22–23; leadership quotas, gendered, 187, 271; masks used by, 111f, 111–12; Michigan State University chapter, 11, 41; militancy of, 82–83, 86, 92, 96, 104, 127; New York City chapter, 85, 204; Northern California chapter, 42, 51, 83, 102, 179, 185, 267, 283n95; and Nowruz celebration at Iranian embassy, 78–79; overview of, 81–88; "People's Living Conditions, the Reason for Struggle," 92–93; Philadelphia chapter, 178; political culture of, 29–30; and political parties, 85–86; prehistory of, 35; radicalization as transnational process, 28, 33–34; school attendance discouraged, 189; self-defense campaigns, 97; shift from reform to revolution, 87–93, 139; Shi'i Muslim majority, 30–31; split (1975), 13, 101, 203, 294n41; splits within, 86–87, 104; Statue of Liberty, Iranian occupation, 1–4, 2f; students return to Iran, 30, 109–12, 179, 252; as targets of anti-Arab violence, 156–57; Texas-Oklahoma chapter, 83, 178, 204–5; United Nations demonstration, 80; University of Illinois chapter, 90; Washington, DC, chapter, 83, 85, 151, 186; "We continue the struggle" poster, 66, 67f; "Why the Shah Should Not Be Invited to UCLA," 95–96; women leaders in, 83–84
Iranian United Nations Mission at Rockefeller Center, 109
Iran-Iraq War, 261, 263–64
"Iranophobia," 125
Iran Report (ISA quarterly journal), 156, 165
Iraq, 261, 263, 269
Islam: repressive outcomes of revolution not inherent to, 221–22; Shi'i mythology, repackaging of, 195, 223
"Islamic republic," as concept, 219–20
Islamic Republic of Iran, 18–20, 166, 295n8; constitution, 220, 232–33; gains made by women in, 234–35, 297n62; permanent migration from, 247; referendum

establishing, 254; retribution, law of, 241; women's sexuality seen as threat, 200–201, 223; women targeted by state, 216. *See also* hostage crisis (1979); Iran

Islamic Republic Party, 254

Islamic Revolution of 1978–79, 53–54

Islamophobia, 21, 23, 125, 216

Israel, 152, 154–66

Jaleh. *See* Behroozi, Jaleh; Pirnazar, Jaleh

Jangalis, 40

Jewish Defense League, 157

Jewish Iranians, 45–47

Jila (student activist), 190, 198, 202–3

Johnson, Lyndon B., 92

"June 5th" uprising, Iran, 53–54, 58–59

Kalantari, Khosro, 128–33, 172, 289n6

Karim, Persis M., 18

Kate (white American leftist), 143, 174

Kaviani, Zohreh (student in West Germany), 83

Kazanjian, David, 36, 140, 250

Kelley, Robin D. G., 193–94

Kennedy, John F., 44, 90

Kennedy, Robert, 89

Kennedy administration, 89, 283n91

Kermani, Manizheh Ashraf Zadeh, 210

Kermanshah, Iran, 37–41

Khaled, Leila, 210, 294n63

Khalkhali, Ayatollah, 259–60

Khane-e Iran (Iran House) (ISA headquarters), 47, 84–85, 87, 108, 131, 156

Khayam, Zohreh (student activist), 52–57, 87–88, 141–43, 152; activism in Iran, 225, 227; on female guerrillas, 210–11; on gender issues, 185, 202; marginalization, feeling of, 268; and NUW, 240–41; on Palestine, 162

Khomeini, Ayatollah, 25–26, 53–54, 58, 219–20, 242; family laws of 1967 suspended by, 225, 238; hostage crisis as turning point for, 255–56; jailed for denouncing Shah, 91; oppressive reforms, gendered, 225–28; populist amalgam of religious and leftist ideas, 244–45

kinship, alternative, 83, 190–93

Klein, Christina, 75

Kowsari, Hamid (student activist), 36, 42–45, 96, 129, 131–32, 138, 145, 239; on mimicking proletariat, 196; return to Iran, 257–58, 266–67

Kramer, Paul, 73, 76

Ku Klux Klan, 125

Kurdish movements, 222, 256

Kurzman, Charles, 299n13

Lahuti Khan, Abulqasim, 39–41

Lazreg, Marnia, 207–8, 209, 211, 294n55

Leahy, Margaret, 130, 131, 133

Lebanon, Israeli raid into, 157

Left: calls for punishment of opponents, 259; "dirty laundry" debate, 19; failure, narrative of, 27, 29, 247; failure to clarify morality issues, 182; gender politics of, 15–16, 19, 29, 182; Iranian, before coup, 42; mistaken assessments by, 58, 61, 86, 216, 239, 242–43, 249–50, 252–53, 263–68; "new," Iranian, 60; patriarchal attitudes, 14, 221, 238, 293n16; racialized movements, 237; suppressed in US, 109–10; underground parties, 13, 31; US, 29; women's betrayal by, 4, 223–24, 231–32, 235–38; women's sexuality seen as threat, 200–201, 223; women's support for Khomeini, 240, 242. *See also* belonging, revolutionary; genealogy, leftist; revolutionary affect; solidarity

Left, Iranian: after revolution, 219–22; assumed alliance with Iranian government, 19; dismissal and denouncement of women's movement, 222, 235, 239; existing hierarchies reproduced by, 16–17, 221, 237, 244, 272; fragmentation and disorientation of, 30, 239; gender consciousness in, 188; in hiding, 256, 258, 267; limitations of, 25–26; ongoing history of, 61–62; opposition to anti-imperialist clerics, 220–21; persecution of by Shah, 25; Stalinist approaches, 221; support for anti-imperialist clerics, 220; two cohorts of, 35

"left melancholia," 249–50

liberation movements, 3–4; affective attachment to, 71–72; Afro-Asian connections, 29, 40–41, 136, 143–54; attachment to liberation of others, 11; feminist and gay, 13, 194. *See also* anticolonial movements; anti-imperialism; antiracism

The Limits of Whiteness: Iranian Americans and the Everyday Politics of Race (Maghbouleh), 23

Lippman, Walter, 73

Los Angeles Times, 112, 118–20

loss: of biological kinship ties, 192–93; conservative manifestations of, 248; engagement with, 7–8, 27–28; melancholic attachment to, 36, 139–43; memories of personal and global, 253–54; politicized, 247–48; revolutionary vs. majority of diaspora, 261–62. *See also* memory; resistant nostalgia

lotti figure, 144

Lowe, Lisa, 97, 284n5
Lumumba, Patrice, 151

Maghbouleh, Neda, 23, 278n68
Maira, Sunaina, 97
"mania," 142
Manifest Destiny narrative, 97
Maoism, 13, 85–86, 135, 178, 195, 197, 221; Black, 193–94
Mao Tse-tung, 178, 183, 194, 195
martyrdom, 195, 211
Marxism: Iranianized, 41; Third World, 13–14, 85, 135, 158, 180; "woman question" in, 182, 186
Marxism-Leninism, 13, 49, 86, 135, 196, 221, 271
masculinization, 10, 14–16, 181, 198–200, 244, 247, 271
"masses," 180, 195–96
masterwords, 235
Matin, Mahnaz, 225, 237
Matin-asgari, Afshin, 81, 86, 120, 249, 255, 277n65
Matin-Daftari, Hedayat, 237
McClintock, Anne, 180, 193, 214, 234
McDonald, Larry, 114
McKay, Claude, 40
media: *Ayandegan* banned in Iran, 255; and backlash against Iranian students, 116–20; coverage of protests in US, 102–4, 108, 112–22; exposés of Iran in, 104–5; human rights, focus on, 114; masks, commentary on, 112; "model minorities" celebrated by, 74–75; not in line with State Department, 107–8; portrayals of students as unruly and ungrateful, 114–22; publicization of attacks on students, 113–14; *60 Minutes*, 107–8; student newspapers, 6, 101, 112, 114. See also *Daily Californian* (UC Berkeley); *Resistance* (ISA magazine); *Washington Post*
melancholia, 7, 27, 28, 32, 145, 173; and discredited affect, 58; and heightened activity, 142; as individual, 250–51; "left melancholia," 249–50; and militancy, 139–43; refusal to accept defeat, 35–36; refusal to forget US role in Iranian police state, 70–71; resistant nostalgia as, 35–36
memory, 33; body's affective capacity for, 6; collective, 31, 35, 251; diasporic, 34–35; "duty of," 35, 37; as embodied archive, 36–37; forbidden, 263, 268; of freedom, 250, 253, 254, 263; idealized, 87; of possibility, 251–54. See also resistant nostalgia
Meydan-e Shush neighborhood, 144
Michigan State University, 11, 41

middle- and upper-class Iranians, 52, 58; affluent women students in ISA, 205–6; concern for poor Iranians, 10; high school attendance in US, 50, 55–57; as revolutionaries, 72. See also students, Iranian
migration, and memory, 34–35
migration, Iranian, 17, 18, 28; ISA members as part of first wave, 22; normative association between memory and place, 34–35; permanent, 247. See also "imperial model minorities"; students, Iranian
militancy: body as site of, 139–40; "culture of," 176–77; gendered performance of, 145; of ISA, 82–83, 86, 92, 96, 104, 127; joint organizing, 141–42; and melancholia, 139–43; not inherently masculinist, 29, 137
Mina (Iranian student), 176–77
Mitchell, Nick, 99
Moallem, Minoo, 182–84, 196, 197, 210, 223, 294n63
"Mobarez," Mohommad, 101
Mobasher, Mohsen, 125
"model minorities," 28, 74, 280n13, 280n15. See also "imperial model minorities"
modernization: attributed to Shah, 69, 90; clothing as symbol of, 184, 196–97; economically polarizing, 74; gender politics of, 14, 53–54, 76, 184, 185, 196–97, 206–7, 223; and patriarchy, 184, 244, 271; traditionalism against, 53; Western-backed authoritarian, 22, 50
Moghadam, Nasser, 48
Moghissi, Haideh, 182, 187, 188, 214, 221, 224, 293n16, 295n67; on Tehran women's uprising, 227
Mojahedin (Islamic guerrilla group), 86, 104, 178, 256, 262, 263
Mojaher, Nasser, 225, 237, 238
Mosaddeq, Mohammad, 37–39, 42, 52, 78, 142, 224, 237; house of looted, 49; ISA demand for healthcare for, 88
Mossavi, Mir-Hossein, 261
Mostashari, Jalil, 11, 14, 33, 34, 36, 37–41, 133–34
mostazafin (oppressed) versus *mostakberin* (the oppressors), 220
Mostofi, Nilu, 277n61
Mottahedeh, Negar, 222, 224, 297n50
Mouvement de Libération des Femmes Iraniennes: Année Zéro, 6, 228–34, 297n57; anti-hijab narrative imposed on, 228; counter-reading of, 217–19; mistranslation of Persian audio, 217, 230–31; violence omitted from, 233; "Year Zero," contested interpretations of, 228–34

Mubarak, Hosni, 27
Muñoz, José, 25, 248, 278n72
Museum of Contemporary Art (Tehran), 261
Muslim Students Association, 124–25, 134

Naber, Nadine, 22, 277n60
Naghibi, Nima, 229
Najmabadi, Afsaneh, 294n46
Nateq, Homa, 236, 238
National Democratic Front (NDF), 255
National Front (Jebhā-ye mellī-e Īrān)
    (Mosaddeqi), 37, 85, 160–61, 178, 241
National Front Abroad in Europe, 220
nationalism: "Aryan," solidarity as alternative
    to, 157–58, 166; challenges to, 98, 125;
    "conservative principle of continuity,"
    180; family as metaphor for, 193; forms
    of, 35, 235, 278n68; minority, 137; "na-
    tional time," 180, 190; in US university
    curriculum, 97–98; xenophobic, 116, 119,
    125–26
National Lawyers Guild, 102, 103
National Security Council, 90
National Union of Students of France, 86
National Union of Women (NUW), 225, 238,
    240–41
National United Committee to Free Angela
    and All Political Prisoners, 151
New School for Social Research, 85
New Statesman, 90
Newton, Huey, 146, 149, 194
New York Times, 118, 119, 121, 124
Nixon, Richard, 80, 169–71
Nixon Doctrine, 169–71
Nkrumah, Kwame, 151
Nodjoumi, Nicky, 109, 148f, 233, 252, 259–62
Non-Aligned Movement, 136, 290n13
non-Iranian activists, 173–74, 195–97
"norms of respectability," 137
nostalgia. *See* resistant nostalgia
Nowruz (Iranian New Year) celebrations, 78,
    84, 109, 160
nursing students, Iranian, 232–33

observers, sent to Iran, 105–7
Occupy Wall Street, 33
October: Ten Days That Shook the World (film),
    113
Odeah, Camelia, 157, 158
oil boom, 1970s, 83, 100
Old Testament parables, 194–95
Oman, 163–66, 164f, 165f, 210
"On the Question of Splits in the Iranian Stu-
    dents Association," 86–87

oppression: and affect, 134, 141, 157–58; class,
    237; gender and sexual, 17, 19–21, 136, 178,
    181–82, 186–88, 199–200, 207, 209–10,
    214, 216–18, 223, 231, 237–39, 244–48,
    271–72; hierarchy of within Left, 16–17,
    221, 237, 244, 272; intersecting forms of,
    6, 11, 14, 16–17, 20, 26, 136–39, 157, 218,
    277n51
Organization of African Unity, 153
Organization of Communist Unity (Sāzmān-i
    vahdat-i kummūnisti), 220–21, 241
Organization of Solidarity of the People of
    Africa, Asia, and Latin America, 135
Organization of Tehran University Students
    (OTUS), 80
Orientalism, 18–19, 20, 23, 216, 281n26; of area
    studies programs, 100; Cold War, 75–76
Oskooi, Marzieh Ahmadi, 208–10, 213
Oslo Accords (1993), 159
Other, 12, 76, 100, 126

Pahlavi, Farah (Empress), 209, 211f
Pahlavi dynasty (1925–79), 21
Paidar, Parvin, 15, 21, 181, 255, 299n21
Paknejad, Shokrollah, 161
Palestine, 154–66, 210; effect of US-Iran
    relations on, 154–56; ISA members as
    targets of anti-Arab violence, 156–57; and
    Islamic Republic of Iran, 166; "one-state
    solution," 159; women's involvement in
    struggle, 174
"Palestine Group," 149, 161
Palestine Liberation Organization (PLO), 156,
    157, 258
Palestine Solidarity Committee (UCLA), 162
Palestinian liberation movement, 134, 135
pan-Muslim affiliation, 23
patriarchy, 16, 174, 214; as central to racism
    and capitalism, 217–18; and family, 179,
    185, 193; and Iranian revolution, 229, 238,
    245–46; and Left, 14, 221, 238, 293n16;
    and modernizing regime, 184, 244, 271;
    women's self-sacrifice expected, 213.
    See also gender
pax Americana, 98
Paykari, Haydar "Radical," 101
People's Front for the Liberation of Oman, 163,
    165–66
"People's Living Conditions, the Reason for
    Struggle" (ISA), 92–93
Persian Empire, 23, 75
"Persian imperial identity," 23, 70, 75, 133
Philippines, 169
Pinochet, Augusto, 141–42

180, 191, 192; loss of members, 239–40; separate March 8 celebration, 242; spokespeople outside Iran, 258; support for Khomeini, 221; Third Line, 197, 294n41

Revolutionary Student Brigade, 1

revolutionary subjectivity, 7–9, 14, 27, 29–30, 41, 71–72, 76, 180, 198; alternative forms of, 244, 247, 271; centrality of affect to, 71–72; estrangement from, 198; and gender, 180; masculinist forms of, 10, 14–16, 198, 244, 247, 271. *See also* subjectivity

revolutionary time, 29, 278n80, 292n1; sociality and gender sameness, 179–83; social reproduction in, 189–93

"Revolution Until Victory" (documentary), 158–59

Rezavi, Haj (student activist), 149

Rhodesia, 153

Ricoeur, Paul, 35, 37

right-wing, US, 114, 118

Riverside City College (California), 124

Roy, M. N., 40

Russell, Bertrand, 114

Russian Revolution of 1917, 34, 40, 41

Samiian, Vida, 84, 120, 162, 183, 224, 241

Sanasarian, Eliz, 226

San Francisco Iranian consulate, ISA occupation of (case of "the 41"), 112–13, 150, 192

San Francisco Moratorium March, 169

San Francisco Sheraton Palace Hotel sit-ins, 145

San Francisco State College protest (1967), 5, 45, 128–32, 130f, 132f, 137–39, 145; Third World Liberation Front (TWLF), 138–39

San Jose State College seminar, 158–59, 159f

San Luis Obispo University (California), 102

Sartre, Jean-Paul, 44, 47, 114

SAVAK (Sāzmān-e ettelāʾāt va Amniyat-e Keshvar), 9, 48, 64–65; CIA education of, 73, 97, 299n27; informants in US, 108–11; Israeli training of, 154; *lubia* ("string bean") as code word for, 107; parents pressured by, 108, 191, 192; persecution of dissidents in Iran, 149; *Resistance* pamphlet on, 107; students, interaction with, 69; US activities of, 89, 96–97, 107–8, 114–15, 126, 146; in US prisons, 133; violence instigated by, 115; wanted list, 257. *See also* torture

Schneider, Ann, 173

Seale, Bobby, 149

Secret Service (US), 115

self-determination, struggles for, 134–35, 158, 166, 171, 173–74, 194, 244

self-sacrifice, 270; appeal of ultimate, 207–13; and arrests, 264; and collectivities, 180–81; *fadaiyan* ("self-sacrificers"), 60; gendered, 180, 189–90, 193–97, 207–9, 244; new act of as honor, 236; and solidarity, 133, 137

Senate Select Committee on Intelligence, 108

sexuality: communal living experiments, 204–5; dating outside group forbidden, 202–3; as "private," 202; reproduction, 189–90, 203; "sexual revolution," 202; and surveillance, 201–7, 214, 244, 294n55; women's seen as threat, 200–201, 223

Shadman, Dariush, 90

Shah, Mohammad Reza Pahlavi, 1, 10, 17, 25; *60 Minutes* interview, 107–8; 1967 family laws, 225, 238; activists meet, 50; cancer treatment in US, 123; CISNU banned by, 82, 110; commemoration of monarchy, 62, 92–93; feminism, co-optation of, 14, 238; financial gifts to universities, 100; honorary degrees awarded to, 95–96, 98–99, 101; "image problem," 104; installed by British, 37–38; mass marches against, 244–45; as "modernizer," 69, 90; nostalgia for regime of, 23, 27, 30, 249–50; parliament suspended by, 89; popular uprising against (1952), 38–39; tear-gassed in Rose Garden, 116; US complicity with dictatorship of, 1, 3; US tours, 87, 90, 92, 110, 114–16, 117f, 129, 171; as watchdog for US interests, 22, 81, 134, 156

Shah, Reza, 37, 41

Shahnaz (student activist), 26, 121, 160, 197–98, 200, 202, 241–42; as political prisoner, 265–66

Shannon, Matthew, 89, 277n65

Shariati, Ali, 223

Shayegan, Leyli (student activist), 204, 224

Shayegan, Mother, 210

Shiʿism, 37, 144, 248; martyrdom in, 195; populist version of, 219–20

Shohat, Ella, 263

Shokat, Parviz (student activist), 48–51, 79, 84, 129, 146–49, 179, 197, 239

Siahkal guerrilla assault (Gilan province), 60, 91–92, 211

Sina (Iranian student), 69–70, 76, 81, 144–45, 157, 162, 180–81, 188, 203; memory of possibility, 251–52

"sister revolutions," 136

60 Minutes, 107–8

sociality, revolutionary, 179–83, 192, 195, 214

"US-Iran conflict," 24, 68

US-Iran relations, 271, 284n5; dictatorship and imperialism at impasse, 23, 269; government and bilateral agreements, 82; and Iran's invasion of Oman and Yemen, 163–66; and Israeli occupation of Palestine, 154–56, 166; "special relationship," 71–72, 77, 89, 92, 100, 126, 152; students' inability to support, 93–94; US "advisers" in Iran, 171, 283n95; US weapons sales to Iran, 163–65, 164f, 165f, 170–71. *See also* United States

US National Students Association, 282n73

US News and World Report, 108

Vance, Cyrus R., 122

Vietnam, 12, 45, 55–56, 134, 166–72, 268, 300n38; liberal moratorium movement, 167, 168f; memories of victory, 253, 254; parallels with US interventions elsewhere, 171; political prisoners in South Vietnam, 169, 170f; solidarity with antiwar groups, 172; Tet Offensive, 169. *See also* antiwar movement

"Vietnamization" of war in Southeast Asia, 169–70

Vietnam Veterans Against the War, 1

voting rights, 53–54, 91, 184

Wallace, Mike, 107

War of Sugar in Cuba (Sartre), 44–45

"war on terror," 23–24, 91, 124, 216

Washington Post, 12, 108, 114–16, 123

"Western values," 52, 54, 218; and gender, 14–15, 177, 182, 184, 198, 223, 229, 243, 271

West-toxified/West-toxification, as terms, 15, 229, 297n51

White Revolution, 90, 91, 93, 283n91

Whitten, Les, 108

"Why the Shah Should Not Be Invited to UCLA" (ISA), 95–96

Williams, Raymond, 7–8

women: and affect, 29–30; bourgeois forms of femininity, rejection of, 10; executed by Shah's regime, 210; and "gender

sameness," 15–16, 29, 179–83, 200–202, 223; genealogy of revolutionary feminism, 217–18, 245, 271–72; in guerrilla movement, 210–12, 211f; Iranian society said to be oppressive to, 16; and masculinist forms of revolutionary subjectivity, 10, 14–16, 198, 244, 247, 271; Palestinian, 174; political prisoners, 149, 265–66; questioning of gender roles, 52–53; ridicule faced by in Leftist groups, 83–84; self-sacrifice expected of, 180, 189–90, 193–97, 207–9, 244; and solidarity, 29, 136–37; voting rights, 53–54, 91, 184; Westernized bourgeois image of, 14–15; working class and peasant in Iran, 187. *See also* gender; Tehran women's uprising (March 1979); women's movement in Iran

women-of-color feminism, 14, 19–20, 136–37, 235, 272, 276n49

women's movement in Iran, 217–19, 221–22; as continuation of revolutionary affects, 222–23; as diasporic inheritance, 245; disorder created by, 222; fragmentation and decline of, 239–43; hesitation of caused by lack of support, 237–38; separatism alleged of, 236, 237, 245, 272; "Year Zero," contested interpretations of, 228–34. *See also* Tehran women's uprising (March 1979); women

Women's Organization of Iran (state-sponsored), 185, 223, 229, 230

Wong, Victoria, 98

working-class Iranians, 63–65, 144–45, 203; students, 83, 195

Wu, Hui, 207

xenophobia, 29, 116, 122–26

Yemen, 163

Young, Cynthia, 13, 135–36

Zahedi, Ardeshir, 75, 77–79, 88, 89, 93

Zahedi, Fazlollah, 48

Zahraei, Babak, 113

Zaim, Siamak, 266–67